Born a Child of
Freedom, Yet a Slave

Norrece T. Jones, Jr.

Born a Child of Freedom, Yet a Slave

Mechanisms of Control and Strategies of Resistance in Antebellum South Carolina

Wesleyan University Press
University Press of New England
Hanover and London

The University Press of New England

is a consortium of universities in New England dedicated to publishing scholarly and trade works by authors from member campuses and elsewhere. The New England imprint signifies uniform standards for publication excellence maintained without exception by the consortium members. A joint imprint of University Press of New England and a sponsoring member acknowledges the publishing mission of that university and its support for the dissemination of scholarship throughout the world. Cited by the American Council of Learned Societies as a model to be followed, University Press of New England publishes books under its own imprint and the imprints of Brandeis University, Brown University, Clark University, University of Connecticut, Dartmouth College, University of New Hampshire, University of Rhode Island, Tufts University, University of Vermont, and Wesleyan University.

The epigraph on p. xi is excerpted from the book *homegirls & handgrenades* by Sonia Sanchez. Copyright © 1984 by Sonia Sanchez. Published by Thunder's Mouth Press.

Printed in the United States of America

∞

LIBRARY OF CONGRESS CATALOGING-IN-PUBLICATION DATA
Jones, Norrece T., 1953–
Born a child of freedom, yet a slave : mechanisms of control and strategies of resistance in antebellum South Carolina /
Norrece T. Jones, Jr. — 1st ed.
p. cm.
Bibliography: p.
Includes index.
ISBN 0-8195-5213-5
1. Slavery—South Carolina—Condition of slaves. 2. Slaves—South Carolina—History—19th century. 3. Plantation life—South Carolina—History—19th century. 4. South Carolina—Race relations.
1. Title.
E445.S7J66 1990
975.7′00496073—dc19 89-5458

5 4 3 2 1

This book is dedicated to the Asbury, Jones, and Simpson families of South Carolina and especially to Aunt Bea and my late Aunt Laura (Mrs. Laura J. Simpson).

Preface

At the end of my first college research paper, Dr. Elinor Hoag wrote, "This is the germ of a book." I did not take her seriously nor think a great deal more about "The White Man's Attempts to Pacify Blacks During Slavery" until beginning graduate school. Considering almost twenty years have passed since freshman year at Hampton Institute (now University), my fascination with slave control has been little short of an obsession. Many have helped fuel and sustain that interest. A very special tribute is due to Dr. George M. Fredrickson, who directed my doctoral thesis—from which this study grew—at Northwestern University. His willingness to allow me to unravel the complexities of slave control with a free but firm hand, his continuing friendship, and his brilliance have meant more than he will ever realize. Nor can another member of my dissertation committee, Dr. Sterling Stuckey, know fully the impact his scholarship and intellectual vigor have had on me. Without his incisive questions and determined suggestions, much would be absent in this book.

During the interim between graduate school and the transition of a thesis into a book, I have benefited from an extraordinarily generous group of scholars. In almost every instance, I was introduced to them through the letters of a stranger—myself. Their kind acceptance of my intrusion was a warm and wonderful introduction to the profession. I must thank them all wholeheartedly and there are many: James A. Anderson, Sidney M. Mintz, David R. Roediger, Phyllis Boanes, Peter H. Wood, George A. Rawick, William Green, Victoria Swigert, Lawrence Goodwyn, and Brenda Stevenson. I hope this study does justice to their contribution.

No research project, of course, is possible without the assistance and guidance of many archivists and librarians. Of the many fine and helpful guides, special mention must be made of Allen Stokes at the South Caroliniana Library, who not only buffered the culture shock of antebellum script, but led me to many invaluable sources. I must also thank Anne Denato at the Waring Historical Library, Sylvia Render at the Library of Congress, and Sue

Bass at the Cabell Library of Virginia Commonwealth University. Financial support from the following foundations and institutions was also appreciated: the National Fellowships Fund, a National Endowment for the Humanities Summer Stipend, a Ford Foundation Fellowship for Minorities for Work in Residence at the Newberry Library, and a Virginia Commonwealth University Educational Leave Grant.

Friends and relatives too numerous to mention have been shamelessly abused while completing this project. Their help in proofreading and in providing much-needed moral support can never be repaid—particularly that of my parents, Mr. and Mrs. Norrece T. Jones. From graduate school until present, my former neighbor, novelist Rose Jourdain—whose own work makes history come alive—has been both a friend and an inspiration. Bringing *Born a Child of Freedom, Yet a Slave* to its conclusion was patiently directed by the director of the Wesleyan University Press, Jeannette Hopkins. Her razor-sharp intellect, wit, and demands have contributed immeasurably to this work. The challenge and friendship which grew from each will always be valued. The steady typing and retyping of Gene R. Dunaway, Diane Marshall, Cindy Hartzler-Miller, and, most especially, Janie Ghee and Amanda Marrion were done with a professionalism and kindness difficult to match. Finally, throughout all the years of ups and downs, doubts and more doubts, my friend and fellow Carolinian, Betty Session, has given me more than words can express.

Richmond, Virginia   NORRECE T. JONES, JR.
September 1988

Contents

Illustrations

Distribution by race in South Carolina,
1788–1860, page 2

following page 128

Charleston, South Carolina, slave auction
Diagram of slave ship, *Brookes*
Slave deck of the bark *Wildfire*
Hold of the "blood-stained" *Gloria*
Notice of estate sale of slaves in Charleston, 1859
Notice of slave auction in Charleston, 1833
South Carolina slave auction
Slave with back scarred by whipping
Gang of slaves force marched to market
Metal mask used to punish runaway slaves
Bloodhounds attacking fugitive slaves
Fugitive slaves
Brutus, an ex-slave, at his home
Family of freed slaves

I have come to you tonite out of the depths
   of slavery
   from white hands peeling black skins over
   america;
I have come out to you from reconstruction eyes
   that closed on black humanity
   that reduced black hope to the dark
   huts of america;
I have come to you from the lynching years,
   the exploitation of black men and women by
   a country that allowed the swinging of
   strange fruits from southern trees;
      . . . .
   I have come to you tonite as an equal,
     as a comrade, as a black woman
     walking down a corridor of tears,
     looking neither to the left or the right,
     pulling my history with bruised
     heels,
     beckoning to the illusion of america
     daring you to look me in the eyes to
     see these faces, the exploitation of a
     people because of skin pigmentation;
I have come to you tonite because no people
   have been asked to be modern day people
   with the history of slavery, and still
   we walk, and still we talk, and
   still we plan, and still we hope and
   still we sing;
      . . . .
I have come to you to talk about our inexperience
   at living as human beings, thru death marches and camps,
   thru middle passages and slavery
   and thundering countries raining hungry faces;
I am here to move against
   leaving our shadows implanted on the
   earth while our bodies disintegrate in
   nuclear lightning;
      . . . .
I am here. and my breath/our breaths
   must thunder across this land
   arousing new breaths. new life.
   new people, who will live in peace
   and honor.
           —SONIA SANCHEZ, *homegirls & handgrenades*

Born a Child of Freedom, Yet a Slave

Distribution by race in South Carolina, 1788–1860. The Carolina Low Country (the districts of Georgetown, Charleston, and Beaufort) had the heaviest concentration of blacks. *Courtesy of Sandlapper Publishing Co., Inc.*

Introduction

There is a serious void in the literature on slavery about the control of slaves in the American South. Although historians have addressed the issue, they have done so in mere chapter-length treatments or focused narrowly on a single component of this extremely complicated subject.[1] Much emphasis has been placed on cruel lashings and executions to the neglect of psychological forces frequently more devastating in their consequences and more effectual in spurring "good" behavior. Slaves' fear of being separated from family members and loved ones, for example, made the sale of "miscreant" or "incorrigible" slaves the most powerful long-term technique of control—short of death—that masters possessed. Yet the threat of sale has generally received little more than passing mention as a weapon leveled against captive blacks.[2]

The only monograph devoted specifically to the control of any North American slaves was written in 1914 by H. M. Henry. His work, *The Police Control of the Slave in South Carolina*, was concerned primarily with the legal aspects of slave management. He determined that the harsh and ruthless nature of many laws stemmed from the "barbaric character" of blacks themselves.[3] Despite the hollow analysis, his study did contain a comprehensive survey of the judicial measures passed to compel the good behavior of slaves. But laws can only reflect the desires of their creators. And, to the slave, such decrees constituted nothing more than "a compact between his owners."[4]

What were the mechanisms of control that contained or suppressed discontent? Which were most "successful"? How were slaves affected? And what role did slaves play in preserving or endangering the dominant position of their owners? Although there has been an outpouring during the last three decades of works on slavery, these works have focused more on the mind of the master, on masters' impact on slaves, and on how masters regarded their human chattels. Even studies devoted to slave life have tended to concentrate so heavily on slaves' rich and autonomous communities and the bonds therein that the context in which both developed is often neglected. The results have been tragic, for neither masters nor slaves acted in a vacuum and no one aspect of slave life can reveal fully the totality of the world that slaves survived.

Ironically, incomplete examinations of the institution of bondage or the individuals at its helm have not been as damaging as the distortions of slave culture in certain broad works on slavery. U. B. Phillips, for instance, in 1918 accepted all overt appearances of slave contentment, saw them as evidence that the beguiling remarks of "southern patriarchs" were true, and arrived at the conclusion that antebellum slaves were happy in their relationship with "loving" masters. According to Phillips and Henry, any efforts at controlling slaves were instituted primarily to crush the venality and viciousness of certain aberrant individuals, not to suppress resistance to enslavement.[5] They would have concurred with Walter Fleming, in *Civil War and Reconstruction in Alabama* in 1905, that African-Americans were but "wax in the hands of a stronger race."[6]

Even so perceptive a scholar as Kenneth Stampp, who understands the issue of control, fails to delve deeply enough into the culture of slaves. In *The Peculiar Institution* of 1956, which is still one of the best broad works to date on slavery, Stampp said about slave familial relations and functions:

> Not only did the slave family lack the protection and the external pressure of state law, it also lacked most of the centripetal forces that gave the white family its cohesiveness. In the life of the slave, the family had nothing like the social significance that it had in the life of the white man. The slave woman was first a full-time worker for her owner, and only incidentally a wife, mother and homemaker. . . . Parents frequently had little to do with the raising of their children; and children soon learned that their parents were neither the fount of wisdom nor the seat of authority. . . . The husband was not the director of an agricultural enterprise; he was not the head of the family, the holder of property, the provider, or the protector. . . . The male slave's only crucial function within the family was that of siring offspring.[7]

Eugene Genovese, who has recognized and appreciated the importance of slave culture more than any of the preceding historians, molded his very influential study, *Roll, Jordan, Roll* of 1974—a book subtitled *The World the Slaves Made*—around the paternalist ideology of planters. As a result, the mechanisms of control so central in the lives of bondsmen faded into the background of an otherwise powerful work.[8] It should be obvious that whether one is interested primarily in masters or slaves, the testimony of slaves is crucial. Perhaps if Peter Kolchin, in his critically acclaimed *Unfree Labor* of 1987, had paid closer attention to the unfree labor and analyzed more carefully the mind of the slave, he would have avoided following in the footsteps of others. According to Kolchin, former slaves remembered slavery "in the abstract" as dreadful; he argued further that "slave families faced forced separations more than serf families, not so much because of the good or bad intentions of the owners but because of differing customs stemming from two very different historical experiences."[9]

In my research of South Carolinian slaves, I found few blacks who needed to think abstractly about the nature of bondage or who viewed the heinous act of family separations as ever possibly being rooted in the "good" intentions of the parties responsible. One of the problems with writing regional or comparative studies is the almost inevitable dependence on secondary sources. Consequently, one is forced to cite the primary evidence of others who used that data with different questions in mind. Of course there is nothing necessarily wrong with such an approach, but it can lead to sweeping assertions about the entire South based on a scattering of examples from a few states.

By examining a particular state, as this book does, one not only is able to test generalizations about slave control, but to tap more thoroughly crucial archival sources. South Carolina is especially conducive for both: her antebellum racial demography and her bountiful manuscript depositories provide rich and piercing insights about the tremendously complex world created by those held captive and by the free. And, on the issue of patriarchal relationships, it is clear that if they existed anywhere, the Palmetto State would have been the place. The size of her plantations and the worldview of the white men and women who struggled to maintain them made South Carolina an ideal setting for those patriarchal relationships admired and romanticized by many nineteenth and twentieth century scholars.[10]

In 1857 an English traveler, James Stirling, described South Carolina as "the centre of Southern aristocracy." It was the home of the most outspoken, vain, and self-conscious proclaimers of aristocratic virtues and lineage.[11] Because the state's two principal agricultural pursuits, rice and cotton production, were most profitable when farmed on extensive plantations, the wealthiest and most powerful sector of the slavocracy reigned over vast estates with hundreds of slaves. It comes as no surprise, therefore, that while the Palmetto State was only sixth in aggregate slave population in 1850, it was first both in the number of masters owning more than 200 slaves and in the number of masters owning between 100 and 200 slaves. Although the average number of slaves per plantation for the state in 1857 was 15.04, the majority of slaves lived on estates with more than twenty bondsmen. Throughout this study, I will concentrate primarily on these large plantations, for it is there that one finds what was most typical in the slave experience.[12]

During the first decade of the eighteenth century, blacks gained numerical supremacy over whites in South Carolina, and this remained a prominent factor in the state's demography throughout the antebellum period. In 1850, for example, slaves comprised 57.5 percent of the total population, but in some large slaveholding districts there were more than two slaves for every white. The districts of Georgetown, Charleston, and Beaufort, comprising the famous Carolina Low Country, were areas with the heaviest concentration of blacks. Slaves in Georgetown were between 85 and 89 percent of the population from 1810 to 1860. The role this numerical superiority played in the strategy and tactics of blacks was not missed by slaveowners. Almost from the beginning, the masters were terrified by this black majority—particularly its equalizing effect on the military advantages that whites unequivocally possessed.[13] It fired their imaginations with new and increasingly ingenious mechanisms of control.

However difficult it is to capture adequately the distance and enmity bred by the ownership of men, one must do so, for in the thinking of most slaves no act or gesture could bridge the gap between their status as chattels and that of masters as owners.[14] Legislative records, private correspondence, and records of savage punishments reveal as much by demonstrating the perennial concern of white Southerners with the management and suppression of a hostile black labor force.[15] Nevertheless, there exists enough antebellum literature and postwar recollections of idyllic relations between masters and slaves to present historically a nonexistent world. The only way to prevent such distortions and documented make-believe is to view the Peculiar Institution primarily through the eyes, ears, and mouths of slaves themselves. From these sources one finds the persistent themes of escape and pursuit, sale and family separations, and resistance and sadistic punishments.[16]

As in any society sustained by oppression, there was much the oppressed would have liked to escape. Throughout the slave quarters and urban dwellings of South Carolina, for instance, there were sufficient numbers of mulattoes to make clear what many masters and their hirelings, overseers and other whites, chose to pursue. Needless to say, the knowledge of rapes, and of the callous sale of lives so produced,[17] compounded the antagonism inherent in a community of enslavers and slaves. Perhaps nothing more effectively buttressed the wall dividing the two than this abuse of black women and the severance of kinship ties. These aspects of slave life, as well as the ideas and behaviors of masters, abound in a wealth of South Carolinian research materials.

Some of the most valuable sources are ex-slave autobiographies and the narratives of black Carolinians. There are special problems with these narratives,[18] however, because many of their authors spent only their earliest years in bondage and, as Eric Perkins points out in his review of Genovese's *Roll, Jordan, Roll*, children "seldom felt paternalism's harsh and brutal side."[19] An incident recorded in 1865 by Mary Boykin Chesnut reflects this shortcoming vividly. She wrote of the close relationship between a young slave boy and his beloved mistress:

Sally Reynolds told a short story of a negro pet of Mrs. Kershaw's. The little negro clung to Mrs. Kershaw and begged her to save him. The negro mother, stronger than Mrs. Kershaw, tore him away from her. Mrs. Kershaw wept bitterly. Sally said she saw the mother chasing the child before her as she ran after the Yankees, whipping him at every step. The child yelled like mad, a small blackamoor.[20]

Another difficulty with the black narratives stems from the time and circumstances of the interviews. They were recorded in the 1930s, a time of widespread segregation and other forms of racial oppression. The interviewers were usually white, and, in addition, some were related to the ex-slaveholders under discussion. It is scarcely surprising that a number of blacks hesitated to speak of the harsher features of the Peculiar Institution or of the cruelty of their former masters. Also, those who edited the interviews, which seldom were taken verbatim, frequently deleted descriptions of the most brutal aspects of slave experience. Such selective reporting and the fact that most interviewers were young white women undoubtedly has resulted in censorship or self-censorship of many incidents of rapes, white parentage, and family separations. Further, some of those interviewed were living in the homes or on the property of benevolent white families who had granted them permission to stay there.[21] Many expected to receive money for their interviews or aid in obtaining government pensions.[22] All of these circumstances make it highly probable that any statements exposing the brutality of planters were true. If historians pay close attention to the age of those being interviewed and the realities surrounding the exchange, these sources along with ex-slave autobiographies can be of invaluable service.

An additional lode to mine for slave testimony is the folklore that slaves imparted and bequeathed to generations of black Americans. Many scholars have advocated its use, but few historians have actually used it. In consequence, the innermost feelings and attitudes of slaves have generally remained buried in the rich oral histories they preserved throughout the South.[23] The depth of insights contained in these important documents has been demonstrated brilliantly by Sterling Stuckey in his poignant essay, "Through the Prism of Folklore." He argued,

> My thesis, which rests on an examination of folk songs and tales, is that slaves were able to fashion a life style and set of values—an ethos—which prevented them from being imprisoned altogether by the definitions which the larger society sought to impose. This ethos was an amalgam of Africanisms and New World elements which helped slaves, in Guy Johnson's words, "feel their way along the course of American slavery, enabling them to endure. . . ." In short, . . . a very large number of slaves, guided by this ethos, were able to maintain their essential humanity. I make this contention because folklore in its natural setting, is of, by, and for those who create and respond to it, depending for its survival upon the accuracy with which it speaks to needs and reflects sentiments. I therefore consider it safe to assume that the attitudes of a very large number of slaves are represented by the themes of folklore.[24]

Stuckey's assumption is given firm support in the folklore of slaves from diverse communities whose similarities of themes and message are striking. Frederick Douglass, who was born a slave on a Maryland plantation in 1817, recorded this ode he heard among his fellow slaves:

> We raise de wheat,
> Dey gib us de corn;
> We bake de bread,
> Dey gib us de cruss
> We sif de meal,
> Dey gib us de huss;
> We peal de meat,
> Dey gib us the skin,
> And dat's de way
> Dey takes us in.
> We skim de pot,
> Dey gib us the liquor
> And say dat's good enough for nigger.
>
>> Walk over! Walk over!
>> Tom Butter and de fat;
>> Poor nigger you can't get over dat;
>> Walk over![25]

Put more succinctly, a former South Carolinian slave born in 1857 recited, "Naught is naught and figger is a figger, all for de white man and none for de nigger."[26]

Folklore reveals more candidly than the narratives the mind of the slave. The veiled scorn of former slaves in the 1930s interviews, for example, became outright hostility in the lore shared by slaves and their descendants. The ruthless practices of threatening to sell and of selling slaves were the topic of many of these ballads and tales. One of the most graphic was "Old Man Rogan."

Ole Man Rogan nuse to sell nigger in slavery time. . . . He ain't beat a nigger much, and he guin him plenty to eat, and he bring 'em here in drove and he have 'em chained together, but he have curious ways. . . . He always buy ooman wid chillun, and ooman wid husband, and ain't nobody can buy from Ole Man Rogan mother and chile or man and ooman. He great pleasure been to part. He always love to take er baby away from he ma and sell it, and take he ma somewhere else and sell her, and ain't luh 'em see one another again. He love to part a man and he ooman, sell de man one place and sell de ooman another, and dat look like all Ole Man Rogan live for, and when he ain't 'casion 'stress dat er way, he been onrestless. He love to see a man wid he head bowed down in 'stress, and he love to see chillun holdin' out dey arms cryin' for dey mother, and he always looked satisfied when he see tear runn' down de face of er ooman when she weepin' for her chile. And

Ole Man Rogan die on Boggy Gut, and ever since den he spirrit wander 'cross de big swamps to Congaree. Whether it be God or whether it be devil, de spirrit of Ole Man Rogan ain't got no res'. Some time in de night if you'll set on Boggy Gut, you'll hear de rattle of chains, you hear a baby cry every which er way, and you hear a mother call'n for her chile in de dark on Boggy Gut.[27]

Although slaves could only imagine endless wandering for so brutal a man, many planters evidently saw such individuals in a different light. The consequences of these divergent views and their roots have convinced me that while no model or analogy can portray accurately the horrors of slavery, a view of bondage as a state of war comes closest. Such an analogy not only allows one to perceive lucidly the depth and complexity of the hostilities it stirred, but helps to avoid any puerile interpretations of slave words and actions. The nineteenth-century historian, philosopher, and activist Richard Hildreth, for instance, saw far more of the essence of slavery than most white abolitionists and not a few twentieth-century scholars by using a state-of-war model in his study *Despotism in America*.[28]

Like many others who utilize models, Hildreth could not always resist fitting data into a preconceived model. Nevertheless, through this lens he was able to see the reality behind the masks of servility slaves wore before masters. He did not, for example, confuse slave appropriations and prevarications with infantile or nihilistic behavior, but saw in them the normal acts of survival and resistance that one would expect from men at war.[29] He states:

Falsehood . . . is a condition of open war . . . and if by bold lying, vociferous protestations, and cunning frauds, they can escape some threatened aggression, . . . [and] so secure some particle of liberty from the prying search and greedy grasp of despotism, why blame them for acts, which in like cases, all the world has justified and has even exalted to the character of heroism?[30]

For Hildreth there was never any doubt that "the only cure for slavery" was "freedom."[31]

CHAPTER ONE

The Challenge of Control

Freedom from absolute, arbitrary power is so necessary to, and closely joined with a man's preservation, that he cannot part with it but by what forfeits his preservation and life together. For a man, not having the power of his own life, cannot, by compact or his own consent, enslave himself to any one, nor put himself under the absolute, arbitrary power of another to take away his life when he pleases. Nobody can give more power than he has himself, and he that cannot take away his own life cannot give another power over it. . . .

This is the perfect condition of slavery, which is nothing else but the state of war continued between a lawful conqueror and a captive. For, if once compact enter between them, and make an agreement for a limited power on the one side, and obedience on the other, the state of war and slavery ceases as long as the compact endures; for, as has been said, no man can by agreement pass over to another that which he hath not in himself, a power over his own life.

JOHN LOCKE[1]

The abstractions of Locke were translated daily into a harrowing reality by the enslaved of South Carolina. The challenge slaves posed reveals dramatically the war inherent in the conquest of masters. Whether the battles waged between these captors and captives meet the criteria for war of modern theorists on the subject is not the point, for in the thinking of slaves they most decidedly were entangled in a grim and endless war. Of equal importance is the acknowledgment that, on almost all physical fronts, members of the plantocracy were victorious. Not only were they successful in preventing the majority of slaves from reaching their ultimate goal—freedom—but also in keeping most confrontations nonviolent, at least those that originated with slaves, for few organized and armed black assaults ever progressed beyond the planning stage.

Although no comprehensive study has been made of the costs these victories entailed or the multifarious techniques and mechanisms by which they were accomplished, the costs were tremendously high. In addition to the great sums of money spent to suppress and control slaves, much blood was spilt and combatants on each side sustained and suffered incalculable mental turmoil and duress. In this chapter I will explore the sources of those costs, how planters responded to them, and the threats to slave control from outside the slave community.

The essential and eternal issue in the war between masters and slaves was the slaves' desire for liberty. It was this quest for freedom that on the one hand made necessary every strain of control and on the other hand intellectually bound the first African enslaved to the last African-American freed.

Like their forebears, untold thousands of whom were maimed and murdered in the effort to make them slaves, the men and women who survived the forced migration to South Carolina and the rigors of life there demonstrated repeatedly an insatiable desire to be free by pursuing every conceivable means, from individual and mass desertions to insurrection. And despite the failures of the vast majority, the hope of freedom was kept alive in their folklore, oral histories, religion, and dreams.[2]

A knowledge of this thinking, decision, and resolve allows one to grasp how difficult the task was of creating productive, loyal, obedient, and contented slaves. Masters struggled relentlessly to make just such slaves, and the conflicts that ensued constituted the bedrock of slavery. This situation differed significantly from that experienced by Native Americans—another people of color robbed and displaced by whites during the course of the nineteenth century. What white Americans primarily wanted from them was their land. By military and legal means this was accomplished, and, whether genuine or bogus, treaties frequently were signed with these victims of white repression. The treaties alone reflected not only a greater respect for Indians, but an acknowledgment of their independence of thought and spirit.[3] There were no treaties with the black oppressed: by force of arms and infinite other physical and psychological controls, masters sought to capture the very souls of slaves.

Many planters were almost psychotically possessive in regard to their human property. In explaining his decision not to purchase an "insubordinate slave," R. F. W. Allston, a large South Carolinian slaveholder, declared, "I like to be kind to my people but I imperatively require of them honesty, truth, diligence and cheerfulness in their work, wherever and whatever it is."[4] Many masters were obsessed with having slaves who appeared to love them as well as to be happy in performing their unrequited toils, and they believed adamantly that when such behavior was absent, slaves had become "demoralized" and "law and order" abeyant.[5]

To preclude such lawlessness and its intellectual and physical costs, planters tried desperately to instill in slaves a sense of duty, gratitude, and loyalty. Modern research and experiments by social psychologists validate the wisdom behind these efforts. Herbert Kelman, for instance, found that a public acquiescence to another's power and desires without a private identification with or internalization of that other's will required a constant surveillance of the party being influenced and a primary dependence on negative sanctions. He labeled this latter type of induced behavior "compliance."[6] Masters, of course, would have preferred a conformity based on a slave's identification with them and the rewards such a relationship provided or ideally on an internalization of slaveholders' values and beliefs. They failed to produce either in all but a minority of slaves. As a result, the rules of behavior or "norms" established by planters were constantly being broken and a formidable body of controllers had to be employed for the scrutinizing and punishing of their much-proclaimed "people."[7]

Distinguishing compliance from identification and internalization refines the discussion of slave behavior, for "accommodation," the term that has long plagued the study of slaves, encompasses *all* types of conformity and, more hazardously, suggests in popular usage an acceptance of one's status or condition. An understanding and adoption of the Kelman terminology makes more specific the meaning of slavery and explains, in part, why the battle for slave minds was so persistently and strenuously fought. How that and other struggles developed requires a brief overview of the key developments in the eighteenth century, for it was then that both slave challenges and planter responses acquired their most enduring and basic shape.

As noted in the introduction, nothing bore greater consequences for masters and slaves than the existence and growth of a black majority. The composition of that black mass is of special importance for, between 1720 and 1740, it changed from a population in which only 5 percent of the black adults had been on South Carolinian soil for less than a decade to one where 50 percent of the black men and women were relatively recent imports.[8] These slaves came largely from Africa and their influence in South Carolina as elsewhere suggests a direct correlation between the presence of African-born slaves and the probability of heightened unrest and rebellion. Certainly the "breaking in" or "seasoning" of new arrivals put additional pressures on an already strained environment. Whatever the cause, there were repeated discoveries of slave conspiracies to revolt throughout the first half of the eighteenth century.[9] These were not, however, the only sources of the mounting tensions between white controllers and the individuals they chose to subdue.

Besides sporadic acts of arson, there were many instances of poisonings. Substantial evidence existed that Africans had brought with them a deadly knowledge of herbs. While these two acts—arson and poisoning—were difficult to detect or prove, everyone could see readily the disappearance of the valuable property one historian has aptly described as "slaves who stole themselves." Although desertions had always been a problem in colonial South Carolina, the 1733 decision by Spanish authorities to liberate all slaves from British territories who arrived in their Florida possession, St. Augustine, increased further the number of escapes. In response to these developments, white Carolinians relied, as usual, on force, but, in addition, strengthened legislation addressing the control of slaves. To assure, for example, that masters' pecuniary interests did not overshadow their control-mindedness, public funds throughout the eighteenth century were increasingly used to compensate owners for slaves executed as well as to finance such corrective measures as brandings, whippings, and the cutting off of ears.[10] In order to deter the ever-growing number of runaways, members of the legislature voted in February 1739 to employ two scouting boats to patrol their southern coastline for the following nine months. They recommended also that large bounties be offered for the capture of black absconders in the all-white colony of Georgia. Adult males, "women, and children under twelve were to bring £40, £25, £10, respectively, . . . and each adult scalp 'with the two Ears' would command £20."[11]

Despite these efforts, on September 9, 1739, the most serious rebellion to occur in colonial America commenced at Stono, South Carolina. When it ended, more than sixty lay dead and all the gnawing fears of a white minority had coalesced into a steadfast commitment to prevent any future revolts. The uprising began with the meeting of about twenty slaves at the Stono River in St. Paul's Parish.[12] They first broke into a store, confiscated arms, and began marching toward St. Augustine, killing almost two dozen whites in the process. As other slaves joined them, "two drums appeared; a standard was raised; and . . . shouts of 'Liberty!'" rang out from the marchers.[13] Although some of the insurgents—whose total number ranged from sixty to one hundred—eluded capture for over a year, most were killed either in the pitched battle waged with militiamen on the first day of the uprising or during the weeks thereafter when cornered by pursuers. And according to one report concerning the fate of some vanquished rebels, planters on September 9 "Cut off their heads and set them up at every Mile Post they came to."[14] Grisly warnings to blacks contemplating freedom became a tradition in South Carolina.

The already tightening controls governing blacks were made even more constricting after the Stono Rebellion. A comprehensive and elaborate Negro Act was passed a year later and, despite some revisions, remained the principal legislation prescribing slave behavior until the conclusion of the Civil War. This 1740 act did more than any other colonial law among South Carolinians "to curtail de facto personal liberties, which slaves had been able to cling to . . . during the first three generations of settlement."[15] Besides detailing a closer surveillance of blacks, the act, along with other governmental decrees, systematically promoted slave collaborators by providing rewards for informants and other slaves drawn into the camp of masters.[16] Furthermore, because of laws rooted in the belief that certain private punishments may have contributed to the rebellious tendencies of slaves, planters could now be penalized for barbarities such as scalding, burning, castrating, and extracting the tongues or eyes of slaves.[17] One must emphasize, however, that there was no characteristic among slaveholders more deep-rooted and persistent throughout the history of slavery in South Carolina than the belief that they as slaveowners could do whatever they wanted with their property. Although as time passed, public opinion no doubt deterred many from inflicting the more sadistic punishments, a cool rationality had to be present for such outside influence to work. Unfortunately, it was rarely operative when an individual was in a state of rage or what nineteenth-century judges would later gingerly label "heat and passion."[18]

In light of the foiled uprisings and closer watch by a determined white slavocracy, the future could not have seemed bright for those held captive during the eighteenth century. The massive influx of Africans, however, must have bolstered the spirits of some with their tales of life in freedom and memories of a world still real and significant to a broad spectrum of blacks. But with these newcomers also came constant reminders of white power, for every day brought a fresh example of how men and women were made slaves. One foreign observer reported:

> As to their general Usage of them, 'tis monstrous, and shocking. To be sure, a *new negro,* if he must be broke, either from Obstinacy, or, which I am more apt to suppose, from Greatness of Soul, will require more hard Discipline than a young Spaniel: You would really be surpriz'd at their Perseverance; let an hundred Men shew him how to hoe, or drive a Wheelbarrow, he'll still take the one by the Bottom, and the other by the Wheel; and they often die before they can be conquer'd.[19] (Emphasis in the original.)

Those surviving the whips and spurs that prodded them developed with others, both seasoned and not, a cautious and circumspect outlook that can best be expressed as "Things cannot get better, they can only get worse." As the 1700s came to a close, more and more slaves had adopted this view and it contributed in interesting ways to keeping their war against masters nonviolent. Fewer conspiracies were uncovered, and none put into effect, but pacific tactics of resistance continued and a new wave of slaves joined fellow captives in their belief that a Christian God would free them.

Perhaps nothing served enslavers better than the fear and cautiousness a century of brutal repression had instilled. Both no doubt contributed to the growth during the 1800s of an enemy within: slave betrayers. While planter campaigns to divide and rule were partially responsible for betrayals, so, too, like oppressed peoples everywhere, slaves faced the timeless battles of maintaining their ranks and keeping fortified the courage and confidence needed to overcome antagonists of varying strengths. Through work slowdowns, collective thefts, and aid to runaways, African-

American bondsmen continued to demonstrate remarkable unity in their pursuits against masters.

The most visible and costly exception to this unity, at least in nineteenth-century South Carolina, was the inability of slaves to prevent slave collaborators from revealing to their masters information on conspiracies to revolt. This treachery undoubtedly stopped many potential insurgents from divulging to other slaves their boldest and most dangerous dreams of insurrection. There is much evidence of other collective acts of resistance where secrecy was preserved and assistance provided. Slave desertions, a major problem in the new century, were not only individual acts of revolt. Those who escaped could not have stayed out for long periods or reached free states without the aid and silence of fellow blacks. While the risks of helping or accompanying runaways were less grave than the risks of following those who plotted rebellions, they were still severe. Corporal punishment or imprisonment could result, and even death if one were caught absconding by the men delegated to reenslave them. Testimony from both blacks and whites report cases of runaways killed by slave catchers or by the hounds trained specially to assist them. Some catchers ordered their dogs to bite those captured as a warning and as training for future slave hunts. One tracker fed his hounds the heart of a black he had caused to be hanged.[20]

Although the majority of slaves chose not to risk the hazards of desertion, they confirmed their opposition to slavery not only by supporting those who fled but also by serving as accomplices to slaves engaged in acts of nonviolent resistance. Thefts were the most common crimes among slaves, and no occupational, religious, or social body of these blacks lacked its share of active participants.[21] It was a way of getting back at masters for stealing their labor, energies, and freedom. Some might see such appropriations as a means of making slave diets adequate, but alternatives like fishing, hunting, gardening, and paid work for neighboring farmers were more productive as sources of food. Masters knew as much; they were also aware that slaves rarely stole from their fellows.[22] But they did not understand the true nature of thefts. Instead, they saw them as evidence of an immorality and ingratitude peculiar to blacks. With some exasperation, the influential Charles Pinckney declared, in 1829, that slaves' depredations of rice amounted to 25 percent of the gross average of crops, and "this calculation was made after fifty years experience, by one, whose liberal provision for their wants, left no excuse for their ingratitude."[23] All thankfulness aside, slaves kept challenging masters by taking what slaveholders deemed their own, and the situation seemed to worsen as the antebellum period crawled with increasing vigor toward its cataclysm in gray and blue.[24]

In other ways also, long before the Civil War, enslaved blacks made their sentiments clear about bondage and the inhumanity it spawned. Arson was one time-tested mode of black protest, at once the most costly act of resistance for planters and the safest for perpetrators. Few suspects ever confessed and few were caught in the act. Individuals may have planned and executed their attacks alone, but only with the collective approval of fellow slaves, for without such an unspoken mandate, it seems unlikely that "negroes, big and little," would have grown so "notorious for being careless with fire."[25] Fear of losses through arson kept planters alarmed and chronically on edge.[26] One Samuel Porcher Gaillard was threatened by an incorrigible runaway with a plan to burn his house. Gaillard accused this slave of having already burned another house of his. He earlier replaced him with stock in a bank, and concluded tersely, "I ought to have sold him 6 years ago."[27] Six months later his home was set on fire again and he wrote in his plantation journal of November 24, 1856, "Two of my house servants are strongly suspected, [but] as yet cannot place it upon them."[28]

Floride Calhoun had written on February 15, 1842:

My Dear Husband, I fear from your last letter you have not received the half of my letters, one in particular, in which I mentioned having heard little Sawney [?] was in [the] goal (sic) in Daniels Ville, Georgia . . . and that I thought he ought to be sold out of State. . . . Mr. Davis . . . said he did fire his tent, and nearly burnt him up; he showed me the scars, on his hands, and that he [Sawney] ran off as soon as he set [the] fire.[29]

While some arsonists apparently also had intentions of murder, it appears that most sought only to destroy the homes and other property slaveholders had derived from slave labor.

Planter wealth in urban areas seems to have been a special target.[30] For six months beginning on Christmas eve of 1825, a fire was set every night in the opulent city of Charleston. In a single fire more than $100,000 worth of property was lost. The only culprit ever caught during this or any of the other conflagrations was a slave woman named Winnie, discovered in June 1826 trying to fire her master's home.[31] Although most slaves never turned to arson, almost all concealed a burning indignation about their enslavement and the illegitimacy of those whose authority was rooted in it. When a ninety-eight-year-old former chattel was asked why slaves were beaten, in striking contrast to her other milder testimony, she replied "rather vehemently": "Just because they wanted to beat 'em; they could do it, and they did."[32]

In comprehending the war against masters, one is tempted to focus on physical attacks and bloody insurgencies, but as Sidney Mintz wisely warns, bound men and women "like all human beings everywhere, were beset by all of the ordinary demands of living—to sleep, to love, to eat, to understand and to explain, to survive."[33] Such functions took on monumental proportions within the confines of slavery: anyone surviving could suffer a crippled psyche or what one enslaved mother deplored, a broken "constitution."[34] But lives infused with remarkable mental health thrived in the slave community, sustained by an autonomy, a moral and spiritual independence that bound slaves together in a society of souls that remained intact from their lives as slaves. This autonomy was fiercely struggled for and tenaciously preserved. The steadfastness and resourcefulness of slaves in the battle to free themselves psychologically as much as possible from the totality of their masters' control has never been fully told. This stems most likely from the arena in which that struggle occurred. It was fought largely on a psychological battleground where ideas burrowed deep and stayed entrenched despite the onslaught of enemy advances. More important, in all the varied campaigns between these contestants, that mental war front never toppled, for it was there and only there that black combatants could usually win. Slaves did not escape unscathed. The ability of masters to flog at will, to shatter familial bonds, and to rape both married and single loved ones had a devastating effect on many. At a bare minimum, scarred bodies, auctioned flesh, and the presence of mulattoes were evidence of the costs of being unfree. With such penalties for simply existing, it is not hard to understand why some slaves began to hate themselves, to distrust each other, and to identify with masters. What is extraordinary is how and why far more did not. The answer to those questions gives form to a war long denied.

Slaves everywhere were relentless in their quest for an autonomous world safe and distinct from the world they were forced to live in, but those on large plantations had all the advantages: there one could elude controls and controllers more easily. It is probably no coincidence that the first slaves to abandon their masters at the outset of the Civil War were precisely those who had had the greatest difficulty in securing a sense of autonomy. As Joel Williamson argues:

> The inclination of domestics, mechanics, and laborers in the extractive industries and on relatively small plantations to leave their masters at the first reasonable opportunity while agriculturists on the larger plantations remained suggests that desertion correlated very closely with the degree of proximity that had existed between the slave and his owner.[35]

But whatever the size of the plantation, bound men and women found ways to win some sort of autonomy.[36] And some even learned how to vanish in the very midst of whites without the latter's knowing they had ever disappeared. Just as foreigners may distance themselves from unfriendly hosts by speaking in an "alien" tongue, many Low Country South Carolina slaves conversed in Gullah and thereby entered a world the uninitiated could seldom penetrate. Scholars have long debated the origins and morphology of this language but have neglected its role in creating private space.[37] Even after slavery, those in command of this language could evade outsiders. Mason Crum wrote that few whites knew what these Negroes talked about because they were "timid among strangers"[38]; however, a history of those blacks and of the language they spoke suggests that exclusivity and not timidity was at the root. With more insight than she may have realized, one of the earliest teachers of Sea Island blacks recalled the first day of class when her Gullah-speaking pupils "*evidently* did not understand me."[39] (Emphasis added.)

The black linguist Lorenzo Turner, who researched extensively among Sea Island blacks in the 1940s, found that there were far fewer African words and names in his early recordings than appeared later, when he was no longer an outsider. Equally instructive was his experience during a field trip to which he had invited a white colleague. His guest prompted one informant to terminate all discussion because he was offended by the "tone of voice" used. When Turner returned to the islands several weeks later, he "was confronted on every hand" with a question translated as "Why did you bring the white man?"[40] It was an inquiry time had not softened.

In 1842, the Reverend C. C. Jones admonished:

> Persons live and die in the midst of Negroes and know comparatively little of their real character. The Negroes are a distinct class in community, and keep themselves very much *to themselves*. They are one thing before the whites, and another before their own color. Deception towards the former is characteristic of them, whether bond or free. . . . It is habit—a long established custom, which descends from generation to generation.[41] (Emphasis in the original.)

Slaves and their descendants needed this autonomy, for without such a psychological underpinning no principle of independence could have been implanted nor any struggle for freedom sustained. Their success prompted one of the most relentless contests between masters and slaves: the battle for slave minds.

Slaveholders demanded infinitely more from their slaves than labor; to assure a sense of duty and servility, the enslaved had to be convinced that their owners were all-knowing, all-merciful, and all-powerful. Consequently, slaves were bombarded with words and deeds telling them that they sprang from savages and could be nothing but slaves.[42] Enslavers reasoned correctly that any people believing these tenets would be loyal and grateful to those who guided them through their hopeless existence. They understood also that the slave community had to be infiltrated early, for another group—slave parents and adults—was simultaneously implanting a very different set of concepts often long before many in the quarters knew what bondage meant.

Conquerors everywhere have recognized the advantages of captivating the young. Those proselytizing the "heathen" in Africa, for example, concentrated their missionary efforts among the children[43] and, as a result, did a great service to the unrobed that followed, wanting more. Similarly, Southern controllers and their religious wing acted in clever collusion to eliminate nasty habits, stubborn views, and dangerous potentials for rebellion.[44] It was a formidable challenge, because for at least the first six to eight years of a slave's life, black parents were in control.[45] Children were usually fed, clothed, and schooled by parents, siblings, grandparents, cousins, or miscellaneous "adopted" kin. In their homes and those of other bondsmen, slave children learned of the intrinsic humanity, natural intelligence, and superior morality of black folk. Children were taught to judge themselves by how well they adhered to the norms and values of the men and women who inhabited the quarters. Being mannerly toward the aged, obedient to parents, and respectful of all community members were the traits most rewarded.[46] According to thirty-six-year-old Lillie Knox of Murrells Inlet, S.C., some of the old "slavery time" people were living proof of the wisdom in these lessons. In 1936 she told what former Low Country slave Maria Heywood said about "manners":

She say when she [Heywood] a little girl they have to tote water in a pail. Have to tote water so far! Old people all cripple up. Walk on a stick in that deep, King Road sand. Aunt Maria tell me 'bout how she totin' water—way from the spring to the Big House—and she'd met one them old women, and they say: "Dater (daughter), give the old woman a drink!" And Aunt Maria say the old person'd say: "Tank you, dater! You'll have long life!"

She say she never couldn't refuse when the old people ask for a drink, not even when the sand deep, and the sun hot, and she know if they take the drink it mean she have to walk clean back down the hill, and up the hill, for another bucket. But some the girls wouldn't let the old people drink out their bucket, and Aunt Maria say they'd tell em: "Go long! You nasty no manners thing! You'll never live out you day!" And you know Aunt Maria say all them girls GONE, and she one leave! [left][47]

Service and loyalty to their families and black neighbors must have been drilled repeatedly in young ears. These and other early messages subconsciously confirmed by their life experiences as slaves no doubt explain why the ostensibly most content and pacific slave could suddenly change. Masters and their hirelings were often attacked, murdered, and threatened by the men and women they sought to control. For a wide range of reasons, the frequency and extensiveness of such violence has been grossly underestimated. Although most agree that Southerners, fearful of abolitionist propaganda, increasingly kept reports of slave assaults and slayings out of the press, there has been a tendency to acknowledge that subterfuge and move on. If one stops, however, and explores the full range of historical sources *collectively* as well as uses a bit of common sense, it becomes evident that the control of slaves was a very dangerous vocation. That risk and how accustomed many became to it can be grasped indirectly in the nonchalant recordings of certain free Carolinians. In a terse note to his father, Joseph Miller declared, "There [?] is to be three negroes hung in town to day for killing their master. I have nothing of importance to communicate."[48] John Ashmore wrote the following in his farm journal on February 5, 1856: "Difficulty with Pompey—who used violence upon me."[49] Why such observations and actions seemed unexceptional to some is revealed in an almost encyclopedic assortment of documents; together they establish that slave efforts to injure or to kill whites were common.[50]

Part of the blame for inaccurate assessments of slave violence lies in the sources frequently culled for evidence. Court records provide many insights, but, if viewed alone, have major shortcomings. Most South Carolina slaves, for instance, were tried in the magistrates and freeholders courts convened throughout the state. Unfortunately, the only extensive surviving records are for the districts of Pendleton, Anderson, and Spartanburg—all up-country communities. But the bulk of the black population was concentrated in the Low Country. And even if adequate court transactions could be found elsewhere, these documents would pose other problems.

Planters had a great deal to lose if they reported slaves who attacked them, for "grievously wounding, maiming, and bruising a white man" was a capital offense.[51] While executions did not necessarily follow such convictions, they certainly occurred. That some masters found life with proven dangers preferable to pecuniary loss is clear, in part from the decision of legislators to compensate owners for slaves executed. Although it may not have been legal until 1843 to receive compensation for slaves found guilty of murder or rebellion, some slaveholders did. Charles Prioleau, Hannah Tait, and Francis Kinlock, the owners of three slaves executed for their involvement in the 1829 Georgetown slave insurrection, each received $122.45 in December of 1829. But, no matter what crime executed slaves had committed, slaveowners never received full value for their human chattels because they were held partially responsible for their behavior. Lawmakers and others in the white community argued that a slave properly controlled would never harm a master. Thus, the social stigma of having an "uncontrolled" or poorly managed slave no doubt kept many from taking violent slaves to court. And because the compensation for an executed slave was small, some wealthier slaveowners may have chosen not to petition authorities for it at all.[52]

The greatest obstacle to uncovering slave assaults and murders ironically is both the least discussed and the most obvious: success. While some slaves killed in fits of anger, others planned meticulously to rid themselves of their targets without arousing any suspicion or, if suspicion was inescapable, by pointing the blame elsewhere.[53] Poisoning seems to have been a favorite mode of dispatch, from the seventeenth century on.[54] Other tactics were more complex and more daring. The slaves on one South Carolina plantation conspired to kill a heavily armed but lone overseer in a surprise attack. After bludgeoning him to death, they carried the body on his horse to "an unfrequented, adjoining swamp" where both were "reduced . . . to ashes." The fate of that particular controller would never have been discovered if a young slave witness had not, years later, betrayed the older slaves involved. Because the owner, like many slaveholders, considered overseers to be among the most irresponsible of whites, he had simply assumed his employee had tired of the job and unceremoniously departed. But there was no arrest or conviction. "The matter ended," wrote the contemporary who recounted this near-perfect murder, because the master of those responsible reasoned, "the sacrifice of some valuable negroes, would not restore a lost overseer."[55]

Although it is easy to cite the specifics preceding and following certain slave attacks, none necessarily explains fully what lay behind them. A threatened punishment or an actual attempt, for example, was sometimes violently repulsed, but why then? It seems unlikely that a majority of the slaves who reacted in this fashion had never experienced chastisement or a warning of one before. The abruptness with which many compliant and patently nonviolent slaves changed strongly suggests a suppressed rage capable of shattering all passivity. Implicated in and executed for an 1831 "attempt to raise an insurrection" was one Ned who had been owned from childhood by Robert Cuningham. Throughout those years there had never been "any cause of . . . suspicion against him of a capital nature."[56] In another instance, John T. Kirby's "good boy and faithful servant" almost killed him when he tied and began to lash his son.[57] How and why these "good boys" became transformed into fearsome men still is being debated.

Perhaps most terrifying to whites were the endemic group and interplantation murders committed by slaves,[58] for such killings denied them the psychological comfort of attaching individual motivation to solitary circumstances. It was unclear, in one instance, whether two bondsmen murdered their master because of rewards promised by "neighboring" slaves or because of a prior decision. In either case, they not only did the job, but almost succeeded in making it appear accidental.[59] Such calculated and studied attacks made it all the more difficult to hide from the horrible truth that seemingly anything or nothing could snap the constraints that bound a slave. Note the case of Clory:

> I'll always 'member Clory, de washer. She was a mulatto with beautiful hair she could sit on. . . . One day our missus gone in de laundry an find fault with de clothes. Clory didn't do a t'ing but pick her up bodily an' throw 'er out de door. . . . Afta dat she begged to be sold fur she didn't want to kill missus, but our master ain't nebber want to sell his slaves. But dat didn't keep Clory from gettin' a brutal whippin'. Dey whip' 'er until der wasn't a white spot on her body. Dat wus de worst I ebber see a human bein' got . . . I t'ought she wus goin' to die, but she got well an' didn't get any better but meaner.[60]

Whether such active resistance was spurred by individual anguish or collective fury did not matter as much to controllers as how to prevent it. Never far behind that perennial struggle was an unfathomable terror. It was most palpable whenever planters and nonslaveholding whites perceived a rise in slave rebelliousness, or worse, heard rumors of slaves conspiring to revolt. Both substantially explain the periodic bloodletting they almost ritualistically engaged in during the time span of this study.[61] No matter how unfounded the claim or how spurious the source, the threat of an insurrection could trigger interstate hysteria that rarely was quelled until some black body had been sacrificed. And so that cycle went: deadly fear, black deaths, and appeals for more funds toward slave control.[62] In response to the last, militias were formed, arsenals refurbished or built, informants rewarded, and compensations dispensed to those whose chattels lost their lives in the struggle for freedom.[63]

While the costs of slave control continued to mount, other tolls—nonfiscal but as taxing—escalated also. The nightmare of blacks on the rise prodded at least one Carolinian to carry loaded pistols with him to bed. The precaution cost him his life. In a letter on the excesses white fears of black rebellions had caused over a thirteen-year period, South Carolinian Anna Hayes Johnson wrote:

> At the time . . . of the projected insurrection a gentleman by the name of Micale—a very promising young man—was so much alarmed at the news that he always slept with a pair of pistols under his head—the morning of which I am speaking he rose early and taking the pistols from his pillow he . . . struck one of them accidentally . . . and it immediately went off and blew out his brains.[64]

Less dangerous safeguards settled others at dusk. Adam Hodgson, writing in 1820, declared that someone was stationed each night on a Charleston church steeple "to watch and give the alarm in case of fire, as the *inhabitants are never free from the apprehension of an insurrection . . . in the confusion of a premeditated or accidental conflagration.*"[65] (Emphasis in the original.) From poor whites to planters, the "principal topic" and subject most "interesting" was "how to control negroes."[66] Herbert Aptheker captured well the mind of the white South when he depicted "a machinery of control" constantly in motion.[67]

Unfortunately for the ruling class, an elite dominated by planters but including merchants and lawyers, potentially dangerous groups other than slaves themselves complicated the never-ending war. Challenges from South Carolina's nonslaveholding and small-slaveholding whites, free blacks, and antislavery Northerners caused controllers in the state to search for the best means of neutralizing or thwarting the perceived threat from outside the slave community. The reliance primarily on force in their defense against slaves was deemed neither plausible nor as yet necessary to employ with the other orders of society. Instead, they began a war of words to convince all—including slaves—that bondage was not only the best system imaginable, but absolutely essential.[68] So successful were their campaigns that the patriarchal worldview they brilliantly disseminated endured throughout the years of slavery and much of the twentieth-century scholarship devoted to it.

According to this ideology—an amalgam of paternalistic, pro-slavery, and racist ideas—enslavers were benevolent patriarchs who cared for, protected, and cherished their slaves. In return, supposedly grateful and loyal servants labored happily and diligently to please their beloved masters. Here was an ideology designed to obscure reality. And the South's ruling class succeeded in this: ultimately, practically all white civic, political, and religious leaders sounded a harmonious chord that rejoiced in this divine system of government. As one such voice proclaimed, "God in his good Providence has brought these heathen to our very doors;—they are around our very hearth stones, and in our dwellings, with relations existing between us, which . . . devolve upon us obligations and duties as solemn and responsible as those we owe to our children."[69]

Obviously, the practical advantages of this ideology to slaveholders were multifold. It deflected attention from such unpatriarchal practices as abandoning or selling old and decrepit slaves while admonishing those who embarrassed the regime with unabashedly cold fiscal moves. Angered by the attention abolitionists were bringing to sales and family separations, Governor James Henry Hammond countered loudly that keeping families together "had always been" a "prime consideration" among slaveowners, but even when impossible, it mattered little, for Negroes were "both perverse and comparatively indifferent" about their families. He perhaps never heard the pitiful wails of black loved ones awaiting their fate at the festive human markets crammed with white buyers.[70]

The contrast between the world reflected out of a patriarchal looking glass and the images slaves saw was recounted by an ex-chattel whose master "allus kept more dan 200 head of slaves." George Fleming, born in Laurens County, recalled that his master never had to whip much because "he would say if dat nigger didn't walk de chalk, he would put him on de block and settle him. Dat was usually enough, 'cause Marse mean't dat thing and all de niggers know'd it."[71] Physical chastisement and the threat of sale reveal much about the worldview of planters and about the relations among masters, slaves, and those between. Each brutality was justified with paternalistic jargon. As one noted patriarch declared, "To manage the slave, without an occasional resort to the lash, is as much a matter of impossibility—as to manage

children without it."[72] And despite repeated urgings by slaveholders against excessive lashing, overseers and drivers became
notorious—thanks largely to the propaganda of their bosses —
for brutalizing slaves. Paternalism not only spared planters from
having to justify an oppressive system of force, intimidation, and
ceaseless struggle, but it cast all responsibility for that reality elsewhere.[73]

No matter who slaveholders blamed, physical coercion by way
of the lash was the most effective and frequently used day-to-day
mechanism of control, for to sell every misbehaving slave would
have been a Pyrrhic victory. Unfortunately, as James Anderson
brilliantly argued in "Aunt Jemima in Dialectics: Genovese on
Slave Culture" scholars like Eugene Genovese have allowed the
theoretical smokescreen of paternalism to hide the "violent repression . . . at the core of minority subjugation in America."[74] In
Roll, Jordan, Roll, the work in which Genovese presents the paternalism thesis in most detail, he fails to distinguish between
paternalism as an ideology and as a way of life. Moreover, he
never substantiates the acceptance or internalization of paternalism by those whose sanction was essential, namely, the slaves.[75]
That there were masters who did everything in their power to
realize the patriarchal ideal is not in dispute. Even at financial loss,
some masters struggled to provide for, to protect, and to prevent
the breakup of families among their slaves.[76] So strong were those
commitments that despite the awakening Henry William Ravenel
had to have experienced during the Civil War, he still could write
in May 1865, "As they have always been faithful and attached to
us, and have been raised as family servants, and have all of them
been in our family for several generations, there is a feeling towards them somewhat like that of a father who is about to send
out his children . . . to make their way through life."[77]

A formidable range of factors precluded the cementing of widespread paternalistic bonds in South Carolina. Not least among
them was distance. Because of the feared sickly season and "country fever" between May and November, most ruling-class planters
from the eastern and middle portions of the state departed for
healthier climates. Large numbers of bondsmen had contact with
overseers alone for almost seven months of the year, and overseers
were not known to foster many paternal links.[78] Only "close living

of masters and slaves" could develop a sense of paternalistic duty.[79] As contemporaries frequently noted, even when planters resided on their estates they seldom had contact with any but the domestics and other elite slaves. This is undoubtedly the reason why privileged slaves were the only blacks most planters remembered in their nostalgic recollections.[80]

The celebrated "faithful old house servant" is, not surprisingly, portrayed most often by masters as the grateful recipient of their paternalism. This classic black stayed with the owner throughout the war, remaining loving, loyal, and devoted to the end. Such characters appear almost solely on the pages of romantic memoirs, for during the antebellum period domestics were criticized constantly for their incompetence, treachery, and dishonesty.[81] The house servants of the aristocratic and politically prominent R. F. W. Allston family "were a terrible trial" to the relative taking care of Mrs. Robert Allston, a new mother who had become ill "after childbirth." Her daughter, Elizabeth Pringle, wrote, "Aunt Mary had no patience with incompetence, . . . and mamma had to hear hourly of their [house servants'] shortcomings, which she knew only too well already."[82] Even those domestics purchased or hired out to work in urban hotels received poor marks. During a January 7, 1855 visit, a Charleston guest wrote:

> One particular want appears to me evident in negro minds and character: they have no consciousness of the fitness of things. I suffer now from the cold wintry weather here; and upon my begging Blackie for a better fire in my room, in the civilest, most anxious tone, he asked whether I would not like some iced water? (Knowing this to be a luxury in hot weather, he would never consider that it might be less acceptable in cold.) We have lately had black chambermaids in all hotels. They are perfectly good-natured, and officiously anxious to help us in all matters in which their assistance is not required. "Let I do this, Missus," and "Let I do that," when perhaps it is hard to induce them to do what is really wanted—to light the fire when we are cold, or to bring a little warm water when clean hands would be a luxury.[83]

What little evidence one finds to support the contention that blacks internalized the paternalist ethos comes almost exclusively from white sources and implicates only the *top* of the domestic hierarchy, that is, the mammies, butlers, and body servants.[84] It is perhaps for this reason that mammies received such lengthy and romantic treatment by Eugene Genovese.[85] Yet several factors militated against master-slave relationships of mutual obligations and sincere reciprocity even within these three groups of house slaves. Close proximity to one's owner could result either in a deepening of positive feelings or in a sharpening of tensions. Furthermore, privileged blacks were part of the broader slave community and subject to internal pressures to conform to *its* norms, and loyalty to slaveholders was certainly not a standard the masses of slaves advocated. Slaves of the household had families of their own: their greatest obligation was to them. Metta Morris Grimball noted that Patty, a mammy of the dutiful stereotype, who remained with her throughout the war and some time after, departed promptly when "sent for by her son & Husband."[86] When one considers the mind and culture of the slave community, it is not difficult to comprehend why a keen observer of the newly liberated at Port Royal "once," and once only, heard "uncontrollable laughter among the Colored" when she and her party remarked, "Your Massahs said they loved you."[87]

While the ruling class failed to persuade most slaves to join them in patriarchal bliss, they did win over most nonslaveholding and small-slaveholding whites. No aspect of the patriarchal ideology was as effective in this as its racist component. Whites had to stand united if civilization was to be spared the pollution and destruction of barbaric blacks. So fervently did the elite warn of the dangers both freed and free blacks posed to white jobs, women, and lives that its members earned legitimacy and credibility as leaders articulating the collective will of white Carolinians. It was a different story, however, when ruling-class whites argued in republican detail how classless and democratized white society had become through the enslavement of blacks.[88]

Patriarchs both knew and feared the effect their control of the courts, their monopolization of the best lands, and their ownership of the majority of slaves had on introducing dangerous class divisions. How uncertain and troubled those breaches made them was only thinly veiled in the well-rehearsed sermon the Reverend William O. Prentiss delivered to the South Carolina state legislature in 1860. After the usual rantings about the innate servility and contentment of slaves, he declared, "If time allowed me . . . I could prove to you . . . the absurdity of believing that dangerous combinations could be formed by him with badly disposed white persons, with whom our police regulations do not permit him to be intimately acquainted."[89]

Laws against the absurd unthinkable did not prevent it. From colonial times onward, poor whites socialized with, broke the law with, and, most alarmingly, sometimes communicated and interacted with slaves in a way that strongly suggested a shared hostility toward bondage.[90] Just how far this could and occasionally did take nonslaveholders is one of the most woefully neglected areas of scholarly research. In 1862 twenty-four residents of Marion District petitioned to the governor against members of one family, and others, who "for many years" had harbored fugitives, traded with slaves, and recently made clear both their ability and willingness to "incite an insurrection among the slaves."[91] Another incident, not precisely dated, offers another glimpse into this important class division. Writing from Cokesbury, South Carolina, a woman discussed the uncovering of a plot that led to five blacks being sentenced to hang and that implicated twenty white men in their conspiracy. She described the whites as "all *southern born*, the poor white *trash* who have associated with negroes and are jealous of the higher classes and think insurrection will place all on [an equal] footing [and] get [them] some plunder in the bargain."[92] (Emphasis in the original.) These are only two instances of behavior the elite had long before encountered.[93] Through the years, similar experiences reinforced a truth that those studying antebellum and postbellum race relations have sometimes failed to remember, that control of blacks demanded control of whites.

In his study, *The Ruling Race*, historian James Oakes argues that scholars have underestimated the potential nonslaveowners and small slaveholders had for class mobility.[94] But on the way up, the economic interests of nonelite whites conflicted sharply enough with those of planters that they threatened the effectiveness of the multitudinous controls prescribing slave behavior. Black Carolinians, who understood this only too well, were adept at exploiting the divergent economic forces that assisted them in gaining autonomy and, also, prized commodities like tobacco and alcohol. For a white without slaves, much money, or learning, it was exceedingly difficult to resist bartering with and buying from slaves their extensive inventory of "appropriated" goods, a temptation no doubt fueled to a degree by the aristocratic disdain with which many planters regarded their lesser brethren. Slaves both perceived and appreciated the class dynamics at work; it is hardly likely that poor and middling whites did not also.[95]

As was often the case, elite whites were either too frightened to acknowledge or too blind to see the active role slaves played in nurturing markets and divisions advantageous to themselves. The following 1850 petition from "Sundry Citizens of Barnwell District to Increase the Punishment for Illicit Traffic With Slaves" reflects not only the frustration the most advantaged whites felt in attempting to curtail the pervasive trading with slaves, but their racist view that blacks were passive. It states in part:

> Your Petitioners are confident in the opinion that more injury—far more, both to the morals and property of the community is received through the instrumentality of dishonest white persons tampering with our slaves and inciting them to plunder, than is done by any other system of open or secret dishonesty. The owner of the property is defrauded of his just gains and the slave is made the vehicle through whose hands the stolen property is passed. Thus, though [through] the base and nefarious means used, the slave is made the fit instrument of crime, and being trained to every violence, he too often eventually becomes an assassin or incendiary. His mind corrupted, his body diseased, he either fills a premature grave by the effects of disease or through the administration of justice, expiates his crime on the gallows, while the promoter and partner of his guilt escapes with impunity and in defiance of the law.[96]

Harboring fugitives was another crime that compromised slave control. Whites were repeatedly implicated in advertisements as potential harborers of runaways; neither liberal rewards for their conviction nor patriotic appeals seemed to do much good. While some small slaveholding and nonslaveholding whites risked prosecution primarily to exploit the labor of runaways, others most assuredly were expressing genuine empathy for those who escaped.[97] To be sure, such miscreants never seriously threatened elite rule, but they did cause considerable uneasiness.[98] So too did another potentially dangerous group—free blacks.

Unlike the lower white orders whom planters could cajole with a shared racist identity, generous offers of ginning facilities, social gatherings emphasizing the rich possibilities of a slaveholding society, and jobs increasingly reserved for whites only, blacks without masters proved a more troublesome presence. Not only did

they bely patriarchal essentials, but participated in all the illegal-
ities discussed above.[99] How these walking contradictions were
dealt with will be discussed later. The plantocracy had many
weapons to keep each danger in check, perhaps none more consistently effective than the vast array of controllers under their
control.

Members of the slaveowning elite employed both whites and
blacks to aid them in suppressing and managing an unwieldy
slave-labor force. The most successful—for reasons enslavers never
quite understood—were the black drivers who supervised slave
labor and served as a punitive arm of their owners. The reasons
for the greater receptiveness of slaves toward these controllers
were complex, but had much to do with the figures immediately
above and responsible for the performance of the drivers: the
overseers. For the enslaved, drivers were the lesser of two evils.

According to the testimony of slaves, most overseers did not—
contrary to William Scarborough—treat "Negroes in their charge
fairly well."[100] Indeed, accounts of the brutality of overseers made
those concerning drivers pale by comparison. That explains no
doubt why slaves more often attempted to cause the dismissal of
overseers than the demotion of drivers, contriving this frequently
with the aid of drivers whose easy access to the ultimate controller—the slaveowner—gave complaints force. The job of overseers
was, for such reasons, the most difficult in the control hierarchy.[101]
South Carolinian B. T. Sellers reported an 1860 incident that captures just how difficult the job could be:

> Their has been quite a riot at Mrs. Smiths, on this river, a short time
> ago, it appears, that the Overseer (Palmer) floged the Driver, whereupon the
> son-in-law of Driver, assaulted him (Overseer) & beat him soundly, literally
> stripping him of his clothing . . . *Palmer* . . . it is said beged the *Negros
> pardon,* as negroes had threatened to report his past conduct to Mrs. Smith.
> . . . where their is so many Negroes, & but so few white in Summer, I think
> that this matter ought to concern every planter on the river.[102] (Emphasis in
> the original).

Overseers were expected to do the impossible: planters demanded slave compliance without slave injuries, bountiful crops
with limited resort to lashings, and faithful service despite poor
pay. Added to these difficulties were the physical dangers overseers
faced each day. When black captives killed or attacked, overseers

often were the victims.[103] One contemporary argued that masters suppressed news of such murders because they feared that publicizing them would put overseers in a better bargaining position for higher wages.[104] In light of how disparagingly masters spoke of overseers, it is questionable whether that would have been sufficient. The attitudes of planters toward overseers were usually class-related, and slaves rarely forgot it. One slave, Dinah Cunningham, recalled:

> My white folks was no poor white trash. . . . Good marse and good mistress had heap of slaves and overseers. One overseer name Mr. Welch. De buckra folks dat come visitin', use to laugh at de way he put grease on his hair, and de way he scraped one foot back'ards on de ground when they shake hands wid him. He never say much, but just set in his chair, pull de sides of his mustache and say "Yas sah" and "No sah," to them dat speak to him. He speak a whole lot though, when he get down in de quarters.[105]

While overseers had guns to protect themselves from slaves, they could do little to combat the ridicule and disdain of planters. They did, however, have strong advocates among the white majority. Planter success in employing these nonelite whites to do most physical controlling was aided considerably by their ambition to join the elite. Many adopted an outlook and behavior more control-minded than that of the ultimate controllers. By overlooking this dimension of lower class aspirants and the extraordinary possessiveness of planters toward their chattels, scholars have failed to see also how important the law became in maintaining white unity.

The legal apparatus of South Carolina played a crucial role in precluding fratricidal battles among the strata of white society. Nowhere was this clearer than in cases involving the generally poor and nonslaveholding whites delegated to patrol. On the one hand, planters wanted patrollers to do their duty in making sure slaves were not wandering about at night without permission. On the other hand, when patrollers "corrected" errant slaves, masters could become enraged. When one considers the temperaments[106] and possessiveness of those involved, what on the surface seemed innocuous could have triggered bloody confrontations with a stark class dimension. And some affluent slaveholders made it clear that neither patrolling nor patrollers were welcome. When a

Mr. C. W. Jones notified the wealthy Louis Manigault of his up-
coming "Patrol Duty," Manigault responded:

> I myself am now *exempt* from every thing pertaining to military Duty
> *not only* in *South Carolina* & Georgia but in the *United States*. . . . More-
> over, you need not trouble yourself concerning my plantations, Gowrie &
> East Hermitage. _for altho' In Our Community true it is that Law & Order
> should ever reign paramount. _still the *Master* when on his place is *the one*
> to examine into his own property & When not there himself *then* his Over-
> seer who has his Confidence & who represents him during his absence _ &
> I Can not allow any new regulations.[107] (Emphasis in the original.)

As petitions to the legislature and court cases repeatedly reveal,
the power of the State kept masters, slaves, and those between on
a war-torn but secure terrain.[108]

Besides providing an alternative to armed resolutions, the court
system assured that planters who were either too lenient or too
cruel would encounter the community's displeasure. The most
significant law to enhance the welfare of South Carolinian blacks
was an 1821 amendment making the murder of slaves a capital
offense. One must be extremely careful, however, in evaluating
this and other reforms, for the record of South Carolina courts
in bringing criminal planters to justice is poor. The greatest hin-
drance to convictions was the applicability of the following 1740
provision to the 1821 amendment: ". . . if a slave suffered in life
or limb, or was cruelly beaten or abused where no white person
was present, or being present, shall neglect or refuse to give evidence—in every such case the owner or person having care and
management of the slave . . . shall be adjudged guilty, unless he
can make the contrary appear by good and sufficient evidence, *or
shall, by his own oath, clear and exculpate himself.*"[109] (Emphasis
in the original.)

Nonelite controllers found additional safeguards in the courts.
Overseers attacked by slaves could seek redress—from peers—if
their employers failed to take action. Slaves undisciplined at home
would find the State intervening.[110] Finally, legal mechanisms and
a powerful corps of white volunteers also kept the potential threat
of free blacks in check. Despite their effectiveness, efforts were
made to control them more completely. Just a year before the
Confederate rebellion, legislation was proposed to place South

Carolina's free blacks in bondage. As this reality drew closer, a member of the free brown elite warned a friend, "What is to come will be worse."[111] In some ways it was, but nothing could compare with the horrors that the black unfree and the shallowly free experienced before white America went to war—this time with itself.

CHAPTER TWO

The Threat of Sale
The Black Family as a Mechanism of Control

The fundamental principles upon which the system is based, are simply these: That all living on the plantation, whether colored or not, are members of the same family, and to be treated as such—that they all have their respective duties to perform, and that the happiness and prosperity of all will be in proportion to the fidelity with which each member discharges his part. I take occasion to inculcate repeatedly that, as the patriarch (not tyrant) of the family, my laws, when clearly promulgated, must be obeyed —that, as patriarch, it is my duty to protect their rights, to feed, clothe and house them properly—to attend to them carefully when sick—to provide for all their proper wants—to promote peace, harmony and good feeling, as so far as practicable, their individual comfort. *On the other hand, the servants are distinctly informed that they have to work and obey my laws, or suffer the penalty.* (Emphasis added.)

Southern planter, 1853[1]

Mother, is Massa gwine to sell us tomorrow?

Slave folk song[2]

The plantocracy of South Carolina attempted various methods of pacification and repression to cow African-American slaves into submission, but the most effective long-term mechanism of control was the threat of sale. Blacks feared the realization of that portentous suggestion more than any other mode of punishment, for while they could endure the pain of chastisement through whipping, it was more difficult to suffer the grave psychological injuries that stemmed from the severance of familial bonds through sale. Memories of that traumatic experience would linger long after the wounds of a sadistic beating had healed. Parents who were sold would worry about the welfare of children growing up without a mother and a father. Slave men and women heard frightening tales from masters about the dangers of life in other states or in other parts of the same state where they might be sold.[3] Charles Ball, for instance, who was sold more than once before he was transported from Maryland to a South Carolina plantation in 1805, recalled:

I shall never forget the sensations which I experienced this evening on finding myself in chains, in the state of South Carolina. From my earliest recollections, the name of South Carolina had been little less terrible to me than that of the bottomless pit. In Maryland, it had always been the practice of masters and mistresses, who wished to terrify their slaves, to threaten to sell them to South Carolina; where, it was represented, that their condition would be a hundred fold worse than it was in Maryland.[4]

The removal of recalcitrant and incorrigible bondsmen was a time-tested and widespread custom. As one judge said in 1833, "The owners of slaves frequently send them off from amongst their kindred and associates as a punishment, and it is frequently resorted to, as the means of separating a vicious negro from amongst others exposed to be influenced and corrupted by his example."[5] One planter who owned about one hundred and thirty-five slaves was so pleased with this method of chastening blacks that he urged his heirs to continue the practice. He left instructions in an 1855 will that the "young negroes be kept on one of his plantations, and . . . to sell any of them that are turbulent or otherwise troublesome."[6]

Reliance on punitive sales had long been a tactic used by masters to rid themselves of noncompliant slaves. In 1740 the wealthy South Carolinian Robert Pringle sold "a Very Likely Young Wench" to Portugal for the sole reason that "she had a practice of going frequently to her Father and Mother, who Live at a Plantation I am Concern'd in about Twenty Miles from Town from whence there was no Restraining her from Running away there & Staying every now & then."[7] This savage and brutal mode of disciplining "execrable," "indifferent," or simply "bad" slaves was employed throughout the antebellum period and was even quite common during the Civil War.[8] Such sales were sanctioned by almost all in the white community and received particular approval from the religious sector.[9] With the exception of the Society of Friends, every denomination in the South had compromised with slavery until by midway in the nineteenth century religious leaders were either silent or offered divine justification for the traffic in human chattels.[10] One prominent Presbyterian preacher and slaveowner in South Carolina argued that nothing human was being sold, only the right to "labor and service." "When we buy and sell them," he declared, "it is not *human flesh and blood* that we buy and sell, but we buy and sell a *right*, established by Providence, and sanctioned by Scripture, to *their labor and service for life.*"[11] (Emphasis in the original.)

Slaves knew that much more was at stake than the sale of labor. Susan Hamlin, who was born in 1833, recounted after she was freed the heartrending sorrows and screams of slaves who were torn from loved ones and of others who had discovered that a sale was coming. Hamlin, who had been a house servant at the Charleston home of Edward Fuller, told of a couple who were married one night and learned the next morning that the wife had been sold: "De gal ma got in de street an' cursed de [owner] fur all she could find. . . . De police took her to de Work House . . . an' what become of 'er, I never hear."[12]

It is crucial to note that not only familial ties but also the land on which black men and women had toiled, loved, borne children, and buried their dead acted as a powerful centripetal force that made the prospect of sale all the more horrifying. Many observers, both before and during the war, remarked about the magnetism of African-American birth and burying places.[13] Charles Nordhoff, for example, said that ex-slaves displayed "the same strong local attachment . . . characteristic of the black freedmen in the British West Indies."[14] When Union forces evacuated Edisto Island, just off the coast of South Carolina, in 1862, Laura Towne, the Northern schoolteacher who had come to teach liberated blacks, recorded: "A few old people had determined not to leave the home they loved so much, and they waited on shore till the last moment and then came hurrying down."[15] It is understandable, therefore, that most newly freed slaves returned to the area they had lived in while in bondage.[16] Funeral rites and burial grounds hold great importance in African-American culture. As late as the 1950s, some descendants of slaves arranged to have their remains interred on the plantations where their forebears rested.[17] Referring to blacks who had been slaves held by her relative R. F. W. Allston, Patience Pennington commented:

> Every year more hands leave the plantation [at Chisora Wood] and flock to the town, and every year more funerals wend their slow way from the town to the country; for though they all want to live in town, none is so

poor but his ashes must be taken "home"; that is, to the old plantation where his parents and grandparents lived and died and lie waiting the final summons. . . . The whole family unite and "trow een" to make up the sum necessary to bring the wanderer home; and even the most careless and indifferent of the former owners respect the feeling and consent to have those who have been working elsewhere for years, and who perhaps left them in the lurch on some trying occasion, laid to rest in the vine-covered graveyard on the old plantation.[18]

Such attachments were in all likelihood stronger before emancipation. An individual sold might be separated not only from the birthplace and burial grounds so important to black Carolinians, but removed perhaps forever from parents, cousins, aunts, uncles, grandparents, siblings, and friends. Bitter memories of such separations remained for years. The pain could still be seen in the tears of aging men and women who recalled lost kin and in the invectives expressed by ex-slaves and their descendants about the whites who commanded the inhuman domestic and international slave trade.[19] At least for slaves, their disdain of masters as a whole often inspired a blanket distrust of whites in general.[20] A slave whose master or mistress did everything possible to prevent sales and to minimize lashings was still a slave. Resentment of this reality contributed to the steady flow of errant slaves streaming into distant states. So extensive was the influx of "undesirable" slaves into the Palmetto State that in 1847 a group of citizens from Charleston appealed to the legislature to limit admission of "vicious slaves." Their petition demonstrates how widespread that market had become as well as how prevalent the belief that "docile" local slaves were prodded to mischief by recalcitrant outsiders. Their appeal stated in part:

Your petitioners . . . shew That the persevering efforts, in some parts of our Union, to intermeddle injuriously with our slave population furnish increased motives for vigilance on our part, not only in repelling interference from abroad, but in a stricter government of our slaves at home is liable to mischievous disturbance from the importation of vicious or criminal slaves from other states. That as laws have been passed by the states South West of us prohibiting the importation of slaves into those states merely for Sale and not the property of residents or immigrants passing through them. [sic]
This State and the City of Charleston in particular, have become the common place of meeting between the slave dealer from places north of us and the purchaser South West of us. That the motive of the Slave dealer is not only to approach as near as he can to his buyer, but to remove the slave

as far from his old range and from notorious bad character, as possible. That while on sale here many vicious slaves are palmed upon careless or confiding citizens among us, and their mixture with our own has had a sensible influence upon the docility and usefulness of our slaves. That your petitioners are not to be confounded with those inimical to Southern interests who oppose the removal of slaves from state to state under any circumstances. *We propose* to confine the admission of Slaves into this State, to those brought here by their owners, residents in this State and those the property of emigrants passing into or through this State and we propose to prohibit under proper sanctions the introduction of slaves into this state *merely for sale.* . . .[21] (Emphasis in the original.)

Most masters chose not to accept the fact that blacks who were native-born and free from "outside forces" could be refractory. They continued to delude themselves that they could preserve the purity and peacefulness of their slaves by keeping out all troublemakers. Slaveholders continued exercising, therefore, the powerful lever of deportation not only to accomplish this objective, but to warn bondsmen that they were not the subjects of idle threats.[22] To be sure, the mere presence of non–South Carolinian slaves proved the seriousness of remote planters, but the departure of local, native-born neighbors who failed to heed their owners' warnings was evidence of the sudden uprooting *all* slaves could face. The consequences of R. F. W. Allston's orders, for instance, would not have missed the attention of blacks:

Appropos of sales you enquire what Brass is to do. I sent him up to split Rails, and told him upon his repeated failure that he must go to the vendue table [auction block], whenever he could not do this. Now if any one about you is going to Charleston, give Brass a new shirt and send to Robertson Blacklock and Co. to be turn'd into money, forthwith. It is the best thing to be done with Brass. There must be no fuss about it, or noise, or notice.[23]

Needless to say, sales, either effected or threatened, would have been less meaningful to someone who lacked the bonds of friendship and family. South Carolinian enslavers learned this lesson early when, as a cost-saving measure in 1714, they experimented with deportations instead of their traditional solution of executions of slaves who committed crimes. Within three years, slaveholders revoked the law establishing the policy of deportations after they discovered that it prompted slaves "to commit great numbers of robberies, burglaries and other felonies, well knowing they were to suffer no other punishment for their crimes, but transportation, which to them was rather an encouragement to pursue their villanies."[24] In a black population largely male and single, planters during the first quarter of the eighteenth century had to find other methods of control.[25] The next century, however, brought new life to an old experiment.

By 1800, Africans and African-Americans generally had enmeshed themselves in an intricate and extensive network of kinship ties that commanded a loyalty so powerful that the atmosphere was ripe for masters to impose more successfully a compliance based on slave fears of banishment. Indeed, until the Confederacy lost its war, the prospect of being sold, whether for profit or punishment, hovered over all those in chains. This most-feared possibility was made real in innumerable ways. Not only did planters threaten to sell slaves who persistently refused to comply, but they saw to it that insubordinate slaves, as well as other bondpeople, constantly witnessed auctions and the endless processions of human chattels driven by diverse whites to distant destinies in captivity.[26] While one could choose not to watch such scenes, there very likely were black neighbors who had traveled on and remembered well each step of that route.

Jacob, a slave who belonged to Charles Manigault, would not have taken lightly the message from his master delivered to him after he had spent three weeks in solitary confinement while in jail and received a whipping for being "a bad disposed Nigger." Manigault's "compliments" were to be given to Jacob with notice that if he did not change for the better, New Orleans would be his destination—a marketplace, Jacob was reminded, where "several of the gang" had already been sent for "their misconduct, or their running away for no cause."[27] Although it is not possible to determine the exact number of punitive sales, virtually all sources indicate that the communication network among blacks was so efficient and extensive that most slaves were probably aware of those that did occur. As former slave Isaiah Butler declared, everyone knew the meaning of "I'll put you in my pocket, sir!"[28]

During the summer of 1863 some men owned by Plowden C. J. Weston, a planter on the Waccamaw River near Georgetown, tried to escape to Union forces. As a result of this "bad conduct," Weston decided to "dispose of them" because "he could never consider them as his people again." Elizabeth Collins, the English companion of Mrs. Weston, said about that event: "They were each sold to different people,—sold from their wives, poor things, who felt it very much at first; but the contented mind of the black people causes them soon to forget."[29] In grave contrast to the impression Miss Collins had of their mnemonic abilities, African-American slaves retained lucid memories of relatives and friends torn away from them and the circumstances under which they occurred. Newly freed slaves spoke constantly of "transported" family members, and the authors of slave autobiographies were frequently most graphic when describing how loved ones were lost to the notorious "trader."[30] Charles Ball, for example, wrote mournfully of witnessing his mother "dragged . . . towards the place of sale" after he was "snatched . . . from her arms." Years later, he wrote, "Young as I was, the horrors of that day sank deeply into my heart, and even at this time, though half a century has elapsed, the terror of the scene returns with painful vividness upon my memory."[31] In a different way, but with the same effect, Caleb Craig, born in 1851 on a Blackstock, South Carolina, plantation, recalled, "My mammy name Martha. Marse John soon give us chillun to his daughter, Miss Marion. In dat way us separated from our mammy. Her was a mighty pretty colored woman and I has visions and dreams of her, in my sleep, sometime yet."[32]

Craig was not unique in experiencing lurid flashbacks of sales and family separations: other ex-slaves—both in the nineteenth and the twentieth centuries—expressed similar sentiments and emotions.[33] Sylvia Cannon was eighty-five in 1937 when she cried about the unknown fate of her brothers sold while in bondage. Mrs. Cannon said: "I see em sell some slaves twice fore I was sold en I see de slaves when dey be traveling like hogs to Darlington. Some of dem be women folks looking like dey gwine to get down dey so heavy."[34] A large number of slaves would have had cause to weep over some relative who had vanished in the interregional slave trade. Despite such losses, the black family survived as an institution, for the ideas and principles guiding it were anchored in traditions so deep-seated and binding that they could endure even after familial links had been severed. To understand its survival and the full impact of sales, one must examine concepts of kinship in Africa as well as in North America, which made the black family the single most powerful source of support among slaves.

Sidney Mintz and Richard Price suggest in their brilliant anthropological study that "certain widespread fundamental ideas and assumptions about kinship in West Africa" may have been retained and shared by enslaved Africans landing in the Americas. The two scholars noted also that "the aggregate of newly-arrived slaves, torn from their own local kinship networks, would have continued to view kinship as the normal idiom of social relations."[35] Such beliefs could have been passed on easily to the descendants of indigenous Africans held captive in South Carolina, for on many plantations generations of particular slave families lived and flourished.[36] This was especially true in the district of Georgetown because after the 1780s "very few slaves [were] brought in from outside" its borders and apparently fewer were exported to foreign parts than in other areas.[37] Numerous sources indicate that native-born Africans were often the transmitters of social norms and history both to their progeny and to members of the broader society.[38]

One such African evidently so inspired his daughter, for many years later her young mistress remembered, "Often we children would . . . listen with rapt absorption to Maum Hetty's tales of the Guinea Negroes of whom her father was one before he was brought as a slave to Carolina. Sometimes she taught us scraps of native African songs, and when we were able to count to ten in African we concluded that our education was complete indeed."[39] What the Maum Hettys of the South added to their lessons to blacks in private, however, was a different story. Collectively, they instilled in black children and young adults familial obligations that reached far beyond the typical white American nuclear family. These and other norms—particularly those dictating what were acceptable marital bonds—distinguished slaves from members of the planter class. In his massive study of the black family, Herbert Gutman found that slaves adhered to rigid rules of exogamy in their selection of mates, while the men and women of the slaveholding elite often married first cousins. Because he found similar patterns, mores, and norms among slaves on quite disparate plantations, Gutman concluded that those patterns were influenced neither by slaves' occupation nor by the type of planter on the estate. He therefore discarded the ever-popular "mimetic theories of Afro-American culture."[40] It is my belief that because of the strength of the black family, sale and the threat of sale acted as a major determinant of slave behavior. Sold slaves not only disseminated and unified slave culture, but graphically demonstrated the reality behind each threat of sale.

Sidney Mintz was correct in arguing that "within the structure of a slave society the slaves were required to engineer styles of life that might be preserved in the face of terible outrage."[41] The black family did engineer such survival strategies. It was an extremely cohesive and resilient unit that demanded from its members numerous obligations and infinite devotion. Slave parents, for example, played certain economic roles, such as vegetable gardening and hunting, that were essential to the procurement of adequate food for their offspring. Moreover, although other relatives gave some assistance, fathers and mothers were responsible for the bulk of their children's socialization. So intense was loyalty to one's family that Union officers found it difficult initially to recruit blacks into the army because they feared to leave loved ones unprotected. Once freedmen did enlist, it was difficult sometimes to retain them because, as one observer noted, "A negro thinks to go and see his family the height of happiness."[42] Thus, the magnetism of African-American kinship ties sometimes irritated the self-proclaimed friends of the slave, just as it infuriated his adversaries almost perennially.

The family was, ironically, not only at the base of masters' most effective control mechanism, it was the source also of their most persistent aggravation, the runaway. Contemporary publications and correspondence are replete with cases of absconding blacks who were thought to have deserted in order to reunite with relatives.[43] Such knowledge must have simply added to the frustration of many masters, for it did not always help in retrieving their property. "A black fellow named Ned," for instance, was still evading capture almost a year later despite his master's careful listing in a runaway advertisement of "relations" that the thirty-two-year-old plowman and wagoner had living "at Mrs. Bird's, at the Rocks, at Dr. Wilson's, on the State Road, and at Moorer's in St. Mathews Parish."[44] Half a century earlier, John Davis recalled about his travels in South Carolina:

> The Charleston papers abound with advertisements for fugitive slaves. I have a curious advertisement now before me.—"Stop the runaway! Fifty dollars reward! Whereas my waiting fellow, Will having eloped from me last Saturday, *without any provocation,* (it being known that I am a *humane master*) ... *Will may be known by the incisions of the whip on his back*; and I suspect has taken the road to *Coosohatchie,* where he has a wife and five children, whom I sold last week to Mr. Gillespie."[45] (Emphases in the original.)

Analogous suspicions about why and where bondsmen ran were expressed throughout the antebellum period. In 1829 monetary compensation was offered for the apprehension of "George, Celia, and Sarah." Their owner declared that "there is every reason to suppose the wenches are harboured on John's Island, from whence they came, and where they have connexions . . . and that the fellow George, who has runaway since has joined them, the whole being of one family."[46] There was, of course, no single reason for slave desertions, but it is interesting that members of the immediate family often escaped together.[47]

Enslaved husbands, wives, daughters, and sons shipped great distances from each other rarely forgot those left behind and frequently pursued every method of ending the separation. In an effort to join family members in South Carolina a Samuel Tayler wrote the following letter to his former mistress:

> My Dear Mistress　　　I have been in this City about three years and belong at present to Mr. Sam'l Jerques, merchant. I was sold for $1,900. He is remarkably kind and gives me a fair opportunity of making pocket money. But still my mind is always dwelling on home, relations, & friends which I would give the world to see. As times now are, I suppose I may be purchased for about 10 or $11 hundred dollars. If you my Dear Mistress, can buy me, how happy I would be to serve you and your heirs; I beg you will write me how *all* my relations are, and inform them that I have enjoyed uninterrupted health since I came here. Rember me also to Sarah, my ma ma, and Charlotte, my old fellow servant & Amy Tayler.
>
> I would be glad to belong to my young mistress, Mrs. Parker in case you should not feel disposed to take me.[48]

Some slaves never gave up the hope of reuniting with loved ones many miles away. Pitiful efforts were still being made long after

Emancipation. Black newspapers well into the 1870s and 1880s were filled with "Information Wanted" sections carrying appeals from mothers, fathers, sisters, brothers, and children who refused to abandon the glimmer of hope that they might yet find family members who had been torn from them in bondage.[49] Charles Gatson pleaded for "information of his children, Sam and Betsy Gatson" in 1870. He wrote, "They formerly belonged to Washington Fripp, of Newhaw, South Carolina; were carried to Charleston and there sold by a trader to go far South, it is supposed to Mississippi or Louisiana. They are now about twenty-two to twenty-five years old, and were taken away in 1861."[50]

The behavior of blacks during the Civil War offers further testimony to the strength and binding character of African-American kinship ties. In the face of tremendous odds, which ranged from possible sale to Cuba[51] to murder, whole familes, not merely individuals, were the most common venturers to Union lines. Charles Nordhoff observed in 1863, "They have strong affection for their children. It is well known that few men run away to us alone; as a rule they come off bringing with them their wives and little ones—often from great distances, and at frightful risks."[52] Almost all Northerners who visited Port Royal, the place of convergence for thousands of contrabands, commented similarly and noted the great skill and diligence with which freedmen sought relatives sold off or by some other means taken from them while in servitude.[53] Although for the first time in their lives these slaves could feel secure in keeping their families intact, many nevertheless sacrificed all and hazarded possible permanent separation by joining the Union Army's fight against their oppressors.

African-American men in the army continued to demonstrate a role as providers and as heads of families while they served. The soldiers in Thomas Higginson's black regiment in South Carolina, for example, "intrusted him, when they were paid off, with seven hundred dollars, to be transmitted by him to their wives, and this besides what they had sent home in other ways,—showing the family-feeling to be active and strong in them."[54] It appears that the overriding concern of black patriarchs, whether in fighting in the Yankee army or while serving as cooks, body servants, and laborers for Confederate troops, was the care and future welfare of their families. One Stephen Moore wrote this while accompanying his officer-owner in the Confederate ranks:

Dear Wife   I take the present opportunity of writing you a few lines to let you know how I am getting on. I am as well as common and hope these few lines may find you all well. I was rite smartly vext til Minus come here. He said you was all well and that gave me satisfaction. Tell Minuses Mother that he is in a half mile of me. I can see him any time I want too. He is well. I will try to come home in 2 or 3 weeks if I can get off. You and Elihue must gather me about 40 chickens when I come home. I will have the money to pay for them. I am making money every day. Tell Numer and Ransom they must sea to my children & sea that they mind theirs mother & tell Elihu like wise . . .

Tell Synthy and Chany I am very much ablige to them for the word they sent me by Minus. Tell Lizabeth, Nelly and Gracy I thank them for this compliments they sent. Tell Mother I will send her money as soon as an oppertunity will admit. Tell Mr. Hill [overseer] I want to see him as well as any body else. Tell him to please take this letter & read it to Rachel. I will thank you to take this letter and read it to all my people. Tell Rachel I have bought a fine watch for her [but] I have no way to send it & will keep it and bring it when I come. . . . Tell Rachel if she needs any money to write to me when Elihew write. The money is not to be made it is all ready made. I have 3 meals of victuals to cook a day and the rest of the time is mine. If you don't spend the money I send you keep it for me when I come hom. Rachel pay Gracy 30 cts for me, pay Noah 25 cts for me, pay Numer one dollar & a half & I will settle the balance when I come. Write sone.[55]

The role slave mothers and, particularly, slave fathers played in the acquisition of food for their families made the threat of sale all the more intimidating. While most scholars do stress the adequacy of slaves' diet, few note or address the significance of why and how it became so sufficient.[56] Planters in South Carolina generally furnished only a peck of corn per week to each slave to be ground into grits or meal. All sources indicate that this quantity was constant between 1800 and 1865. Other staples, such as potatoes or rice, were sometimes substituted for corn and a small portion of salt was allotted on occasion.[57] Masters rarely provided any meat other than bacon, and that usually not weekly. Although there is some scant evidence that the amount of meat given during this period increased slightly from about a pound per week to three, no data have been uncovered to establish that there was any change throughout the years under examination in the sporadic and infrequent distribution of that luxury.[58] At least on seventeen plantations, it was not until the 1851 death of the proprietor, Nathaniel Heyward, that the more than one thousand bondsmen on these estates began receiving *any* form of meat, and this was due to the benevolence of the new master, Charles Heyward.[59]

Historians of U. B. Phillips's caliber never failed to cite the rules for management of planters like James Henry Hammond, who left instructions that workers be given "three pounds of bacon or pickled pork every week."[60] Unfortunately, Mr. Hammond kept no records that would indicate whether these orders were in fact carried out and, if so, how often. Documents of this nature would, of course, be the most definitive. The present writer, however, studied the detailed accounts of meat distribution for three South Carolinians over periods of nine, six, and eight months.

William Ervin Sparkman, of Springwood plantation in Georgetown District, possessed one hundred and two laborers in 1845.[61] Between March 31 and December 25, 1844, he furnished meat to blacks on three occasions: July 28, August 18, and September 8. He specified the amount allotted for the week of July 28 alone, at which time appeared the entry "3 lbs meat a piece." The type of viand was described simply as "meat," except on the 18th of August, when "bacon" was designated. On December 26, undoubtedly as part of the Christmas celebrations, slaves received "10 lbs Beef, 1 pt. lasses, & tobacco." For an interval of nine months, workers received meat from their master during four weeks only.[62]

The eleven slaves owned by Dr. J. Rhett Motte, of Exeter Plantation in St. John's, Berkeley, were supplied with meat once a month for all but two months, January and April, during a six-month period ending June 30, 1850. Dr. Motte gave no quantities and referred simply to "meat" on all but one occasion, when he cited "bacon" as part of the provisions on June 16.[63] John Milliken, the proprietor of Mulberry Plantation, "one of the oldest establishments on Cooper River,"[64] kept complete food-allotment records from December 1853 to March 1854 and from January to April 1857. During this time, excluding January 1857, he gave a monthly meat allowance of unknown measure and twice presented a "big pot," probably containing some meat. It is interesting that there was no mention of a "big pot" in 1857 and that, beginning in February of the same year, the weekly distribution of corn, rice, or potatoes was reduced to only three weeks during each month.[65] All slaveholders were looking constantly for ways to trim the costs of feeding laborers, and perhaps this was one method. An 1856 "Bill to alter and amend the Law in relation to the trial of owners . . . for not furnishing their slaves with sufficient clothing or food" indicates that planters of this type were prevalent enough to warrant this retention and expansion of the 1740 Act penalizing such behavior.[66]

Slaveowners may possibly have distributed such sparse rations because they believed blacks had different nutritional needs from whites; some, at least, used this as their rationale.[67] James Henry Hammond explained on November 6, 1847, that they needed fat and salt and strong drink:

> Negroes must be kept hardy; they will not *bear* fine treatment; if they were furnished with fine houses and feather beds they would often sleep out at night and thus danger of exposure would be greatly increased. The food of negros should be strong and stimulating; their nature requires stimulants Fat and salty. bacon is the best meat they can get. Fresh meat is poisonous in summer.
>
> Strong drinks are good for negros; they require something to stimulate them.[68] (Emphasis in the original.)

Not all South Carolinians were satisfied with the type of food slaves received. One planter wrote, "It is only necessary to inquire of the physician, or to consult any medical work, to be convinced that an improper attention to diet, is one of the most prolific causes of disease among our negroes."[69] Ironically, H. Perry Pope, a medical student in Charleston, presented a thesis one year later urging masters to add meat to slave provisions. As a positive incentive to this policy, he noted the substantial superiority in growth of domestics' children, who ate generally the remains of meals in the Big House, over that of field hands' offspring, who survived on the comestibles supplied by owners and whatever their parents could produce.[70]

Obviously, planters differed in their views about slave food. But the most crucial judges are those who had to subsist on it. Jacob Stroyer, born in 1849 on a large plantation near Columbia, South Carolina, recalled bitterly the "mush" children were fed at the summer residence of their owner. He and all other children "too small to work" were taken each May or June to that vacation

home and separated from family members who remained to labor
on the plantation about four miles away. What "the slaves called
mush" was corn flour; it was served usually with either "a gill of
sour milk" or molasses. That "seldom changed diet," as well as
loneliness, no doubt, made the children "anxious for Sundays to
come, when our mothers, fathers, sisters and brothers would bring
something from the plantation, which, however poor, we considered very nice, compared with what we had during the week. . . .
Among the many desirable things our parents brought us, the most
delightful was cow pease, rice, and a piece of bacon, cooked together," a mixture they called "hopping John."[71]

While such supplements pleased the young Jacob, a plethora of
evidence indicates that most slaves considered their food allotment
insufficient and complained frequently about its quality and quantity—particularly the paucity of meat.[72] John Jackson, who was
enslaved by Robert English in Sumter district, said he was fed
"twice a day," but protested:

All we got to eat then was three corn cake dumplins and one plate of
soup. No meat unless there happened to be a rotten piece in the smoke
house. This would be given to us to make our soup. Why the dogs got better
eating than we poor colored folks.[73]

Another former slave declared that the males on his plantation in
Beaufort District "didn't have time to frolic 'cause they had to
fin' food for the family; master never give 'nough to las' the whole
week."[74] An awareness of these conditions enables one to understand why the struggle for food is such a consistent theme in
African-American folklore. As Charles Joyner observed, blacks
"like folk groups everywhere, remembered what they found memorable, used what they found usable, and forgot what they found
forgettable."[75]

In order to make their daily fare adequate, American bondsmen
demonstrated remarkable resourcefulness and industry. Slaves
were the de facto owners of garden patches around their homes
and/or on other parts of the plantation where a wide assortment
of vegetables were grown. Planters sanctioned and encouraged this
practice universally in South Carolina and even allowed men they
did not own to keep and farm such land on their estates if their
wives were there.[76] Others foraged for wild greens. And many
raised poultry, or sometimes hogs, which they either saved for

family consumption or sold in order to procure certain luxury food items. But the principal method of obtaining the much-coveted meat and fish in their diet was by hunting and fishing by which the men procured rabbits, raccoons, oysters, shad, trout, and clams. Both males and females appropriated foodstuffs from their masters, but they also acquired delicacies through "legal" pursuits, such as the manufacture and sale of baskets, bowls, ladles, and the like, and through paid labor during free time which enabled them to purchase many of the desired articles not furnished by slaveholders.[77] Charles Pinckney was not far from correct when he said of the enslaved worker: "When his owner is barbarian enough to withhold the necessary food, he has always intellect, and generally opportunity to supply the deficiency."[78]

It is clear that slave parents supplied a large percentage, if not the bulk, of their families' food. The fulfillment of this vital function explains why mothers and fathers were particularly apprehensive about threatened sale. They would have been tempted inevitably to ask, "Will our children be provided for as well if either of us is sold?" In view of the dreaded day that they might be separated, parents began instructing children early in certain techniques and stratagems of survival. The first lessons taught to young bondsmen were strict obedience to elders and silence unless spoken to or addressed in some manner. Laura Towne did not think blacks were "harsh" to their offspring, but commented that, "They have a rough way of ordering them that sounds savage. When you speak to a child who does not answer, the others say, 'Talk, talk. Why you not talk?'—in the most ordersome tone to the silent one."[79] Growing accustomed to imperious commands was part and parcel of being a slave. Moreover, it was imperative that each child learn how to hold his or her tongue, for a careless slip could bring down the wrath of masters on all. This was probably the reason bondsmen did not "allow their children under certain ages to enter into conversations with them."[80] In the eyes of the enslaved, the home was the safest training ground for teaching these modes of combating white repression.

There is some evidence that slaves instructed their youngest progeny to view masters as evil and powerful adversaries with whom they should have as little contact as possible. In reference to his former owner, John Collins recalled, "De slaves whisper his name in fear and terror to de chillun when they want to hush them up. They just say to a crying child: 'Shet up or old Nick will ketch you!' Dat child sniffle but shet up pretty quick."[81] Contemporary travelers observed frequently that slave children were afraid of whites and would run away at their approach.[82] A native South Carolinian, fearful about how outsiders might view this, suggested that

> Young servants should not be suffered to run off and hide when the master comes up, or any other white person; they should be taught to stand their ground, and speak when *spoken to*, in a polite manner; have them well clothed and this thing is more easily accomplished. A lot of ragged little negroes always gives a bad impression to strangers, and is often the cause of their running away and being hard to manage when grown. Talk to them; take notice of them; it soon gives them confidence and adds greatly to their value.[83] (Emphasis in the original.)

As young laborers grew older, their parents entrusted them with the more difficult and dangerous lessons of prevarication and appropriation. Juvenile blacks were such good students that one of the major impetuses among planters for the religious proselytizing of young slaves was the hope that it would neutralize their "negative" home influences. The ruling class was not very successful, however, for the descendants of slaves continued to internalize antiservile characteristics. To inculcate various stratagems, mores, and values, African-American slaves relied heavily on a didactic, as well as an entertaining, folklore.[84] In this regard things do not appear to have changed greatly when Julia Peterkin early in the twentieth century became mistress of an Orangeburg District plantation once owned by Langdon Cheves. She observed:

> The training of children is concerned chiefly with self-preservation in this world and preparation for the life to come. They are taught to provide for the needs of their bodies, to save their souls and to abide by the ancient customs, beliefs and rules of conduct handed down from generation to generation by word of mouth. In the hot summer evenings when they sit on cabin doorsteps with their parents, or in the winter time around fires that burn in the wide chimneys, time not whiled away with singing is often spent listening to the old folk tales which are rich in negro philosophy, and sparkle with negro ideas of wit and repartee. Many of these tales teach some simple moral lesson. The people who treasure these stories have no books, have never seen a play or moving picture, have never read a newspaper; but

whether the stories are of men or of beasts, they invariably portray the same human traits and problems that make worth-while literature and plays and moving pictures.[85]

In much the same fashion, slave children learned not only how to "lib on de fat uv de land," but how to share with fellow blacks. They were instilled with principles of cooperation and assistance, illustrated most dramatically during the Civil War when, as a result of the benevolence of blacks, few orphans went uncared for. In addition, slaves generally were taught to treat elders with great reverence and to address them with honorific titles such as "Daddy" and "Maumer." Blacks of the same age group referred to each other as "Bro" (brother), "Titty," (sister), or "Co" (cousin), which caused Northerners trying to discern actual blood ties no small confusion. These traditions and mores stemmed most likely from the efforts of African-Americans to assure the well-being of children who might be separated from *real* parents.[86] Gutman states that "fictive, or quasi, kin" bound

unrelated adults to one another and thereby [infused] enlarged slave communities with conceptions of obligation that had flowed initially from kin obligations rooted in blood and marriage. The obligations to a brother or a niece were transformed into the obligations toward a fellow slave or a fellow slave's child, and behavior first determined by familial and kin obligation became enlarged social obligation. Just as the fictive aunts and uncles may have bound children to quasi kin, so, too, the ties between a child and its fictive adult kin may have bound children's parents to their fictive aunts and uncles.[87] (Emphasis in the original.)

Such attitudes and beliefs undoubtedly helped more than anything else to preclude the divisive tendencies inherent in an excessive loyalty to *particular* families, especially when one's own might be sold.

Obviously, young slaves were learning more than simply what adults demanded of them: they also began to perceive what adults expected of each other. It would have been difficult to miss the great importance older blacks placed on inquiries about one's family as part of all greetings. Similarly, children gradually would have learned that those who best provided for their families, and who verbally thrashed and even physically assaulted a mysterious and amorphous group known simply as "buckra" or "whites," were for some as yet undetermined reason considered pillars of the community.[88] To be sure, much was unclear to the young, but these early messages no doubt had an impact.[89] So, too, must the names and titles slaves gave one another, for once entering interracial settings the pervasive "Sirs," "Madames," "Mrs.," and "Mr.'s," whom black youth both knew and admired, were reduced—despite age and status—to "boy," "girl," or a generic "nigger."[90] The psychic damage done could not be erased, but in a multitude of ways prior to this awakening, young blacks had been subtly, explicitly, and continuously taught that, regardless of their status in the broader society, there would be dignity and respect among themselves.

Another way of instilling self-esteem in a humbling environment was in selecting the names of children. Recent scholarship has established the tremendous role those name choices played in cultivating individuality and distinctiveness.[91] Tragically for fresh African arrivals, however, a psychological denuding occurred with the expunction of their names at purchase. According to Gabriel Manigault, whose grandfather owned over two thousand slaves:

> Upon naming a negro a card upon which it was written was tied around his neck and it was a common thing to see a planter in his fields, go up to a field hand, whether man or woman and insert his forefinger under the collar of the shirt to draw out the card. . . . This of course was only done for a short time, and became unnecessary as soon as the darkey could pronounce his name.[92]

Not all imports learned so quickly. It is not by chance that eighteenth-century runaway advertisements were replete with African names—some cited beside the English names that certain fugitives had doggedly rejected.[93] Even later, many held tenaciously to their African names or adopted surnames equally symbolic of an independence and identity long repressed. Toward the end of the antebellum period, young Jacob Stroyer recalled his father's having a surname "he could not use in public" because the last name of his owner was Singleton. What made the elder Stroyer's act illegal, his son discovered, was "that to allow him to use his own name would be sharing an honor which was due only to his master, and that would be too much for a negro, *said they,* who was nothing more than a servant."[94] (Emphasis in the original.)

Black fathers and mothers throughout South Carolina and elsewhere broke the law; they did so not only to preserve a measure of autonomy for themselves, but also to instill in their children a spirit of independence. These unlettered but driven educators hoped that this spirit and the various techniques of survival they taught would one day congeal among the young into a base from which yet another generation could launch their people's seemingly endless struggle for freedom. In their thinking, the key prerequisite for that legacy was knowledge. As a result, they labored continually to learn as much about the world around and beyond them as possible. The postwar mania of freedmen for learning was no less real during slavery. Those responsible for the control of slaves were confronted too often with slaves who could read, decipher, and convey craftily their findings. Southern controllers watched closely any setting in which a dangerous "progress and diffusion of knowledge" might occur.[95]

In 1838 more than three hundred South Carolinians from the districts of Abbeville and Edgefield lashed out against the proposal of a missionary to preach to blacks. They argued:

> Some of the negroes will attend your meetings for religious improvement; others from idle curiosity; and a few of the more daring and intelligent, with restless spirits, to impart to each other every whisper that reaches them of the progress of Abolition, and the glowing prospect of their liberation. . . . When the last census was taken, the black population exceeded the white upwards of sixty-one thousand five hundred. We consider the common adage true, that "knowledge is power." . . . Intelligence and slavery have no affinity for each other.[96]

With the last view in mind, lawmakers repeatedly passed legislation prohibiting the written instruction of slaves. The recurrence of such laws and the uncovering recently of extensive correspondence by ex-slaves fighting in the Civil War make it clear that neither threats of maimings nor severe beatings prevented some slaves from becoming literate.[97] Most, of course, never did, but masters feared those who succeeded because they sometimes aided escapes and other illegal travels by forging passes and obtaining information belying planter myths about the impossibility of blacks surviving as free men and women. That slaves could escape, survive, and overcome a hostile white world were insights not a few black adults had acquired. Young blacks were both the beneficiaries of this knowledge and the ones who could make the most troublesome use of it. The enslaved thus taught their owners a bitter lesson: while they with relative ease could maintain a predominantly illiterate mass beneath them, it was far more difficult to keep an ignorant one.

Although slave elders succeeded in capturing some autonomous space and the minds of most among them, they did so under a complex system of controls that made each unservile move a serious risk. In such a setting, they could ill afford to shield their children indefinitely from the looming dangers. Consequently, children received many perplexing, contradictory, and paradoxical messages. Two family histories provide stark insights on the contradictions in slave responses to danger. George Cato, the great-great-grandson of Cato, leader of the Stono Rebellion of 1739, described the risks his ancestor had been willing to take:

> As it come down to me, I thinks de first Cato take a darin' chance on losin' his life, not so much for his own benefit as it was to help others. . . . Long befo' dis uprisin', de Cato wrote passes for slaves and do all he can to send them to freedom. He die but he die for doin' de right, as he see it.[98]

But the descendants of Robert Nesbit, who had been acquitted of insurrection charges during the Denmark Vesey conspiracy of 1822, learned why their forebear failed to help Vesey, though he was his friend and fellow "property-owner." Israel Nesbit wrote:

> My great-granddaddy never take no part in de plannin', 'cause he tried all de time to show Vesey he was headin' to a fall and was playin' wid dynamite. . . . Granddaddy say dat de loyalty of de slave to his master was so deep under de skin of de slave, dat it was even stronger than de long dream of freedom.[99]

Obviously, young slaves in the transition from childhood to adolescence had much to question and to resolve. How, for example, would they have reconciled tales of their people's courage and strength with the lacerated backs of so many among them? Some explanation, too, had to be forthcoming when loved ones were sold, slave rebels killed, or everyone in the quarters punished. Was it worth emulating slave and free black heroes if it meant death or shipment to worse circumstances? The discord and ambiguity such questions raised is reflected in the testimony of ex-slaves who were still children at the outbreak of the Civil War. Reuben Rosborough said, "My marster was a kind and tender man to slaves. You see a man love hosses and animals? Well, dat's de way he love us, though maybe in bigger portion." Still, he had to concede that his master "was good enough to buy my old gran' mammy Mary, though she never could do much work."[100] With similar reasoning, Ellen Renwick concluded her owner was "good": he "didn't whip . . . much."[101]

While distinguishing between "good" and "bad" masters implicitly seems to legitimize planter rule, most slaves never sanctioned the authority of slave ownership. They lived and usually died, however, in a war zone that made accurate comparative assessments of their oppressors vital. An owner who fed more, parted family members less, and left wider channels open for autonomy had to be preferred over one who often did the opposite. Differences were always on the minds of those in chains, yet despite variations in treatment, a slave was a slave. This was the crucial constant. Through their words and actions, the unfree consistently brought that point home. Rarely did they allow any kindness or humoring to blur the reality that the principal objective and motive of planters was the enrichment of their pockets and their power. Nor is it coincidental that ex-slaves so often referred to themselves as beasts of burden when they described their former owners' behavior. One former slave could not resist adding a pungent note to her recollections of slave food: "Us had all us need to eat. . . . Marse like to see his slaves fat and shiny, just like he want to see de carriage hosses slick and spanky when he ride out to preachin' at Ainswell."[102]

However ignorant planters might be of such sentiments in the slave community, they were keenly aware of slaves' devotion to their families and cognizant of how effectively that affinity could be exploited. Adele Petigru Allston settled on the following plan to control workers after three children of "a highly favoured servant"[103] had absconded toward the end of the Civil War.

I think Mary and James should be taken up and sent to some secure jail in the interior and held as hostages for the conduct of their children. And they should understand that this is done by the police of the country, who require that the older negroes should endeavour to influence the younger ones to order and subordination while this war lasts, and that they will be held responsible for the behavior of their children. For this course to have the best effect it ought to be universal, and ought to be required by the police of the country. I wish you to show this letter to Col. Francis Heriot and consult him as to what course he thinks best. If he thinks it best to make an example among the old people whose children have deserted, then let a cart or wagon be ready as soon as the search of the houses is over, and

Mary and James sent off. Some place of confinement would be the best . . .
letting them understand they would have to remain there until the end of
the war, and desertion or rebellion in any of their children would be laid at
their door. If this is done let them not have a day or an hour on the place
after it is fixed on. Let them have no communication with any of their family
except in presence of a white person, and put their children who have never
learnt to work at once to learn. It does not seem to me reasonable or right
to leave negroes in the enjoyment of privileges and ease and comfort, whose
children go off in this way. I am persuaded it is done with their knowledge
and connivance.[104]

Members of the plantocracy realized also the conservative effect
of marriage and, for the most part, encouraged such unions.[105]
Holland McTyeire, a Baptist minister who supported this policy
observed that

Local as well as family associations . . . are strong yet pleasing cords
binding him to his master. His welfare is so involved in the order of things
that he would not for any consideration have it disturbed. He is made
happier and safe; put beyond discontent, or temptations to rebellion and
abduction; for he gains nothing in comparison with what he loses. His
comforts cannot be removed with him, and he will stay with them.[106]

The gravitational pull of the connubial relations of slaves was
revealed most vividly to Captain and Mrs. Basil Hall while traveling through South Carolina in 1828. They witnessed a slave
coffle of about twenty-five individuals, two of whom were "bolted
together." When one of the men was asked the reason for the
chains, he replied quite happily, "Oh sir, they are the best things
in the world to travel with." His companion said nothing. Upon
further inquiries, Captain Hall learned that the silent bondsman
had a wife on a neighboring plantation whose owner refused to
sell her and, thereby, caused their separation. To prevent desertion, "the wretched husband was . . . shackled to a young un-
married man, who, having no such tie to draw him back, might
be more safely trusted on the journey."[107] If the single male were
to wed, he would undoubtedly remember the distraught partner
en route to his new home and very likely behave without misconduct so as to avoid following in those shackled footsteps.

American planters were not the first enslavers to recognize the
pacifying influence of conjugal and other family attachments. As
early as 1527 Spanish authorities had enacted a measure to promote marriage among slaves. They reasoned that this "would calm

them down," decrease the number of runaways, and prevent "unrest."[108] The Jamaican ruling class also noted the greater manageability of blacks who were married and, significantly, often placed indigenous Africans with Creole families during their "seasoning" process. Referring to this practice, Bryan Edwards, author of an 1801 study on the British West Indies, stated that within eight or ten months "new people . . . begin to get well established in their families, their houses and provision-grounds; and prove in all respects as valuable as the native or creole negroes." He described further the great desire of creole slaves to bring the "raw" Africans into their families and observed that:

> The strangers too were best pleased with this arrangement, and ever afterwards considered themselves as the adopted children of those by whom they were thus protected, calling them parents, and venerating them as such; and I never knew an instance of the violation of a trust thus solicited and bestowed.[109]

Slaveholders in the United States directed recent purchases, both domestic and foreign, to reside with families in their possession, but there is no way of determining whether this was done for reasons of control or of economic convenience. Whatever the case, the consequences were the same: slaves forged pseudo-kinship bonds quickly and adjusted rapidly to the ways of the plantation.[110] When Charles Ball arrived in South Carolina he was told to live at the home of Nero, a slave with a wife and five children. The following excerpt from *Fifty Years in Chains,* illustrates how swiftly one could become "part of the family."

> I could make wooden bowls and ladles, and went to work with a man who was clearing some new land about two miles off—on the second Sunday of my sojourn here, and applied the money I earned in purchasing the tools necessary to enable me to carry on my trade. I occupied all my leisure hours, for several months after this, in making wooden trays, and such other vessels as were most in demand. These I traded off, in part to a storekeeper . . . and for some of my work I obtained money. Before Christmas, I had sold more than thirty dollars worth of my manufactures; but the merchant with whom I traded, charged such high prices for his goods, that I was poorly compensated for my Sunday toils, and nightly labours; nevertheless, by these means, I was able to keep *our family* supplied with molasses, and some other luxuries, and at the approach of winter, I purchased three coarse blankets, to which Nero added as many, and we had all these made up into blanket-coats for Dinah, ourselves, and the children.[111] (Emphasis added.)

Although the black family was the source of the planters' most effective control mechanism, it was also, for slaves, the greatest mitigation of the harshness and severity of bondage. John Jackson spoke angrily of the many sadistic and humiliating beatings he received as a slave, but stressed the following turning point during "those horrible times": "I growed up and married when I was very young, and I loved my little girl wife. Life was not a burden then. I never minded the whippings I got. I was happy."[112] The kinship networks created by African-Americans helped shield bondsmen from the dehumanization inevitable in any slave society. Slaves could depend on familial relations—both real and fictive—when in need, and however futile it may have been, protection sometimes from white oppressors.[113] Yet the family served as a pacifying institution as well. Gutman suggests that slave women bore children in part because they were aware that evidence of their fertility might persuade masters not to exchange them for more "profitable" servants.[114] Because a slave, once informed of the owner's decision to sell, could do little to alter the decision other than to appeal to the owner or practice self-mutilation,[115] many slaves sought to prevent separation from loved ones by abiding by the rules of the plantation. Not a few slaves regarded obedience as a fair price to pay for keeping their families intact.

Some slave elders, without any *direct* external pressure, taught their progeny lessons that can be classified as "internal controls," in the sense that they kept community members "out of trouble" and "peaceful."[116] Aaron Ford, a former slave, recalled these guidelines and instructions he received from his grandfather throughout his sixteen years of servitude:

I remember my grandfather all right. He de one told me how to catch otters. Told me how to set traps. Heard my grandfather tell bout whippin slaves for stealin. Grandfather told me not to take things dat were not mine. If a pile of corn was left at night, I was told not to bother it. In breakin corn, sometimes people would make a pile of corn in de grass en leave it en den come back en get it in de night. Grandfather told me not to never bother nothin bout people's things.[117]

One slaveholder, David Golightly Harris, received help from his slaves when he "had difficulty with Matt," one of his slaves.

I tied him [Matt] up and gave him a gentle admonition in the shape of a good whipping. I intended to put him in jail and keep him there until I sold him but he seemed so penitent & promised so fairly *& the other negroes promising to see that he would behave himself in future* that I concluded that I would try him once more.[118] (Emphasis added.)

For exactly two months, Matt's neighbors, some of whom were certainly his relatives, were able apparently to constrain him, but, finally, he was converted into cash. Harris noted that Matt himself "was willing to be sold."[119]

Perhaps the most telling statement on the role of the family came in 1863 from Jim, a slave captured by Union forces with his master on Bailey's Island in South Carolina. Laura Towne described Jim as "sad" and recorded his declaration that "he would not give up the wife and children now on the Main for all the freedom in the world."[120] Familial bonds militated against and sometimes prevented revolutionary fervor. The difference in the number of men and women who ran away reflects this phenomenon indirectly. According to one scholar, at least 80 percent of all runaways were males between the ages of sixteen and thirty-five. He posited that mothers were more unwilling to defect because of their stronger attachment to children, whereas many young men had yet to assume the responsibilities of marriage and fatherhood and therefore felt less obligated to stay.[121] Although some bondsmen fled to the North, the majority simply remained "out" near their homes and often for remarkably long periods of time through the assistance of their families and friends.[122] While this was a constant annoyance to planters, it did not hurt their pockets as much as the loss of captive laborers who obtained permanent freedom above the Mason-Dixon line. Again, African-Americans' family ties guaranteed and protected the property interests of the ruling class.

It is not difficult to imagine the influence masters had over slaves with mates and kin on other plantations: they had the power to withhold the passes that bondsmen were required to carry when absent from the estates of their owners. Although most blacks probably did not wait for such "permission," they still would have needed, on occasion, the sanction of planters, and good behavior was undoubtedly a major criterion.[123] Mrs. Benjamin Perry, for example, promised the visiting mother of Delia, a fifteen-year-old servant, that Delia could visit her at Christmas "if" she was "a good girl."[124] Members of the plantocracy did help slaves sometimes to see relatives and to keep their families together,[125] and it is highly unlikely that such aid was unappreciated or forgotten by blacks. In the eyes of the enslaved, kinship ties were of paramount importance and worthy of infinite sacrifice. In this lay the force of masters' threats to sell. Not surprisingly, those slaveholders who made it a habit of "transporting" unruly and incorrigible blacks were known to have "well-ordered people" who gave "little trouble."[126] The threat of sale was the most effective long-term mechanism of control.

CHAPTER THREE

A System of Rewards and Punishments

No question can possibly be more interesting to the Southern planter than the slave question, nor can any thing more deeply affect the agricultural prosperity of South-Carolina and Georgia than the state of subordination in which our slaves are kept. . . . A state of rigid discipline does not require frequent punishment, but the contrary; that good disciplinarians, that is, men who punctually visit misconduct with the requisite notice, like a good military officer, seldom have occasion to punish at all—while the relaxed, sentimental *covert abolitionist,* first begins by spoiling his slave, next becomes severe, which is followed by running away, this again by enormous depredations, ending in the transportation of the unhappy negro; who would have been, under a good master, (that is one who would have compelled good behaviour,) a valuable labourer, increasing his master's wealth.

Editor, *Southern Agriculturist,* 1829[1]

When examining the various control mechanisms devised by South Carolina's ruling class, it is difficult to speak of rewards without discussing punishments, for they were frequently no more than different sides of the same coin. Both were contrived in an effort to achieve optimal productivity and to repress the involuntary work force, both physically and mentally. Because planters considered everything from basic necessities to customary rights as privileges to be withheld at will, it is not an exaggeration to state that, in many cases, rewards were simply punishments not realized.

Good crops and hence good profits were, of course, the overriding concerns of the white elite. The elite was dependent, therefore, on disciplined enslaved masses to assure its own wealth and well-being. Contemporary sources abound with complaints about the reluctance of blacks to work and the poor quality of their labor, and slaveholders' various strategies to stimulate them to more effort. Frustrated masters decried especially the necessity of keeping constant vigilance over laborers and of guarding against feigned illnesses.[2] Work-related faults, such as lateness and slovenliness, were cited most often by South Carolina ex-slaves, by planters, and by travelers as the reasons for the chastisement of slaves.[3] After encounters with black captives in South Carolina and Georgia, Amelia Murray, a visitor from England, complained that despite slaves' eager and cheerful offers to help, they could never fulfill or understand her most basic needs without tedious and time-consuming instructions. She concurred with a fellow Englishwoman that "one white servant would do the work of three blacks" and that without recourse to the lash, slaves "would be utterly unmanageable."[4]

In 1853 Frederick Law Olmsted watched while twenty or thirty "toiling" but incompetent South Carolina slaves were "encouraged" by an overseer with a whip:

The overseer rode about them on a horse, carrying in his hand a rawhide whip, constantly directing and encouraging them, but as my companion and I, both, several times noticed, as often as he visited one end of the line of operations, the hands at the other end would discontinue their labor until he turned to ride towards them again. Clumsy, awkward, gross, elephantine in all their movements . . . I never before had witnessed, I thought, anything more revolting than the whole scene.[5]

As if the half-hearted efforts at work were not annoying enough, many blacks often pretended to be sick and unable to work. One observer traveling from Orangeburg, South Carolina, declared that determining whether a slave was "really sick" or simply "shamming from indolence" was "the most delicate" task masters faced. It was a task the Reverend C. C. Jones in 1842 labeled "vexatious."[6]

So widespread were feigned illnesses that a medical student at the Medical College of South Carolina devoted more than two-thirds of his 1850 senior thesis to methods of discovering such "impostures."[7] After warning the "young Physician" to be constantly on guard, he advised:

As a general rule, the garrulity of a sick negro is a good evidence of imposture; the loud groans and exclamations, ejaculations, tossing turning rapidly in his bed are all circumstances which should excite suspicion. . . . Through anger and malevolence Negroes will sometime feign concussion of the brain. This will always alarm the masters, as they only feign this when they are beaten for their negligence. A negro man was carriage driver to one of my neighbours; he was much addicted to sleeping at his post. On one occasion his master struck him with the butt end of the whip on the head.

The negro immediately fell back speechless. . . . On the arrival of the Physician, the negro was still stupid but exhibited some signs of intelligence [and] on enquiry, it was ascertained that since he had come home, he had eaten heartily. His pulse was good, of natural force and number to the minute. . . . The conclusion of the Physician was that there was nothing the matter except a stubbornness of disposition which should be corrected immediately by the whip. This being done, the negro was cured almost immediately.[8]

To counter the objectionable habits of captive workers, slaveholders attempted to merge the interests of the enslaved with those of the enslavers. In addition to garden plots around slave homes, for example, a large number of planters granted bondsmen as much land as they could handle elsewhere, in most cases to grow corn. Crops raised in this fashion were generally purchased by masters at market value—a practice which acted further to draw blacks closer to the Peculiar Institution, for they viewed their "property" and possessions more seriously than one might imagine. Such industry during the after-hours—that is, when slaves' time was not engaged by their masters—made it possible to buy certain luxury items for loved ones.[9] When one Low Country slaveholder expressed "fear" in April of 1849 that his corn crop would "not hold out . . . to feed the Negroes till August," he resolved, "I must try to get a barrel of molasses & some other articles to try and buy some corn from the negroes."[10]

Having crops of their own to tend prodded some slaves to finish the chores of masters quickly and efficiently. The ruling class thereby gained an additional mechanism of control, for they could now assign blacks added tasks as punishment which would consume their customary free time. Readers of the *Southern Agriculturist* learned the multiple advantages of this policy from R. King, Jr., overseer on one of the largest and most productive Georgia Sea Island plantations. King made errant slaves dig stumps or clear away trash "in their own time" and assigned "no before-day work, only as punishments":

Every means are used to encourage them [slaves], and impress on their minds the advantage of holding property, and the disgrace attached to idleness. Surely, if industrious for themselves, they will be so for their masters, and no Negro with a well stocked poultry house, a small crop advancing, a canoe partly finished, or a few tubs unsold, all of which he calculates soon to enjoy, will ever run away. . . . Many may think that they lose time, when

Negroes can work for themselves; it is the reverse on all plantations under good regulations—time is absolutely gained to the master. An indolent Negro is most always sick, and unless he is well enough to work for his master, he cannot work for himself, and when the master's task is done, he is in mischief, unless occupied for himself.

King claimed he used "the lash, least of all" and that his "most severe" punishment was "confinement at home six months to twelve months, or longer."[11]

Just how precious slaves' free time was becomes clear when one examines the extensive market system blacks created among themselves and the interracial market they expanded significantly. Such a trading network was evident even in the seventeenth century. It helped blacks to dispose of the goods they had made, grown, caught, and sometimes stolen during the after-hours. Obviously this market posed both benefits and dangers for planters. To limit the risks, an early law of 1686 sought to ban any trade between slaves and free people that had not been approved by the slave's owner, but such legislation evidently failed, since strikingly similar edicts continued to be enacted during the nineteenth century.[12]

While some slaves may have hastened their pace working for masters in order to pursue after-hours endeavors, far more persisted in ploddingly slow toil for others, refusing to put forth any more energy than the bare minimum those wielding the whips demanded. Members of the plantocracy never ceased trying to cross carrots with sticks. Among the more positive inducements to work were a varied assortment of rewards. Coin and cash gratuities were given frequently for jobs well done or for "extra" labor during the after-hours.[13] Jesse Williams of Chester, South Carolina, recalled his master's giving him a "shinplaster" the first time he picked a hundred pounds of cotton and then promising another for every repeat performance. With a little aid from plants heavy with dew, Williams was able to make eighty cents that year.[14] In a similar vein, Charles Ball reported both a carrot and a stick:

> On all estates, the standard of a day's work is fixed by the overseer, according to the quality of the cotton, and if a hand gathers more than this standard, he is paid for it, but if on the other hand, when his or her cotton is weighed at the cotton-house, in the evening, it is found that the standard quantity has not been picked, the delinquent picker is sure to receive a whipping.[15]

Monetary incentives may not have been very large, but they were highly valued. The extensive market created by African-Americans for goods like tobacco and liquor has not received a great deal of attention by historians, but an abundance of evidence indicates that vast numbers of slaves became addicted to tobacco, and not a few to alcohol.[16] One scholar citing Edward Pierce, the Northern Treasury Department agent who worked among Sea Island blacks in 1861, argued that slaves considered tobacco "the chief necessity of life."[17] So great was the demand for it and liquor that a planter wrote in the November 1836 *Southern Agriculturist*, "They [slaves] are always found ready to barter away their whole weekly allowance to some neighbouring dram shop, for a gallon of whisky, or a pound or two of tobacco."[18] To be sure, a significant portion of the money earned by slaves fell into the hands of the infamous storekeepers who traded with them illegally, that is, without owners' permission.

Perhaps to curtail or at least to limit such transactions, some planters preferred to bestow on "worthy" servants fancy garments and cooking or eating utensils, like forks and spoons. The aunt of Elizabeth Pringle rewarded the slaves on one South Carolina plantation with thread, buttons, and tea if they curtsied as her carriage passed; the recipients had to be fast, for she dispensed these goods from her passing coach. Planters allocated meats and liquor on occasion for meritorious behavior.[19] James Henry Hammond stipulated in his plantation rules that "a ditcher who does each task *without occasioning annoyance for a week* receives on Wednesday night an extra pound of meat."[20] (Emphasis added.) Another slaveholder, John Gabriel Guignard, wrote in an 1829 letter that periodically he liked to indulge his "Fellows" with a dram or two of whiskey for working well.[21] Slaves participating in the interplantation corn-shuckings so prevalent in South Carolina were usually rewarded with both culinary delights and spirituous drinks.[22]

Awarding of sporadic holidays was another instrument of control employed to pacify slaves. In addition to "half-tasks" on Saturdays and no mandatory labor on Sundays, bondsmen occasionally received day vacations for barbecues or relaxation. They used these brief respites for a wide range of activities, from competing in foot races and wrestling matches to attending church.[23]

Many visited friends and relatives. Robert Smalls, the illustrious Reconstruction-era black Congressman and war hero who had escaped to Union forces with a sixty-thousand-dollar Confederate ship, told the American Freedmen's Inquiry Commission in 1863 that slaves who lived in the country cared more about family than city dwellers did and would "often walk fifteen miles on Saturday night to see a cousin."[24] Social activities such as parties were not uncommon and were often sanctioned by their masters. As one contemporary student of South Carolina slavery revealed, these events made slave management easier because "innocent amusements, when under proper regulations, and when partaken of with moderation, conduce to morality and virtue."[25]

The effectiveness of these festive occasions in deflecting slaves' attention from the hardships of bondage was noted by Charles Ball. He described the activities "at the laying by of the corn and cotton."

> I doubt if there was in the world a happier assemblage than ours, on this Saturday evening. We had finished one of the grand divisions of the labours of a cotton plantation, and were supplied with a dinner, which to the most of my fellow-slaves, appeared to be a great luxury, and most liberal donation on the part of our master, whom they regarded with sentiments of gratitude, for this manifestation of his bounty.
>
> Our quarter knew but little quiet this night; singing—playing on the banjoe, and dancing, occupied nearly the whole community, until the break of day. Those who were too old to take any part in our active pleasures, beat time with their hands or recited stories of former times.
>
> A man cannot well be miserable, when he sees every one about him immersed in pleasure; and though our fare of to-day, was not of a quality to yield me much gratification, yet such was the impulse given to my feelings, by the universal hilarity and contentment, which prevailed amongst my fellows, that I forgot for the time, all the subjects of grief that were stored in my memory, all the acts of wrong that had been perpetuated against me, and entered with the most sincere and earnest sentiments, in the participation of the felicity of our community.[26]

While the laying by of the crops and the Fourth of July were major holidays, the main event of the year was Christmas. It was a period of great celebration and a time during which most planters allowed blacks at least three or four days of vacation. Besides an abundance of much-coveted meats and whiskey, slaves usually received gifts, from pretty handkerchiefs to cash.[27] Peter Clifton, who was born a slave on a plantation between Kershaw and Camden, South Carolina, in 1848, remembered Christmas day as a time when "every woman got a handkerchief to tie up her hair. Every girl got a ribbon, every boy a ballow knife, and every man a skin plaster."[28] Richard Jones, a former field hand and boatman, interviewed when more than a hundred years old, recalled receiving much larger sums on the Union, South Carolina, plantation of Jim Gist:

> Marse allus carried a roll of money as big as my arm. He would come to de Quarter on Christmas, July 4th and Thanksgiving, and get up on a stump and call all the chillums out. Den he would throw money to 'em. De chillums got dimes, nickles, quarters, half-dollars and dollars. At Christmas he would throw ten dollar bills. De parents would take de five and ten dollar bills . . . but Marse made [dem] lett de chilluns keep de small change.[29]

Some masters shrewdly chose the twenty-fifth of December as the date to "give" bondpeople their yearly supply of blankets and winter clothing.[30] The Reverend Irving Lowery, formerly enslaved by John Frierson in Sumter district, described how eagerly slaves awaited these gifts. Frierson made an annual trip to purchase the garments. Lowery wrote:

> That night their slumbers were filled with dreams and visions of new suits, new shoes, new caps and new dresses. But these things were not given out until Christmas morning. And while this glad day was perhaps only a month off, yet the month seemed longer, the days seemed longer and the nights seemed longer than at any other season of the year. The anxiety, the longing and the solicitude for the dawn of Christmas morning is indescribable.[31]

Planters could thus arrange to appear loving and magnanimous before "their people"—even when furnishing basic necessities.

Although slaves enjoyed all the delicacies and presents associated with Christmas, they liked most the opportunity to visit with kin living elsewhere. Many saw them at no other time. Masters legitimized these journeys and other travels by issuing general passes during the holidays.[32] David Harris, for instance, wrote on December 22, 1858, "This morning I gave my negroes passes for Christmas, telling them to be at home by Wednesday."[33] Hammond recorded in 1831: "Negroes all up. Gave them a pound of tobacco each for Christmas & their shirts & 2 pipes with permission to go where they pleased . . . until Wednesday morning."[34] Blacks took advantage of this freedom. John Cornish, a

New England teacher and minister en route from Walterboro to Grahamville, South Carolina, recorded in his diary on December 26, 1839, "I met Negroes traveling in all directions with loads upon their backs & heads of rice, potatoes, fowles &c. going from one plantation to another to spend Christmas with their wives, their Husbands, & families."[35]

But, of course, the greatest incentive was emancipation. John Belton O'Neall, a prominent South Carolina judge, argued that it was the "only reward" slaves appreciated.[36] Members of the plantocracy were prohibited from granting this most-esteemed prize for good behavior and faithful service after private manumissions were outlawed in 1820.[37] Alarmed by "the great and rapid increase of free negroes and mulattoes [from] migration and emancipation," South Carolina legislators ruled in 1820 "That no slave shall hereafter be emancipated but by act of the Legislature."[38] Thus, guilt-ridden dying masters could no longer appease their consciences by freeing slaves in a surge of deathbed humaneness.

An examination of eighteenth-century runaway advertisements illustrates how effectively the prospect of liberty could subdue certain favored slaves. Ads announcing runaway slaves in the *South Carolina Gazette,* for example, show that very few skilled craftsmen, domestics, or personal servants deserted. It is not coincidental that these were the most likely to succeed in securing their release.[39] But even after being prohibited by law, some planters did continue to try to emancipate "deserving" slaves. They resorted to secret agreements with heirs and executors to assure de facto freedom for favored bondsmen. An 1841 law, however, declared such covert contracts null and void. In consequence of the 1820 and 1841 enactments, a slave could anticipate manumission *only* for extraordinary acts of collaboration such as betrayal of plans for insurrection, and even this was not always enough.[40] Despite his disclosure of an 1829 slave conspiracy, the backing of 101 white petitioners, and a favorable legislative committee report, Abram, a slave betrayer, was never freed.[41] Dutiful slaves like Abram must have discovered sometimes that it was easier to negotiate freedom from a master than from a large and shifting legislature.

In 1829 the editor of the *Southern Agriculturist* urged his readers "to remember that a slave in a state of insubordination is an enemy," but "in a state of perfect subjection . . . is a kind, willing, good-humored, and useful friend."[42] To keep their slaves willing and good-humored, most masters relied far more heavily on punishments than on rewards. The former ranged from physical torture to psychological terror, and *all* segments of white society concurred that some form of either, if not both, was essential.[43] Thomas C. Law, the secretary of the Darlington District Agricultural Society, declared that the "rod" could not be dispensed with because blacks were "naturally indolent" and required "compulsion to labor."[44] Charles Jones, the famous Presbyterian clergyman from Georgia dedicated to the evangelization of slaves, recognized that the manner of controlling bondsmen was "too much physical in its nature" but asserted that "to discard an appeal to the principle of fear—the fear of punishment . . . would be running contrary to all governments in existence, both human and divine."[45] Even one twentieth-century scholar used such antebellum views to rationalize slavery's sadistic treatment of its human chattels. He believed that "the cruelty" to blacks was "in some measure . . . justified by the fact that nothing but the fear of a certain and severe physical punishment for misdoings could hold most slaves in check."[46]

Whether coercing bondsmen to labor or simply to "behave," the principal objective of planters was to attain hegemony over the lives of slaves. The whip was the most active weapon in the ruling-class arsenal. Charles Ball described the staff and its lash in detail:

> The staff is about twenty-two inches in length, with a large and heavy head, which is often loaded with a quarter or half a pound of lead wrapped in cat-gut, and securely fastened on, so that nothing but the greatest violence can separate it from the staff. The lash is ten feet long, made of small strips of buckskin, tanned so as to be dry and hard, and plaited carefully and closely together, of the thickness, in the largest part, of a man's little finger, but quite small at each extremity. At the farthest end of this throng is attached a cracker, nine inches in length, made of strong sewing silk, twisted and knotted, until it feels as firm as the hardest twine.[47]

Hickory switches, leather straps, wooden paddles, and the butt end of the lash were substituted sometimes for this kind of whip.[48]

The procedure of chastising slaves was varied but, on occasion, could be brutally unique. Charlie Grant, for example, who was born in 1852, recalled: "De overseer, he pretty rough sometimes.

Tie de slaves clear de ground by dey thumbs wid nigger cord en make dem tiptoe en draw it tight as could be."[49] The majority of blacks, however, were bound by their wrists and then raised completely off their feet with a heavy rope attached to a tree, post, or ceiling. Another popular method was to beat slaves as they lay prostrate. To make everyone "comfortable" in this position, holes were dug to accommodate the stomachs of women "in the family way." Although masters generally applied the lash on bare backs only, they were not always so selective. The defendant in the State v. Harlan, convicted primarily for having whipped a slave not his own, had used "a little India rubber whip" to inflict between two and three hundred stripes "on the property of another . . . from the calves of his legs to his shoulders."[50] The slave who survived this scourging not only had been out with documented permission—a pass from his master—but was "uniformly pronounced to be a *submissive negro.*"[51] (Emphasis in the original.)

Blacks were castigated usually for negligence at work, but many other "transgressions" could bring a flogging, among them "insolence to a white man," "retailing spiritous liquors," running away, and "sutting and vexsatious language."[52] Some planters formulated scales designating the degree of wrongdoing for their wide assortment of "crimes." In his plantation book, Andrew Flinn declared:

The following is the order in which offences must be estimated & punished—1st Running Away 2nd Getting drunk or having spirits 3rd stealing Hogs 4th Stealing 5th Leaving Plantation without permission 6th Absence after Horn blow 7th Unclean House or Person 8th Neglect of mule 9 Neglect of tools 10th neglect of work The highest punishment must not exceed Fifty lashes in one day.[53]

An identical list was adopted and enforced by Hammond until he raised the maximum number of lashes per day to one hundred in his plantation rules for 1857–1858.[54]

Not a few masters advocated whipping blacks periodically regardless of their behavior. A Mr. Moody, a member of the ABC Farmer's Club of Beech Island, South Carolina, explained that punishment should be scheduled every Saturday night.

Negros would not bear good usage. The better you treated them, the worse their conduct would be. . . . The best plan would be to give them 25 or 30 lashes a piece every Saturday night anyhow, which probably keep them straight until Monday morning, and then watch them close all the week. . . . The men should have 25 lashes on Saturday night and the women 30 for the women were worse than the men.[55]

Slaves often felt the wrath of their owners simply because the owners were unhappy, intoxicated, or just in the mood.[56] Although still a child when freed, Victoria Perry remembered that she had been as scared of her former master, Bert Mabin, "as she was of a mad dog." When Mabin was angry at any one slave on his farm near Newberry, South Carolina, he would beat them all—"tie them to a post or to a tree, strip off their clothes to the waist, and whip them till he got tired." In addition to those indiscriminate beatings, Mabin lashed her mother regularly and severely. Many nights Victoria awoke to her mother's cries and prayers, in great pain from the whippings she had received that day. She frequently saw her mother's clothes "stick to her back . . . because she 'bled' so much." The only consolation of mother and daughter was faith. The mother believed, and convinced Victoria, "Some day we are going to be free; the Good Lord won't let this thing go on all the time."[57]

While there is no way of determining the frequency with which planters beat slaves, it is clear from a wealth of evidence that the vast majority engaged in some flogging occasionally. Furthermore, practically all slaves *knew of* whippings and were probably reminded personally often enough not to forget such powerful incentives to work correctly and well. Indeed, nowhere was the communication network among slaves more conspicuous than in the dissemination of information about chastisements and other acts of cruelty. George Rawick, whose exhaustive research and editing of North American slave narratives is unsurpassed, declared, "One can almost conclude that whippings were daily affairs on most plantations by simply counting the number of interviews that mention whippings, and we know that such material was often deleted." He added, "If the ex-slaves had one thing in common, it was their universal consciousness and hatred of whipping."[58]

Memories of these punishments became embedded firmly in the minds of those enslaved and were passed on from generation to generation in folklore and by word of mouth.[59] One tale that captured the horrors of bondage, ideas about Africa and Africans, and the ever-popular escape motif—this time without its pursuit component—was "All God's Chillen Had Wings." Caesar Grant, a black carter and laborer from John's Island, shared this tale with John Bennett, a white "transient resident" of Charleston who published it in 1943. After recalling a time when "all Africans could fly like birds," Grant told the story of a Southern plantation on which the slaves were beaten brutally and worked to death. One day a new gang of slaves was brought from Africa to replace those who had died. When the driver began whipping these slaves, an old man among them shouted something neither the driver nor the overseer understood: "And as he [the old man] spoke to [his fellows] they all remembered what they had forgotten, and recalled the power which once had been theirs. Then all the Negroes, old and new, stood up together; the old man raised his hands; and they all leaped up into the air with a great shout; and in a moment were gone, flying . . . beyond the wood, beyond the river, miles on miles, until they passed beyond the last rim of the world and disappeared in the sky."[60]

Few slaves permanently escaped or completely forgot the world of bondage. Robert Toatley, who was given as a wedding gift to his master's oldest child, remembered the whippings of that earlier time:

De biggest whippin' I ever heard tell of was when they had a trial of several slave men for sellin' liquor at de spring durin' preachin', on Sunday. . . . They was convicted, and de order of de court was: Edward to receive 100 lashes; Sam and Andy each 125, and Frank and Abram 75 lashes. All to be given on deir bare backs and rumps, well laid on wid strap.[61]

It was not unheard of for a slave to be beaten to death. A slave could receive anywhere from a few licks to several hundred stripes.[62] In March 1865 Henry, "a strong boy but of a weak mind" was convicted of burglary. The jury "mitigated" his punishment because the house he broke into was unoccupied; consequently, "no life [had been] endangered." The slave Henry was sentenced only to "be imprisoned for two weeks and to receive Three Hundred lashes each week well laid on—his bare back."[63] Three years earlier, Laura Towne wrote in her diary about the liberated blacks of St. Helena Island:

We saw there one woman whose two children had been whipped to death, and Mr. Wells said there was not one who was not marked up with welts.

He had the old whip which had a ball at the end, and he had seen the healed marks of this ball on their flesh—the square welts showed where it had taken the flesh clean out. Loretta of this place showed me her back and arms today. In many places there were ridges as high and long as my little finger, and she said she had had four babies killed within her by whipping, one of which had its eye cut out, another its arm broken, and the others with marks of the lash. She says it was because even while "heaviest" she was required to do as much as usual for a field hand, and not being able, and being also rather apt to resist, and rather smart in speaking her mind, poor thing, she has suffered.[64]

The grapevine and personal observation taught the enslaved that all planters, however "different," were potential sadists capable of unleashing barbarities whenever they chose. The memory or prospect of such treatment assured the good behavior of not a few individuals. Former slave Ryer Emmanuel, for instance, reported that "Ma was whip twice en she say dat she stay to her place after dat."[65] Even Ball, who was unafraid to risk his life in daring efforts to flee captivity, wrote, after describing both the regular and extra floggings on his master's estate, "I was careful, for my part, to conform to all the regulations of the plantation."[66] Fear of lashing led Susannah, who had been the seamstress of a Sea Island planter, to declare, "I was quite satisfy if dey didn't lick me. I would work or do anything for them if dey would n't lick me." Her sickliness and her much-needed skills were probably more responsible than faultless deportment for being spared the lash. When her owner, a cruel taskmaster who not only bought and sold slaves indifferently, but refused to provide meat, shoes, or "Sunday clothes," "threatened to shoot" the hogs she owned and was raising to provide for her family, Susannah replied, "No massa, you cawnt do it. What can I do for our children's winter shoes and our salt if our pigs are shot? You cawnt do it—you cawnt do it." He did not.[67]

Whipping was just one method of chastening errant bondsmen. Confinement in prisons, stocks, and various other contraptions was punishment of another sort. Many planters kept private jails or at least buildings which could be used as such; others relied on public institutions.[68] Perhaps the most well-equipped and busy of these was the Charleston workhouse. A slave could be sent there with a note from his owner, receive a designated number of lashes, and then be locked up or returned home—all without blemishing the character of the master. It saved sensitive residents with an eye toward the North from administering whippings in sight of the city's constant stream of visitors. This fear of inadvertently providing suspected abolitionists with antislavery propaganda probably explains why the whipping-room of the workhouse, popularly known as the "sugar-house," was made of "double walls filled in with sand so that the cries could not be heard in the street."[69] Once again, criticism from without had no more effect on the oppressed within than to make their treatment a more hidden and secret affair.

To make sure that the guests of the workhouse did not relax, the city council decided to erect a treadmill there in 1825.[70] Duke Karl Bernhard of Saxe-Weimar-Eisenach, touring Charleston between the 11th and 19th of December, 1825, described two tread-wheels then in operation:

Each employs twelve prisoners, who work a mill for grinding corn, and thereby contribute to the support of the prison. Six tread at once upon each wheel, while six rest upon a bench behind the wheel. Every half minute the left hand man steps off the tread-wheel, while the five others move to the left to fill up the vacant place; at the same time the right hand man sitting at the bench, steps on the wheel, and begins his movement, while the rest, sitting on the bench, uniformly recede. Thus, even three minutes sitting, allows the unhappy being no repose. The signal for changing is given by a small bell attached to the wheel. The prisoners are compelled to labour eight hours a day in this manner. Order is preserved by a person, who, armed with a cow-hide, stands by the wheel. Both sexes tread promiscuously upon the wheel. . . . The negroes entertain a strong fear of the tread-mills, and regard flogging as the lighter evil! Of about three hundred and sixty, who, since the erection of these treadmills, have been employed upon them, only six have been sent back a second time.[71]

Stocks of various sizes to accommodate men, women, and children were common features in private jails.[72] One planter kept a slave whose only crime was running away to rejoin his wife in the stocks for six weeks "in a miserable hovel, not weather-tight."[73] Some masters evidently felt that the effect of such imprisonment compensated for the loss of labor. As late as 1937, Peter Clifton, then eighty-nine, still retained vivid memories of this mode of correction: "Well, they put de foots in a stock and clamp them together, then they have a cross-piece go right across de breast high as de shoulder. Dat cross-piece long enough to bind de hands of a slave to it at each end."[74] Robert Smalls knew of one slave-holder who added a special twist not soon forgotten by those so subjected. The planter had one set of stocks built over another; individuals placed in the top one were compelled "to take a large dose of medicine" that "caused them to filth down upon each other."[75]

Some members of the plantocracy constructed small cells where occupants could neither sit nor lie.[76] "De sweatbox," for example, was said to be "made de height of de person an' no larger. Jus' large 'nough so de person wodn' hab to be squeezed in. De box is nailed an' een summer is put een de hot sun; een de winter it is put in de coldest, dempest place."[77] The Massachusetts colonel of a black regiment, Thomas Higginson, discovered a somewhat similar contraption while on a raid in South Carolina. He found this apparatus "perfectly unintelligible till the men explained all its parts: a machine so contrived that a person once imprisoned in it could neither sit, stand, nor lie, but must support the body half raised, in a position scarcely endurable."[78] It is possible that what Higginson examined was a "screw box," a device used not only to press bales of cotton but, in some cases, to punish blacks. Eliza Carson of Rafter Creek, for instance, confined refractory slaves in a press of this type so tightly that victims were unable to move until released in the morning when they were whipped and put to work.[79]

During the 1830s, the Society for the Advancement of Education, at Columbia commissioned N. Herbemont to study "the moral discipline and treatment of slaves." He found, among other things, that slaves considered "solitary confinement . . . the most severe punishment short of death."[80] Although many masters were aware that blacks hated isolation, few comprehended fully the reasons for the intensity of their feeling.[81] Insubordinate blacks to be incarcerated were confined usually as soon as they completed their daily tasks, that is, at the beginning of the after-hours. While planters knew of the various endeavors pursued by bondsmen during this period, they did not realize the true significance of them to the enslaved. The wide range of activities engaged in outside of the master's fields, from providing for one's family to visiting and socializing with friends, were essential for preserving slaves' self esteem. It was in the after-hours that slaves achieved their greatest autonomy and were able to maintain a more positive self-image. It was not the solitude that blacks loathed so deeply, then, but the time at which it occurred.[82]

Because nearly all of a slave's personal affairs had to be attended to between dusk and dawn, American bondsmen were in many ways a "night people."[83] It should come as no surprise, therefore, that the same time period remained central in the lives of blacks even after emancipation. One superintendent among the freedmen noted that "the road in his district was more crowded and more people passed, in one night than in three days."[84] While some slaveholders promoted, or at least sanctioned, "innocent amusements" during the after-hours, most did not concern themselves with happenings in the quarters so long as day-time productivity was not affected. Owners almost universally condemned *interplantation* socializing, but slaves exercised an incredible degree of mobility and continued their nocturnal travels and festive meetings despite such ruling-class prohibitions.[85]

The inability of slaveholders to keep their property at home was reflected in this 1804 letter to the editor of the Charleston *Courier* from an anonymous "Bye Stander":

Being on Beale's wharf last Sunday morning about 6 o'clock I must confess I was astonished to see about forty negroes, men and women arrive in one boat from Sullivan's Island. Curiosity led me to enquire what such a number had been amusing themselves with during the night, and I found they had been dancing and carousing from Saturday night until near sunrise the next morning, to the number, I was informed, of about one hundred. A lady who had missed a mulatto fellow of her's, caught him when coming out of the boat; and a gentleman the Saturday previous, caught his wench who had been gone a good many weeks. I wish to know why a stop is not put to the boat-men, plying between this and the Island, carrying negroes to the Island without a pass . . . our negroes going to or coming from the country must have a pass, and I can assure you one is more necessary for the Island. I leave it to your abler pen, Mr. Editor, to hint what mode ought to be adopted to put a stop to this growing evil—should you think proper to do so . . . you will befriend your fellow-citizens.[86]

The type of question posed by this South Carolinian was raised thousands of times again, but no one ever seemed to find an adequate answer to the problem of restraining the movements of slaves.

Not a few African-Americans were perfectly content, however, simply to remain at home after toiling most of the day for others. Singing songs and telling stories to family members and neighbors were gratifying and soothing to tired workers. Colonel Higginson witnessed the satisfaction among black soldiers during the Civil War. He observed, "Give these people their tongues, their feet, and their leisure, and they are happy. At every twilight the air is full of singing, talking, and clapping of hands in unison."[87] Blacks on the plantation did more during the after hours than unwind: they took advantage of this time to pass on their history, culture, mores, and lore to the next generation. The young thus learned of their people's struggle and the old rejoiced in retelling and singing their stories and songs.

Teachers and students dramatized collectively the popular South Carolina slave saying, "De buckruh hab scheme, en de nigger hab trick, en ebery time de buckruh scheme once de nigger trick twice."[88] A black schoolgirl on St. Helena Island told folklorist Elsie Clews Parsons in 1919:

Once upon a time there was a old man in slavery. He told his master that he was cripple and couldn't work. So the man let him stay home to take care of his children. One day the master went away. When he came home, he find the man play on his banjo,—

"I was fooling my master
seventy-two years, An' I
am fooling him now."

He was singing this song away on his banjo. His master caught him. So the old man went to the doctor Negro. The next day he was to be kill'. When his master start to whip him, none of the licks touch. And he had freedom.[89]

Historian Lawrence Levine writes, "For all the limitations imposed upon slave tricksters and all the hazards they faced, it is not difficult to understand the pleasures slaves derived from their exploits. . . . [They] continually made the whites look foolish and always seemed one step ahead of them.[90]

Home itself was slaves' greatest joy, for it gave individuals a feeling of autonomy and independence. When Ball was ill, he preferred to stay in the quarters rather than going to the sick room because, at home, "*I was my own master.*"[91] (Emphasis added.) Blacks guarded the exclusiveness of their private domain and were none too happy when whites came. Traveler William Russell wrote after passing the domiciles of William Henry Trescot's "people":

"The old negroes were mostly indoors, and came shambling out to the doors of their wooden cottages, making clumsy bows at our approach, but not expressing any interest or pleasure at the sight of their master and the strangers."[92] Northern missionaries working among newly freed bondsmen seem to have been no more welcome. A. M. French wrote:

If, for instance, persons approach the huts of the field hands, they are met at the door by the whole family, who stand right before it, and with bows, courtesies, and docile actions and words, would beguile you from entering. This, however, they have tact enough to make appear as a mere matter of course . . . but still no way can you possibly open to enter the hut, until you say decidedly, "I will go in, if you please."[93]

In a doctoral dissertation, Bobby Jones made the cogent observation that "those who paint slavery with a continuous stream of doleful and sombre colors underestimate the resiliency of the human spirit and its capacity to adapt to the most trying environment."[94] Parties, drinking, gambling, and dancing were pastimes which few ex-slaves failed to remember in their narratives and autobiographies. The popularity of dancing accounts, in part, for the great prestige of fiddlers.[95] Prince Baskin, a short, dark black man interviewed late in the nineteenth century, had been both the driver and the fiddler on a South Carolina plantation. He recalled, "When I ben a-courtin' I nebber 'lowed no man to get de benefit ob me. . . . I allers carry off de purties' gal, 'cause you see, Missus, I know how to play de fiddle an' allers had to go to ebery dance to play de fiddle for dem."[96]

Needless to say, there was a certain escapist quality to many of the pursuits in and beyond the slave quarters. The status (and money) someone gained in gambling diverted one's attention briefly from the demeaning position of enslavement. An abundance of evidence indicates that large numbers of slaves lost no opportunity in drowning their miseries with liquor.[97] Determined to curtail both the drinking and mobility of slaves, the officers of the Society of Vigilance petitioned the South Carolina legislature to revise the patrol laws:

We think that a ticket given to a slave ought to state where he is going as well as how long to be absent and that a pass and repass as it is called ought not to be lawful. We are satisfied that negroes having tickets to pass and repass such a length of time without stating where they are going are

in the habits of visiting grog shops and other places where they would not
be willing to be seen by their owners and where their owners are not willing
for them to go but having a pass & repass cannot be lawfully whipped by
the patroll.[98]

Some may feel that it is contradictory to speak of a relentless
and perennial struggle between masters and slaves while acknowledging the seemingly noncombative and pacific life-styles of slaves
in the quarters, and the unequal battle. Slaves did act both offen-
sively and defensively in their struggles with the plantocracy, and
even activities in slave homes were part and parcel of that contest.
Slaves were consciously and subconsciously more on the offensive
during the after-hours when they had a measure of autonomy.
Every mode of behavior antithetical to the ideal type desired and
promoted by planters was encouraged and advanced by blacks
after hours. They spent these moments doing everything which
was conducive to instilling and preserving a positive self-image
and a healthy psyche: disparaging their oppressors in story and
song, stealing or firing the property of those foes, and dodging
them while on forbidden journeys were just a few such pursuits.
In the story, "Gullah Joe," the narrator recounted the treachery
and ruthlessness of whites who tricked Africans into slavery and
"brung us to dis country."

When I been a boy, a big vessel come nigh to my home. An' it had white
folks on it an' dey hab all kind er bead an' calico an' red flannel, an' all
kind er fancy thing. An' dem white folks gee a heap er thing to de people
er by tribe an' entice 'em on de boat. . . . An' one day dey hab de boad
crowd wid mens an' womens an' chillun, an' when dey find dey self, de boat
was 'way out to sea. An' some er dem niggers jump off an' dey was drowned.
But dem white folks overpowered dem what was on de boat, an' th'owed
'em down in de bottom er de ship. An' dey put chain on 'em an' make 'em
lay down moest of de time.

Dey been pack in dere wuss dan hog in a car when dey shippin' 'em. An'
every day dem white folks would come in dere an' ef a nigger jest twist his
self or move, dey'd cut de hide off him wid a rawhide whip. An' niggers
died in de bottom er dat ship wuss dan hogs wid cholera. Dem white folks
ain' hab no mercy. Look like dey ain' know wha' mercy mean. Dey drag
dem dead niggers out an' throw 'em overboard. An' dat ain' all. Dey th'owed
a heap er live ones wha' dey thought ain' guh live into de sea.

An' it look like we been two or three month in de bottom er dat ship.
An' day brung us to dis country an' dey sell us. . . . I is a ole man now . . .
but when I thinks er my tribe an' my friend an' my daddy an' my mammy
. . . a feelin' rises up in my th'oat an' my eye well up wid tear.[99]

Ridiculing whites was an old tradition among black Carolinians. During a clandestine dance on the outskirts of Charleston in 1772, sixty slaves mocked their owners in dance and, probably, the "curious anecdotes" accompanying it. According to an anonymous writer in the *South Carolina Gazette,* "the entertainment was opened by the men copying (or *taking off*) the manners of their masters, and the women those of their mistresses, and relating some highly curious anecdotes, to the inexpressible diversion of that company."[100] (Emphasis in the original.) With considerable glee on the night of July 17, 1851, Marion, a slave owned by Colonel E. S. Ervin, not only "assaulted & struck repeatedly" a patroller, but then "broke from the custody of the patrol" and fled laughing all the way. The State saw nothing funny in his adventure. Why Marion was sentenced to no more than "a moderate whipping of forty stripes" may be explained by the prominence of his owner and Joseph Cox, Esq., who had "charge" of the slave.[101]

Perhaps not so much out of choice but a certain helplessness, masters were basically on the defensive at night. They tried simply to limit slave travels[102] and depredations during the brief interim before their implacably offensive strategy was put into effect the following morning. This daytime plan encompassed every ruse, stratagem, and machination imaginable to maximize the productiveness of a reluctant work force. Bondpeople switched primarily to defensive tactics at sunrise: they wore all the masks necessary to avoid or at least check the frequency of the lash and did as little labor as possible by waging slowdowns and by malingering.

The great importance of the after-hours and holidays to African-Americans was not unnoticed by members of the ruling class. Many found that assigning additional tasks during these "free" periods was an extremely useful device. Plowden C. J. Weston said that "the stoppage of Saturday's allowance, and doing whole task on Saturday, will suffice to prevent ordinary offences."[103] Gaillard also noted the salutary effect of extra toil. In his plantation journal for Thursday, July 24, 1856, he wrote:

> Gave most of the negroes to day to work their own crops there are 10 who have without good cause laid up much during the hoeing season & having some of them runaway as a punishment would not give these 10—So put them to finish the 2 acres left in 16 acres after that to list slips ground.[104]

On December 26 and 27, 1853, John Milliken of Mulberry Plantation, declared a "Holiday for all hands except Ned & Paris / who for bad conduct & neglect of work / were kept at Sawpit."[105] This mode of correction affected more than the individual disciplined, for the welfare of one's family was jeopardized when any member who was contributing to the procurement of adequate food was detained. Once again, familial responsibilities prodded many to behave in such a fashion that they would not be hindered from providing for their loved ones.

It was not always necessary to dictate more work as punishment. Sadistic masters found effective ways to make normal loads much heavier. Irons weighing as much as sixty pounds were sometimes chained to the legs of errant bondsmen.[106] Langdon Cheves explained the reason for this burdensome appendage when discussing a recently captured absconder. He recommended a "light Iron" for the deserter, which Cheves suggested "ought to be changed every 3 or 4 weeks" so that "if he were to runaway again, he would find some difficulty in getting it off & if he should not succeed in that it would distinctly indicate him as a Runaway."[107] Slaves who stole themselves were subjected, after capture, to iron collars with long prongs and steeplelike frames occasionally which made *all* movement onerous. In an 1863 interview, a former South Carolina field hand, Harry McMillan, suggested that neck irons were sometimes used even before a slave fled. When asked about punishments, he said, "The punishments were whipping, putting you in the stocks and making you wear irons and a chain at work. Then they had a collar to put round your neck with two horns, like cow's horns, so that you could not lie down on your back or belly. This also kept you from running away for the horns would catch in the bushes."[108] Ball, for example, met a brutally beaten black hiding in the woods with an iron collar and an iron rod that extended "from one shoulder over his head to the other." It formed an arch towering three feet over the hair of the victim. Three bells were fastened to the top. This "frightful figure" was fleeing from an owner who had torn the flesh off his back so often that "the natural colour of the skin had disappeared, and . . . scarcely any of the original back remain[ed]."[109]

It is remarkable that such deterrents did not stop more slaves. A newspaper advertisement for Dinah, a slave woman, hints both at how determined many escapees were and their pre-liberated demeanor. Despite "an iron on her right leg" and a face "much marked . . . by the whip," Dinah fled one winter, taking her nine-year-old son.[110] The extensive use of irons and an apparent worry about how those appendages might be interpreted by outsiders were revealed in an 1806 Charleston ordinance:

Be it ordained, That it shall not be lawful for any owner, or for any other persons, having the control of slaves, to permit or suffer any slave to appear in the streets, or any public part of the city in irons, or with an iron or irons put round or on the neck, head, legs, hands or any part of the body: Neither shall it be lawful . . . to permit or suffer any such slave to appear in the streets, or any public part of the city, without sufficient clothing.

There was, however, an interesting caveat, "That nothing in this Ordinance extends to fugitive slaves who have escaped from the country."[111]

In devising new methods of disciplining slaves, planters were truly ingenious. One slaveholder would tie the hands and feet of a slave and then place him across a rail fence. From that tenuous position, the sufferer was pushed or shoved while spectators looked on amusedly as he struggled to land without injury.[112] Another master ordered his cook to eat a raw chicken liver simply because she had accidentally dropped the liver of that evening's meal in the fire.[113] Freed blacks and others described masters who frequently doused the whipped and lacerated bodies of slaves with red pepper and saline solutions.[114] For those who had applied these washings, ex-slave Solbert Butler could only imagine an eternal place where "dere can't be no rest." Butler had been enslaved on one of the Bostick (a large slaveholding family) plantations in Garnett, South Carolina. Years later, he still remembered: "Dey planted cotton, corn, peas, potatoes, rice—an' dey'd lick you! All de time, dey'd lick you. After dey'd lick 'em until de blood come out, den dey'd rub de red pepper and salt on 'em. Oh, my God! Kin you say dem as done sech as dat aint gone to deir reward?"[115]

Curtailment or complete denial of food allotments was a more widely practiced punishment.[116] When two slave carpenters killed one of his hogs, Dr. Henry M. Holmes, an aristocratic South Carolina planter, "whipped them and ordered each of them to have a hundred lashes more." The two ran away. Lucy Ruggles, governess to the Holmes children, recorded in her diary typical

Holmes punishments of the sort that probably awaited them if captured: "He frequently locks them up in a dark room—chains them to a chair and gives them nothing but a little gruel once a day sometimes for a month or more."[117] Another prominent planter, John Blount Miller of Sumter District, declared in his plantation rules that "if a small negro runs away the meat of the family must be taken away or withholden until return," but "if a grown one the *meat of all* must be taken away or withholden."[118] (Emphasis added.)

The most severe forms of chastisement were, of course, torture and murder. One antebellum visitor to South Carolina wisely challenged the common belief that the economic interests of masters precluded them from mistreating their slave property. "This reasoning," James Stirling wrote, "assumes, first, that slave-owners will take an intelligent view of their own interests; and, secondly, that they will be guided by the passion of gain rather than by other passions."[119]

The measures necessary to control slaves left little room for compassion and often led to a hardening of feelings toward those being suppressed. Acts of brutality became all the easier once one ceased to identify or empathize with blacks and began to regard them as subhuman beings.[120] Moreover, the inability of slaves to testify against whites and the right of whites to exculpate themselves from any charges of abuse encouraged further the cruel and inhumane handling of living chattels.[121] Still applicable in the 1800s was the provision discussed in chapter one that any white who maimed, "cruelly" beat, or killed a slave could "*by his own oath, clear and exculpate himself.*"[122] (Emphasis in the original.) White controllers thus had a license to murder.

The concerted efforts of Southerners to hide the less attractive features of their slave society caused an almost total censorship of information in local publications about the more hideous aspects of the system. This incessant campaign of suppression and the steadfast refusal of other native sons to interfere with the "personal" affairs of slaveholders assured that only the most atrocious cases of slave abuse ever reached the courts. Even then, masters were hardly ever sent to the gallows for killing a slave. They were usually subjected to no more than a fine which, incidentally, could not exceed five hundred dollars. If one confined his or her barbarities to private estates and did not damage *another's* "property," the prospect of suffering any consequences at all was extremely remote.[123] Indeed, one examination of the trial records from eighteen of South Carolina's forty-six districts reveals "that only sixteen of seventy-one prosecutions for slave murder resulted in conviction, and that only one of those convictions carried the death penalty."[124] The commitment of the jury foreman in the State v. M'Kee not to "convict the defendant, *or any other* white person, of murdering a slave," (emphasis added), was apparently shared by many other South Carolinians.[125]

Much the same attitude prevailed in cases involving less fatal incidents. In 1807, a Dr. Fairchild "took in and cured a female slave" who had been beaten savagely by her owner with "an iron on her leg of fifteen pounds weight." He was suing for compensation. Although Dr. Fairchild had informed a justice of the peace about the slave and received instructions from him to give her medical treatment, the defendant refused "to furnish the wench with clothes and necessaries, . . . was outrageously angry, and threatened to sue the plaintiff for harboring his slave." Fairchild acted first, but "the jury found for the defendant."[126]

When one considers that overseers usually had to obtain special permission from planters before inflicting any exceptionally cruel chastisement, it is ironic that the overseers have been held more responsible for the sadistic treatment of slaves than those who hired and directed them.[127] One slaveholder, Edward C. Johnson, demanded in his plantation rules of 1850 that "no *unusual* punishment . . . be resorted to without the employer's consent."[128] (Emphasis added.) Similarly, Hammond ordered, "The overseer is strictly enjoined never to kick or strike a negro with his hand or a stick unless in self defense. No unusual punishment must be resorted to without my consent."[129] While many subordinates undoubtedly failed to ask consent, the history of slaveowners indicates that large numbers of masters would have gladly granted their requests. Contemporary and more recent sources are replete with examples of "patriarchs" subjecting "their people" to horrors unbefitting even to wild animals. Rosa Barnwell wrote the editor of the *Liberator* in 1862 about her experiences as a slave "for more than twenty years" in South Carolina. She described a fellow slave who had been "almost butchered" by her master: "he took a bowie-knife, and thrust it into the fleshy parts of his shoulder until the flesh was turned inside out." Miraculously, he survived and ultimately escaped to Washington, D.C.[130]

Piercing with forks, burning with tar, skinning with knives, and killing outright with whips and pistols are well-documented methods in which planters tormented and murdered blacks.[131] After being accused by a mulatto "friend" of attacking a white woman, Ball narrowly escaped being skinned alive. Although a timely confession by the true culprits spared Ball's life, he nevertheless had to suffer the preliminaries to that "most horrible of tortures."

The overseer, and the gentlemen, all followed; and as soon as the cellar door was closed . . . I was ordered to pull off my clothes and lie down on my back. I was then bound by the hands and feet, with strong cords, and extended at full length between two of the beams that supported the timbers of the building. . . . "Before you are skinned, [the doctor said] you had better confess your crime." The doctor, during this time, was assorting his instruments and looking at me—then stooping down, and feeling my pulse, he said, it would not do to skin a man so full of blood as I was. I should bleed so much that he could not see to do his work; and he could probably cut some large vein, or artery, by which I should bleed to death in a few minutes: it was necessary to bleed in the arms, for some time, so as to reduce the quantity of blood that was in me, before taking my skin off. He bound a string round my right arm, from which the blood ran in a large and smooth stream.[132]

Not all tortures resulted in scarred and bloodied bodies: some masters discovered ways to cause immense suffering without marring the surfaces of their human property. A friend of the South Carolinian exile Sarah Grimke would punish a slave by making him stand with one ankle in a strap attached to his neck, "so that the least weight of the foot . . . would choke the person. . . . The pain occasioned by this unnatural position was great; and when continued . . . for an hour or more, produced intense agony."[133] But there was no scar. Whether mild or severe, such disciplinary actions or simply news of them convinced many African-Americans further that things, indeed, could only get worse.

During the early 1830s, "an immense assemblage of slaves" was gathered in Greenville, South Carolina, to witness the burning alive of a bondsman named George. Fugitive slave Moses Roper remembered:

a pen of about fifteen feet square was built of pine wood, in the center of which was a tree, the upper part of which had been sawn off. To this tree

George was chained; the chain having been passed round his neck, arms, and legs, to make him secure. The pen was then filled with shavings and pine wood up to his neck. A considerable quantity of tar and turpentine was then poured over his head. The preparations having been completed, the four corners of the pen were fired, and the miserable man perished in the flames. When I was last there, which was about two years before I left America, for England, not only was the stump of the tree to which the slave George had been fastened, to be seen, but some of his burnt bones.[134]

Few whites protested the torture and murder of unlawful slaves. Some whites, however, were appalled at how slaveholders could butcher slaves illegally and escape public censure. Thomas B. Chaplin, a Low Country planter near Beaufort, discussed at length an 1849 case that illustrates more than any other incident the ease with which one could torture a fellow human being and receive de facto approbation. He recorded the following on a cold day, February 19, 1849:

I received a summons while at Breakfast to go over to J. H. Sandiford's . . . and sit on a jury of inquest on the body of Roger, a negro man belonging to Sandiford . . . there were 12 of us together (the number required to form a jury). We were sworn by J. D. Pope Magistrate and proceeded to examine the body, we found it in an out-house used as a corn house, and meat-house. . . . Such a shocking sight never before met my eyes, there was the poor negro—who all his life had been a compleat cripple, being hardly able to walk & uses his knees more than his feet, in the most shocking situation but *stiff dead*, he was placed in this situation by his *master*, to punish him, as he said *for impertinace* . . . this *poor cripple*—was sent by his master (as Sandifords' evidence goes) on Saturday the 17th inst before day light—(cold & bitter weather, as every one knows—tho Sandiford sais, it was *not very* cold!) in a paddling boat down the river to get oisters and ordering him to return before high water & cut a bundle of marsh. The poor fellow did not return before ebb tide—but he brought 7 baskets of oisters & a small bundle of marsh (more than the primest of my fellows would have done, Anthony never brought me more than 5 baskets of Oisters & took the whole day) His master asked him why he did not return sooner & cut more marsh. he said the wind was too high. his master said he would whip him for it, & set to work with a cow hide to do the same the fellow hollowed & when told to stop Said he would not as long as he was being whipped for which impertinance he rec^d 30 cuts. . . . Sandiford then had him confined—or I should say murdered in the manner I will describe. . . .

This man, this demon in human shape, this pretended Christian—Member of the Baptist Church—had this poor cripple negro placed in an open outhouse—the wind blowing through a hundred cracks—his clothes wet to his waist—without a single blanket & in freezing weather with his back against a partition shackels on his wrists & chained to a bolt in the floor and a *chain* around *his neck*—the chain passing through the partition behind him & fastened on the other side. In this position the poor wretch was left for the night. . . . The wretch returned to his victim about day light the next morning & found him as any one might expect dead—Choked & strangled—frozen to death, murdered. The verdict of the jury was that Roger came to his death by choking by a chain put around his neck—*having sliped from the position in which he* was placed.[135] (Emphases in the original.)

Orlando Patterson, in his prodigious study, *Slavery and Social Death,* offered keen insights on why slaveowners around the world felt little or no remorse about killing their slaves. He states:

Perhaps the most distinctive attribute of the slave's powerlessness was that it always originated (or was conceived of as having originated) as a substitute for death, usually violent death. . . . Archetypically, slavery was a substitute for death in war. But almost as frequently, the death committed was punishment for some capital offense, or death from exposure or starvation.

The condition of slavery did not absolve or erase the prospect of death. Slavery was not a pardon; it was, peculiarly, a conditional commutation. The execution was suspended only as long as the slave acquiesced in his powerlessness.[136]

The assault on slaves was not only physical but mental. The plantocracy realized that without capturing the minds as well as the bodies of their workers, all efforts at control would be futile. They, therefore, launched an elaborate and systematic psychological campaign aimed at instilling in the enslaved a sense of inferiority and a feeling of deserved dependence on the ruling class. Slaveholders themselves tried always to pose as omnipotent, benevolent, and totally in command so that bondsmen would be reminded constantly of their base position in white society and of the judiciousness of that state. Masters were particularly insistent that overseers behave with an aloofness, confidence, and calm like their own.[137] Plowden C. J. Weston, for example, ended his plantation rule book with this statement:

The Proprietor hopes the Overseer will remember that a system of strict justice is necessary to good management. . . . Every person should be made perfectly to understand what they are punished for, and should be made to perceive that they are not punished in anger, or through caprice. All abusive language or violence of demeanor should be avoided: *they reduce the man who uses them with a level with the negro,* and are hardly ever forgotten by those to whom they are addressed.[138] (Emphasis added.)

Even in defeat, planters and their managers attempted to look victorious and supreme. After slaves had stolen practically all their stock of hogs, two prominent slaveholders in 1818 and 1859, respectively, decided to make contracts with the thieves "permitting" them to raise hogs for their personal consumption and sale.[139]

To illustrate their strength and power, slaveowners compelled blacks to witness the flogging, torture, and execution of fellow bondsmen. These displays had to have been a powerful inducement to pacific behavior since slave onlookers would have experienced vicariously the suffering of their brethren and, thereby, the fearful might of their masters. Nothing was more painful psychologically than to stand by and watch as friends, loved ones, and relatives underwent such agonizing punishment. While some slaves intervened, most concluded that such efforts were useless and looked on helplessly and with mental anguish.[140] The young Victoria Perry was so frightened when her mother got whipped that she suppressed her tears for fear that she too "would get whipped if she cried."[141] When William Boswell, the overseer of Spartanburg slaveholder John Zimmerman, tried to whip a slave named Sally, she struggled with him and told her son to call Levi, his father. Boswell succeeded in tying her to a tree, but her husband Levi and shortly thereafter another slave, Simmon, "came up like tigers."[142]

Levi told the overseer that Sally "was his wife and that he would unloose her or commit murder at the root of that tree." Simmon said he would do it himself because she was "my Colour and when ever I see one of them tied he would loose them at the risk of his life." Boswell called for his gun "to shoot them"; members of his family brought it and an axe for good measure. The two families fought, Boswell was disarmed, and Sally was untied. A wounded Boswell went and appealed to his employer who apparently did not live on the plantation. Although Zimmerman offered to beat the slaves personally and granted Boswell permission to whip them first to "his full satisfaction," Boswell declined. Believing Simmon could be hanged "for choaking his wife," Boswell "dident feel like whipping." He "wanted to law the negroes" and succeeded.[143]

The State blocked the overseer's vendetta and Zimmerman's slave was spared the noose, but the three slaves were lashed severely and each black man imprisoned for a month.[144] Whether slaves resisted or watched passively as fellow captives withstood or perished in any number of brutalities, ultimately they were suppressed physically, if not spiritually. The defeat was even worse when one was forced to be both a spectator and an instrument of the chastisement. A respectable Charlestonian frequently ordered "brothers to whip their own sisters, and sisters their own brothers."[145] It is not difficult to imagine the added degradation of victims when they were not only whipped before an audience of their peers or even their family, but ridiculed so when completely nude.[146]

Because most members of the plantocracy believed firmly that punitive examples were the best preventive medicines for prospective rebels, black Carolinians by the thousands were on occasion forced to witness an execution, usually by hanging. To make sure that one did not miss the point of these exhibitions, slaves were often sentenced to die at the scene of their crimes. Condemned blacks were sometimes dressed in "grave clothes," then carried through the community seated upon the coffins that were shortly to be their final home. Such masters were clearly determined to make each killing, whether by noose, or torch, or axe, a spectacle viewers would not soon forget.[147] Eighty-two-year-old Violet Guntharpe was still talking in 1937 of a slave boy named John who had killed his master, Captain Thorn of Grimkeville, South Carolina, and "throwed his body in de river." According to Guntharpe, "when they find his [Thorn's] body they ketch John . . . give him a trial by six white men, find him guilty and he confess. Then they took de broad axe, cut off his head, mount it on a pole and stick it up on de bank where they find old Captain Thorn. Dat pole and head stay dere 'till it rot down.[148]

The refusal of planters to inter the corpses of "dangerous" or simply "nonexemplary" slaves was a typical means of deterring blacks from following any similar "unhealthy" precedents.[149] Such terror tactics must have been fairly common in some regions, since Reverend William P. Hill recorded his own experience, of April 9th, 1847, quite nonchalantly:

AM. 8 clock left for Orangeburg C.H. Went out of my way mistaking my road[;] passed by where a negro was executed for murder and robery-1st hung and the[n] decapitated the gallows being reared on the place where the murder was committed. [H]is head was placed on a spike on the top of the gallows—Stopped at Mr. J. Whetotone's for dinner. . . .[150]

Despite all such physical and psychological atrocities, many bondsmen, nevertheless and remarkably, steadfastly refused to become
the mere puppets of which owners dreamed.

Many African-American slaves considered absconding their most
effective mode of resistance. A song slave laborers sang at work
reflects that threat. Sam Polite, a former slave, born in 1844,
remembered it this way:

> Go way, Ole Man
> Go way, Ole Man
> W'ere you bin all day
> If you treat me good
> I'll stay 'till de Judgment day.
> But if you treat me bad
> I'll sho' to run away.[151]

While excessive labor, severe beatings, and undesirable tasks prodded some to flee, many others needed no motivation but the prospect of freedom and the end of involuntary toiling for others.[152]
The threat of punishment, however, was cited most often as the
reason blacks ran away and the source of their willingness to
endure the grave privations and dangers of "being out."[153] Therefore planters usually did not warn those marked for chastening,
but seized them by surprise and *then* castigated them for any
misconduct.[154] Illegal departures were so widespread that certain
measures of slaveholder response became traditional. Individuals
returning on their own accord, for example, were generally exempted from corporal punishment.[155]

But some masters adhered only to their own customs; James
Henry Hammond, for instance, ordered that the two runaways
who returned to him voluntarily on October 17, 1839, receive
"three lashes for each day" they were absent, that is, from the
26th of August or fifty-two stripes. Hammond then instituted a
rule that deserters thereafter receive ten stripes "for each day if
caught & Three if they come in."[156]

To survive the more gruesome features of bondage, enslaved
workers sometimes turned to the less oppressive members of the
ruling class.[157] Because they themselves could not testify against
whites in the courts, blacks sought the assistance of sympathetic
slaveholders for redress or relief from cruel and sadistic masters.
Lewis Mitchell, a young bondsman fleeing from a particularly

brutal mistress, implored the aid of Henry W. Ravenel. Upon arrival at Ravenel's estate in Aiken, South Carolina, Mitchell said "he could not return home he was treated so badly." As reported by Ravenel, Mitchell said that he had not eaten for two days and had "stayed last night in the woods covered by some straw — that when he is at home he sleeps in an open fowl house with one or two ragged blankets, & that she does not give him enough to eat, & beats him. He has all the appearance of a starved & ill-treated person—Eyes dull & heavy, cheeks sunken & skin shriveled & weak voice. I have given him a good meal & will go in to Aiken tomorrow & represent the case to the authorities—If there is a law of humanity, it should not be tolerated."[158]

Many slaves wanted to use "friendly" whites to secure pardons or milder punishments for absconding.[159] Eugene Genovese says that such appeals by servants "strengthened the doctrine of paternalism among the whites as well as among themselves."[160] While it may indeed have strengthened white paternalism, there is little evidence supporting such a consequence among blacks in South Carolina. African-Americans wore a wide variety of masks on occasion and they most prized those pretenses that reduced the severity or number of lashes anticipated for some misdeed. In such patently unpatriarchal societies as Jamaica, the practices of white intercession were extremely common both during slavery and the four-year apprenticeship period before freedom was granted in 1838. Joseph Sturge and Thomas Harvey, authors of *The West Indies in 1837 . . .*, found that in Jamaica it was customary "for repentant runaways to get an intercessory letter from some friend of their master, or even from a stranger, to save them from punishment."[161] Bondsmen in Jamaica and in America were taught certain manipulative skills very early to deceive or influence whites in their behalf. These ploys and ruses do not, in themselves, necessarily reflect any paternalistic relationship between slave and master.

Large numbers of bondsmen decided not to await the assistance of benevolent outsiders, but chose to remedy their problems by attacking, and some by killing, the men behind the whip.[162] Dr. A. Burt of Edgefield District, for instance, was murdered when he attempted to punish one of his slaves. The doctor "had broken off a branch of a peach tree" and inflicted "a few stripes, when the negro seized an axe and almost instantly killed him."[163] A significant portion, if not the majority, of all murders by blacks were, interestingly, not a result of impulse but plotted and carried out by two or more of the victim's slaves working together.[164] Members of the plantocracy feared such calculated acts of violence more than any other type of resistance. Not only did such aggression cause injuries and deaths, but they dealt a lethal blow to ruling-class pretensions of omnipotence and superiority. Blacks witnessing these slayings learned how guns, knives, and bare hands alone could "equalize" the various strata of society. Neither the executing nor the torturing of their guilty comrades would erase that lesson.

It was not necessary, of course, for African-Americans to watch their oppressors bleed, suffer, or die in order to achieve a sense of equality or parity with the power elite. Quite to the contrary, they felt morally, physically, and intellectually superior to slave-owners long before displays of this nature.[165] Slaves considered the mere holding of fellow human beings in bondage immoral, wicked, and sinful.[166] Black Christians looked at themselves as the only true believers and questioned seriously whether any whites would enter heaven.[167] Harriet Martineau, a noted British traveler, remembered the slaves on one estate "taunting their mistress with, 'You no holy. We holy. You no in state o' salvation.'"[168] What a few blacks said publicly was surely expressed by many others in private.

American bondsmen took great pride in their strength and in their agricultural skills. The largest muscles helped determine whether the master's tasks would be completed early enough to pursue other interests and that ability may very well have raised a man's eligibility in the eyes of women.[169] Those seeking mates would have considered who could contribute most to a family in which a collective effort was essential for adequate provision of one's children and each other. Former slave I. E. Lowery revealed much about slave men and women in his description of the festive interplantation log-rollings that planters sponsored:

A log-rolling always meant a good dinner . . . lots of fun, as well as a testing of manhood. The testing of manhood was something that everybody was interested in. . . . The slave women were concerned: for they wanted their husbands and sweethearts to be considered the best men of the community. Then, too the men took great pride in the development of their muscles. They took delight in rolling up their shirt sleeves, and displaying the largeness of their arms. . . . If one fails to lift his part, he is said to have been "pulled down," and therefore becomes the butt of ridicule for the balance of the day. When the women folks learn of his misfortune, they forever scorn him as a weakling.[170]

How well one could work was an important determinant of status in the slave community. Charles Ball illustrates this graphically:

I had ascertained, that at the hoe, the spade, the axe, the sickle, or the flail, I was a full match for the best hands on the plantation; but soon discovered, when we came to the picking of cotton, that I was not equal to a boy of twelve or fifteen years of age. I worked hard the first day, and made every effort to sustain the character that I had acquired amongst my companions, but when evening came, and our cotton weighed, I had only thirty-eight pounds, and was vexed to see that two young men, about my own age, had, one fifty-eight, and the other fifty-nine pounds. I hung down my head, and felt very much ashamed of myself, when I found that my cotton was so far behind that of many, even of the women, who had heretofore regarded me as the strongest and most powerful man of the whole gang.[171]

Blacks, as an agrarian people, were gratified by watching the products of their hands grow and flourish. Moreover, it was advantageous psychologically to observe how dependent the ruling class was on their brawn, knowledge, and ingenuity. Historian Eric Perkins sheds additional light on the meaning and importance of work to slaves:

In the work of Hegel and Marx, the dialectic of lordship and bondage is mediated by labor. The freedom of the master comes from his dependence on the labor of the slave. Through his labor, the slave comes to possess an idea of freedom just as the master. But unlike the master's idea of freedom, which is based on another, and not himself, the slave's [sic] realized himself and his freedom through labor.[172]

As Alexandre Kojeve notes in *An Introduction to the Reading of Hegel*: "Through his work, therefore, the Slave comes to the same result to which the Master comes by risking his life in the Fight: he modifies them, starting from the idea he has himself. In becoming conscious of this fact, therefore, he becomes conscious of his freedom, his autonomy."[173]

The work arena was not the only area in which blacks felt supreme. Behind a mask of docility and an esoteric vocabulary incomprehensible to whites, they flaunted an intellect, considered among themselves far superior to that of planters. Although not schooled formally, slaves believed they held the secrets of the soil and of nature and harbored an abundance of mother wit that few whites could equal. There were, of course, some bondsmen who did not look at themselves so positively. It was among this group that planters were no doubt the most successful in recruiting collaborators through which to divide and rule.

CHAPTER FOUR

Tactics of Divide and Rule

Speaking of the driver, brings me to notice my management of him more
particularly. I always required of him, that he should dress himself better
than the other negroes. This caused him to maintain a pride of character
before them, which was highly beneficial. Indeed, I constantly endeavoured,
to do nothing which would cause them to lose their respect for him. With
this view, I made it a rule never to scold or lecture my driver before the
other negroes for any inadvertence or fault. . . . The more the driver is
kept aloof from the negroes, the better. The truth is, he cannot maintain
too much pride in his conduct towards them. Once let them believe that
they are his equals, and all control is lost.

An overseer, 1836[1]

Just as European imperialists penetrated Africa, in part by playing tribe against tribe and brother against brother, so too did
North American planters invade the minds and quarters of their
slaves with stratagems to divide and rule. Both in the East and
in the West, white transgressors were aided in their ploys to control indigenous and imported populations by the divisions that
existed already within their domains or communities. The loyalty
of slaves to their own families, for example, kept South Carolinian
bondsmen entangled in endless feuds with others. When the
American Freedmen's Inquiry Commission in 1863 interviewed
Harry McMillan, a forty-year-old former field hand from Beaufort, South Carolina, about his life as a slave, he was asked what
a young black male would do if "struck by another?" McMillan
responded, "If he is injured bad the relations come in and give
the boy who injured him the same hurt. I would tell my boy to
strike back and defend himself."[2] African-Americans considered
familial ties so binding and inviolable that the offending of one
member usually resulted in the outrage of the entire clan. Although pseudo-kinship networks and communalistic values precluded much internecine strife, some battles were inevitable. No
common foe, however pernicious, could absorb all the anger,
hatred, and frustration endemic to any crowded and oppressed
community. Indeed, as the ongoing history of blacks in the United

States continues to show, the struggle to maintain unity and to overcome all that is self-destructive are alarmingly timeless battles.

In antebellum South Carolina, some bondsmen, either through their industriousness or position, were able to maintain life-styles that aroused the jealousy and envy of others.[3] Charles Ball made the following telling remark when discussing the greater frequency with which he was able to obtain meat as a consequence of his after-hours exertions:

> It may well be supposed, that in our society, although we were all slaves, and all nominally in a condition of the most perfect equality, yet there was in fact a very great difference in the manner of living, in several families. Indeed, I doubt, if there is as great a diversity in the modes of life, in the several families of any white village in New York, or Pennsylvania, containing a population of three hundred persons, as there was in several households of our quarter.[4]

According to Reverend C. C. Jones, slave families grew "jealous and envious of their neighbors" because "some essay to be *leading* families."[5] (Emphasis in the original.) Another white contemporary, whose father owned a plantation with 110 slaves in the Piedmont section of South Carolina, wrote that, "Like the white people, the negroes, though slaves, had their petty jealousies." He cited "two or three men on the plantation who did not like Unc' Essick," the slave foreman, "for no other reason than that he was promoted over them."[6]

The general absence of data or discussion in the historiography of slavery about fights among blacks is remarkable when one considers the plethora of such data in contemporary sources, at least in South Carolina. From ruling-class correspondence to criminal court records, a picture emerges of slave altercations as common occurrences, which not infrequently ended in serious injury or death.[7] In July 1840, blacks owned by Colonel Thomas Sumter, Jr., in Stateburgh raised such a commotion "quarreling," perhaps after a long night of socializing, that they awoke his wife at five o'clock on a Sunday morning.[8] Some slave altercations involved whites more directly. One cost an overseer his job. David Gavin, a South Carolina planter, wrote in 1860:

> Henry Syphret my overseer and girl Betsey had a fight yesterday and I settled with him last night and he left this morning. It seems the negroes Mike, Big Jim, Little Mary & Betsey had a fight Sunday night, Mike was

jealous of Big Jim and his wife Little Mary, Syphret quelled the affray and not being over his ill humor yesterday had a fight with Betsey. He is very steady but is not much account amongst hands, he does not know when negroes are working, without at plowing, for none of my work went on as well as that, every thing else is behind, He is some better than none but not much, but I do not know where to get another overseer, and I need one.[9]

The consequences were more severe on another plantation where a slave named Sam accused a fellow bondsman, George, of taking his hammer. George, whom both blacks and whites described as the least "tempered of the two," killed him with an axe.[10] Not all conflicts ended fatally. In 1851, David W. Moore, a Spartanburg slaveholder, charged a slave named Bassett with "assault & Battery on Joseph a negro slave his property." The two bondsmen fought when Bassett struck Joseph with a "large stick" after Joseph asked him "what he had been abusing *his wife for*."[11] (Emphasis in the original.)

H. Perry Pope discussed the competitive spirit of some South Carolina slaves, and the violence that competitiveness occasionally aroused, in his 1837 thesis at the Medical College of the State of South Carolina. In a "Dissertation on the Professional Management of Negro Slaves," he wrote:

Boatracing they are extremely fond of, and it is surprising to see the efforts they will make to obtain the Victory; and the distance they will row, before they will acknowledge themselves beaten. Christmas is a favorite time for this with them, as at that period a great number of Boats meet in the neighboring Cities, either in carrying the Crop to Market or in bringing supplies for the Plantation, it occasionally happens a Negro will exert himself so much to obtain or keep the ascendency in a race, that medical aid is required, and some are known to have seriously injured themselves from over exertion, formerly it was not an uncommon thing to hear of a general fight at one of the above racing matches, but of late it is very rare.[12]

Struggles over women, marital disputes, and suspected adulterous behavior are cited most often as the cause of physical confrontations.[13] With considerable braggadocio, eighty-seven-year-old Anderson Bates recounted how he had physically overcome seven slave competitors vying for the "sugar lump of a gal" whom he eventually married on a plantation of more than one hundred slaves near Jenkinsville.[14] Unfortunately, such conflicts sometimes continued even after marriage. In 1815 Billy, a slave member of the Welsh Neck Baptist Church, not only attempted "to commit adultery" but "offered violence to the woman's husband who detected him in his design." Billy was "excluded [from] the church."[15] When Poyas John, the slave of a large Low Country planter, thought in 1858 that a runaway called Hercules "had been with his . . . wife," John confronted him, they "quarrelled, and [John] shot him." Hercules, who had "been about the neighborhood for several years," lived long enough to tell who shot him.[16] For this murder, John received the unusually severe sentence of twelve months in solitary confinement at the Walterbourough jail, thirty-nine lashes "the first Monday in each month," and, "at the expiration of which time," sale out of state. Reflecting upon the trial and its outcome, John's owner, J. B. Grimball, wrote in his diary that there was nothing in John's favor but "his own previous good conduct . . . the bad character of the Runaway . . . and the fact that he probably believed that Hercules had lain with his wife—and probably rightly believed so." As Grimball saw it, "These three things were all that could be said for him."[17]

Acts of violence were given the de facto sanction of the ruling class through lenient prosecution of parties involved in "black-on-black" crimes. If, for example, a bondsman killed or attempted to kill a white, he faced almost certain death.[18] When Paul and Bacchus, two "able bodied fellows & above the average value of negroes," murdered their overseer in 1838, they went to the gallows.[19] George, the axe-killer, however, was charged with "manslaughter" and sentenced only to two months' imprisonment and fifty lashes "every Wednesday morning."[20] When blacks attacked and sometimes killed their own, they were sentenced usually to no more than three months of solitary confinement, corporal punishment, and possible sale out of state.[21] Some planters considered even these disciplinary actions too severe for slaves' aggressions upon fellow blacks.

Edward Carew pleaded with the legislature to shorten the jail term of a bondsman named Isaac who had murdered his wife Kettura. Carew, the owner of Isaac, argued that there was no premeditation and that quarrels "between a negro and his wife" were "of frequent occurrence," worthy only of "moderate" correction":

The Case is not distinguishable from many others of conflict between people of this description. No such violence was used by the Prisoner as should have excited an apprehension of fatal consequences. This appears as well from the testimony, as the Judgement of the Court. The death of Kettura may be regarded in some measure as accidental since there was no injury inflicted sufficient in nine cases out of ten not have been attended with such an effect. Indeed the evidence only shews a common instance of a quarrel between a negro and his wife which are of frequent occurrence and not deemed to merit more than moderate correctin [sic].[22]

The lawmakers of South Carolina evidently concurred with Carew, for the slave Isaac was sentenced to just twenty-five lashes and three months in prison.[23] This was indeed a far cry from the gallows.

Folklore passed down from slavery to freedom by learned if unschooled black elders provides further evidence of the divisions among slaves. The pervasive "brer rabbit" tales, for example, portray the protagonist usually as a furry Robin Hood who stalks and vanquishes larger animals for the benefit of all. He does, however, also employ his infinite wisdom and skills to exploit fellow creatures on occasion with a ruthlessness thought possible only from the most despicable beasts of the forest.[24] In "Buh Rabbit an De Tarruh Beasties," our hero not only lies about the illness of his wife to avoid helping stockpile food for the winter, but steals the products of these "comrades'" labor for himself.[25] Similar inconsistencies and contradictions characterize the leading figure of another folk series about the adventures of a crafty servant named John. While John exemplifies courage and brilliance in outmaneuvering slaveholders, he sometimes resorts to the same fiendish methods of his oppressors. To escape drowning one day, John tricks an innocent old lady into substituting herself for him in a sack that the master plans to put him in and throw in the river. As a result of this treachery, the poor woman dies.[26] Although the folklore of African-Americans encourages unity and cooperation among the weakest members of society, it often reveals the troublesome presence of disruptive individuals whose depravity or avarice leads them to betray their fellows.[27]

An examination of slave attitudes toward "conjuration" discloses further the existence of persons of evil intentions who can be stopped only by opposition, either in the form of physical confrontation or protective charms and amulets. This system of magic, divination, and herbalism, referred to as "conjuration," was practiced extensively in slave communities throughout the

New World. Mysterious illnesses, foiled love affairs, and other inexplicable unfavorable occurrences were often attributed to the conjuring or "hagging" of some black enemy.[28] William McCaa, a medical student at the University of Pennsylvania, recorded the following incident in his 1823 senior thesis:

> A practitioner of my acquaintance was called to visit a negro fellow some few miles from town. When he saw him he had a ligature around each thigh, drawn so tight as nearly to impede altogether the circulation; he said that "one of his fellow servants had bewitched him! and placed in his legs a number of crawfish, which he was endeavoring to prevent from getting into his belly," after much persuasion he took off the strings and in a few days was relieved of his rheumatism; but he always afterwards viewed with a cautious eye the person who bewitched him.[29]

In another incident, Jim, a slave belonging to an Alexander Norwood, was excluded from the Welsh Neck Baptist Church in 1826 after beating "an aged Woman" to death with a "Grape Vine" for supposedly having practiced witchcraft on him.[30]

The awe with which both skeptics and believers viewed conjurers is an indication of their influence over slave laymen. Large numbers of slaves undoubtedly were consoled and comforted by these canny interpreters of the supernatural. As historian Albert Raboteau understood it, conjure was a theory not only "for explaining the mystery of evil, but . . . for doing something about it. . . . Because the conjure doctor has the power to 'fix' and to remove 'fixes', to harm and to cure, it was possible to locate the source of misfortune and *control it.*"[31] (Emphasis added.) Such preventive or retaliatory measures must have given many slaves a sense of order in and authority over their lives. The retention of similar beliefs and practices after slavery offers further testimony to this assertion.[32]

The self-repose achieved by some slaves by this or other means came often at the expense of others and did much to stir disharmony in the black community. One might think that the prevalence of these divisive tendencies would have precluded the need of planters to create additional havoc in the quarters, but slaves' private battles did more to spread a general mistrust and suspicion of each other than to inspire any allegiance or loyalty to masters. Indeed, American bondsmen maintained such a unified front against slaveholders that the white elite found it difficult to crack the wall of silence that separated them from their "people."

Although there are accounts of slaves who revealed voluntarily the names of slave thieves and the whereabouts of runaways, far more evidence in South Carolina indicates that slaves refused, generally, to do so. In a desperate effort to discover whether his slave Squire had stolen from him, Joel W. Ashford of Winnsboro wrote his fellow slaveholder Dr. James Milling in Rocky Mount, Louisiana. Milling, formerly of South Carolina, had moved his slaves to Louisiana in 1859 and Ashford wanted him to interrogate one of them, Wash, a close friend of Squire. Recognizing the customary difficulty in obtaining such information, Ashford told Milling to tell Wash that "if he did tell on him now it would make no difference him being so far away." Whether Milling succeeded is not clear, but slaves collectively kept their lips sealed regularly enough to make whites lament what some described as a "free masonry" silence among them. It was the "one point" that the Reverend Jones concluded slaves were "scrupulous" about: "They make," he wrote, "common cause, as servants, in *concealing* their faults from their owners. Inquiry elicits no information [for] no one feels at liberty to disclose the transgressor; ... the matter assumes the sacredness of a 'professional secret.'"[33] (Emphasis in the original.)

To hamper the annoyingly cooperative spirit among the enslaved, the ruling class attempted to instill in slaves an avid individualism that was intended to pave the way for collaboration. Garden plots and task labor were implemented in part to achieve that goal. Masters assumed that such familial and personal pursuits would divert a slave's attention away from oppression and also help them to combat the hostile collective will they felt most palpably whenever slaves labored in groups. Both peer pressure and lashes determined the productivity and pace of captive workers. Controllers fought that pressure in many ways. Swift and vigorous punishment awaited any "criminal" assistance to brethren in need.[34] On July 18, 1832, James Henry Hammond "had Rose, Charles, Caroline & Mle Goodwyn flogged for harbouring Nancey & Abram."[35] Some slaves must have refused to lend a helping hand to suffering friends and neighbors for fear of such brutal repercussions.

A slave foreman caught cooking a stolen sheep told Ball of a personal experience that details graphically the costs and challenges in achieving black unity. To deter other slaves from thievery, the foreman was flogged almost to death in front of a crowd of neighboring masters and their slaves who had been invited to witness his punishment. The slave was then taken to the kitchen, doused with scalding "red pepper tea," and greased down "from the neck to the hips." There he was left, powerless and alone. He remembered, "Such was the terror stricken into my fellow-slaves, by the example made of me, not one of them dared to approach me during this night." Things could have been different: he had planned to divide his rare prize, "when cooked, between my fellow-slaves (whom I knew to be as hungry as I was) and myself."[36]

Members of the plantocracy found that disciplining all of their bondsmen for the "crimes" of one encouraged blacks not only to suppress antiservile behavior but also to ferret out the guilty ones. Not a few masters made it clear that the innocent would be spared if wrongdoers were turned over or came in voluntarily.[37] Slaveholder Thomas Pinckney told in 1822 how a Colonel Huger prevented the depredation of fruit and "other delinquencies" by pursuing the following course with captive laborers.

In addition to their usual supply of provisions he issues weekly to every task able working hand three pounds of salt meat & a proportionate quantity to those who do less than a task, and in case any of his fruit is stolen and the *black people will not discover who is the thief* he stops the weekly issue of the meat until he thinks the withholding is sufficient punishment, but as these people love meat still better than fruit he has seldom had occasion to resort to this measure.[38] (Emphasis added.)

Dr. Henry M. Holmes, of Cordesville, South Carolina, was equally harsh to his chattels after a slave deserted. He made those remaining on the estate do the work of the absconder on Sunday— the one day they were normally off. Moreover, as the governess of the family noted, the field hands, who had nothing "but dry hominy and sometimes potatoes and soup once a week," were to be denied even that until the runaways had been "found and brought back."[39]

Of all the strategies designed to divide and rule, none was as agonizing as the forcing of bondsmen to taunt, lash, and kill one another. Not only was the slave's basic powerlessness reinforced thereby, but allegiance to fellow blacks was shattered temporarily by having to torture, either physically or psychologically, respected friends and loved ones.[40] In 1818 six boatmen on a Sea Island plantation were "compelled . . . to whip each other till they all had received a severe flogging" for the unpardonable crime of permitting a guest's clothes trunk to get wet.[41] Edward S. Hammond, the son of the renowned governor and senator James Henry Hammond, found this method of turning servant against servant immensely funny. On June 7, 1857, he wrote in his diary, "Adopted a novel punishment for Edward & Hardy—tying their left hands together & giving each a switch in the right. They were both soundly whipped while I could not restrain laughing."[42] This humiliating custom was not new to the nineteenth century. A 1740 South Carolina legislative act authorized constables to order slaves to inflict corporal punishment on other blacks. Resistance to such an order could mean twenty lashes, compliance a five-shilling reward.[43]

Besides using sporadic and random selection of laborers to do their punitive work, masters beginning in the colonial period carefully recruited and groomed a number of bondsmen as drivers. These, sometimes called foremen, became an extremely influential and powerful group of slaves.[44] Southern white mythology has portrayed these accessory bondsmen as vile and vicious lackeys who ruthlessly suppressed their brethren, but they would be more accurately depicted, in the main, as respected leaders among blacks who aligned themselves most often with the slave community. As previously stated, planters desperately wanted slaves who identified with or, ideally, had internalized their, the planters', interests. They also constantly sought controllers who could inspire work with little resistance, and fidelity without harmful "correction." Ironically, the individuals who did this best came from the oppressed themselves: they were the slave drivers.

It was the driver's job to supervise slave labor, to mediate conflicts within the quarters, and to punish those who failed to conform.[45] Not surprisingly, a myopic emphasis on the last responsibility has revealed much, but hidden more. Although the whip, as rice planter D. E. Huger Smith asserts, was the "emblem of authority" carried by drivers, it was used far less than many assumed. Drivers generally had to get permission before inflicting corporal punishment and, even then, frequently were limited in the number of lashes they could apply.[46]

While masters recognized the importance of drivers, much evidence suggests that they never grasped fully why these foremen were so successful. Planters and other white observers repeatedly failed to see that drivers were able to tap into an immense well of black cultural and political ideas that ideally suited them to get results without compulsion. Whereas masters and overseers rarely could expect anything more from slaves than compliance based on constant surveillance and a reliance on force, drivers could exploit their racial and religious identities, and even their age, to gain slave conformity.

Drivers lived among their charges; together, they succeeded in making each other conform to a commitment to black unity and a reverence for the older members of the slave community. It is not by chance that on the slave lists and other records of planters, drivers frequently were described as "old." They also were almost always listed first. Such positioning and the praise given them by both blacks and whites—obviously for different reasons—reflect the extraordinarily high regard in which they were held.[47] Richard Jones of Union, South Carolina, recalled, "We had a 'driver,' a older person, dat showed us how to do everything right. Marse never let him over-work or hurry us. We liked him—'Uncle July Gist,' we called him and dat was his real name, too."[48] Because there were major advantages in being a driver, it seems reasonable to assume that those who held such positions used everything at their disposal—including race and age—to keep and to maintain them.

Slaves did not, however, obey or cooperate with drivers out of any blind racial loyalty or deference to age. There were very real advantages in having a black driver supervise one's labor. *Someone* would serve in that capacity. Drivers not only were aware of the norms and aspirations of the slave community but significantly contributed to both. Generations of slaves had instilled the unfree with a staunch esprit de corps. Their message evidently stuck. Time and again the deftly cracked whips of drivers somehow missed, meats were stolen by drivers and shared, and religious meetings could be found with drivers articulating the slaves' most respected and important prayers.[49]

Austa French, who accompanied her minister-husband to Port Royal during the Civil War, spoke glowingly of a deeply religious driver. This "very tall and strongly built Colored man, with an exceedingly fine, manly expression" once received a hundred and fifty lashes for "not driving harder than he possibly could." Early in the 1860s he discussed with her his life as a driver:

I was driver many years; cou'dn't help it—had to do it. When task not done, dey all get whipp'. I, too, for um; I'se had mo'n one thousand lashes in my time. Had to whip chil'n, too, so awful; dey break plate, or fall 'sleep, waiting for do something, or for Massah, gi' 'um twenty, thirty, lashes. Massah say—"you go barn, whip dis Nigger"; I go; know de poo' chil'n hain't done not'ing; don't describe it.

So sorry for poor little chil'n, 'cause can't get away from Massah, no how! no way! neber! So I tells 'um: 'scream while I whip somet'ing else, wid all my might.' Massah hear; t'inks it's dem. People know 'twasn't. If dey tell, and Massah hears it, I gets fifty or mo' lash, awful! But mus' try to save chil'n, eben if I did suffer so.[50]

Keen insights about the character of certain drivers as well as the complex bonds of family and community that shaped their behavior are found in the diary of Thomas Chaplin. On October 16, 1850, he wrote, "My fellow Sanchos took himself off on Monday last, on account of [the driver] Isaac's attempting to flogg him for beating his daughter Mary—Sancho came in today—Note Isaac has never been able to find it in his *tender heart* to find a *whip* to make my negroes do their work—but as soon as one of his family was molested he could directly *feel* it his *duty* to inflict punishment."[51] (Emphases in the original.) Drivers like Isaac, Uncle July, and others did much to ease the lives of fellow blacks. They not only could exploit their past kind deeds, but promise a better future due, in part, to malaria-carrying mosquitoes and the yearly flight of fearful whites.

Drivers knew that slaves valued autonomy little short of freedom and probably worked out deals with them that assured longer terms of white-free rule than the sickly season alone. Their exertions and ability to negotiate with masters evidently were successful, for not a few planters defied the law and left drivers in charge. The absence of planters and the arrangements in which overseers, if employed, resided somewhere other than on the plantation must have made the work of drivers easier.[52] But that was the problem. However benevolent and lenient drivers were, they contributed mightily to planters' control of their slaves. It was part of their job to discipline their neighbors, and to refuse meant risking the punishments all slaves faced when they disobeyed orders. While most slaves understood the dilemma of drivers, they could not help but note, with dismay, the ease with which planters had infiltrated the slave quarters with individuals who, for whatever reason, owed *some* allegiance to their oppressors.

This disquieting realization became a living nightmare when slaves encountered drivers or black overseers who had internalized their owner's values and savagely beat, brutally worked, and sexually assaulted those beneath them. June Johnson had been enslaved on a plantation with a black overseer who managed the estate without any permanent white presence. Their master, Tom Robertson, resided in Columbia four or five miles away. According to Johnson, Robertson "didn't see us much" and "the nigger overseer . . .took 'vantage of his bein' 'way." She said, "De overseer was a nigger and de meanest man, white or black, I ever see. Dat nigger would strut 'round wid a leather strap on his shoulder and would whip de other slaves unmerciful. He worked us hard from sunrise to sunset every day in de week, 'cept some Saturday evenin's."[53]

Dr. J. Milton Hawks, a Northern physician working with the Union forces and the National Freedman's Relief Association on North Edisto Island in 1862,[54] examined a patient who had been so severely whipped by a driver six years earlier that "he was left senseless on the field." Dr. Hawks wrote to his wife, "He has never been able to stand since, and appears idiotic . . . he sits in the dirt, covered with an old carpet . . . with a pile of sweet potatoes in reach—these he pokes into the fire and roasts and eat as he wants—It is a disgusting sight.[55] Treacherous, brutal, and divisive slaves like the one Hawks heard of and Johnson survived threatened the slave community. Perhaps the greatest achievement of African and Creole slaves was keeping such black oppressors impressively outnumbered. In so doing, they went far toward winning their most timeless battle.

In a wide variety of ways, slaveowners tried to instill elite slaves such as drivers, domestics, boatmen, and craftsmen with feelings of superiority over the masses, that is, the field hands.[56] By distributing special garments or extra materials to particular workers, slaveholders created a hierarchy of dress that corresponded roughly to the status they assigned to each occupation.[57] In October 1809 John Ball, a planter in St. John's Berkeley, gave his driver and boatmen each a "fearnought great coat" that cost him "$7 1/2 each."[58] The only slaves who received seven or more yards of cloth on the Goose Creek plantation of Francis S. Parker were evidently the carpenter and the driver. Quamina, who served as Parker's driver from at least 1850 to 1859, also received "a Great-coat."[59] In a book about his family's rice plantations and slaves, Duncan Clinch Heyward wrote, "Every field hand was given five and a half yards of gray cloth, and a smaller quantity for each of his or her children. . . . The drivers, carpenters, and other head men, *to distinguish them from the rest,* were allotted six and a half yards of blue cloth and one of white. They were also given overcoats."[60] (Emphasis added.)

There is no way of determining whether this stratagem of planters was solely the product of their ingenuity or simply the exploitation and accentuation of a dress code already existing among slaves. Gus Feaster, a former slave who had served in various capacities from coachman to field hand for the Thomas Anderson Carlisle family of Union, gave a detailed account of how slaves dressed and looked at camp meetings which did not seem tied necessarily to instructions or special gifts of clothing from whites. According to Feaster, who was born in 1840, "De gals [who] come out . . . fer de camp meeting . . . took dey hair down out'n de strings fer de meeting. In dem days all de darky wimmens wore dey hair in string 'cep' when dey 'tended church or a wedding. At de camp meetings de wimmens pulled off de head rags, *'cept de mammies. On dis occasion de mammies wore linen head rags fresh laundered.*"[61] (Emphasis added.) Whatever the source of slave ideas about style and proper attire, there is no doubt that masters and other controllers pursued a deliberately divisive clothing scheme. On General Bratton Canaan's plantation near Winnsboro only the driver was given "de honor to wear boots"; the other slaves wore shoes with "wooden bottoms."[62]

Until one considers the poor quality and limited quantity of garments supplied to most bondsmen, it is difficult to appreciate the great importance of clothing. Charles Ball described the 168 field hands he labored with as "a wretched looking troop" amongst whom "there was not an entire garment."[63] The contrast between these individuals and those who toiled in liveries at the

Big House was readily apparent. The house servants of the Allston family "wore dark green broadcloth coats with vests trimmed in silver braid and red facings with trousers of green plush."[64] Needless to say, the general paucity of adequate clothing made all slaves extremely conscious of clothes.[65] Not a few planters believed the self-esteem of slaves to be so entwined with dress that their perception of themselves would rise to a dangerous level if they were permitted to wear or carry certain apparel. Authorities in Camden, South Carolina, forbade slaves to appear in any material "finer than negro cloth, duffils, kerseys, osnaburgs, blue or check linen, or coarse garlix."[66] The ruling class at Greenville enacted a law prohibiting blacks, both free and slave, from smoking "a segar in any street" or walking "with a cane, club, or stick, (except the lame, infirm, or blind,)."[67]

Besides distributing extra and fancier garments to favored occupational groups, masters provided elite bondsmen with additional bonuses, such as lighter workloads, better and more food, and the privilege of hiring themselves out without, in some cases, relinquishing any part of the profits.[68] The greatest benefit, however, of an upper-echelon position was the security it gave one's family. It appears that elite blacks were less likely to be sold in nonpunitive transactions. Not only had planters spent a substantial amount of time training them, but the cost of securing comparable slaves on the open market became increasingly prohibitive during the nineteenth century. The proximity of privileged servants to members of the plantocracy enabled them to plead against the sale of their own children and relatives. The greater familiarity of planters with these bondsmen assured them of other special treatment and consideration on occasion, such as the purchase or hiring of mates separated by different owners. Personal appeals from the slaves in closest contact with masters may explain why they generally were sold or bequeathed in family lots, in contrast to the masses of slaves who usually were divided and dispersed at will without any thought to the severance of their kinship ties.[69]

"Good" Negroes were hard to find, and they frequently came with families, as an 1828 dispatch to John C. Calhoun illustrates graphically:

I have delayed replying to your letter of 11th Ulti[m]o relative to the purchase of three house servants in the full expectation that I should have been able to meet with such as you want. But am sorry to add that after mak[in]g every enquiry & seeing all the Negroes for the last three weeks that have been advertised for sale, I have not seen or heard of one that would . . . answer your purpose, certainly none that I would purchase were I in want of them myself. It is a difficult thing to meet with a good Negro, *for sale*. There are many offered for sale very capable, but not to be depended upon, wanting honesty & sobriety. . . . Another great difficulty is to procure single Negroes, for in nine cases out of ten where a house servant, Cook or chamber maid is offered for sale you will find some family attached to them.[70] (Emphasis in the original.)

Most elite slaves did not have to wait until market day to realize the advantages they had over other slaves in keeping their families intact and happy. Almost from the outset, privileged blacks reaped certain benefits for loved ones. The brides or grooms of such servants could anticipate receiving elaborate Big House weddings with sumptuous dinners and parties provided by their owners.[71] An overwhelming amount of evidence indicates that such couples could place at least some of their children in upper-echelon positions.[72] A former slave domestic named Lucy had followed in her mother's footsteps and worked as a house servant at the Richardson family "Big House" in Greenwood, South Carolina. Lucy had planned for her daughter to do the same. She explained in a postwar interview, "I was housemaid befor freedom, an' my fus' chile bawn right thar. Fixin' ter raise dat gal ter wait on Missus too, but de times change so."[73]

Henry Coleman knew firsthand how a privileged slave parent or parents put a child·on an elite course. "Time I got big enough for to run aroun' in my shirt tail," he recalled, the senior Colemans found him a pair of trousers so that his mother, apparently the cook for their Fairfield owners, could "put him up over de white fokes table."

In dem [days] de dining room wuz big and had de windows open all de summer long, and all de doos stayed streched too. Quick as de mess of victuals began to come on de table, a little nigger boy was put up in de swing, I calls it, over de table to fan de flies and gnats off 'en de Missus victuals. Dis swing wuz just off 'n de end of de long table. . . . Well, when I got my pants, my maw fetched me . . . to git up in [the master's] swing.

Armed with a "fly brush" made of long peacock feathers, Coleman served in this capacity until he "got bigger" and "got to be house boy."[74]

Marriage to an important slave often led to special favors and rights. Note the following message from S. H. Boineau to Charles Heyward:

I would here inform you that ever since Mathias has been driving. I have never allowed his wife but the half of every Saturday. I find it works well and *his wife is not so idle as drivers wives generally are and by no means so badly spoiled.* I look upon a drivers wife upon a plantation having half of every day a great nuisance. [So] do instruct me whether Mathias wife is to be allowed the same liberty that March will claim for his wife or if March's wife shall be brought to the Standard that Mathias wife now hold. You know that Mathias has no family but his wife who is ordily and one of the most faithful women on the place, but will soon be ruined if she has to be idle half of every day throughout the year.[75] (Emphasis added.)

Although one may debate whether all such practices were conceived primarily to divide and rule or simply to inspire devotion and productiveness, there can be no question about the basic desire of slaveholders to create strife among slaves. The power elite hoped that such dissension would deflect the hatred of bondsmen from the enslaver to the enslaved and, in the process, create a human warning system that was not only faithful to members of the plantocracy but committed to their physical and financial well-being. Nowhere is the evidence for these contentions stronger than in the case of domestics and field hands. Some planters disallowed domestics to associate with field hands; others discouraged any connubial unions between the two.[76] Many contemporary narratives and more recent historical accounts concur for the most part that masters were successful in causing house servants, on one hand, to look down upon field laborers and, on another, to look up to and emulate slaveowners.[77]

In his comparison of field slaves and house slaves, Joseph Ingraham, a Northerner who had lived in the South, claimed that "The domestic servant is more sprightly, better clad, more intelligent and animated, apes polite manners, and imitates the polished airs of the well-bred 'white folk.'"[78] Historian C. W. Harper wrote in 1978 that because house servants were "reared with the white children and indulged by the master and mistress," they became "very much attached to the white family, and very faithful."[79] Another historian argued "privileged slaves" like domestics had "so identified themselves with their masters and their race that their values and ideals were identical."[80]

Not surprisingly, the manor house employee described by these scholars and antebellum observers was an obsequious, cringing, and pampered turncoat who would betray a fellow slave for little more than a hand-me-down garment or a flattering remark. The reasoning behind how this legendary figure came into existence is both specious and, to a degree, racist. Since domestics were forced to defer to whites more often than field hands were, they purportedly internalized what the majority of slaves only wore externally, that is, a fawning and docile mask of servility. Similarly, the mere proximity to ruling whites drove house servants inevitably to copy their "superiors" and to discard the inferior racial traits and customs blacks supposedly possessed.[81] To be sure, some domestics did become Sambos, but their numbers were far smaller than slave historiography and mythology would have us believe.

Much of the confusion about the behavior and character of house servants stems undoubtedly from the oft-proclaimed friendships developed during childhood with residents at the Big House. Because the offspring of elite slaves often followed in the footsteps of their parents, favored youngsters began work frequently doing small chores around the manor house. They were usually assigned also to play with *and* watch over the children of masters.[82] Although these tasks could nurture close and lasting relationships,[83] it appears that in reality they rarely did so. There were too many temptations for infant and juvenile whites to abuse the dictatorial powers delegated to them by virtue of their position and color. Such disparities in authority and rank generally precluded bonds of *mutual* trust and friendship. The black playmates J. G. Clinkscales remembered in his nostalgic "reminiscences" could not have shared the joy their young master felt in whipping them while they were "hitched" to his wagon and spurred to kick, rear, and snort "like real horses."[84] Ex-slave Rebecca Grant recounted what happened to her as a little girl when she failed to call an owner "master." Grant was about eight years old and living at her mistress's Beaufort Big House where she scrubbed floors and polished brass. One day, the mistress sent her to pick up a package from the store: it contained a "raw cowhide strap bout two feet long." Grant learned its purpose when she returned home and her mistress demanded, "You can't say 'Marse Henry', Miss? You can't say, 'Marse Henry'!" Grant answered, "Yes'm. Yes'm. I kin say,

'Marse Henry'!" and probably never forgot the proper way to address Henry, her mistress's son. "Marse Henry," Grant said, "was just a little boy bout three or four years old. Come bout halfway up to me. Wanted me to say, Massa to him, a baby!"[85]

Unfortunately for young black guardians, what John Hope Franklin has described as a fierce and pugnacious spirit appeared very early among South Carolinians.[86] One former subject, Henry Gladney, recalled that in the "heart and mind" of "Little Marse John," he "was just a little dog or monkey . . . to pet or kick as it pleased him."[87] I. Jenkins, another source of considerable unhappiness in childhood, reminisced merrily about the pain he caused James and Primus, two slaves "set apart to 'mind'" him:

> They were older than I, and their sole duty was to be responsible for my welfare—no small job. . . . I made that half-grown boy's life [James] one of sunshine and shadows—particularly shadows. His desire to please me, his charge, his chum, on one side, and his fear of the consequences if he were too lax in his care, on the other, left him problems to solve that should have made a diplomat of him.[88]

To illustrate this point, Jenkins referred to an instance when he refused to climb down from a treetop:

> James cajoled, used blandishments, made promises of the most extravagant and impossible kinds to lure me to earth. I jeered at him and derided him. Finally he went off and reported: "Missus, I can't get Junior to come down." The order was snapped back: "Go, bring him!" James finally had to climb and bring me down. I resented it by howling, "Jeems hurt me!" And the burden rested on poor James to disprove it.[89]

Clearly, an individual working under a puerile ruler learned quite quickly what it meant to be a slave, and, unfortunately, pupils were taught more often than not through a series of castigations sparked by their sometimes friendly masters.[90]

Another major source of misconception about domestics lies in the material advantages they had over field hands, benefits supposedly at the root of their much-purported attitudes of superiority. To be sure, certain gains were attained from working at the Big House. Meat and clothing were more available there as a result of planters' willingness to give house servants what remained on or what had been discarded from their plates and wardrobes.[91] Nevertheless, domestics were subjected to many unfavorable conditions that should warrant some rethinking about the relative position of house and field slaves. Those toiling in the manor, for instance, labored longer hours than field hands and were under constant surveillance, conditions that caused workers and their families considerable distress. Unlike the majority of bondsmen, whose day usually ended with the completion of their tasks, domestics were compelled to remain in the evening and serve at dinners and parties and for any unexpected guests. Sundays, when there was a habitual procession of visitors, were particularly busy—a custom that caused at least one white minister to denounce "the engrossing engagements of houseservants even on the Lord's day."[92]

Naturally, enslavers considered the comfort of their families most important. Domestics therefore were denied on occasion the pleasure of attending to their significant others.[93] Louisa Davis, the wife of a field hand who lived on another plantation, declared, "My husband was a slave of de Sloans and didn't get to see me often as he wanted to; and of course, as de housemaid then, dere was times I couldn't meet him, clandestine like he want me. Us had some grief over dat."[94] Obviously, the nocturnal and illicit travels so popular with slaves would have been more difficult for a laborer who was on call night and day. This perhaps explains why the children of a domestic rather than the mother were caught making a surreptitious trip to reunite briefly the members of a family split by different owners. To prevent detection during their visit, the mother hid them "under her bed." Her bed was in the master's kitchen. Even this contact may have ended, for when the owner of the children discovered their activities he charged her master with "harboring or feloniously stealing his negroes."[95]

While field hands had to be on the watch usually for a driver and an overseer, house slaves had to look out always for the mistress, the master, the children, and sometimes even the guests of these imperious figures. The eyes that tracked their every move belonged often to persons who were not only jealous and brutal, but vindictive. Frustrated Southern women commonly took out their anxieties on house servants—particularly those suspected of catching the master's fancy. Such misgivings and their consequences may be the reason why female rulers were depicted frequently as the most stringent and sadistic of the manor-born.[96] Fannie Griffin, who was in her twenties when freed, had been owned by Joe and Grace Beard. She described Joe Beard as a "good man" who owned six slaves—"three men and three women." Griffin recalled, "I was de youngest slave, so Missy Grace . . . keep me in de house most of de time, to cook and keep de house cleaned up. My massa was good to all he slaves, but Missy Grace was mean. . . . When she go to whip me, she tie my wrists together wid a rope and put that rope thru a big staple in de ceiling and draw me up off de floor and give me a hundred lashes." According to Griffin, even when she and others "ain't done nothing bad," her mistress still would whip a whole "heap of times."[97]

The greater constraints and pressures on domestics help one to understand why large numbers of field hands dreaded "promotion" to the Big House. In 1828 Basil Hall was told by a well-informed driver that "every where the slaves preferred the field-work," because it was "definite in amount" and "left them a certain portion of the day entirely to themselves." Hall observed:

This privilege has become, virtually, a right in many places; and so far, is a spark of freedom in their dark night of bondage; whereas the house slave, from being liable to every call, early and late, sometimes fancies himself less free.[98]

More autonomy was only one reason why field hands wanted to remain in the open air: they took pride in using their agricultural skills and in their capacity to provide for loved ones without imploring whites to vouchsafe leftovers and hand-me-downs. Also, there appears to have been a feeling among some bondsmen that house work was effeminate.[99]

Most domestics, however, apparently had no desire to leave their posts.[100] Stephen, a house servant of the Mackay family at Walnut Hill, was outraged when told he was going to be put in the fields. In a letter to George Mackay, Robert Mackay reported, "I have just informed Stephen of my determination to place him in the field to-morrow—he says if I put him there *that he will not stay home,* as he has never been brought up to *such work,* and that he rather I would give him a *Ticket* to search out a *new master* and that if such be really my determination he must tell me beforehand *that he will go away.*" (Emphases in the original.) Stephen's threats fell on deaf ears, for Mackay concluded, "I am determined to place him in the field to morrow let the consequences be what they may."[101] Many domestics considered relocation, especially outside, a demotion because it meant, in part, the cessation of certain intangible but highly treasured benefits. Those working at the Big House gained considerable knowledge about life beyond the plantation through listening to the conversations of their well-traveled owners. Furthermore, the chosen few who were taught to read were usually members of the household staff. This privilege countervailed the more unpleasant aspects of domestic labor, for slaves considered literacy an attainment little short of freedom.[102] What they could not learn about the larger world by eavesdropping and reading, house servants frequently discovered empirically while accompanying members of the plantocracy to the various locations they visited for health, pleasure, or business.[103]

Domestics found compensation also in knowing that *if* their immediate family "behaved," in all probability their offspring would be spared the unhealthy and often deadly toils of labor in South Carolina's mosquito-ridden rice fields. Thus, one was not always being snobbish in repudiating outdoor labor, nor implying necessarily that those doing such work were inferior or less worthy. Any slave accustomed to doing a particular job would find it difficult, if not traumatic, to begin a new one in a different milieu. Eking out an existence under slavery was such a long and torturous process that few desired to experience it more than once, for in bondage there were no trials and errors, just *faux pas* and lashes.[104]

While there is documentation that some house servants considered themselves better than field hands, it is far from extensive or conclusive.[105] Indeed, what stands out, at least in the testimony of blacks, is the relative absence of statements indicating hostility between domestics and the masses of slaves. Certainly, there were enough factors militating against the development of such strife or attitudes of superiority among *any* bondsmen. The slave community exerted considerable pressure on its members to stand united and firm against the white minority. Servile blacks who were suspected of collaborating or becoming too familiar with their oppressors were either ostracized, physically accosted, or killed. It was undoubtedly for these reasons that the identities of slave traitors were guarded so carefully by the ruling class.[106]

In an instance when they failed, not only the collaborator but her owner too was seriously threatened. Petitioners from the district of Georgetown appealed to the legislature to manumit a slave, Henrietta, and to compensate her owner, Mrs. Ann Paisley:

The Petition of the undersigned for themselves and on behalf of their constituents the Inhabitants of Prince George & All Saints Parish respectfully sheweth That Mrs. Ann Paisley of Prince George is the owner of a negroe woman named Henrietta—that on or about the 20th of July last, *Charles* one of the Ring leaders in the late conspiracy in this quarter, having in her presence made use of some threatening expressions in anticipation of the intended insurrection, the said Henrietta made known the same to her mistress and directly after to the Intendant of the Town who thereupon took counsel. . . . That in consequence of the above information given by the said Henrietta the blacks were very generally excited against her; an evidence of which was the attack made upon her by a negro man named Joe, who was tried for the same and executed. . . . That Mrs. Paisley being a widow and living alone is in daily fear of some act of revenge being exercised toward her by the black population on account of her said Henrietta our informant.

Now your petitioners, in consideration both of the expediency of rewarding the fidelity thus exhibited . . . and of the necessity of affording her efficient protection—pray your Honorable Body to manumit the said woman . . . and to make such appropriations as may appear to you just . . . for the indemnification of Mrs. Paisley.

There is no indication whether the delegation succeeded, or whether Henrietta survived.[107]

Besides the pressures to conform to slave norms, other factors helped to deter attitudes and behaviors that served white oppressors. Large harvests, economic hardships, and planter whims assured that elite slaves would perform a variety of tasks on occasion that ranged from cotton picking and hoeing to waiting on guests and tending coaches. These labors and the prospect of them made it difficult for an individual to look down upon an occupational group that he or she could be working alongside at any time.[108] The embarrassed proprietor of one estate explained to a visitor who had to put his horse away himself, "at this season of the year, the planters were so hurried by their crops, and found so much difficulty in keeping down the grass, that they were generally obliged to keep all their servants in the field; that for his part, he had been compelled to put his coachman, and even the waiting-maids of his daughters into the cotton fields, and that at this time, his family were without servants, a circumstance that had never happened before!"[109] Sam Mitchell, born in 1850, said in his later recollections that his father had been a carpenter, "but w'en dey was no carpentry work to do on de plantation, he plow."[110] Planter James Hopkinson declared in his rules for the driver, "As he has no regular work, *he will be expected to lend a helping hand,* when it does not interfere with his other duties."[111] (Emphasis added.)

The periodic shifting of the enslaved from one job to another did, then, keep the various strata of bondsmen in frequent contact with each other, despite the apparent insularity of regular jobs. Indeed, practically every slave had a close friend or relative working in some position considered either below or above the one he or she held under the Peculiar Institution.[112] Gladney, who had been given to a young John McCrorey, "just to wait on him and play wid him," remembered also "choppin' cotton and pickin' cotton and peas 'long 'side mammy in de field." His father "stayed at de blacksmith shop, work on de wagons, shoe de mules and hosses, make hinges, sharpen de plow points and fix de iron rings."[113] Jacob Stroyer said that although the family from which his mother came consisted primarily of skilled and privileged bondsmen, including blacksmiths, carpenters, and drivers, his mother was forced "to take her chance in the field with those who had to weather the storm."[114]

In addition to the relatives field hands would have had throughout the plantation hierarchy, many no doubt maintained confidential and even intimate associations that went back as far as childhood with members of the domestic staff. On many plantations it was customary for boys and girls to labor around the manor before most of them were deployed outside, which generally occurred at the age of twelve. The relationships these youngsters developed with the children who remained captive in the Big House often continued despite sunup-to-sundown separation.[115] Such social and familial connections did more than anything else to deter the sharpening or hardening of class lines, for as stressed earlier, African-Americans regarded their kinship bonds as sacred and would have hardly disowned or disparaged a "lesser" relative. The strength of the black family in shaping and directing behavior was demonstrated by two representatives of the "colored aristocracy" when they chose not to flee Union troops with their owners in order to stay with relatives who had decided to abandon their rebel masters. According to Laura Towne, in 1862, "they would have gone with their masters, both of them, but they had relations whom they did not want to be parted from, 'except by death.'" Interestingly, although they told Towne that it "seemed like they couldn"t be happy widout white ladies 'roun'," each "wanted to go North" if their former owners "were to come back."[116]

Familial ties and the interacting social, religious, and economic lives of blacks thus did much to prevent the antagonisms so sought after and encouraged by whites. Not only did the vast majority of slaves live, play, and worship together, but they traded with each other as well.[117] Elite bondsmen who held greater access to urban and country markets often played the role of middlemen to the rural masses. John Berkley Grimball recorded the following incident after receiving a dispatch in Charleston from his overseer sent by way of a slave messenger:

> [Mr.] Farran's letter enclosed a note which our Cook-Kit had written to his Father accompanying a jug of Whiskey which he sent up to retail on the Plantation. Kit acknowledged the writing and as it is against well known regulations, to trade with Spirits amongst the people, I was obliged to have him corrected.[118]

On February 24, 1826, an A. M'Kab ordered "all persons sending negroes up the Pee Dee with Flats and Boats . . . to . . . label the jugs of liquor they may be permitted to take, *as they are so much in the habit of trading with the plantation negroes they will be taken away.*"[119] (Emphasis added.) Due to the grave dangers in volved in such transactions, it is probable that many bonds of mutual trust and friendship were forged among these illicit buyers and sellers. Surely some feelings had to develop among the partners in "crime" who attended parties, church, and, on occasion, chores together.

Nothing, however, slowed planter designs to divide and rule more than the unity created by the punitive system all bondsmen knew and tried to evade. To those who forgot, it was a painful reminder that a slave was a slave regardless of rank; this knowledge strengthened the cords binding each chattel to the next. Contrary to popular belief, elite blacks were subjected to as much castigation, if not more, than the masses of slaves. White employees who became jealous of skilled bondsmen often sparked fights with them in order to find grounds for correcting the "uppity" and "impudent" blacks.[120] Stroyer warned his readers "not to think that those" slaves with trades "were free from punishments." Indeed, "some of them," he wrote, "had more troubles than the field hands."

> At times the overseer . . . would go to the shop of the blacksmith or carpenter, and would pick a quarrel with him, so as to get an opportunity to punish him. He would say to the negro, "Oh, ye think yourself as good as ye master, ye _____." Of course he knew what the overseer was after, so he was afraid to speak; the overseer, hearing no answer, would turn to him and cry out, "ye so big ye can't speak to me, ye _____," and then the conflict would begin, and he would give that man such a punishment as would disable him for two or three months. The merciless overseer would say to him "ye think because ye have a trade ye are as good as ye master, ye _____; but I will show ye that ye are nothing but a nigger."[121]

Domestics, especially, were victimized as a result of their greater visibility and function as scapegoats for every fault and misadventure of ruling whites. And, they lacked the advantage that field hands often had of being chastised twenty-four hours *after* any wrongdoing was discovered. Plowden C. J. Weston instructed his overseer that no punishment was "to exceed 15 lashes," that permission was required for any "severer punishment," and that "24 hours" should "elapse between the discovery of the offence, and the punishment."[122] Perhaps John Peyre Thomas's overseer did not have the patience for such a cooling off period; he was reprimanded for "whipping the Negroes improperly & when in a passion."[123] There was no superior to subdue or temper the impulsive rage of those who owned their victims. This explains, in part, why house servants were punished usually when their master or mistress was in the heat of passion.[124]

The severity with which an upper-echelon slave could be disciplined was relayed graphically to the American Freedmen's Inquiry Commission in 1863 by a former chattel named Solomon Bradley, who had served in the Palmetto State as a blacksmith and cook. Bradley recounted vividly an incident he witnessed on the plantation of a Mr. Farrarby.

> I went up to his house one morning from my work for drinking water, and heard a woman screaming awfully in the door-yard. On going up to the fence and looking over I saw a woman stretched out, face downwards, on the ground her hands and feet being fastened to stakes. Mr. Farrarby

was standing over and striking her with a leather trace belonging to his carriage-harness. As he struck her the flesh of her back and legs was raised in welts and ridges by the force of the blows. Sometimes when the poor thing cried too loud from the pain Farrarby would kick her in the mouth. After he had exhausted himself whipping her he sent to his house for sealing wax and a lighted candle and, melting the wax, dropped it upon the woman's lacerated back. He then got a hiding whip and, standing over the woman, picked off the hardened wax by switching at it. Mr. Farrarby's grown daughters were looking at all this from a window of the house through the blinds. This punishment was so terrible that I was induced to ask what offence the woman had committed and was told by her fellow servants that her only crime was in burning the edges of the waffles that she had cooked for breakfast.[125]

However tempted one might be to believe that the savagery unleashed for such an innocuous error was unique, it was not. Spilling milk, breaking dishes, and a variety of other kitchen peccadilloes could and often did trigger barbaric responses from slaveowners throughout South Carolina.[126] So common were acts of brutality on the slaves who prepared and served the meals of the Holmes family that the governess was moved to declare in her diary, "I sometimes think Mrs. H loves to see them whipped as much as she loves her dinner. And yet she is a *woman!*"[127] (Emphasis in the original.)

The most important slaves on the plantation, the drivers, were also made to suffer the lash. Some slaveholders preferred to correct drivers in private, but they did nevertheless get beaten.[128] A headman belonging to the extraordinarily wealthy and aristocratic Langdon Cheves received a flogging of seventy-five stripes, which his owner described as "perfectly harmless to him."[129] Whether or not an individual was injured physically, however, is insignificant compared to the psychological scars that were probably more painful and certainly more enduring. These wounds taught both the victims and the witnesses the futility of trying to escape bondage by climbing up the occupational slave ladder. It was perhaps for this reason that Lydia Smalls, the mother of the famed war hero Robert Smalls, "forced her son to watch a slave being whipped" in order to make him "realize the meaning of slavery" and "the full indignity of his position" even as the "pampered pet" of a wealthy planter.[130] Moreover, all chattels could be threatened with sale, particularly if they broke the fragile paternalistic contract, enforced by the self-proclaimed patriarchs of the South.

Thus, through observation and experience, black slaves of every status understood the harsh realities of servitude and the need to maintain an impregnable phalanx in their war against masters and mistresses.

An impressive array of evidence indicates that the combined influences of African-Americans' kinship ties, social lives, and corporal punishment worked to create a remarkably united black front. The communication network among slaves, which so frightened and dismayed enslavers, could not have come into existence or survived without the cooperation of privileged bondsmen. If members of the plantocracy had been successful in divorcing favored servants from the masses, surely the favored ones would have kept the conversations and movements of the ruling class in confidence. But this was not the case.[131] When Benjamin Russell, an ex-slave born in 1849, was asked how captive workers got news, he replied, "Many plantations were strict about this, but the greater the precaution, the alerter became the slaves, the wider they opened their ears and the more eager they became for outside information. The sources were: Girls that waited on the tables, the ladies' maids and the drivers; they would pick up everything they heard and pass it on to the other slaves."[132]

These chattels kept their brothers and sisters abreast of the master's financial state also and provided them with some idea of whether sales and family separations were likely as a consequence. They also often gave advance notice of patrol activities and warned individuals marked for punishment to beware. But at no time was the contribution of upper-echelon blacks to the communication network more in evidence than during the Civil War when political developments in the North, troop movements in the South, and planter reactions everywhere were shared with the slave masses. Obviously, there was more to the refusal of servants to shut doors than met the eye.[133]

While most intelligence traveling through the slave grapevine was the result of espionage at the Big House, there were other sources. The Reverend I. E. Lowery remembered the role his extremely popular friend and fellow slave, Jimmie, played in enlightening "the folk" during slavery:

Jimmie was something of a privileged character on Mr. Frierson's plantation. It is true, he had to work in the field along with the other hands.

Sometimes he dropped corn and peas; sometimes he thinned corn and cotton; and sometimes he hoed or plowed. But when Mr. Frierson would go off on business in his buggy, Jimmie had to go along and drive him. When his daughters went to church, or to make social calls, he went to drive them, and to care for the horses. So Jimmie had the privilege of attending all the big meetings, the weddings, and the parties of the white folks. All this proved to be of considerable advantage to him in gaining knowledge and information. Frequently on his return from some of these trips, the slaves would gather around him—old and young—to hear him tell what he saw and heard. And for days these things would be discussed by the body of slaves.[134]

Besides sharing their experiences, some bondsmen also imparted adventures and insights obtained from the written page. Will Capers, for instance, a slave cabinetmaker who read "all the papers," held a "secret night-school" for his less fortunate brethren.[135]

The cooperative spirit reflected in the relations between upper- and lower-echelon slaves was visible in other areas as well. American bondsmen considered it a "religious duty" to aid blacks who were homeless, hungry, weak, or needy.[136] This principle of mutual help was demonstrated daily in the collective work habits of field hands. Despite the individualistic task system imposed by whites, slaves customarily assisted slower members.[137] Richard Mack declared that after the completion of his assignment he helped "others with their task so they wouldn't get whipped."[138] Former planter Henry Ravenel told readers in *The Yale Review* that slaves who finished their tasks first "were always generous enough to help out the others and they all generally left the field together."[139] Even when beyond the boundaries of the plantation—and the law—slaves could anticipate assistance. Fugitives who were evading planters almost universally received support from fellow blacks.[140] James Henry Hammond ordered two domestics into the fields for having aided escapees.[141] All prospective collaborators knew that to betray the identity or location of a slave "miscreant" sought by masters guaranteed arousing the ire of "street" residents, that is, blacks in the quarters, who practically without exception regarded such disclosures as sacrilegious and sinful. It is not surprising, therefore, that slaveholders were kept busy devising new ways to lure blacks into their corner and thus to offset the aggravating code of silence.[142]

If the mores, values, and interests of each status group had indeed been so antagonistic that they rent the bonded community with crippling divisions, one would have expected to find quite different behavioral patterns. Most contemporaries of the period, however, reveal a stunning unity of thought and action among servile workers. In my research, for instance, there were as many complaints about the obstinacy, obtuseness, and tardiness of elite blacks as of field hands. Furthermore, malingering and the need for constant surveillance appear to have been as big a problem with the former as with the latter.[143] Nor is there evidence that privileged slaves were any more docile, loyal, or trustworthy than the black majority. On the contrary, drivers, domestics, and other "confidential servants" deserted, robbed, and assaulted whites just as frequently as the masses of slaves.[144]

More than a month after their escape, James Erwin of Barnwell District was still seeking the capture of two slaves who had absconded from his plantation on November 9, 1828. One had been raised as a "waiting man" and Erwin wanted him back, dead or alive:

> Sam is about 5 feet 7 inches high; of a dark complexion, stout built, and about 28 years old; Sam has been r[ai]sed a waiting man, and is one of the worst of Negroes, having repeatedly armed himself and eloped, and on one of those occasions stole between 5 and $600. He has now between 90 or 100 shot in him, which he received about 5 months since; whilst runaway, he has been guilty of conduct even more atrocious than this—in short, he is a villain of the most consummate kind. When they went away they carried with them two double barrel guns, two pistols, a dirk, a violin, ten dollars in cash, with some articles which they obtained by breaking open a store. Fifty Dollars will be given for Sam and the articles, or One Hundred Dollars *if delivered alive* with the articles.[145] (Emphasis added.)

Such rebelliousness both before and during the Civil War makes it difficult to understand how the legendary passivity and sycophancy of elite slaves could have gained the acceptance it did in postwar literature. Not only were members of this group generally the first to abandon their masters when the troops appeared near, but those remaining attained notoriety often as the most deceitful, fractious, and treacherous among the captive population. Nevertheless, the myth of the "faithful old servant" has persisted.[146]

While the social, cultural, and economic lives of blacks kept all but a small minority of bondsmen from wandering into the camp of planters, some did wander. The exact number cannot be determined, but it is clear that the individuals who did so were remarkably effective in breaching the ranks and exciting distrust. These collaborators helped masters convict servants accused of everything from gambling on Sunday to plotting insurrections. They played a role also on occasion in capturing runaways and other servile malefactors.[147] Word of slave betrayers must have filtered back to the slave community, especially after court cases where a fellow black was convicted, in part, because of slave testimony. The fate of Charles, a slave charged with "Gambling and Fighting," is unclear, but three slave witnesses to what apparently had been an interplantation game provided damaging evidence to those hearing his Spartanburg case.[148] "Yellow Frank," a slave owned by a D. Cain in St. John's Parish, accused several slaves of assisting him in an 1829 "attempt to poison D. Cain." Frank was hanged after his trial, but he caused other slaves to go to court. One defendant was "whipped & croped; two others were sentenced "to be sold, out of the State."[149]

Although there were many reasons why a slave might connive with his or her oppressor, the hope of monetary compensation or manumission undoubtedly was high on the list.[150] When the residents of St. John's Berkeley & St. Stephen's Parishes were plagued by a band of "desperate Runaways," William Dubose of the Pineville Police Association advised that through "secret Offers of Reward to certain Negroes, their Agency and Assistance might . . . be obtained." Dubose's hunch proved correct, for he was able to report later "that by the active and ready co-operation of a Fellow called Billy . . . a Plan had been devised" that resulted in the death of the gang leader and three members. For this exceptional fidelity, Billy received the grand sum of forty-seven dollars.[151]

Many collaborators neither asked for nor even thought of financial gains because they were too busy thinking about how best to save their lives. Some slaveowners would stop at nothing to ferret out culprits and to macerate dissent. Such planters gave prisoners the simple choice of informing or dying, though less heartless rulers later commuted that ultimate sentence to lengthy periods of incarceration and deportation. And, needless to say, there were servants who without any of the above "incentives" informed willingly with truths or lies in hope of shifting the bulk of the blame elsewhere.[152] Although no longer a resident of

Charleston, W. H. Wilson, a white contemporary of the Denmark Vesey scare, remembered well the behavior of blacks at that time. "As usual in such cases," he wrote, "as soon as it began to be realized that the plot had been discovered, there were enough of the weak hearted coming forward to testify in hopes of getting clear, and no difficulty was experienced in securing sufficient evidence for the conviction of the leaders."[153]

Some bondsmen, of course, were genuinely concerned about the welfare of particular planters and warned these individuals of any events or plans that might endanger their safety.[154] Furthermore, there had to be at least a few slaves whose self-image and attitude toward other blacks were so poor that they needed the recognition and respect of whites to feel "equal" or even human. Naturally, approbation of this sort required proving one's loyalty through endless acts of "fidelity." How many bondsmen collaborated will never be known, but the mere presence of these renegades sparked much distrust and wariness within the slave community. Ball refused to tell his neighbors of a fugitive he met and befriended in the woods because he said, "Experience had made me so well acquainted with the dangers that beset the life of a slave, that I determined, as a matter of prudence, to say nothing to any one."[155] If an individual was afraid to converse about a runaway, it is not difficult to imagine how fearful he would have been to speak of any revolutionary or insurrectionary leanings. This ironic mistrust of fellow bondsmen nurtured inevitably the rooting cautiousness already characteristic of so many slaves.

Charleston, South Carolina, slave auction. Note mothers with children; when sold, families were almost always separated. *Courtesy of the Valentine Museum, Richmond, Virginia*

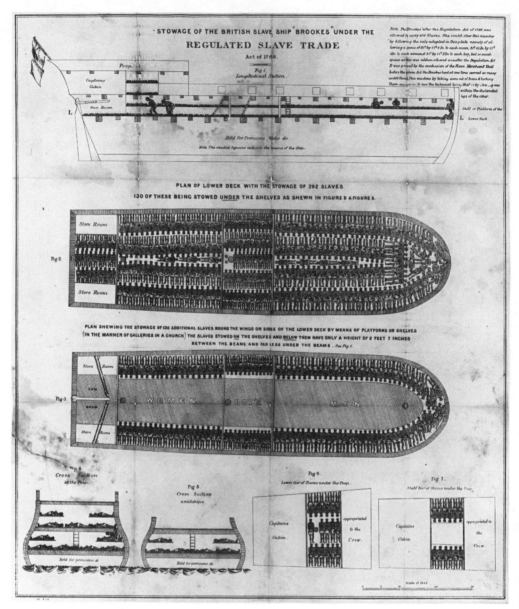

Diagram of slave ship *Brookes*. Before regulation, the ship carried many more slaves than shown here, stowed by placing one "within the distended legs of another." *Courtesy of the Library of Congress*

(Left) Slave deck of the bark *Wildfire,* brought into Key West, Florida, April 30, 1860. Cartoonists chose not to depict slave suffering—note the smiling faces. *Courtesy of the Library of Congress*

Hold of the "blood-stained" *Gloria,* carrying slaves to America. *Courtesy of the Library of Congress*

ESTATE SALE!

A REMARKABLY PRIME AND ORDERLY GANG

OF

85 NEGROES,

Accustomed to the Culture of Rice and Provisions,

ON WACCAMAW RIVER.

BY P. J. PORCHER & BAYA.

On MONDAY the 24th day of January, 1859,

AT 11 O'CLOCK, A. M. WILL BE SOLD AT

RYAN'S MART, Chalmers-st,

IN THE

CITY OF CHARLESTON,

A REMARKABLY PRIME AND ORDERLY GANG

OF

EIGHTY-FIVE NEGROES

Accustomed to the Culture of Rice and Provisions on Waccamaw River, among which are valuable

COOPERS, CARPENTERS, DRIVERS AND HOUSE SERVANTS.

CONDITIONS OF SALE.—One-third Cash; balance in one and two years, secured by bond, mortgage and approved personal security, with interest from day of sale, payable annually. Purchasers to pay P. J. P. & B. for papers.

(Left) Notice of estate sale of slaves in Charleston, 1859. Slaves skilled in rice production, brought to South Carolina from the "Rice Coast" of West Africa, were highly valued after the late 1770s, when the South Carolina economy depended largely on rice exports. *Courtesy of the South Caroliniana Library, University of South Carolina*

Public Sale of Negroes,
By RICHARD CLAGETT.

On Tuesday, March 5th, 1833 at 1:00 P. M. the following Slaves will be sold at Potters Mart, in Charleston, S. C.

Miscellaneous Lots of Negroes, mostly house servants, some for field work.

Conditions: ⅛ cash, balance by bond, bearing interest from date of sale. Payable in one to two years to be secured by a mortgage of the Negroes, and appraised personal security. Auctioneer will pay for the papers.

A valuable Negro woman, accustomed to all kinds of house work. Is a good plain cook, and excellent dairy maid, washes and irons. She has four children, one a girl about 13 years of age, another 7, a boy about 5, and an infant 11 months old. 2 of the children will be sold with mother, the others separately, if it best suits the purchaser.

A very valuable Blacksmith, wife and daughters: the Smith is in the prime of life, and a perfect master at his trade. His wife about 27 years old, and his daughters 12 and 10 years old have been brought up as house servants, and as such are very valuable. Also for sale 2 likely young negro wenches, one of whom is 16 the other 13, both of whom have been taught and accustomed to the duties of house servants. The 16 year old wench has one eye.

A likely yellow girl about 17 or 18 years old, has been accustomed to all kinds of house and garden work. She is sold for no fault. Sound as a dollar.

House servants: The owner of a family described herein, would sell them for a good price only; they are offered for no fault whatever, but because they can be done without, and money is needed. He has been offered $1250. They consist of a man 30 to 33 years old, who has been raised in a genteel Virginia family as house servant, carriage driver etc., in all which he excels. His wife a likely wench of 25 to 30 raised in like manner, as chamber maid, seamstress, nurse etc., their two children, girls of 12 and 4 or 5. They are bright mulattoes, of mild tractable dispositions, unassuming manners, and of genteel appearance and well worthy the notice of a gentleman of fortune needing such.

(Right) Notice of 1833 slave auction in Charleston. During the 1830s domestic sales of slaves increased, and hence separation of slave families increased also. "Mulatto" girls and women were often valued as potential concubines for buyers. *Courtesy of the South Caroliniana Library, University of South Carolina*

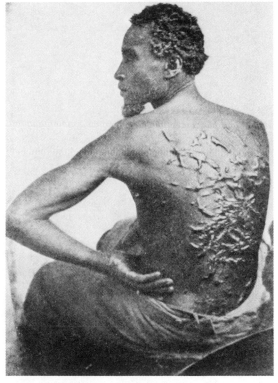

(*Above*) South Carolina slave auction and freed slaves, in foreground right. *Courtesy of the Library of Congress*

(*Right*) Slave with back scarred by whipping, the most common form of punishment. *Courtesy of the South Caroliniana Library, University of South Carolina*

Gang of slaves force marched to market. *Courtesy of the South Caroliniana Library, University of South Carolina*

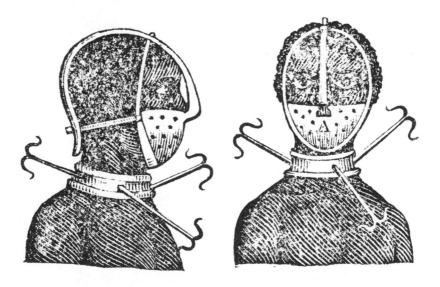

Metal mask, probably used to punish and as a deterrent for runaway slaves; the hooks around the neck would prevent escape through the vines and trees of swamps, and the mouthpiece served as a muzzle. *Courtesy of the Library of Congress*

Bloodhounds and hunters attacking a family of fugitive slaves; "nigger dogs" were trained to help capture runaways. *Courtesy of the Library of Congress*

Fugitive slaves. *Courtesy of the Library of Congress*

Brutus, an ex-slave, at his home, Palawana Island, South Carolina. Many tended to stay in the same area after Emancipation. *From the Penn School Collection, permission granted by Penn Center, Inc., St. Helena Island, South Carolina*

Family of freed slaves at their home. *Courtesy of the Valentine Museum, Richmond, Virginia*

CHAPTER FIVE

Slave Religion
The Dialectics of Faith

If slavery be inconsistent with the genius and spirit of Christianity, (as has been more frequently asserted than proved,) how shall we account for the total silence of its founders on the subject? At the period of the Christian era, it had long prevailed in various modifications over the known world. Yet in all the special instructions of our Saviour, in all his general references to the old Law, not one word condemns the practice. More recent scriptural authority is found in the writings of the great Apostle of the Gentiles. His instructions are even more minute than those of his master; is it possible that St. Paul, amid his multifarious directions, descending to the minutiae of domestic arrangement and female attire, would have omitted so important a topic, had he considered it a moral evil? In writing to Philemon, to intercede for his fugitive slave, Onesimus, (who had been converted by his preaching, whilst he was a prisoner at Rome,) he had the Apostle deemed it such; especially when we consider the eminent piety, 'the love and faith towards the Lord Jesus, and towards all saints,' which he ascribes to Philemon, the master of the runaway.

Christian enslaver, 1829[1]

Thar's a day-a-comin'! Thar's a day a-comin'! I hear de rumblin' ob de chariots! I see de flashin' ob de guns! White folks' blood is a-runnin' on de ground like a riber, an' de dead's heaped up ... high! Oh, Lor'! hasten de day when de blows, an' de bruises, an' de aches, an' de pains, shall come to de white folks, an' de buzzards shall eat 'em as dey's dead in de streets. Oh, Lor'! roll on de chariots, an' gib de black people rest an' peace. Oh, Lor'! gib me de pleasure ob livin' till dat day, when I shall see white folks shot down like de wolves when dey come hongry out o' de woods!

Enslaved Christian, c. 1850[2]

No topic about the systems used to control slaves is more controversial or subject to more debate than the role, if any, played by Christianity in subduing the enslaved. The uncertainty and forensic character of that issue lies often in the Christian religion itself, or can, depending on one's interpretation. Christianity has been adapted to virtually any disposition, cause, and group. This remarkable flexibility undoubtedly explains the apparent relevance of Christian tenets and their incredible influence on much preindustrial and contemporary history, not only in the American antebellum South. Both rulers and the ruled have historically found comfort and support in, for instance, the written word of the Lord. Antebellum planters believed not only that they had received biblical sanction to enslave other men but also that they would be bountifully blessed for placing those subjects under *His* command.[3]

While certain religious beliefs were used to pacify slaves, the mode in which they were used can be grasped only by understanding thoroughly what such tenets meant to opposing parties of master and slave. In masters' hands, Christianity became a litany of secular commandments that sanctioned slavery and glorified white supremacy. The faith forged by slaves rejected bondage and condemned those supporting it. How the Christianity of slaves between 1800 and 1865 could bolster rebelliousness, but simultaneously diminish any revolutionary potential will be the focus of this chapter.

Slaveholders felt assured that in both word and deed the Almighty upheld their kingdom of African thralls and multiracial freemen.[4] Slaves thought God promised them freedom. With such a malleable faith, it is not surprising that members of each group could find *something* to thank their Heavenly Father for "causing" or at least not preventing. Masters expressed gratitude after reaping good crops or in reflecting upon healthy servants; the enslaved praised the Lord for giving them the strength to endure their subjugation and endless toil.[5] Neither of these two perspectives was necessarily antithetical to the production of profits for the ruling order.

Nowhere was the magnetism of the extraordinarily enticing three-in-one deity of Christianity more in evidence than before and after attempts at insurrection. Rebelling servants sometimes cited the Old Testament, especially, during recruitment efforts as proof of the Almighty's support for revolutionary thrusts toward freedom, but masters always could look back at foiled uprisings as divine endorsements for *their* position and struggle in maintaining the Peculiar Institution. Rachel Blanding of Camden, South Carolina, wrote to her cousin on July 4, 1816, "Our Village and neighbourhood has been in great confusion for two days past owing to the fear of an insurrection of the blacks and nothing but the interposition of that Being to whom we are indebted for all our mercies has saved us from destruction."[6]

Anna Hayes Johnson, daughter of the famed jurist William Johnson, exclaimed after the discovery and suppression of the 1822 Denmark Vesey plot that "nothing but the merciful interposition of our God has saved us from horror equal if not superior to the scene acted in St. Domingo."[7] One prominent minister even called for a special day of thankfulness "publicly acknowledging" the "Divine Interposition" that had been so "conspicuous" in the prevention of that well-organized revolt.[8]

Planters were so convinced of their license to oppress that they decided to share the details of this heaven-sent dominion with those they persecuted. There was some skepticism initially about the prudence of proselytizing among a captive labor force. During much of the eighteenth century some masters believed baptism might dictate physical emancipation. Despite clerical denials that this was true, the apprehension persisted along with the view that conversion made slaves less tractable. Many masters throughout the colonial as well as the antebellum periods were fearful that religious meetings of servants would be used to transmit incendiary ideas or, worse, guidelines on how to effect them. Such forebodings among the ruling class were reflected in legislation and in the reluctance of chattel owners to finance adequately any missionary efforts.[9] By the third decade of the nineteenth century, however, attitudes toward the religious education of bondsmen had changed considerably. There were several reasons for this new outlook. Most planters became convinced, for instance, that there would be no consequent rise in slaves' literacy—an intellectual weapon slaveholders guarded with military-like secrecy to prevent it from falling into the hands of the enemy. Furthermore, an impressive array of evidence, gathered largely by white clergymen, concluded that "saved" slaves made "better" slaves.[10] Reverend George W. Moore described the "decided change" in the "moral character" of slaves near Beaufort where he had charge of "one of the largest and most prosperous" Methodist missions in South Carolina. He wrote in 1834 that there had been both a decrease in slave thefts and in the consumption of "ardent spirits." Reverend Moore promoted "the power of the voice of conscience" and took pride in its effect:

After one of my sermons . . . a [slave] woman got possession of the key of the house where the molasses was kept. She went to steal some to send to a woman on a neighboring island, and when she had put the key in the door, she stood motionless, having no power to open it, and was found in that position by the driver. I was an eyewitness to her agony. She could neither move nor speak. Afterward she seemed very penitent especially when she knew that I was acquainted with all the circumstances.[11]

The white elite was comforted by such testimony and by the fact that slave converts would be under the discipline and observance of holy controllers on Sunday, the one day most susceptible to iniquitous activities and mischievous travels because slaves were, generally, off duty. As one former slave recalled, Sabbath services were designed for "the spiritual and moral uplift of the slaves as well as to keep them out of devilment, and from desecrating God's holy day."[12] Concerned captors assumed that acceptance of blacks into the church would not only counteract abolitionist criticisms but give all observers the illusion of harmonious relations between devout masters and pious servants.

The plantocracy demonstrated their commitment to the Christianization of slaves by funding missions, building private chapels, and inviting itinerant preachers to preach on their plantations. Those who could not afford or who disapproved of such endeavors ministered directly to the workers or permitted slave worshipers to attend local churches where seats in the galleries had been reserved for them. The denominations most successful in gaining the support of societal lords and devotion of slave souls were the Baptists and the Methodists.[13] Whatever differences in theology or in organizational and ritualistic practices existed between these and other sects were obscured by their white spokesmen who focused almost exclusively on texts that simply echoed variations on a theme of "Pray, obey, and stay!" Both ecclesiastic and temporal masters hoped that what the cowhides of mortals did not achieve, the lash of God would accomplish. By stressing the brevity of life on earth and the impartiality of the Judgment in determining one's *eternal* state, both the temporal power elite and its holy cohorts sought to merge the interests of the enslaved with the enslaver. Every person, regardless of rank, was a child of God held accountable equally for deeds.[14]

Although it is not possible to establish the exact number of slaves who were touched by widely diverse modes of evangelization, some approximations can be made. Historian Luther P. Jackson estimates that "the combined Negro membership of the four major denominations [Baptist, Methodist, Episcopalian, Presbyterian] in South Carolina was no less than 85,000, a figure which represents about twenty per cent of the total Negro population of the State just before the Civil War."[15] One must be extremely careful in using such statistics because records of this nature have often proved inaccurate and, even when relatively accurate, fail to account for the hundreds of servants with no official connection with any church but who nevertheless worshiped the Lord fervently at private gatherings under the direction of revered slaves. When eighty-eight-year-old Charles Davis was asked about his religious education during slavery, he replied, "No 'mam, didn' have no church for de colored peoples in dem days. Just had some of dese big oaks pile up one on de other somewhe' in de woods en dat whe' we go to church. One of de plantation mens what had more learnin' den de others was de one what do de preachin dere."[16]

In addition to religious meetings like those described by Davis, some masters had "colored preachers" minister to slaves in the quarters. Former slave Rebecca Grant recalled, "Didn't have no colored churches. De drivers and de overseers, de house-servants, de bricklayers and folks like dat'd go to de white folk's church. But not de field hands. Why dey couldn't have all got in de church." According to Grant, her Beaufort, South Carolina "marsa had three or four hundred slaves, himself. And most of the other white folks had just as many or more."[17] To accommodate these blacks,

They had colored preachers to preach to de field hands down in de quarters. Dey'd preach in de street. Meet next day to de marsa's and turn in de report. How many pray, how many ready for baptism and all like dat. Used to have Sabbath School in de white people's house, in de porch, on Sunday evening. De porch was big and dey'd fill dat porch! They never fail to give de chillun Sabbath School. Learn them de Sabbath catechism.[18]

Southern missionaries concentrated heavily on young blacks who had not yet been admitted into the church. The South Carolina Methodist Conference reported on January 10, 1856, that, while 10,423 slaves had become members, 6,890 "colored children" were undergoing preparation for this privilege through the religious instruction of catechists.[19] Thus, many more bondsmen than church membership rolls can reveal were influenced by or at least familiar with the teachings of Christianity.

What captive Christians believed is easier to discern than their numbers. Both believing and skeptical slaves considered bondage an evil that would cause the damnation of anyone who advocated or supported it. The adamant commitment of Southern churches and their white constituents to this Peculiar Institution[20] was consummate apostasy to the vast majority of blacks. It was inevitable, therefore, that many servants of the Lord would discard all lessons that were intended to promote the comfort of earthly rulers, convinced that their inhumanity, hypocrisy, and greed deserved nothing more than deprecation and disdain. Individuals who tore asunder husbands and wives, reaped the products of others' sweat, and stole the virtue of innocent laborers could not possibly share the same heaven that the oppressed workers deserved and had striven to reach. This juxtaposition of moral rectitude among bondsmen and depravity among masters is apparent in the folklore of African-Americans.[21] In "Dead Duck and Wounded Duck," a John tale folklorist Elsie Parsons collected on Hilton Head, "an ol' man servan'" named Uncle John was asked by his master while hunting ducks, "why is it de Devil is always after you, an' de Devil never worry me?" Uncle John answered after his owner had "shot into a convey of ducks" and ordered him to "hurry, an' ketch de wounded duck fus'!" Completing his task, Uncle John said, "Now, massah, me ready to give you an answah. See! you say to me, 'Ketch the wounded duck firs',' an' dat is jus' what de Devil say. Say ketch me, because I'm scramblin' to get away f'om him, an' you are de dead duck. De Devil already got you, sah."[22]

"The Slave Barn," a folk poem, captures bitterly the diametrically opposed mores and outlooks of enslavers and slaves:

> Here, right here, is de spot
> De yoke of de ox
> Was wored by de humans—
> Mens an' womens alike—
> Chained to de walls
> In misery an' pain;
> Sold in de daytime
> Wid laughter an' joke
> Like hogs in a pen.

An' de trader live
To die in honor,
Forgiven by de church,
Prayed for, helt up,
He sins forgotten,
He name guin to a school—
To de young as a sample
Of virtue an' trute.

Fore here's a slave barn
Wid memories of sorrow;
An' de name
Of a brute
Handed down wid a lie
Of love.

A little gold to de church,
A prayer in he name;
An' a dog wid out honor
Die wid a name
Equal to a follower of Christ.[23]

The intense enmity expressed in this poem toward the corrupters and abusers of scriptural laws is reflected in numerous other ways. Individuals who plotted revolts, for instance, usually did not plan to spare white preachers. And insurgents on the battlefield found nothing sinful in slaying "saved" persons among the ruling class. According to Blanding in her communication about the 1816 Camden slave conspiracy, "Their thirst for revenge must have been great, it was the wish of some [rebels] to spare some of the whites and they mentioned an Old Gentleman who is a preacher he never owned a Slave and has Time to preaching to them on the plantations *but even him they would not Spare.*"[24] (Emphasis added.) Six years later, an insurrectionist executed with Denmark Vesey declared that Vesey ordered "all the Ministers . . . to be killed except a few who were to be saved and showed the different passages in the Bible from which Denmark preached . . . and they were to be asked why they did not preach up this thing (meaning the passages on liberty-&c) to them before and that they were to be made to tell."[25]

The destruction of church property both during and after the Civil War indicated further how deeply disenchanted some blacks were with planter-led priests and the edifices that symbolized that unholy alliance.[26] The "very handsome and elaborate" chapel bequeathed to W. St. Julien Mazyck by Plowden C. J. Weston, also a slaveholder, was "abused . . . in a most irresponsible manner" by newly freed slaves. Besides destroying the Bible "entirely, they broke the stained glass windows, tore up the books and generally wrecked the building."[27] Interestingly, this was the church ministered by the noted Episcopalian rector of All Saints Parish, the district in which the Weston property was situated. The Reverend Alexander Glennie, who had held that post for thirty years, was the "life-long friend" of Mr. Weston, and "probably the first minister [to undertake] the teaching of the Episcopal faith to the negroes."[28] It was perhaps the memory of the prayer he read so often that triggered the fury of former worshipers:

> Give to all masters grace to keep order and discipline in their families, and to treat their servants with mercy, kindness, gentleness, and discretion; knowing that thou has made of one flesh all the nations of the earth. Give to all servants grace to obey their masters, and please them well in all things; knowing that in thus doing they shall please thee who are the Master over all.[29]

Bondsmen could not be expected to respond very favorably to such requests of the divine.

The heavy concentration of slaveholders in the Episcopal church goes far to explain why enslaved blacks rejected, almost unanimously, fellowship within that body. Even those who did join abandoned the sect with remarkable celerity upon emancipation.[30] But no matter what denomination gained the allegiance of servants, its tenets were refined and reshaped by slave believers to meet their collective needs and interests. African-American men and women saw the Lord always at their side and were convinced that they indeed were *His* Chosen People. God was not only a personal friend but an ally who supported their myriad modes of survival and resistance.[31] The Almighty considered few things more laudatory than defying the dictates of blasphemous mortals—a view most masters never understood or appreciated fully. Without a doubt, here lies the reason in part for the consistent failure of Elizabeth Perry, like so many other slaveowners, to make their property obey or behave "correctly." She relayed the following grievance to her husband, a prominent politician who most likely was in Columbia:

> Delia sleeps in the room with me at night; her only fault is, not coming the instant I call her; and doing immediately what I tell her to do. I read to

her last Sunday some verses in the bible, I selected those that told servants to be obedient to their owners; and one in particular that suited her. "Servants be obedient unto your Masters, and please them well in all things, not *answering again.*"[32] (Emphasis in the original.)

Many captive workers were convinced that they held heaven-sent decrees to feign illness, to run away, to conceal the identities of bonded malefactors, and, most especially, to appropriate the belongings of all manstealing whites.[33] The human property of one Christian replied to the query by a white, "if he thought it any sin to take from his master," that "the Bible says a man has a right to the sweat of his own eye brows and what *he* worked for *he* thought it was no harm to take." (Emphasis added.) This was the retort of a man who "had long been a member of the church" and a leader at the prayer meetings of his fellows.[34] An example equally revealing is found in a slave sermon recorded by the Reverend John G. Williams:

Buckra an nigger skin diffrunt but dem haht is de same color. As ole mossa use ter say, 'dem tar wid de same paddle stick.' Ef dem wite preacher tek de commandiment. 'Dow shall not steal,' fur e tex, all de buckra turn roun an look rite at de nigger, much is ter say: 'Dat fur you stealing nigger,' an dem neber tek a wurd to demself. But ef buckra neber teef, how cum nigger yer? Enty buckra gone in dem ship an steal we an bring we frum we own country an sell we yer? Ef wun buckra steal anudder buckra nigger, an dey ketch de nigger teef, dat buckra sho fur heng. But how bout de teef dat steal nigger not frum e mossa, but frum a fahder an mudder?[35]

With such deft reasoning, it is no wonder that many of the "most zealous pretenders to religion" were often found to be "the greatest rogues" as well.[36]

Southern blacks interpreted the Decalogue differently from their lighter brethren, but they also modified Christian rituals. During the conversion sequence, for instance, bondsmen insisted that one must experience visions in order to attain true salvation, a sharp contrast to the practices of white "plain-folk," those "who were neither rich nor poor," and of aristocrats, both of whom regarded such manifestations as aberrant and little more than the fanatical delusions of primitive minds.[37] This element in slave religion appears with stunning regularity throughout the South. Charles Raymond, a white minister who had spent fourteen years in various cotton-growing states, was overwhelmed by the phenomenon and pondered whether blacks "learned from each other certain formulas, which are perpetuated like traditions among rude and half-civilized nations?" He mused on the possibility that there might be "but one impressional mould, every where homogenous and characteristic of the race, in which all their religious experiences are shaped."[38] The recollections of one contemporary suggest that Raymond was at least on the right track. An ex-slave told this story:

> When I was twelve years old I wanted to join the church. My father told me that I had better not come home unless I seen something. When I joined I didn't see anything, and I was scared to go home, but just as I stepped out the door the heavens opened up and I seed angels flying around. I ran to my father then.[39]

The rigidity with which Christian slaves adhered to such syncretic conventions as well as to those biblical doctrines untainted by others' perverted applications was difficult to match. Both contemporary and postwar observers noted how many saved blacks abandoned not only dancing but the playing of musical instruments as well.[40] Nor should one forget what tremendous sacrifices some bondsmen made to uphold their convictions. A number were harassed or even sold for spreading the word of God, and at least one suffered death following a flailing inflicted solely because he would not "deny his belief in the Lord Jesus Christ."[41] The Reverend Whiteford Smith, D.D., wrote about another slave whose faith cost him dearly. Smith first met the slave, whose name was Sancho Cooper, when he was a college student in Columbia between 1826 and 1830. Cooper was the "trusted servant" of Dr. Thomas Cooper, a well-known "skeptic" and a college president. According to Smith, Sancho's previous owner "had no objection to him except on the score of his religion. He was bitterly opposed to his holding meetings and praying with the negroes on the plantation; and inasmuch as Sancho could not be persuaded to give up his conscientious convictions of duty in this respect, he was threatened and afterward cruelly punished to make him stop praying, and finally sold for no other fault but this."[42]

The unswerving devoutness and commitment of slave votaries can be seen in their contributions to the church of money out of their pitifully limited resources and their assemblage at late-night or early-morning services in their only free time.[43] Religious gatherings during those precious moments of leisure are all the more significant if one considers how fatigued the participants must have been both physically and mentally after long hours of work and little sleep. Nevertheless, they convened—and none too quietly, according to certain witnesses.[44] A correspondent to the *Times* (Charleston) complained in the summer of 1816, of noisy midnight services and warned of the probable evil consequences:

> Almost every night there is a meeting of these noisy, frantic worshippers. . . . Midnight! Is that the season for religious convocation? Even allowing that these meetings were conducted with propriety, is that the accepted time? That the meeting of numerous black people to hear the scripture expounded by an ignorant and (too frequently) vicious person of their own color can be of no benefit either to themselves or the community is certain; that it may be attended with many evils is, I presume, obvious to every reflecting mind.[45]

Not all blacks were so conscientious. Many were as unsaved as they were unimpressed by Christian tenets and preferred outdoor parties to outside prayers. These "heathen" men and women would not accept any God who allowed the brutalities they incurred to continue while watching those perpetrating the evils thrive. They could never kneel to a God or body of beliefs that, in their view, so blinded believers that they alternately promoted and abetted their own subjugation. It is remarkable, therefore, how similar their rationales for the rejection of Christianity are to those proffered by latter-day folk philosophers whose views have been preserved in lore and tales.[46] During his ministry among Southern blacks, John D. Long encountered slaves who would not accept the Christian faith because they suspected "the Gospel to be a cheat, and believe the preachers and the slaveholder to be in a conspiracy against them."[47] Some slave descendants perpetuated other suspicions about Christianity in a folktale called "The Three Dreams." As told by a young black on Ladies Island in 1919, whites were able sometimes to snatch an earthly reward while blacks dreamed of heaven:

> Two mans wen' to a restauran'. It was late, so de man who was keepin' de restauran' sell up ev'ryt'in', had only a piece of chicken. Tony call out, 'De one dream de longes' dream will eat de chicken!' So Boss say, 'All right.' An' after dey lie down an' Tony drop fas' asleep, Boss get up an' eat de chicken. Tony snorin'. Wake up. Call Boss, 'What you dream?' Boss stretch. 'Tell yer dream,' Tony say. 'Yours firs'.' Boss said, 'Tell your.' Tony begin, 'I dream I gone from dis place. Angel Gabriel come down an' put

two wings on me. I fly. I fly. Gates wide open. I fly right in.' Boss say, 'Tony boy, I saw when you flyin', so I ate de chicken.'[48]

Both before and after Emancipation, there were blacks who held greater confidence in conjurers than in Christian holy men. Griffin Whitmire, a former South Carolina slave, recalled how the adults among the more than sixty slaves on his master's plantation would meet secretly on Saturday nights for a "lil' . . . fun frum de white folks hearin'." The revelers "felt no scruples" about stealing a hog each Saturday or continuing their festivities on Sundays because "none o' our gang didn't have no 'ligion." They felt especially confident because a "Conjin 'Doc,'" told them he had put a spell on "ole Marse so dat he wuz 'blevin ev'y think dat us tole him bout Sa'day night and Sunday morning." Whenever the master inquired about their whereabouts, Whitmire claims, "Us would tell some lie bout gwine to a church 'siety meetin'."[49] The existence of such influences throughout the slave community and the numerous advantages associated with church membership or attendance, should cue one to be wary of many who claimed to be sanctified. There is evidence that not a few religious advocates were simply wearing masks of piety to impress masters or to make their incessant "falsehoods" to controllers more credible.[50] In addition, the faithful, however disingenuous, were usually granted permission to travel to wherever the nearest place of worship was and thereby gained access to beloved friends and relations with whom to exchange the latest news.[51]

Divine guises could inspire even greater rewards. Some slaves had to know of whites who not only protested the injunction against teaching chattels to read, but also defied the law so that their servants would be able to discover and share the wisdom of the Scriptures for themselves. The Reverend Robert Fair of Abbeville defended such aberrant behavior by pointing out there was "enough between the lids of the Bible" to make *all* legislation superfluous that sought to "guaranty the stability and perpetuity of the institution of Slavery."[52] Other white proponents of written religious instruction submitted petitions calling for the repeal of the 1834 act prohibiting such training.[53] In an especially moving appeal, petitioners from Chester District decried the statute as an invasion of their *"rights of conscience"* and, thus, "unconstitutional":

Thousands of good citizens are grieved with this law & desire its repeal. . . . It will be a *dead letter* generally & in most cases where it may be enforced, it will be roused by *malicious persons* to punish men better than themselves. . . . It is by no means unusual to hear good citizens say, "I am prepared to *disrespect* such a law. . . ." The *ability to read* which the Legislature seems to dread *now exists,* in probably every plantation in the State. Dozens, yea, hundreds of slaves can now read all over the state & it is utterly impossible even for the *masters* to prevent this, as is apparent in those cases where negroes learn to *write* by *stealth* altho the master is very watchful to prevent this. Besides is it not very questionable whether *intelligence* is more productive of dangerous insurrections than ignorance? Your memorialists soberly believe that the State has less to fear even from *general* intelligence among the slaves (for which we are not pleading) than that ignorance which seems to be contemplated by the law in question, which would make our servants the fit dupes of every Nat Turner who might chance to pass along. (Emphases in the original.)

The memorialists then scornfully asked, "Does chivalrous South Carolina quail before gangs of cowardly Africans with a Bible in their hands?"[54] The rejection by the legislature of this prayer, and of others asking the same, can be interpreted only as an answer in the affirmative, for literate slaves, saved or not, posed a threat to the system.[55]

Distinguishing sincere religiousness from simulated sanctity is a difficult task, for all persons consider self-interest at times and can be driven equally and simultaneously by the rewards of religious behavior and by more selfless sentiments. It would be hard to imagine either a true believer or a false celebrant not harboring thoughts of shaping a master's or mistress's behavior by entering into fellowship with him or her. Slave members of respective congregations did complain occasionally of the abuses they sustained from their church brethren/rulers, but such owners, unlike the quarry, were rarely found guilty. Indeed, whenever the accuser was black and the accused white, the accuser was commonly charged with prevarication and speedily "suspended from the special priviledges of the church."[56] The details and outcome of one such confrontation follow. It led to the excommunication of the slave Judy.[57]

Judy acknowledges she did give ill Language to her Master and Mistress because she had not anough to Eat—given her from them. . . . Evidence from Bro. Johnson by Sister Johnson they prove Judy . . . did say that she had backers in the church which she will not own or deny. . . . Bro. Johnson sayes if he has hurt aney of his Brethrens feelings by whipping his servant, or saying aney thing, or doing aneything, Els he is sorey for it—Sister Johnson says that she is sorey for saying that they would sell Judy. . . . —An attempt was made to git Judy to confess her faults but with out Suckcess or Satesfaction to the Comittee.[58]

The fate of Judy may seem harsh, but to her it most likely seemed a marvelous respite from the sentences generally meted out. She and all others of her status undoubtedly recognized that while one could be readmitted to church, the effects of a severe flogging or of a sale that separated generations were never so foreseeable. Moreover, if the apologies of the Johnsons were sincere and presaged an amelioration in their treatment of Judy, then her banishment from the church may have been a blessing in disguise. This is not to say that Judy or a majority of those who engaged in the Christianizing activities of their owners participated for mercenary reasons. But some did. As instances of slaves selling spirits during religious meetings suggest, at least a few probably attended in order to facilitate their extra-legal business ventures or to partake of such intoxicating pursuits.[59] Also, it is important to note, a substantial number of slaveholders pressured slaves into attending services.[60] Enthralled workers on John Hymie Tucker's Georgetown plantation were driven to the chapel by a threatened denial of their weekly "extras." That strategy, Tucker argued, "attacked the African in his weakest point, and appealed to his appetite for the good of his soul."[61] How many of these coerced worshipers became independent or authentic followers will unfortunately never be known.

Such compulsion was part and parcel of an ever-growing campaign by planters and white religious allies to proselytize black captives. As most engaged in battle understand, however, nothing is ever thrust upon an enemy without cause. Slave soldiers were no exception and sensed the omnipresent net of control, this time cast with religious cords. How members of the plantocracy towed a rich haul despite that awareness has an irony which neither they nor their catch apparently apprehended. What made Christianity such a pacifying force was not the prostituted Scripture propagandized by whites, but the interpretation blacks forged from those and other sacred tenets. Although, for slaves, it was understood as extirpating all ruling-class "misreadings" and as demolishing any elite pretensions about equality with *or* supremacy over "their people," it nevertheless provided an implacable rationale for the century-old and insidious caution that consumed much of the slave community. More directly, it contributed significantly to the further opening of that secret world to intrusions and divisions so advantageous to masters.

These seemingly contradictory elements in the faith slaves adopted can be understood better by recognizing that Christianity has always had the capacity of functioning both as a centripetal and centrifugal force. Individuals confined at the quarters, for instance, were drawn closer together by the frequent admonishments of slave exhorters to unite and "love one another." But the "holier than thou" attitude of black Christians toward whites must have caused some strife also between oppressed Christendom and its "lost" brethren. Certainly, it would not be the first time that unrelenting efforts to make the blind see sparked more friction than mass revelations. In addition, the unspoken oath to protect fellow bondsmen guilty of what slaves collectively considered political crimes, that is, stealing or absconding from masters, was broken occasionally by captives who embraced ruling-class depictions of such acts as moral felonies and, hence, sins.[62] One betrayal of this time-honored trust resulted in the ouster of two black worshipers from the Salem Presbyterian Church. According to its records on August 28, 1831,

Cato Servant of John Shaw, was suspended for Six months for an assault made upon one of the Church members. Jack servant of R. Witherspoon, was suspended for six months for charging the above named Cato with theft and Causing the assault.[63]

To assure that they would not be dependent on themselves or on conscientious slaves alone to expose any black "wrongdoers," white churchmen culled their religious coffers for suitable black aides. Whether they called them elders, deacons, class leaders, or watchmen, their function was the same—to oversee the blessed and to ferret out the wicked among Heaven's most treasured flock. The success and effectiveness of that procedure were disclosed in a document left by an early-nineteenth-century congregation:

The Church attended to the Cases of several black members, who were reported by the black Deacon, Scipio, to be in disorder: & upon the report of a Committee, appointed to enquire into the facts; excluded the following

persons, viz *Molley,* servants [*sic*] of Alex.ʳ Norwood, for turbulent, quar-
relsome temper, which had hurried her into acts of violences, of which there
was satisfactory proof. All labour with her, had proved unavailing. She had
also been guilty of Lying.[64]

Appointees such as Scipio had no authority over whites, but they
held a great deal of power and respect over blacks, who had
usually approved of the appointments and were sometimes even
involved in the picking. This explains, undoubtedly, why slave
worshipers typically asked those selected to lead them in prayer
and biblical instruction at their own covert gatherings. It is important to remember that meetings held without the presence of
a white were illegal. Needless to say, having such a highly regarded
and black-sanctioned officiary under its direction proved most
beneficial to the watchful league of slavers and priests, for, as their
titles reveal, watchmen at root were but godly spies.[65]

The seriousness and dedication with which these slaves pursued
their duties were noted by Charles Raymond in describing a particularly articulate deacon.

> Peter prided himself, not without just cause on the thoroughness and
> infallibility of his discipline. He knew every colored member of his church
> and kept himself accurately informed concerning the habits and endulgences
> of those whom he had any reason to think open to suspicion. No deed
> of darkness, however secretly performed, but sooner or later reached the
> knowledge of Peter. As soon as there was any ground for scandal, the colored
> deacons went to work to sift the rumor, and bring to light any tangible
> wickedness. They were as expert in following all the windings and doublings
> of the delinquent as a trained detective. The negro's accurate observation of
> the doings of their fellows, and the sort of free-masonry which exists among
> them, were made available for the good of the church and the enlightenment
> of the deacons. If the reports were mere scandals, nothing was said to the
> white members; but if the delinquent was fairly proved guilty, the white
> deacons were called in, and the evidence submitted to them; and if thus
> confirmed, a report was made to the white church, and expulsion of the
> offender followed.[66]

White clergymen had made it abundantly clear that they identified with and were committed to the well-being and preservation
of the ruling class. Nevertheless, South Carolinian slaves continually brought personal problems, internecine conflicts, and marital
difficulties before the church. They thereby exposed a disunity
that ultimately could be exploited by the very powers from whom
the complainants sought private redress and communal peace.[67]

Enslaved Christians apparently felt that it was better for the church than individual planters or the parties involved to resolve any dissension. Masters were not known for their justness and did have a history of settling all problems or disputes through caustic means. James Henry Hammond recorded this on the day after Christmas of 1840:

> Fine day. Had a trial of Divorce and Adultery cases. Flogged Joe Good-wyne and ordered him to go back to his wife. . . . Separated Moses and Anny finally—And flogged Tom Kollock. He had never been flogged before. Gave him 39 with my own hand interferring with Muggy Campbell, Sullivan's wife—Did not break him of his Drivership.[68]

Church authorities, on the other hand, would only have expelled such miscreants. Still, the often neglected point is that private slave affairs such as fights, rivalries, animosities, and infidelities, formerly handled internally—unless, of course, masters discovered them first—were now being taken to the masters' unabashed confederates by members in what before had been an essentially closed black community. Thus, masters had one more path to information about life in the quarters and other intelligence of a most manipulable nature.

If there is any question about the willingness of saved slaves to expose fellow slaves suspected of doing what they believed was wrong in the eyes of God and, hence, a moral crime, one need only peruse the extremely rich church records that far too few scholars have exploited.[69] There is no way, for instance, that whites alone could have detected and prosecuted the persistent accusations of adultery without black assistance.[70] Indeed, one wonders how anyone other than friends, neighbors, and voyeurs could have acquired such intimate knowledge of another's sexual and marital practices. Infidelity was universally condemned; no other area of interracial religious concern appears to have sparked such unanimity of opinion. A substantial consensus must also have existed about worldly amusements, for although nonblacks rarely were present at the social events of slaves, they were nevertheless able to learn somehow which "professors" among the revelers had succumbed to the devil and danced, drank, or played musical instruments.[71] Perhaps the biblical dictate to "love thy neighbor" survived such disclosures, but it must have been strained, broken, and sometimes permanently discarded when a culprit discovered who the informant was who caused shameful public censure to surround what had been done in private or in slave groups alone.

Although the convictions of some Christian slaves made them break the slave ranks, most black Christians held fast to the belief that what they considered political "crimes" were both moral and just. It is no doubt for that reason that an "Old member" of the Welsh Neck Baptist Church gave "improper advice" to a fellow slave:

> After Divine Service, attended to the cases of Daniel and Rose reported Yesterday. *Daniel* had been engaged with the husband of Rose, in stealing hogs: which he confessed, And was excluded by Unanimous vote. *Rose* had found out the conduct of her husband, and had reproved him: but from improper advice of an Old member, she had not, as she should have done, promptly made known his conduct. She was placed under censure.[72]

White Christians made no distinction between moral and political crimes. To them, anything that threatened their livelihood was, in the words of Reverend Glennie and others, a "violation of all Christian codes" and, consequently, a damnable offense. This included, of course, the abandonment by slaves or their appropriations of goods, for these acts removed profits which the unshackled argued God had ordained the unfree to produce but not to possess.[73] Naturally, nothing was more sinful and rigorously condemned than assaults on planters or on the institution of slavery.[74] The disciplinary arm of the church came down heavily also on workers who "were not disposed to do their tasks," who showed "a rebellious disposition," or who simply conducted themselves in a "refractory" fashion.[75] Thus, a merger between sacred and secular crimes was consummated and, in the eyes of masters, God's will had been done.

Few scholars today would deny that Christianity is a double-edged sword. There is far too much evidence, however, for anyone to vacillate or equivocate on which side of that blade flashed most often in reference to enslaved blacks. Some bondsmen, like Nat Turner, who was convinced that God had selected him to lead his people to freedom, were moved by their religious beliefs to transcend rebellious acts and plan for revolution. But messianic visions such as Turner's were seen rarely in antebellum slave quarters. The exact role played by Christianity in stirring Vesey, the other insurrectionary leader, cited continually as proof of how Christian doctrines could spark radicalism, is more difficult to discern. In his recruitment efforts, Vesey not only spoke of Old Testament justifications for violent thrusts toward freedom and the injustices of bondage, but also referred to Congressional debates over slavery and the successful methods of Toussaint L'Ouverture. Existing records make it no more valid to assert that Vesey, a class leader in a Charleston church, was divinely inspired to wage rebellion than to claim that the slave who held the identical church rank betrayed the plot because he felt God decried such upheavals. Nevertheless, it is clear that certain interpretations of Christianity could be used to effect revolutionary ends.[76] A ringleader of the Camden, South Carolina, revolt went to the gallows claiming that he was a "professor of religion" guilty of "only one sin . . . and that was he had set down to the communion Table with the White people when he knew he was going to cut their Throats as soon as convenient."[77]

Why the vast majority of captive Christians chose not to apply the lethal edge of that religion can be found largely in the sermons of black and white preachers. The latter, of course, never exposed the cutting side of their sacred sword, but concentrated instead on demonstrating how all God's people suffered alike. A minister writing in the Southern *Presbyterian* (Charleston, S.C.) delivered a discourse entitled "The Hard Way," in which he said:

> This world is a sorrowful place; not one of us ever saw the man yet, that had no sorrow—that had no sickness, no hard, painful work; no danger; nobody to trouble. . . . But in spite of that, *everybody had his trouble*: if your children all live, maybe some of them behave so badly that they have to be sent away, or they keep you afraid something dreadful will happen to them—or maybe they are so sickly, and they suffer so much, that you'd almost rather see them die. If you are strong and healthy, something else goes wrong. You never can say, "Now I'm happy," unless you're a Christian.[78] (Emphasis in the original.)

Black pastors concurred but knew also that no matter how difficult life was for whites, they would never have to endure the apprehensiveness and fear bondsmen experienced with each heartbeat because others legally could destroy their lives, families, and relationships at will. Most bound men and women of God therefore acknowledged in word and deed both the wrongness of human bondage and the correctness of all day-to-day modes of resistance.[79] A blind preacher named Frank was excommunicated for telling a group of servile worshipers that "their principal portion in this world was a peck of corn, a few clothes, and Seven Hundred lashes."[80] A driver and religious leader among the chattels of John Berkley Grimball was admonished because he "permitted Phettus to do bad work—and when spoken to on the subject had been short in his answer, and indeed somewhat impudent." The enraged overseer who reported him told his master also that "he was in the habit of calling the negroes—those at least who were professionally religious, Sister and Brother" and "that the people had prayer meetings regularly."[81]

While such verbal lessons and instructive behavior were detrimental to the ruling class, other elements in the sermons of blacks more than compensated for any "negative" aspects. Slave leaders who covertly and sometimes even publicly made references to the wickedness of bondage emphasized primarily the need for *personal* salvation and the rewards therefrom, that is, immortal bliss instead of ceaseless hell. Black preachers stressed most incessantly that only through endless faith in God the Almighty would they ever be set free, for He alone could unshackle the chains mortals had forged, linked, and anchored.[82] One can dismiss these otherworldly solutions and their conservative consequences as the realistic decision of captive ministers to ward off needless deaths from a collective physical resistance that was doomed to failure because of black military weakness. This "zero chance of success" theme[83] will be discussed at greater length in the following chapter, but it is debatable whether all slaves, wherever they were located, were convinced equally that rebellions would fail on purely military grounds. There is absolutely no question, however, about the awareness of slave religious leaders that *if* any insurrectionary plot were discovered, they would be the first on the list of suspects. Not only did many influential and powerful whites harbor a deep mistrust of them, but treacherous bondsmen posed a threat as well.[84] The Reverend John Dixon Long noted:

> If a colored preacher or intelligent free Negro gains the ill-will of a malicious slave, all the latter has to do is to report that said preacher had attempted to persuade him to "rise," or to run away; and the poor fellow's life may pay the forfeit.[85]

It was therefore in the self-interest of every black spiritual head to discourage all potential revolutionary onslaughts. Although naturally, only the most "trustworthy" of blacks were given permission to exhort or to monitor the behavior of enslaved worshipers, these privileged characters were scrutinized also. If, for example, a report arose of any appointee's giving "offense" in either speech or deed, he was immediately expelled from the church and thereby stripped of the tremendous status his position had brought.[86] This policy of weeding out "dangerous" holy men may have settled into a long tradition, for the scholar and black leader Benjamin Mays, writing in 1933, recounted:

> Not many years ago, the militant Negro preachers in a certain section of South Carolina were silenced by threats of violence, and in some cases actually run out of the county, because their messages were not considered the kind that would keep Negroes in their "place"; but those who preached about heaven, who told Negroes to be honest and obedient, and that by and by God would straighten things out, were helped financially in church projects. They were held up to other Negroes as embodiments of the virtues of true Negro leadership. Such Negroes could usually get a little financial aid to build new churches and renovate old ones, and they were sometimes encouraged by the whites in their efforts to split the church.[87]

Members of the plantocracy had indeed left future elites a valuable lesson, for slave religious leaders, like those coming behind in freedom, held extraordinary influence over their supporters.[88] One former slave born in 1840 remembered the Palmetto State's black clergymen under Reconstruction who influenced even a man's relationship to his wife:

> Mr. Franklin J. Moses was runnin' for governor. Colored preachers was preachin' dat he was de Moses to lead de Negroes out of de wilderness of corn bread and fat grease into de land of white bread and New Orleans molasses. De preachers sure got up de excitement 'mongst de colored women folks. They 'vised them to have nothin' to do wid deir husbands if they didn't go to de 'lection box and vote for Moses. I didn't go, and my wife wouln't sleep wid me for six months. I had no chillum by her. She died in 1884.[89]

Although antebellum and postwar black preachers wielded great power among their devotees, one can only conjecture how much of what they stressed in official sermons and personal communications shaped slave religious thinking or merely reflected it. There are striking similarities between the views extolled by black exhorters and those that permeate slave spirituals—the documents that are the most revealing of slave scriptural interpretations and

religious beliefs.[90] Nothing, for example, was more central in these
sacred folk productions than the quest for, glorification of, and
thankfulness for heaven. In that angelic world lay the antithesis
of life on earth, for with God there would be no more "parting,"
no sparse diets, no "whips acrackin'" or "hard trials" or "stormy
weather." Rewards, however, would go only to those who had
been patient and never lost faith in His ultimate justice.[91] In
"Good News" ecstatic laborers rang out:

> O, good news! O, good news!
> De angels brought de tidings down,
>   Just comin' from de trone.
>
> As grief from out my soul shall fly,
>   Just comin' from de trone;
> I'll shout salvation when I die,
>   Good news, O, good news!
>   Just comin' from de trone.
>
> Lord, I want to go to heaven when I die,
>   Good news, O, good news! &c.
>
> De white folks call us a noisy crew,
>   Good news, O, good news!
> But dis I know, we are happy too,
>   Just Comin' from de trone.[92]

Workers on St. Helena Island[93] sang as if to reinforce that message:

> Tis good for to have some Patience
>   Pattence [sic] patience
> Tis good for to have some patience,
>   To wait upon de Lord
> Cho. [Chorus]
>
> Oh. Banna wont you rise an go wid me
> repeat—repeat
>   · To wait upon de Lord
>
> De ferry boat da waitin,
>   waitin, waiten
> De ferry boat da waitin
>   To wait upon de Lord
>
> Oh, Banna &c.
> Get your ticket ready
>   ready, ready
> Oh get your ticket ready
>   To wait upon de Lord

O Banna
He wait for true believer
   'liever 'liever repeat &c.[94]

Such confident affirmations of final glory and the behavior
needed to qualify are pervasive in the slave spirituals. There one
finds also a constant discussion and description of the Heavenly
Father who will not only free the enslaved, but also wreak vengeance on those satanic parties who were responsible for their
worldly miseries. He was a vengeful God whose ferocity and exploits were verified by Old Testament tales. Neither pharaohs,
lions, nor seas could stop Him, but when the Day of Judgment
came none save the most tested holy men would reap the joys of
His gold-paved and jewel-studded Kingdom.[95] With such an all-
powerful and pugnacious deity, it is no wonder that oppressed
worshipers sang:

We'll soon be free,
We'll soon be free,
We'll soon be free,
   When de Lord will call us home
My brudder, how long,
My brudder, how long,
My brudder, how long,
   'Fore we done sufferin' here?
It won't be long (Thrice)
   'Fore de Lord will call us home.
We'll walk de miry road (Thrice)
   Where pleasure never dies.
We'll walk de golden street (Thrice)
   Where pleasure never dies.
My brudder, how long (Thrice)
   'Fore we done sufferin' here?
We'll soon be free (Thrice)
   When Jesus sets me free.
We'll fight for liberty (Thrice)
   When de Lord will call us home.[96]

Such spirituals have fueled heated controversy over the real
meaning of these sacred songs. Various scholars have argued that
they contained everything from secret warnings about the approach of an overseer to demands for freedom in *this* world.[97]
Albert Raboteau denies that the "spirituals were coded protest
songs," though he agrees that "a particular verse might have a

particular significance for a person at one time and not at another."[98]

It is a common experience for people to refer to a widely circulated and well-known song as "our song" because it seems a particularly apt comment on some situation in their own lives. It is not necessary, then, to believe that the line "I am bound for the land of Canaan" always meant going North to escape from slavery, even though that is exactly what the line signified for Frederick Douglass and his fellows while they plotted to escape.[99]

A great deal of evidence can be mustered in support of this position, for if such lyrics contained cryptic notes, newly freed bondsmen probably would have told Northern missionaries whom they bombarded constantly with detailed accounts of how their remarkable ploys or artifices had deceived and "put on ole' massa." Such reports are rare. Clearly, much can and has been read into the spirituals, but, for the most part, those heavenly compositions were just what they appeared to be—beatific religious sentiments set to music.

While the issue of whether slave Christians were singing of freedom on earth or "up yonder" has been discussed frequently by historians, few have acknowledged and explored the consequences of the adamant belief among saved bondsmen that wherever liberation did occur, God would be the primary actor and instigator. Practically all sources indicate that the interpretation of Christianity to which slaves adhered embraced a philosophy of life that can be summarized best as: If we do all that is humanly possible to help ourselves by appropriating adequate food, slowing down production, and destroying enemy property, and then place absolute trust in His judgment, He will free us. It appears that the overwhelming majority were waiting for some sign or signal from Him—which, incidentally, they interpreted the Civil War as being—before engaging in any armed struggle. When the American Freedmen's Inquiry Commission asked Sergeant Solomon Bradley if he had been drafted by the Union Army, he responded, "I volunteered," and went on, "In Secesh times I used to pray the Lord for this opportunity to be released from bondage and to fight for my liberty, and I could not feel right so long as I was not in the regiment."[100]

Sergeant Bradley was not alone in his entreaties, for countless others among the enslaved implored the Lord continually to manu-

mit them. Indeed, if widespread paternalistic relations existed anywhere, they were between enthralled Christians and their Heavenly Father. They never ceased avowing their loyalty and devotion,
convinced that He, in return, would continue to grant them
strength, protection, and the hope of a better day.[101] Jacob Stroyer,
as a young boy, thought that his father would avenge the severe
flogging he had received from a white groom on the plantation,
but when Stroyer ran to him for help, the elder "very cooly" said,
"go back to your work and be a good boy, for I cannot do anything for you." "That evening," Stroyer recalled,

> when I went home to father and mother, I said to them, "Mr. Young is
> whipping me too much now; I shall not stand it, I shall fight him." Father
> said to me, "You must not do that, because if you do he will say that your
> mother and I advised you to do it, and it will make it hard for your mother
> and me, as well as for yourself. You must do as I told you, my son; do your
> work the best you can, and do not say anything. . . . I can do nothing more
> than pray to the Lord to hasten the time when these things shall be done
> away; that is all I can do. . . ."
> When the time came for us to go to bed we all knelt down in family
> prayer, as was our custom; father's prayer seemed more real to me that night
> than ever before, especially in the words, "Lord, hasten the time when these
> children shall be their own free men and women." My faith in father's prayer
> made me think that the Lord would answer him at the farthest in two or
> three weeks, but it was fully six years before it came, and father had been
> dead two years before the war.[102]

This belief that the Civil War and emancipation were the direct
consequences of their prayers was averred almost unanimously by
emancipated Christians.[103] Some even argued "that the eleventh
chapter of Daniel" had prophesied the war's coming and end.
Thomas Johnson, the author of *Twenty-eight Years a Slave*, remembered assembling and discussing this biblical account with
his literate brethren.

> We often met together and read this chapter in our own way. The fifth
> verse would perplex many of our company and then verses 13–15 would be
> much dwelt upon, for though the former verses spoke of the apparent victory
> of the South, these latter verses set forth the ultimate triumph of the North,
> for did it not say: "For the King of the North shall return and shall set forth
> a multitude greater than the former. . . . so the King of the North shall come
> and cast up a mound and take the most fenced cities, and the arms of the
> South shall not withstand." Thus we eagerly grasped at any statements
> which our anxiety, hope, and prayer concerning our liberty led us to search
> for, and which might indicate the desirable ending of the great War.[104]

The favorable outcome of the war reinforced all the scriptural interpretations and religious beliefs African-American slaves had propagated for years. Not surprisingly, a revival-like atmosphere pervaded the black community. Liberated residents held all-night prayer vigils thanking profusely the Savior who had freed them and the parties who had been sent to do His biddings, frequently referred to in biblical terms.[105] On April 23, 1865, a Northern teacher working among emancipated blacks at St. Helena, South Carolina, wrote in her diary that when Abraham Lincoln died the people were "inconsolable" and refused to believe he was dead: "They prayed for him as wounded but still alive, and said he was their Savior—that Christ saved them from sin, and he from 'Secesh,' and as for the vile Judas who had lifted his hand against him, they prayed the Lord the whirlwind would carry him away, and that he would melt as wax in the fervent heat, and be driven forever from before the Lord."[106]

Perhaps nothing better captures how newly freed Christians interpreted their liberation than the spirituals they created in its honor. Few were more comprehensive than this one:

> Oh! praise an' tanks! De Lord he come
>> To set de people free;
> An' massa tink it day ob doom,
>> And we ob jubilee.
> De Lord dat heap de Red Sea waves,
>> He jus' as strong as den;
> He say de word: we las' night slaves
>> To-day, de Lord's free men.
>>> De yams will grow, de cotton blow,
>>>> We'll hab de rice an' corn;
>>> Oh! nebber you fear, if nebber you hear
>>>> De driver blow his horn!
>
> We pray de Lord he gib us signs
>> Dat some day we be free;
> De Norf wind tell it to de pines,
>> De wild duck to de sea;
> We think it when de church-bell ring,
>> We dream it in de dream;
> De rice-bird mean it when he sing,
>>> De yam will grow, de cotton blow,
>>>> We'll hab de rice an' corn;
>>> Oh! nebber you fear, if nebber you hear
>>>> De driver blow his horn!

We know de promise nebber fail,
    An' nebber lie de word;
So, like de 'postles in de jail,
    We waited for de Lord;
An' now he open ebery door,
    An' trow away de key;
He tink we lub him so before,
    We lub him better free
        De yam will grow, de cotton blow,
          He'll gib de rice an' corn;
        So nebber you fear, if nebber you hear
          De driver blow his horn![107]

While such views may have effectively mobilized the unfree to support Union forces militarily, planters utilized the same tidings in perennial efforts before, and one might argue even during the Civil War to prevent slaves from "rising." In this sense, the Christianity molded by blacks helped to pacify the slavocracy's most holy property. In his discussion of South Carolina plantation missions between 1844 and 1864, a white Methodist wrote that "true" slave Christians were "better servants" and cited their wartime behavior as proof:

The extraordinary conduct of the slaves during the civil war is an inexplicable feature in the history of that great struggle. Inexplicable, we mean, if this evangelizing work of the missionaries is not taken into the problem. Many writers have believed that Mr. Wesley's followers prevented the uprising of the masses of the English poor at the time of the French Revolution. Religion is the strongest tie that unites man to man in the social constitution. . . . [It] is the best safeguard, and the most potent agency for the preservation of civil society. Its operation is uniform. . . . When St. Paul said "we are saved by hope," he uttered a sentiment that touches the lowly sons of toil at every point. . . . "There's a better day a coming" are the words of an old refrain that have girded up the loins of millions.[108]

The alluring faith espoused by captive workers girded them with many psychological comforts. One of its most consoling was to allay their fears about the future—particularly about dying.[109] Just as saved blacks knew God would free them, they trusted Him to determine the best time for their "departure," and felt obliged to submit willingly. Many displayed extreme resignation, calm, and even eagerness on their deathbeds or after the demise of a beloved relative.[110] G. G. Gibbs, a South Carolina planter, reported of dying slaves:

Negroes are generally fatalists, and believe that every one has his time appointed to die, and if it be "come" they expect to die; and, if not, they will get well without medicine. . . . Frequently have I found the patient's bed turned from its position of the day before, in order that he might die "with his face towards the rising sun," and often have I had it restored and informed them that their "time had not come *to go* home," as they call it.[111] (Emphasis in the original.)

On at least one plantation, dying "believers" among its three hundred slave residents sang a special spiritual to announce that "General Jesus" was "sending" for them and they therefore had "to go."[112] It was perhaps this unswerving faith in the omnipotence of God and His supreme beneficence that caused some parents to appear so free of grief at the death of their children. When Elizabeth Botume said to a bereaved father, "I am sorry you have lost Rozsa," his only child, "he answered with a broad smile, 'Oh, we mustn't say that . . .' for such thinking would 'fly in the face of Providence.'" This newly freed bondsman added, "The Massa call my leetle gal, an' him mus' go. If him call him, him wanted him, an' us can't say nothing."[113] There were, of course, other reasons for persons still in chains to behave or respond in such ways. Almost all Christians who were slaves believed that they would reunite in Heaven with relatives who had been sold off and separated from them in the sojourn on earth.[114] Once past the pearly gates, servants anticipated both freedom and eternal glorification. Some mothers and fathers must have felt relief of a kind when a child died, for this meant one less human being to experience the horrors of slavery. Such thoughts and divine expectations kept more than a few slaves living to die.

The belief that God was watching over and protecting them also lightened the burdens of many weary laborers. Nothing was guaranteed in bondage, and even "good" behavior did not assure reciprocal treatment. Imagine, therefore, the psychological benefits of being able to sing "No Man Can Hinder Me," despite all sure evidence to the contrary.

Walk in, kind Sa-viour, No man can hinder me!
Walk-in sweet Je-sus, No man can hin-der me!

2. See what won-der Je-sus done,
O no man can hin-der me!
See what won-der Je-sus done,
O no man can hin-der me! O no man,

no man, no man can hin-der me! O no man, no
man, no man can hin-der me!

3. Jesus make de dumb to speak

4. Jesus make de cripple walk

5. Jesus give de blind his sight

6. Jesus do most anything. . . .[115]

Such spirituals not only encouraged the pious, but reinforced
their essential humanity and worthiness in the eyes of God and
each other.[116] But it was the conversion experience that most in-
ured black Christians to the uncertainties and realities of bondage.
It is not too farfetched to argue that the Lord symbolized and
pledged His protection, as well as His guidance, during these
extraordinary journeys. Those being saved almost always underwent both danger and then rescue as the Lord led them to safety
from the Devil or his minions. The parallel here with the escape/
pursuit motif so widespread in African-American folklore is nothing short of astonishing. Whether experiencing visions or day-to-
day worldly encounters, enslaved blacks apparently saw perilous
conflicts in need of immediate resolution. With conversion, devotees were transformed instantaneously from creatures of the
world to children of God.[117] Born-again men and women often
found that they had gained the strength to finish tasks, endure
whippings, remain sane, and survive all of the ravages of thrall-
dom.[118] As one recently freed slave said when recounting the brutal rapes by masters:

If I didn't know Jesus Christ, I go crazy all dese years! . . . Jesus is my
trust. He keep heart right. If I do right, Jesus take me. When he send for
me, if I can on'ly meet him, I satisfied. Distress and hard labor drive me to
Christ. So heart-broken, tired, heart all fall down inside![119]

The woman in the preceding account may have gone mad, but
for more than a century before whites had begun any extensive
proselytizing, black slave mothers, fathers, and children had survived mentally and spiritually intact without Christianity. To
overemphasize the role Christianity played in preventing captive
workers from becoming "Sambos" ignores the cultural and religious riches Africans brought to this land and implies that the
enslaved were on the verge of being totally demoralized when the
ruling class decided to give them *its* religion. There is no evidence

that such a time ever came during the history of North American captivity, for just as the oppressed elsewhere have persevered without internalizing the masks they wore in order to survive, so too did African-Americans live and grow as whole men and women despite the tremendous odds.

To a significant degree, what kept the spirits of slave Christians so high and their resistance repeatedly nonviolent was the vicarious pleasure they derived from knowing that those who called themselves "masters" were morally inferior and would one day suffer interminably at the hands of Him who accepted nothing less than total morality. By identifying with what Albert Raboteau aptly labels the "archetypal 'Suffering Servant,'" slave holy men bore the daily horrors endemic to all systems of forced labor as their Lord had borne His miseries.[120] A woman, born in 1845, whose mother and father had been separated in a sale that removed her mother and her children to Beaufort, recollected that a vision of Jesus brought her comfort:

My mother say she didn't know a soul. All de time she'd be prayin' to de Lord. She'd take us chillum to de woods to pick up firewood, and we'd turn around to see her down on her knees behind a stump, aprayin'. We'd see her wipin' her eyes wid de corner of her apron, first one eye, den de other, as we come along back. Den, back in de house, down on her knees, she'd be aprayin'. One night she say she been down on her knees aprayin' and dat when she got up, she looked out de door and dere she saw comin' down out de elements a man, pure white and shining. He got right before her door, and come and stand right to her feet, and say, "Sarah, Sarah, Sarah!"

"Yes, Sir."

"What is you frettin' bout so?"

"Sir, I'm a stranger here, parted from my husband, with five little chillun and not a morsel of bread."

"You say you're parted from your husband? You're not parted from your husband. You're jest over a little slash of water. Suppose you had to undergo what I had to. I was nailed to the Cross of Mount Calvary. And here I am today. Who do you put your trust in?"

My mother say after dat, everything just flow along, just as easy.[121]

William Grimes was consoled after being chastised for something he had not done by thinking of a statement Christ made "concerning green and dry wood on his way to death on Calvary."[122] Those divine words and the Day of Judgment implied in them not only prevented ill feelings about his master, but made Grimes more compassionate toward his callous owner:

It grieved me very much to be blamed when I was innocent, I knew I had been faithful to him, perfectly so. At this time I was quite serious, and used constantly to pray to my God. I would not lie nor steal. . . . When I considered him accusing me of stealing, when I was so innocent, and had endeavored to make him satisfied by every means in my power, that I was so, but he still persisted in disbelieving me, I then said to myself, if this thing is done in a green tree what must be done in a dry? I forgave my master in my own heart for all this, and prayed to God to forgive him and turn his heart.[123]

Such mental comforts may indeed have functioned as a "technique of survival,"[124] but is not anything that helps one to continue one's existence within the contours of slavery also, inevitably, a mechanism of control? George Rawick points out that "if a community is not strong enough to overcome adversity today," it will be unable "to struggle tomorrow."[125] While survival is essential for resistance, neither musing nor sentimentality can ever exalt life above freedom. How can survival without a strategy for temporal freedom through temporal means produce anything other than further oppression and avoidance of the struggle necessary to end it?

The great significance Christian chattels assigned to their church membership and any appointments therein made it possible for lay and clerical controllers to exploit those sentiments in far-reaching ways. The broad range of "crimes" for which one could be expelled, for instance, prompted some slaves to behave "correctly."[126] Slaves had to receive permission from planters to join the church, to attend services, to be baptized, and to worship among themselves at plantation gatherings. Naturally, masters could withhold these privileges whenever they saw fit.[127] James Henry Hammond recorded the following such manipulation on December 15, 1831: "Refused to allow Ben Shubrick to join the Negro church at Red House, but promised to have him taken in the church at Maslock (the same I attended last Sunday)."[128] On another occasion, he declared:

Religious troubles among the negroes. They are running the thing into the ground by being allowed to much organization—too much power to the head men & too much praying & church meeting on the plantation. Have ordered all church meetings to be broken up except at the church with a white preacher.[129]

Any slave who wished to exhort or preach was especially subject to the dictates of masters, for such honored positions went only to individuals who had proven their characters to whites beyond question.[130] Leah Townsend discovered this citation in an 1804 church book:

> Agreed to attend on the morrow evening at Sister Elizabeth Connell's to hear Brother Titus exercise his gift, at an hours sun . . . [In June Titus was] allowed to sing, pray and exhort in public, and appoint meetings in the vicinity of the church . . . all his acting to be in Subordination to his master, and that his master council him in particular cases as his prudence may dictate.[131]

Just how seriously black worshipers regarded their church affiliations is revealed in the appeals of such parties to receive "letters of dismission" when being transported, as well as in the pleas of the excommunicated to be readmitted.[132] A slave belonging to O. D. Allen "presented himself before the church and confessing freely and frankly the unchristian course he had followed by running away . . . was restored to the church and all its priviledges."[133] In like fashion, Frank, a bondsman excluded two months "for making false statements," declared

> that he had Considered his Case that he had done Rong and seen his Rong that he had Prayed to God to for give him his rong hoped and believed God had for give him and desired the Commity to for give him stated he felt varry bad in his condition like one alone and without friends desired and wished to be in the Church again.[134]

This "recantation" won him "full fellowship." Needless to say, the power that the plantocracy held over the unfree in its churches "had a most salutary effect" on many black worshipers.[135] The interpretation of Christianity some slaves adopted undoubtedly saved not a few whites from injury and possibly death. One such incident, in which a potentially violent and deadly confrontation was precluded by the religious thinking of a slave follower, has been analyzed by Raboteau. He examined the way in which Solomon Bayley responded to a fellow "Methodist class meeting" member "who was attempting to sell" Bayley's "wife and infant daughter."[136] The sufferer proclaimed how difficult it had been initially

to keep up true love and unity between him and me, in the sight of God: this was a cause of wrestling in my mind; but that scripture abode with me "He that loveth father or mother, wife or children more than me, is not worthy of me"; then I saw it became me to hate the sin with all my heart, but still the sinner love; but I should have fainted, if I had not looked to Jesus, the author of my faith.[137]

With characteristic trenchancy, Raboteau notes:

The attitude which Bayley strove to achieve is as old in the Christian tradition as "Father forgive them for they know not what they do" and as recent as Martin Luther King's articulation of "soul force" and "redemptive suffering."[138]

Slaveholders unfortunately knew exactly what they were doing and continued to profit from the brutal severance of African-American kinship ties while servants like Bayley had difficulty simply deciding whether to love the perpetrators of their oppression. To be sure, Bayley held rather exceptional views, but the mere existence of such black holy men indicates that the religious interpretation of some slaves would have prevented the psychological emancipation needed to wage any revolutionary attacks on the ruling class. Although slaves' faith emanated from a very different source than whites' commandments, it merged perfectly with the endemic cautiousness already gnawing away at the slave community, for what could be more circumspect than placing the fulfillment of one's most heartfelt, but potentially deadly desire, in the hands of another? In my own thinking, human actions alone alter human conditions and if that task is assigned to a supernatural being nothing but psychological changes will occur. This is not to say that men and women cannot be motivated to risk their lives in the name of some perceived savior. History shows they can. But, in the case of American slaves, only rarely did their God ignite the tinders necessary to fire a revolutionary pursuit of freedom. Both slaves and masters had made a haven no mortal would destroy.

CHAPTER SIX

Combatants Suppressed, But Not Controlled

The problem of slavery . . . was a question of wits, the slave to escape and the master to keep him from escaping.

Former South Carolina slave[1]

Hatred to the whites, with the exception in some cases of attachment to the person and family of the Master, is universal among the Slave population. We have then a foe cherished in our own bosoms—a foe willing to draw our life-blood whenever the opportunity is offered.

Charleston *Religious Telegraph*[2]

To be free is the all-consuming desire of the unfree. Equally true, nothing is more dominant in the thinking of masters than how to prevent their human property from wanting, craving, and, most important, gaining freedom. So the war between master and slave began, and so it continued until the defeat of the Confederacy's secessionist rebellion severed the chains that bound Southern blacks. Even before the Civil War, American bondsmen tried every conceivable method of obtaining their liberty. And never, as the evidence in South Carolina makes clear, did the vast majority become "submissive and content" or "passive and quiet," as George Rogers claims they had in Georgetown, South Carolina, by the 1840s.[3] Whether the battle was waged on a psychological plane or on some physical terrain, it raged with but shifting levels of intensity. The thirst for freedom controlled the minds, the dreams, and the fantasies of black chattels. It entranced the slaves on one immense Georgia Sea Island estate when a slave prophetess named Sinda spoke of the future. Addressing seven hundred fellow slave workers, whose lives would have resembled closely that of their South Carolina island neighbors, Sinda predicted the ending of the world. Her vision so seized the imaginations of her followers that "they refused to work," and neither pleading nor flogging could prod them to return. The rich "rice and cotton fields" of their master's domain "were threatened with an indefinite fallow."

Frances Anne Kemble, who recounted this affair in 1839, said production resumed only after the assigned date for the day of liberation had passed and after the fearless Sinda had been whipped mercilessly. "Think what a dream that must have been while it lasted for those infinitely oppressed people," Mrs. Kemble wrote, "—freedom without entering it by the grim gate of death, brought down to them at once by the second coming of Christ whose first advent has left them yet so far from it!"[4]

Chimerical journeys were not the prime means through which the unfree sought freedom. Most no doubt explored and many did pursue the possibility of being freed through manumission, desertion, prayer, and revolt. Only a minuscule number were successful; why this was so merits a thorough examination. Manumission had been, at least during the eighteenth and early nineteenth centuries, the surest and least hazardous path to freedom. In 1800, however, as again in 1820 and 1841, legislation limited and then, eventually, made emancipation virtually impossible in all but the most extraordinary cases.[5] Some masters, through legal and extralegal channels, continued nevertheless to free their slaves,[6] a practice that so annoyed a justice hearing an 1844 suit that he declared with much exasperation:

> This is another of those cases, multiplying of late with a fearful rapidity! in which the superstitious weakness of dying men, proceeding from an astonishing ignorance of the solid moral and scriptural foundations upon which the institution of slavery rests, and from a total inattention to the shock which their conduct is calculated to give to the whole frame of our social polity, induces them, in their last moments, to emancipate their slaves, in fraud of the indubitable and declared policy of the State.[7]

In that same year Colonel George Gill of Chester District died and left his slave Andy "under the care of his son, C. S. Gill." Andy not only was "to have as much land as he could cultivate," but also have "no work imposed on him." After three years of this de facto freedom, Andy attempted to make it legal by purchasing himself from his deceased master's son. The son agreed, accepted payment, and petitioned the legislature both to sanction the sale and to allow Andy "to remain in the State." Andy had "been a faithful servant" and was "now quite old." But Andy's dream of real freedom was never realized. The legislature deemed it "inexpedient to Legislate on the subject."[8]

As long as there were open or furtive means of winning freedom, slaves exploited them. Some slaves relentlessly prodded their owners to release them, as did two house servants owned by Langdon Cheves, an aged South Carolina planter. With good reason, his daughter, Louisa S. McCord, became "convinced" that the prospective freed man and woman had been "tormenting" her "Father about it [emancipation] . . . for a long time."[9] In an April 13, 1856, letter to her brother, Langdon Cheves, Jr., she lamented:

Although I wrote to you yesterday, I must, to satisfy Father, do so again today, merely to make a statement to you upon which he insists. I did not mention yesterday, because I hoped then to avoid bothering you with it, that one particular fancy by which Father is constantly beset, is a determination to free June, Cilla and any child or children they may have. This is a constant, daily sometimes hourly, subject of discussion with them and I am called in to promise and see which I have been obliged to do over and over 50 times, in the most solemn manner, to the servants themselves as well as to Father. I hoped this would satisfy him; but he now insists upon calling in a lawyer to draw up papers &c, and has even named that drunken creature Treadwell whose name he has got from the servants.[10]

It is not clear why, but early in December 1856 Louisa McCord had the slave June, evidently Cilla's husband, confined at the Charleston workhouse and was eagerly awaiting word from her brother before she sold him out of state "in such manner as to prevent his return." McCord was terrified: she feared for her "life or that of [her] children."[11] What June did, threatened to do, or perhaps had continued doing to members of McCord's family remain a mystery, but on December 20, McCord wrote her brother, "Father is perfectly quiet and composed. . . . This confirms my previous suspicion that for some reason June kept up the excitement of his mind in order to have his own way with him. Perhaps I am wrong, but unless accounted for in some such way, the change is singularly sudden."[12]

Because slaves knew that the possibility of freedom depended on their correct behavior and that only faithful and "deserving" servants would be so rewarded, the prospect of liberation became an effective mechanism of control in itself. When legislators banned private manumissions in 1820, such gambles for freedom became more costly. The legislature alone now held the prize and nothing short of the most extraordinary acts of fidelity could move it to free black American captives. Slaves discovered that betraying slave conspirators was their best bet. And, however dishonorable exposing plans for *collective* liberation was, some took the chance and, on occasion, won freedom.[13]

Of all the roads traveled for freedom, none were more trodden than the earthen paths that led away from the plantation. From the beginning of servitude in South Carolina in 1670 until its end, countless numbers of slaves sought either temporary or permanent liberty by absconding. Escape to free territory had become increasingly difficult by the nineteenth century, and at that time most runaways remained in the South, hiding everywhere from abandoned mansions to verminous swamps. Familial anchors as well kept unbound slaves to a Southern route, for to many, freedom without beloved kinsmen was a meaningless deliverance, and group desertions were the hardest to achieve. Women encountered special challenges: because they most often held positions that confined them to the plantation, they found it more difficult to explain being away than men whose wider range of occupations and duties generally could justify their travels. Women had far fewer opportunities for successful flight. But no matter which slaves fled—individual or group, female or male—masters seemed unable to grasp why they had been forsaken. They generally knew, however, where those renegades were heading, and ran them down.[14] Masters assumed that the relatives of runaways could get in touch with them and advertised frequently that the deserters were en route to or already "lurking" around distant relations.[15] Langdon Cheves, years before the prodding of June, ended an inquiry about the whereabouts of a slave defector with the question, "Has he a family?"[16]

Whether slaves sought liberty in order to reunite with relatives or simply to delve more deeply into themselves, the perils of self-theft were phenomenal. Escaped slaves faced the fear of recapture, the punishments sure to follow, and the risks of survival in a hostile environment while evading unrelenting manhunters whose savage "nigger dogs" were often only slightly more ferocious than their masters.[17] In an 1864 interview, fugitive Jack Frowers told what happened to him after he was caught in his first escape attempt in May of 1863:

There were sixteen bloodhounds and twelve men after me, as I found out when I got back to Aiken. . . . Just as soon as Master Holley got me home, he set the dogs to worry and bite me, and the scars on my legs and arms are what they did with their teeth. After he got tired of that fun, he took me to a blacksmith, who put a ring around my ankle, bending the ends in when it was red hot. (A large scar is all around the ankle, showing the mark from the burn of the hot iron.) And then a heavy timber chain was wound twice around my waist, and locked. The chain weighed as much as fifty pounds, and was put next to my skin, and I wore both these darbies four weeks, and got a hard flogging every day beside. . . . When he took off the fetters, I was too lame and sick to do anything, and he laughed at me, telling me I had better "try again to go to the _____Yankees."

Ten months later he did, and this time succeeded.[18]

In light of the hardships runaways faced, it is debatable how many of those who returned unshackled really came back "voluntarily." Surely, individuals arriving on plantations with gunshot wounds, frostbite, and signs of starvation cannot be said definitively to have planned on staying out only temporarily. But it does make clear why all who escaped captivity, whether successful or not, gained the reputation as being the most courageous, clever, and troublesome of slaves.[19] One former slave born in 1852 had heard "tell bout" slaves who "would run away en go in de woods en perish to death dere fore dey would come out en take a whippin."[20] Eighty-eight-year-old Amie Lumpkin, who had once been a slave on a Fairfield County plantation, remembered a runaway who planned to keep on going until he could get home to Africa:

I 'member seein' one big black man, who tried to steal a boat ride from Charleston. He stole away one night from Master Mobley's place and got to Charleston, befo' he was caught with. He tell the overseer who questioned him after he was brought back: "Sho' I try to get away from this sort of thing. I was goin' to Massachusetts, and hire out 'till I git 'nough to carry me to my home in Africa."[21]

In an 1828 letter, South Carolina slaveholder John Gabriel Guignard described a slave deserter whom he suspected belonged to his brother. Guignard was unsure because the slave was still at large although he had been sighted by and spoken with several whites, one of whom had even given him "something to eat." According to Guignard on July 30th, the fugitive had "called at Calhoun's Mills on Friday last on horseback—stated that my Brother was very ill & that he was on his way for me." Neither was true and "in a few hours a man came in pursuit of a stolen horse and found him turned loose a short distance from the mill (the same the negro was on) . . ."[22] Two years earlier, a fugitive who "had been shot, but not killed, and had the shot still in him," was captured and placed in a Chester jail. His owner, an Englishman named William Gray, hired a Guy Raines to transfer his chattel to Columbia where the prisoner had broken into a store earlier and "stolen money." During the trip, "the negro turned sullen and refused to go further." Raines said he gave the slave "five hundred lashes" to "make him go along." When this proved unsuccessful, Raines "tied the negro's legs to prevent him from going off until [he] could go and get assistance."[23]

Before Raines found help to force the negro "along," the black man died. Raines was charged with his death and taken into custody. When the State tried Raines, several witnesses were called upon who had seen the slave shortly before he died. They testified that "the negro bled at the nouse [*sic*], mouth and ears, . . . That the negro appeared to have been severely whipped below the small of the back, . . . That several switches and two or three larger ones lay near, which appeared to have been much worn, also a stick with a small end and a larger end, seemed to have been used." For killing this "notorious runaway," the jury convicted Raines of "'manslaughter' but recommended him to mercy."[24]

Whites rarely had mercy for fugitive slaves. This was especially true for incorrigible runaways who despite all warnings, punishments, and threatened sale fled again. What made such recalcitrance so frustrating to planters was their keen awareness that these deserters could not have escaped or survived without the assistance and support of "devoted" slaves at "home" and beyond. When Raines sought reinforcements to assist him with his charge, he stopped at "the first house down the road" and asked two women there to "go back to the negro and prevent any one from cutting him loose."[25] It is unlikely that he was thinking of fellow enslavers or nonslaveholders when he took this precaution. Controllers knew that slave absconders, some eluding would-be captors for years, could expect food, arms, shelter, and more from sedentary slave friends and strangers.[26] Ex-slave Jacob Stroyer recalled how farm slaves would often kill and bury hounds that were chasing runaways through the cotton or corn fields in which the laborers happened to be working. "In general," he added, "the slaves hated bloodhounds, and would kill them at any time they got a chance, but especially on such occasions as above stated [when in pursuit of blacks], to keep them from capturing their fellow negroes, the runaways."[27]

There is some evidence, in South Carolina and elsewhere, that not all bondsmen supported and admired runaways. Records exist of slaves receiving monetary rewards for helping owners to retrieve defectors.[28] Eugene Genovese stresses the coercion behind some blacks' involvement with those who escaped, but he relies almost exclusively on a single source. In his work on slave revolts, *From Rebellion to Revolution,* he refers to "slaves and ex-slaves" who "left an unattractive picture" of runaways as "parasites, thieves, and murderers who plagued the quarters as readily as the Big House," but cites only *The New Man* by ex-slave H. C. Bruce. According to Bruce, in Genovese's words, "slaves often refused to betray organized runaways not because of a sense of solidarity but because of fear of ghastly reprisals."[29] As I have documented throughout this study, the bulk of all primary data in South Carolina reveals that the overwhelming majority of slaves who aided runaways did so willingly, and apparently reveled in what they perceived as a collective assault on the will of masters. Sometimes that revelry raised insurrectionary fears. In 1860 five slaves owned by the Robert Ottis family of Spartanburg were charged with "Attempted Insurrection." Their crime seems to have been more talk than action, but they did dig a cave on their master's property where slave residents from surrounding plantations as well as fugitives from Spartanburg and elsewhere convened to play cards, drink liquor, and talk of freedom.[30]

One visitor, who "first" spoke of the cave while "being whipped in jail," had been fed and harbored by the renegade hosts. He, and other eyewitnesses, compiled an amazing scenario: one cave dweller had a "double-barrelled Pistol," another had "a single barrelled pistol," and Jerry, one of the defendants, had both a "stick with a spear in it" and a "knife like a bowie knife." All "got their cooking done" at a "Mrs. Moores Quarter." Some, for whom the limitations of freedom in a cave were too constricting, envisioned, discussed, and planned a wider liberty. According to court testimony, a band of runaways in Union "were to rise upon the whites at that place about Christmas." And "at the same time" their cave counterparts "under the lead" of an unnamed

white man with whom they had traded "were to rise upon Spartanburg." Perhaps inspired by this talk and the strong belief of
several deserters that "the North was going to set [them] free,"
one fugitive declared that he "was going to get him a revolver and
would be good for six white men." Such talk brought sentences
ranging from thirty to eighty-five lashes, to be "well laid on the
naked hide." Each was to be "blindfolded" throughout his scourging.[31]

It is not likely that the two bondsmen whom traveler J. S. Buckingham observed being conveyed to trial in 1839 would have fared
as well, if convicted. One was suspected of shooting his overseer
"dead"; the other, "belonging to an adjoining estate," of acting
as his "accomplice." When Buckingham asked several whites
about this feared interplantation crime, he learned that it indirectly involved runaways:

> They alleged that the negroes were often in the habit of stealing cattle
> from their masters' plantations, as well as from the neighboring estates and
> their overseer being a vigilant man, had often detected them; so that to
> remove him, and thus carry on their depredations unmolested, they had shot
> him with a rifle. I inquired what they did with the stolen cattle, when they
> escaped detection; and was informed that they killed them in secret for food,
> some using the flesh themselves, others exchanging it with other negroes for
> rice; and some being given to runaway negroes, who were often secretly
> sustained in this manner by their fellow-slaves, till they could get safely out
> of their hiding places, and effect their escape.

Buckingham correctly concluded from this Low Country incident
that "there must be great sympathy among them [blacks] with
their runaway brethren, to incur the risk of death, to supply them
also with the means of subsistence."[32]

Although few scholars have explored the effect that punitive
sales and deportations had on the militancy and political consciousness of slaves, they have debated widely on the impact of
slave deserters and their reasons for desertion.[33] While runaway
advertisements hint at answers, unpublished records and black testimony reveal a great deal more. These data leave little doubt that
the men and women who fled shared one overriding goal—to be
free. And a substantial number were not only self-emancipators,
but peripatetic dissidents. When these fiery renegades banded together, they sometimes "infested" and terrorized entire communities.[34] A slave owned by Williamsburg planter David G. Rodgers

joined forces with such a band and helped them to perpetrate "nefarious Acts in the area." Rodgers described his escapee as a jack-of-all-trades: a boat hand, "prime field hand," sawyer, and "quite handy in the use of Mechanical Tools." In 1819 armed whites shot and killed him as they tried to capture the troublesome group.[35]

A decade later twenty-three residents of Christ Church described at length to legislators an array of runaways who plagued their parish. Several of these male and female fugitives were led by a slave who had escaped bondage in 1822 and been free ever since. Other fugitives traveled in groups but acted alone:

> One of them in January last [1829] snapped a gun heavily loaded with Slugs at one of your Memorialists, who met him in the woods and immediately shot the negro. Another of these three negroes in October last attacked another of your Memorialists with a knife fifteen inches long, stabbed him in the hand, and would have cut his throat, but for assistance rendered in time to save him. In 1828, runaway slaves were collected from various parts of the Parish, one was killed upon the spot, and another severely wounded for the second time and taken, in January last eighteen slaves the property of your Memorialists went off under their driver and of these one fellow has been shot and killed, while the house of the owner has been pillaged by his own Slaves, ten of whom are still out in a neighboring parish. . . . One negro taken some months ago, declared on his trial, that he had in three weeks destroyed Forty head of Cattle, and many of your Memorialists are altogether prevented from keeping Stock of any Kind, from these causes, after having had large gangs of cattle, sheep and hogs destroyed.[36]

Whether together or alone, runaway slaves cost planters dearly in both labor losses and recovery expenses. Masters suffered psychologically as well: slave escapees brought to the fore the fallibility of each mechanism of control. Neither patriarchal promises nor the certainty of punishment had driven slaves to forget about freedom or the social, political, and religious ideas behind their diverse but persistent flights to achieve it. These mental assaults sometimes became physical, for when those who stole themselves declined reenslavement, they usually fought a life-and-death struggle.[37] The widowed wife of a Low Country overseer learned this when her husband Joseph Chandler Brown and his friend William Dunn attempted to stop "a gang" of runaways "who infested that part of the country." The "said negroes" had guns and shot at their assailants: Brown was "killed on the spot" and Dunn, "desperately wounded."[38]

Late in July of 1806, an Edgefield planter, Mason Mosely, encountered a black one Saturday whose behavior suggested he was a runaway. Moseley took no chance and demanded the suspect "strip off his cloathes" in order to see if he was hiding "any offensive weapon." Moseley had a loaded rifle. After examining the man, Moseley directed him toward his house and followed behind him. Despite these prudent measures, Moseley, according to a newspaper account, "unfortunately [and] inadvertently approached too near to the negro, when he suddenly turned round, closed upon Mr. Moseley, and gave him a fatal stab in [the] belly with a knife, which he had [somehow] concealed . . ." Before his attacker departed, he took "with him the rifle loaded with two balls." Moseley was discovered "laying near a road, with a great portion of his bowels protruded through the wound." He survived until Monday afternoon and retained his faculties sufficiently to leave this description of the "negro fellow": he was "about 5 feet 10 or 11 inches high, between 30 and 40 years of age; the thumb of the left hand off—a scar on one of his thighs; and his back was well marked with stripes—he had a short dark coloured cloth coat, blue pantaloons, good sharp toed shoes and a tolerable good hat—he had with him a large bag, the contents unknown, and a good blanket apparently almost new."[39]

John Rose, a white man from Richland district, fared better than Moseley but suffered a loss at the hand of a runaway who carried a razor. The state senate sympathized and rewarded him with five hundred dollars after reviewing his 1831 plea for compensation. As Rose explained:

A runaway slave named George, the property of a Gentleman of Chester District stole two horses, broke open several houses and committed other offences in Richland District for which a warrant was issued against him but it was found impossible to arrest him. He was at length taken in Columbia on the 4 July last but broke from custody. A hue and cry was immediately raised and your petitioner joined in the pursuit and first overtook the fellone where a contest ensued between them in which the slave cut out your petitioner's eye with a razor blade—The fellone has since been tried, convicted and executed.[40]

Some fugitives—when no one was trailing—paid visits to former captors and others, with plans of revenge. In 1852 Mattison and Stephen, two slaves owned, ironically, by a South Carolinian named John Brown, absconded to Georgia. They decided to return, however, because Stephen "did not want to go off and leave his wife" and Mattison "declined to go until he got some revenge." According to Stephen, his companion tried several times to obtain a gun to kill Brown. Although he failed to get his weapon of choice, Mattison was no less deterred from his mission. Stephen followed. At some point after crossing over to South Carolina, a posse, including their master, cornered them in a cave. One threatened to shoot Mattison unless he surrendered; he responded, "Shoot." His master testified that Mattison "swore he would kill or be killed before being taken." The vengeful Mattison ventured out of the cave, but "a short time afterward . . . was crippled from a rifle shot and was standing against a tree with a limb or club in his hand with which he was defending himself from the dogs." Mattison, who had "frequently [been] in the habits of running away," was indeed "a boy of a bad disposition."[41]

In view of the radical courses taken by not a few slave absconders and the frequency of desertions, it is amazing how steadfastly many planters and their hirelings held to the belief that blacks would have to be prodded by some untoward incident in order to leave. One controller wrote to his employer, "About 18 days ago Two of your Negroes Sharper and Stepney absented themselves from the plantation and I have received notice to day that Sharper is in Hamburg Jail—I did not give you notice of this before as I was uncertain whether they had run away or were only absenting themselves from work and *particularly as they had not reason for leaving no fault being found with them or punishment inflicted.*"[42] (Emphasis added.) So widespread were these inexplicable flights that a prestigious member of the Southern medical community, Dr. Samuel A. Cartwright, entered the field. He found that runaways suffered from a disease known as drapetomania, "or the compulsion to run away from home."[43]

Some slaves were "only absenting themselves" from plantation work. But if most deserters were simply disinclined to labor, it would go against the abundant evidence of the extensive toil of South Carolinian slaves during their after-hours. More important, if escapees only wanted a vacation, they would have returned voluntarily or submitted peacefully when cornered. Instead, one finds time and again disenthralled slaves not only fighting desperately to remain free, but evidently choosing death over shackles.[44] Charles, a blacksmith who told prospective owners that he would "live with" them only if they purchased his wife, refused to surrender when he ran away in 1839. His enslaver—armed with a gun—tracked and found him in the gin house of another planter poised "with a knife in one hand and a club in the other." A fight ensued and Charles, who once told a white man that "no one man ever had or ever should master him . . . [that] he worked for people as he pleased . . . [and] that neither white nor black had whipped him by force," was "shot at" and killed.[45] In 1856 slaveholder David Gavin wrote, "Me & Mr. C. Rumph caught my man Team and Col. J. S. Shingler's Cato with his dogs this evening, Cato severely wounded the two best dogs with a knife or dirk & attempted to cut his own throat."[46]

To facilitate the capture of such rebellious slaves and, at the same time, to advance a time-tested ploy to divide and rule, members of the Pineville Association of St. John's and St. Stephens, South Carolina, introduced a remarkable scheme of offering "suitable rewards" for "the apprehension of Runaways, within its limits." It reveals that a number of male slaves must have been armed, with guns, bayonet, or sword:

1st. An assessment of 6½ cents upon each slave shall be levied as often as necessary— 2d For every Male Slave taken with firearms There shall be paid not more than $30 nor less than $10— with Bayonet or Sword, not more than $10 nor less than $5— 3d For every Male Slave unarmed who shall have been out 12 months or longer $10— 4th For Male Slaves shall have been out not less than 6 months & more than one month not exceeding $5 nor less than $2— For all under one month $2 & For all Female slaves the sum of $2 — 5th Any Person giving Information of any encampment of Runaways—So as to lead to their capture shall receive a reward of $10— 6th If convenient Runaways shall be sent to their owner— if otherwise to the jail of the District with a certificate which entitles the captain to 12½ ct. per Mile.[47]

Although one might conclude from this monetary scale that unarmed runaway slaves were less dangerous and offensive, this was not always the case. In an 1858 petition to the legislature seeking compensation, William Boyd said that

on the 17th day of November last, he saw three negro slaves pass near his house in Laurens District whom from their dress and appearance he supposed to be runaways that he in company with others went immediately in pursuit and by aid of dogs were successful in overtaking them after having run them about ten miles that immediately upon their coming up the slaves made battle by throwing stones at them Your petitioner was of opion that they could not arrest them with safety under their desperate resistance and therefore sent for aid when others came they made the attempt without success as the negroes fought desperately and inflicted several wouds upon him and his comrades. That they however continued their pursuit and made several attempts to arrest, being each time driven back by the heavy stones thrown by the slaves several of which took effect upon your petitioner wounding and disabling him seriously. One stone striking him on the right arm fracturing the larger bone of the same just above the wrist[;] under these circumstances your petitioner discontinued his attack but continued to pursue them until a sufficient force arrived to overpower them. That said slaves refused to surrender until a force of about forty five or fifty men arrived—when they were taken.[48]

Members of the slavocracy did everything in their power both to combat the influence of these "fractious" slaves and to reward their disloyalty appropriately. By making life outside the Peculiar Institution as unsavory and hazardous as possible, they reasoned that fewer slaves would flee. Masters thus almost unanimously condoned the deployment of "nigger dogs" and sanctioned the ruthless punishment of the prey their four-legged troops retrieved.[49] Former South Carolina slave Silva Durant told of the chastening one friend received:

I hear Tom Bostick tell 'bout when he run'way one time. Say he use'er run way en hide in de woods aw de time. Den de o'erseer ketch him one time when he been come back en wz grabbin' 'bout de tatoe patch. Say he gwinna make Tom Bostick stay outer de woods ur kill him 'fore sun up dat day. Tom say dey take him down 'side de woods en strip he clothes offen him. (I hear em say dere plenty people bury down 'side dim woods dat der ain' nobody know 'bout). Den he say dey tie him to uh tree en take uh fat light'ud torch en le' de juice drop outer it right on he naked body. He say he holler en he beg en he ax em hab mercy but dat ne'er didn't do no good. He mock how de tar make uh racket when it drop on he skin. Yuh know it gwinna make uh racket. . . . Ain' uh ne'er hear no hot grease sizzle lak?[50]

While fears of excruciating punishments and dread of the hazards of hiding probably deterred many from fleeing, the prospect of being sold—the ultimate mode of correction short of death—undoubtedly was the most powerful deterrent to flight. Charles Manigault, in a letter about his overseer, wrote, "I must say that my gang has never given *him* any trouble. They have the reputation of being very orderly and of giving little trouble. I always made it a rule to sell every runaway and they are fully aware of *this*."[51] (Emphases in the original.) But that awareness was insufficient for some slaves and thereby spurred the ruling class to forced separations.[52] Slaveowner Charles Chesnut must have been pleased to learn in a September 25, 1835, message that "Isaac Carter is at home and working pretty well. . . . I am glad you have authorized me to sell him. He has run away so often that no reliance can be placed in him. While out last time he plundered so as to make himself notorious. The example will be worth much to you."[53]

To be sure, memories of such examples made many slaves behave, but those recollections must have also stirred images of individuals whose yearning for freedom could not be quenched by threats, lashings, or even by the pleas of loved ones. And, generations later, that spirit was still cherished by those held yet against their wills. Thus, twentieth-century black Carolinians in the folk ballad "An Escaped Convict" reaffirmed:

> Nothin' but a convict
> Loosed from de chains,
> Wid shackles left behind me,
> Wid shackle scars upon me,
> Wid a whip an' a chain
> Waitin' ef dey ketch me,
> Wid bloodhounds an' bullits
> On my trail,
> An' de dangers er de swamp
> In front er me.
> I'll take my chance, brother,
> I'll take my chance.
>
> De rattlesnake an' moccasin,
> De mud an' de briar,
> An' de pizen vine ain' nothin'
> To de danger
> Dat is left behind me.
> Dare is striped clothes
> An' double shackles
> An' a rawhide whip
> All behind me
> So I'll take my chance brother,
> I'll take my chance.
>
> I know dere's a hard, hard road
> Behind me,
> An' dere ain' no road in front;

Dat de mud is heavy,
An' dere ain' much food
To separate my backbone
From my belly.
For I ain' nothin' but a convict,
Wid de scars to prove it.
I'll take my chance, brother,
I'll take my chance.[54]

The chance of freedom preoccupied the collective mind of African-American bondsmen. Although these men and women varied on how best to achieve liberation, they were sure its day would come. Until that jubilee, some found strength in an African past, others in a Christian present, and many in the power and exertions of themselves alone. Black Christians believed sincerely that if they placed all their faith in God, the Almighty, *He* would free them. Some even concluded that prayers alone would bring freedom through divine intervention. These outlooks were developed, or perhaps simply nurtured, by both white and black religious leaders. But slaves referred not only to a deliverance after death, but to one here on earth. Slave preachers helped stifle any such revolutionary potential among the faithful by instilling in them a sense of helplessness and dependence on their ever-guiding Father. This essentially capitulatory view was nowhere better articulated than in a sermon by a slave preacher entitled "Wy Christun Compa To Sheep." That document merits extensive quotation:

Sheep is a po ting to fend demself. Goat kin fight, but sheep can't. Dem's a po weak, helpless ting, an de same wid de Christun. If e inemy tell lie punun, e can't tell lie pun e inemy; if e inemy cuss um e can't cuss e inemy; ef e inemy hut um an do ebil to um e can't hut an do ebil to e inemy; ef e inemy try fur stroy a good name, e can't stroy e inemy good name, fur mebbe e ent hab good name fur stroy. fur ef e try to do to e inemy all e inemy do to him, dat ent like sheep, but mo like goat—a berry fightin ting. An kase de Christun like sheep, berry peaceabul an can't fend demself, dem inemy like sheep-killing dog. pose pun dem an tek de ekwantig ob dem.

An dem buckra dat beat dem nigger onjestly an onmusefully, jes kase de po nigger cant help e self, dems de meanest buckra ob all, an berry much like de sheep-killin dog dat cowud to take sumpn dat cant help e self. Dat berry ting dat de nigger cant fend e self an helpless, mek de gentleman buckra berry pashunt an slow to punish dem nigger. An de berry fack dat de Lawd sheep is po helpless ting, mek de Lawd pity an lub we do mo, an mek we pen pun Him an cry fur Him in de time ob trouble and danejur. An dat wha de Lawd want, fur we feel we own weakness an trust in Him strenk.

De mudder lub de morest de chils dats de weakest an dat need um de morest, and so wid de Sabeyur an e lettle wuns dat pend *only* pun Him.[55] (Emphasis added.)

Some slaves transcended that dependence and asked the Lord only to oversee their own efforts at casting off the shackles mere mortals had attached. They chose the option of armed struggle for freedom. Nor did they look kindly on the white clergymen who failed to note this form of earthly deliverance. "Heathen" slaves needed no biblical justification of the correctness and sanctity of the violent pursuit of freedom.

At no time in the history of South Carolina were the radical potential of Christianity or the dangers of disbelief in sharper focus than during the Denmark Vesey scare of 1822. Just one year before, the nationalistic and antislavery sentiments of free black and slave Methodists had culminated in the erection of an "African Church" on the outskirts of Charleston. Following the lead of the African Methodist Episcopal Church in Philadelphia, oppressed blacks rejected the racism that pervaded their white brethren's church. And certain faithful Carolinians chose to do more. There is evidence that some deacons in the African Church joined the conspiracy for freedom on earth. Vesey had cast his net wide. Just as he found recruitment material in Congressional debates, so he used the Bible itself as an abolitionist tool. His favorite passages were those that sanctioned the slaughter of masters. Joshua, Chapter 4, verse 21, was a favorite: "And they utterly destroyed all that was in the city, both man and woman, young and old, and ox, and sheep, and ass, with the edge of the sword."[56]

Black Christians may not have accepted Vesey's polygamous marriage to several slave women,[57] but many were inspired by his message on freedom. In 1800 while still enslaved, Vesey had taken a chance in a lottery, won, and bought his freedom. But, as one slave reported, "Vesey said the negroes were living such an abominable life, they ought to rise." In his fifties, Vesey set out to help them as well as his own wives and children, who were still unfree.[58]

The plan was a good one. Vesey recruited a disciplined African and Creole leadership whose slave forces were said to number in the thousands. These city and country slaves were scheduled, on July 14, 1822, to mount surprise attacks on the homes, stores, and arsenals of whites in order to procure a more lethal and plentiful supply of weapons. One recruit had a key to the largest suburban storehouse for government arms on the outskirts of Charleston. Vesey was the only nonslave conspirator. His was a pan-African perspective and cadre: his fellow leaders included "Monday Gell, an Ibo; Mingo Harth, a Mandingo; and Gullah Jack, an Angolan."[59] Slaves from numerous occupational groups joined the plot. There were skilled artisans, field hands, and even the purportedly treacherous house servants, whom one rebel leader warned others to avoid. Some refused his advice; they had discovered "pampered" domestics who were willing to poison their masters' wells.[60]

Historian William Freehling, who has laid to rest any misreadings of the evidence that suggest the conspiracy was neither real nor terrifying to whites, offers these insights about the scare and the house servants who contributed to it:

> As the story spilled out to the community, the Domestic Institution seemed shattered. . . . Uncoerced "Sambos," supposedly consenting to patriarchal direction because of "affection and gratitude," were unmasked as anti-"Sambos" ready to coerce their families. Time after horrifying time, those accused had been trusted serviles. . . . When constables came to arrest Harry's coachman, the master "assured them they were mistaken. He could answer for [the man's] innocence. He would as soon subject himself." After hearing the evidence, Harry turned to his coachman. "Are you guilty?" he asked incredulously. "Yes." "What were your intentions?" The coachman, rage on a face where Harry had seen only smiles, whirled on his patriarch. He said that he sought "to kill you, rip open your belly, and throw your guts in your face."[61]

Each white nightmare, save a successful revolt, converged: slave Christians joining with pagans; Africans with Creoles; and field slaves with house slaves. There was even evidence that four whites —all poor—sympathized with and encouraged this union for freedom. One, a Scot named William Allen, was sentenced to twelve months' imprisonment and a one-thousand-dollar fine. Extremely poor, he probably would have remained in jail until his death, for he was too destitute to pay either the fine or the "security for his good behavior" if released. The court was no doubt harshest to this white because of a statement he made to blacks who had "objected" to his participation. They argued that "being a white man, [he] could not be safely trusted by them." In his defense, Allen responded, "though he had a white face, he was a negro in heart."[62]

Freedom for the conspirators was not to be. Peter Devany, a trusted family servant, earned his title and betrayed the black majority. Shrewder masters would not have been completely pleased with this faithful slave, for instead of going first to his master and disclosing the plot, he sought counsel from a free black skilled laborer named William Pencil. One wonders what would have happened if Pencil had persuaded Peter to join the rising, or, failing to do so, had killed him. Vesey and others had pledged death to all informants. Pencil, instead, advised a trip to his master, and Devany followed.[63] So, too, did arrests and tortures. The Intendant (mayor) of Charleston, James Hamilton, Jr., understood exactly what to do. Blacks, he wrote, had to learn that "there is nothing they are bad enough to do, that we are not powerful enough to punish."[64] Just how able and determined they were is suggested in Governor Thomas Bennett's admission that "no means which experience or ingenuity could devise were left unessayed, to eviscerate the plot."[65] A century and a half of practice made them at least as ingenious as our own century's Nazi SS.

When a co-conspirator was being tortured, Peter Poyas, a rebel leader nearby, urged him to "die like a man." Poyas followed his own advice and shouted to oppressed blacks who had been assembled to witness his execution, "Do not open your lips; die silent, as you shall see me do!"[66] Vesey joined him. The fate of the informants is not clear, but at least three lived more comfortably than they had before their betrayals. Both Peter Devany and George Wilson, a class leader in the African Church who provided invaluable service as a spy, were freed by the legislature and given pensions for life. William Pencil was rewarded with one thousand dollars and exempted from taxes.[67]

Although the conspiracy failed, Sterling Stuckey in 1966 wrote, "Vesey's example must be regarded as one of the most courageous ever to threaten the racist foundation of America. In him the anguish of Negro people welled up in nearly perfect measure. He stands today, as he stood yesterday . . . as an awesome projection of the possibilities for militant action on the part of a people who have—for centuries—been made to bow down in fear."[68] It is no small irony that more than two decades after Stuckey's statement, black composer Walter Robinson at Harvard's W. E. B. DuBois Institute for Afro-American Research had just completed and was beginning to stage his 1988 opera, *Look What a Wonder Jesus Has Done*. It is about the life of Denmark Vesey.[69]

In a new preface in 1969 to his 1943 seminal masterpiece, *American Negro Slave Revolts*, Herbert Aptheker said:

> The highest form of protest was rebellion or conspiracy to rebel. This is collective; it involves an all-out commitment with death the sure price for failure and with success not likely. Its development and, especially, its fruition, require enormous care, effort and dedication. It is important to bear in mind; I mean the fact that rebellion and conspiracy to rebel reflect the highest forms of protest. Hence, when this form is present one may properly conclude that it reflects deep and widespread unrest; the insurrection or the plot was, as it were, the flash of lightning, that told of the profounder atmospheric disturbance creating it.[70]

Considerable controversy has surrounded this work. According to Aptheker, novelist William Styron, whose fictional *The Confessions of Nat Turner* struck a deep and lethal vein in the American popular mind, dismissed his study as "beneath serious contemplation."[71] On the twentieth anniversary of *Slave Revolts*, Styron previewed much of his later *Confessions* in a review appropriately titled "Overcome." After attacking the recent "extremist revisionism" in North American slave historiography, Styron classified Aptheker with "those latter-day zealots who demean the Negro's humanity by saddling him with mythical powers of eroticism or other attributes he neither wants nor needs." To Styron, the often "childish" and "irresponsible" behavior of plantation slaves was "no significant commentary upon the character of the Negro but tribute rather to a capitalist super-machine which swiftly managed to cow and humble an entire people with a ruthless efficiency." With the exception of Nat Turner, "the many millions of other slaves, reduced to the status of children, illiterate, tranquillized, totally defenseless, ciphers and ants, could only accept their existence or be damned, and be damned anyway." These "observably docile" African-Americans, says Styron, were "incapable of real resistance."[72] Such views of passive blacks have consoled many throughout history. Racist historiography and historical fiction have added much to that comfort. Both seem also to explain the heated nature and duration of certain debates about the character—past and present—of African-Americans and their history and, especially, about slave rebels, conspiracies, and rebellions.

Writing about Virginian slaves, historian Philip Schwarz makes this observation: "There is a connection between slave insurrections and slaves' often mortal attacks on whites, which historians of slavery, who have focused mainly on the most famous and large slave insurrections, have largely ignored. To those whites who feared slave resistance, any killing or attempted killing of a white authority by a slave looked a little like an insurrection in miniature."[73] Such an insight is of particular importance to South Carolina, where a significant number, if not the majority, of all slave murders of planters were committed by two or more of the victim's slaves. Equally germane is the reality that violent group and interplantation attacks on slaveowners and those in their employ were endemic in South Carolina. The 1824 experience of a Mr. Dawsey reveals graphically how easily one could read insurrection into a collective assault. While serving as overseer for Charles Pinckney, an absentee planter residing in Charleston, Dawsey demanded that the slaves in his charge fence their hogs. Not only did they refuse to do so, they burned the fence he had erected. In retaliation, Dawsey shot two hogs, causing an uproar among the slaves. One bondsman became so outraged that he swore to send Dawsey "to hell" and "be goddamned" if he did not kill him. When Dawsey ordered the driver to restrain him, the driver refused. Not even a bullet stopped the attacking slave.[74]

Although the slave eventually fell, his fellow slaves continued the assault—this time with the gun Dawsey had lost before fleeing to his home.[75] Those in pursuit attempted forcibly to enter, and two, who had reloaded, smashed his windows and "dared him to sho him self" so they could "blo his branes out."[76] It is not surprising that a contemporary writing to Pinckney about this event described it as "nothing less than a fine rebellion."[77]

In this study, the criteria I have used for an insurrection or a conspiracy to effect one are: one, an interplantation conspiracy which had the avowed objective of freeing the people; two, trials held verifying the goal and extensiveness of the proposed or actual uprising; three, executions of at least some of the accused; and four, expenditures incurred by the courts and militia, not only in preventing or suppressing the insurgency but in "correcting" the guilty parties.

Viewed under such guidelines, no revolutionary pursuit of liberty went the distance in nineteenth-century South Carolina. None went beyond mental blueprints. Plans for revolt were drawn in 1816,[78] 1822,[79] and 1829,[80] and, although there is no conclusive, only suggestive, evidence, three other uprisings—in 1805, 1810, and 1831—seem to have been scheduled also.[81] Planters often tried to blot out news of insurrectionary designs,[82] and it seems reasonable to assume that they occasionally may have been successful, and that, therefore, other conspiracies or revolts may have been erased from the historical record.

Excluding the 1805 conspiracy, for which there is inadequate information, each of the plots we know about failed because they had been betrayed by individuals from within the slave ranks. Two years before Nat Turner's 1831 Virginia rebellion, a far-reaching conspiracy was arrested in Georgetown, South Carolina. Despite the suppression of all news about the 1829 plot in the Palmetto State press that year, a contemporary who lived in a town "neighboring" Georgetown revealed some details to writers for the New Haven *Advertiser*. On August 28, 1829, The New York *Evening Post* reprinted an excerpt from the article that appeared in the Connecticut paper:

A dangerous conspiracy was formed among the blacks at Georgetown . . . to massacre the whites. The plan was matured in all its details, and the time fixed for its execution with such secrecy, that no doubts can be entertained of its certain and terrible success, had not one of the conspirators proved faint of heart, and betrayed the enterprise. . . . About 20 of the ring leaders have been arrested, the residue of the slaves disarmed, and a very active and vigilant police system adopted to disconcert any further measures the slaves may attempt.[83]

Some idea of how many slaves were taken up and put on trial is revealed in a letter from South Carolina attorney-general James Petigru to General Joseph W. Allston, a magistrate in Georgetown. Allston apparently had written to Petigru and asked for assistance. In his April 17, 1829, response, the attorney-general said he was "sorry" that Allston's "labors [were] so arduous," but expressed this concern: "I am afraid you will hang half the country. You must take care and save enough for the rice crop. It is to be confessed that your proceedings have not been bloody as yet, but the length of the investigation alarms us with apprehension that you will be obliged to punish a great many."[84] What happened is not clear but on December 3, 1830, Governor Stephen D. Miller appealed to the state House of Representatives for "a guard in Georgetown." The legislature appropriated five thousand dollars.[85]

Whites in Union district were perhaps spared a fateful meeting with the enslaved by an early morning betrayal from a slave. The only records of this fall 1831 conspiracy are a "Report of Committee on Claims" that compensated an Abbeville master for the execution of his slave who had been "implicated in the late attempt to raise an insurrection"[86] and a badly torn letter from a Rosannah Rogers in Union. Rogers wrote her son about the "considerable alarm . . . in this State and in this Neighborhood" on October 29, 1831:

> One of James Hills negroes confessed to his master on tuesday morning the fourth of October that the negroes intended rising that night and every one intended Killing their own white family. The news soon spread but we did [tear] it until late in the evening which frightened us so much . . . that [tear] went to Maybinton that night where there was a great many collected [tear] . . . guarded by some of the men while the rest were riding patrole. . . . There was a great many negroes taken up here and tried but did not do any thing with them. We have heard there were some hung in Abbeville and about Cambridge. It is evident that they intended to make an attempt for all that confessed acknowledged it was to have taken place on the fourth of October.[87]

Whenever the issue of slave revolts is addressed, scholars have tended to consider the South as a whole, every antebellum state, community, and locale combined. They speculate often on why *all* revolts would have failed—usually on military grounds, alone. But the South was not a monolithic whole with common demographic, topographic, and, hence, logistical conditions that were everywhere the same. That reality becomes strikingly clear when one ponders the questions that prospective rebels, in all probability, would have considered. Few individuals anywhere, for example, would have thought it possible to defeat initially either the plantocracy and its supporters throughout the vast South or even throughout their particular state. Most would have contemplated first simply securing their own immediate locations and then speculated on the possibilities to expand. Thus, the question foremost in their minds must have been, "Can we eliminate the enemies occupying the proposed area of attack and then protect that territory?" The answer would have varied in different states, and within certain enclaves within each. In the South Carolina upcountry, for example, captive workers probably would have responded negatively, for they were outnumbered significantly by bellicose whites. Those in the Low Country, however, might well have replied with an emphatic "yes," for their numerical superiority awed even intrepid controllers.[88] It was this predominance, undoubtedly, that led key leaders in the projected 1822 uprising to estimate confidently that the rival "population in Georgetown could be killed in one half hour."[89]

How one weighs such demographic and strategic approximations depends on the unique characteristics of each state. If, for example, communication had been rapid and fluid between slaves in the upper and lower parts of South Carolina, some in the upcountry may have envisioned that aid would be forthcoming and, hence, anticipated an edging of the balance in their favor, for from a statewide perspective the slaves did constitute a decisive majority. It is also likely that rural and urban slaves would have considered each other's strength and commitment. Edward Hooker, a Northerner who relocated to Columbia, kept almost an hourly account of a December 19, 1805, plot in which such factors played a role:

> The town is in considerable alarm this afternoon. . . . A scheme of insurrection has been formed among the negroes on the other side of the river, a few miles above this place, in conjunction with a party below. Their plan is said to be to assault Granby and then come up and burn Columbia; first taking possession of the arms and ammunition deposited in the State House.
>
> The alarm is increasing, and yet nobody seems to know the true state of the case. . . .
>
> One negro who is suspected of being active in the plot has been committed to jail . . . the patroles have orders from the Gov. to take up every one seen out. One poor fellow, it is said, has just been shot dead by the patroles at the north end of the town, and several have been taken up. The town negroes are all in dreadful consternation about the event fearing I suppose that they shall perhaps be butchered by one party or the other in case their country brethren make the attempt.[90]

During the proposed Camden 1816 rebellion, as well as that of Charleston six years later, help was expected from the surrounding areas where slaves were more heavily concentrated. Rebels in Camden planned to invite their country brethren to town under a variety of pretenses on the appointed date of the uprising. A slave's access to or proximity to unsuspecting whites was important, because small numbers critically placed could strike decisively in any insurrection. Reflective planters were therefore justifiably horrified by news of house servants' involvement in each plot, for when they accompanied masters to urban manors, they usually lived in quarters that stood but a few feet from the masters' dwellings and wells. These circumstances, and the fact that, at certain times every year, Low Country planters fled their estates for more salubrious climes, made a number of crucial centers particularly vulnerable to slave attack.[91]

Freehling is again instructive about these urban household threats and why masters in Charleston, after the Vesey conspiracy, could not write publicly of them:

There it was, in thirty four unpublishable words [a conspirator revealed that Gullah Jack was going to give him "a bottle with poison to put into my master's pump and into as many pumps as he could about town and he said he could give other bottles to those he could trust to"[92]], the peculiar nightmare of these peculiar masters. The court censored nothing about ambushes on arsenals. But a single domestic sneaking poison into a domesticity's water was too petrifying to broadcast. . . . A town could guard against surprise attack on arsenals. A modern army guarding modern firepower could crush several dozen slaves armed with pikes. . . . But the individual household assassin hiding behind an accommodationist's mask was invulnerable to Denmark Vesey's collective vulnerabilities. The solitary servile slipping something into the water need not worry about whether pikes could conquer guns. He need have no concern about wide-awake troops outside the slumbering house. And when "his" white family started dying like flies, he would be all weepy solicitude, full of wonder about what strange sickness ailed the master's house.[93]

Because revolutionary slave leaders, as an abundance of sources document, were hardly wide-eyed fanatics, it is reasonable to assume that they gave serious thought to the possibility of failure and to the best course to take in that event. Here again, what they concluded would have reflected the diverse settings in which they struggled. Nat Turner, for instance, whose revolt often has been dubbed the bloodiest—perhaps because whites *too* were killed—

planned on retreating to the great Dismal Swamp that spanned portions of North Carolina as well as his own Virginia.[94] And in the coastal city of Charleston, Vesey, in 1822, accompanying fellow rebels, considered either withdrawing to the woods and doing "all the harm they could" or escaping to Haiti where an earlier fighter had helped gain freedom for its own least privileged people.[95] Surely others, before and after Vesey, must have also contemplated the uses to which the profuse swamps of South Carolina could be put if an assault ended in defeat.[96] Some idea of why and how can be gathered in an 1863 dispatch about some armed runaways:

After several days hunting in the upper portion of Prince Williams Parish without success I on sunday the 25th of Jany moved over into St. Peters Parish. On monday I commenced hunting down Cosawhatchie Swamp, during the afternoon the dogs struck a warm trail which we followed about one mile into the swamp through water and bog sometimes swimming and sometimes bog down when the dogs trailed a negro boy; belonging to the Est. of Harry Youmans, who has been out since August last. [T]he said boy stated that there was two others with him that day and four at the camp seven or eight miles below—all armed with guns and pistols. I started the dogs again in pursuit, followed about six miles when I came to where the negroes had taken to a boat—night prevented further pursuit for that day— next day I took the boy [and] caught a pilot down to the camp but all the negroes had left in a large batteau. I then had to build a raft to follow them; the swamp becoming too boggy for the horses to travel and the water too deep for the men to wade. On the 29th I found the batteau several miles below but the dogs could not take the trail. I have been hunting ever since but without success so far. On the 1st of Feby a gentleman from St. Luke's Parish who lives on the Swamp came to this camp and reported that the day before some runaways had broken into a house in his neighborhood and stole all the ammunition and some provisions—I believe it is a part of the same gang that I have routed.[97]

Although slaves throughout the South may have reached the conclusion, as many believe, that there was "zero chance" of any successful revolt,[98] their reasons could, and often did, vary both subtly and profoundly with their environment. Much evidence suggests, for example, that many more bondsmen possessed and were familiar with handling guns—especially in South Carolina— than has previously been assumed. Moreover, foiled insurrectionists in that state admitted to plans to obtain arms from the homes of masters or ambushed garrisons they believed their formidable numbers could easily match. It is significant also that one of the 1816 plotters had been engaged as a servant by the militia and hence was privy to at least some lessons of war.[99] Obviously, inadequate training and munitions were major obstacles facing blacks, but other considerations posed equally impeding, if not more arresting, barriers to those calling for freedom *now*.

Given the staunch cautiousness that generations of experience had infused in slaves, most risked participation only in endeavors they felt would be successful; this usually did not include insurrection, which historically had brought early and sudden death.[100] This realistic knowledge, and a religion that fed the belief that *God* would free them, narrowed considerably the field of possible revolutionists. But, taking no chances, the ruling class made the fate of those implicated in aborted rebellions as horrible and as memorable as possible.[101] Following disclosure of the Vesey conspiracy, thirty-six blacks were executed—twenty-two hanged on the same gallows with dramatically precise timing. The hundreds of slave spectators witnessed "the unfortunate wretches" being flung to their deaths "at one fatal moment."[102] To emphasize further the gravity of incendiary acts or aspirations no one was permitted to wear black in mourning, a cruel denial to a people who valued funeral rites and respects so highly.[103] It was not softened by reports that the bodies were "to be delivered to the surgeons for dissection, if requested."[104]

An earlier magistrate who presided over the hearings of insurrectionists in Camden decided to bring a condemned man close to death so all could see the awesome power in the hands of whites. He ordered an insurgent to be hanged, but after the victim watched fellow rebels executed and after he was put in place on the scaffold, his sentence was commuted.[105] That psychological torture must have left a permanent mark not only on him, but on those who saw him then and later, for ever thereafter his story personified the danger of revolt. "Rashness" was no doubt moderated by those whose convicted kin were spared the noose but slipped out through deportation "beyond the limits of the United States."[106] But whether one personally had relations sold or hanged was irrelevant: all felt the greater severity in punishment and treatment that immediately followed every insurrectionary scare. One apparent victim of that backlash was a runaway who, while out

in late July of 1816, "attacked and wounded a white man." Tried
at the Kershaw County District Court in Camden, he "(and other
Negroes like him)" were warned of the recent executions in that
community. Abraham, the slave defector, then received a sentence
of imprisonment, after which he was to "be branded publically
on each cheek and forehead with letter *V* in large letters and
further have one half of each ear cut off beginning at top and
cutting to the bottom."[107]

Terror and repressive shock waves were not the only factors
nurturing slave caution: once again the family swung its weight
to the right by bolstering the stability of the ruling class. Indeed,
just as familial attachments kept many bondsmen from deserting,
or at least not going far, so they also precluded a large number
from doing anything that might jeopardize those intimately drawn
ties.[108] Parents, for example, played the leading role in providing
adequate food for their children and therefore would have been
wary of acts that could permanently "remove" them. Sons and
daughters, on the other hand, knew that elders generally were held
responsible for the behavior of their offspring—no matter how
many years those "boys" and "girls" had lived in adulthood. Harriott Pickney, for instance, wrote in 1855:

> Pray tell Sambo that I received the Palmetto and will send him some
> coffee and sugar the next trip by old Beck . . . tell him he dont deserve that
> I should send him the coffee and sugar because he brought up his Sons so
> badly. Tell him that John is still in the woods and that it was a year last
> Christmas since he went. David came in at Christmas and behaved very ill
> directly after.[109]

The Reverend Richard Furman warned, following the actions
taken to "correct" the misdeeds of Vesey, that "in many instances" those who sacrifice themselves for futile causes "pull
down on the heads of the innocent as well as the guilty, an un-
distinguishing ruin."[110] There was always the danger of indiscriminate vengeance, as Thomas Higginson said of the Charleston
conspirators: "They took no woman into counsel,—not from any
distrust apparently, but in order that their children might not be
left uncared-for in case of defeat and destruction."[111]

With this concern in mind, the heavy concentration of Africans
in eighteenth-century and, to a lesser degree, nineteenth-century
South Carolinian plots or rebellions takes on new meaning, for it

is highly unlikely that the attachments which so often restrained Creole slaves had been consummated by recent imports.[112] This does not, of course, belittle the radical effect that "shock and detachment" undoubtedly had on many "raw" arrivals. It simply adds another factor that may have enhanced a greater willingness on the part of Africans to risk all for freedom. Clearly, in their eyes they had nothing to lose but themselves. Some support for this view is found in the gender and age of most runaways throughout the Old South; typically, they were young males, between sixteen and thirty-five years old. A significant percentage were probably free of the stabilizing marital and parental bonds that sober restless spirits everywhere. For whatever reasons, these and others, native Africans were identified closely with contumacious attitudes and vehement antiservile behavior.[113] A traveler visiting a friend near Georgetown in 1810 recorded:

> Our lodging here was rendered unpleasant by the alarming intelligence of a plot which had that morning been discovered by a mulatto boy, who declared that he had more than once heard a collection of negroes (principally Africans) debating on the best mode for carrying a plan of insurrection into execution against the white Inhabitants residing on great Pedee, of which Lynch's Creek is a Branch. They had however concerted their scheme in so clumsy a manner and with so little secrecy that the coloured boy who had as little mercy to expect from them as the white, was able to detect and reveal it. This disclosure supported by other evidence, led to the seizure of the Ring Leaders, some of whom I afterwards learned were punished in a very summary way.[114]

As the above account hints at and data from the eighteenth century confirms, there was a revolutionary tradition among South Carolinian slaves. Another legacy, however, countered this rebelliousness: the persistent record of betrayals from within the slave quarters.[115] African-Americans maintained remarkable unity in the face of whites, but a small group of collaborators broke into that unity. Whether for money, liberty, or simply their lives, certain bondsmen not only revealed the names of slave "culprits," but on occasion helped capture rebels, runaways, thieves, or killers.[116] In June of 1822, the "neighbourhood of Georgetown was infested by a gang of lawless & desperate runaways." One defector killed George R. Ford, a local slaveowner. His slaves Jack and Tom pursued the killer "at every hazzard and arrested" him. The "murderer" was then "taken, brought to trial and executed."

Years later the Intendant and the Town Council of Georgetown appealed to the legislature to reward the "two negro men." It is interesting that neither was ever referred to as a "boy," "slave," or "fellow," although both were still in bondage. In the minds of many whites, collaboration was perhaps the prerequisite for slave males to earn the title of men. Tom and Jack received fifty dollars each.[117]

For some slaves, personal loyalty to their owners was so deep that they needed no incentive to sacrifice fellow blacks in order to preserve their masters' and mistresses' well-being and safety. Scipio, a privileged domestic who appears to have been the body servant of his master, Colonel James Chesnut, warned him of the impending Camden uprising. His good faith was rewarded with freedom, but Scipio never left: he personified the paternalistic ideal. Whether he remained as a paid servant is unclear, but his love of the Chesnuts is beyond question.[118] The small minority of slaves who consummated paternalistic bonds came almost exclusively from the top of the domestic hierarchy. They were the mammies, butlers, and body servants. The nature and consequences of paternalism for slave men are discussed at length by historian Kenneth Stampp:

> This kind of paternalism . . . which often arose from the master's genuine love for his slave, gave its recipient privileges and comforts but made him into something less than a man. The most generous master, so long as he was determined to *be* a master, could be paternal only toward a fawning dependent; for slavery, by its nature, could never be a relationship between equals. Ideally it was the relationship of parent and child. The slave who had most completely lost his manhood, who had lost confidence in himself, who stood before his master with hat in hand, head slightly bent, was the one best suited to receive the favors and affection of a patriarch. The system was in its essence a process of infantilization—and the master used the most perfect products of the system to prove that Negroes were a childlike race, needing guidance and protection but inviting paternal love as well.[119]

Slaves like Scipio surely would have qualified.

In 1838 the Reverend Richard Johnson petitioned the legislature on behalf of another trustworthy bondsman. He had killed a fellow black who was attacking his owner's property. As Reverend Johnson wrote,

> He was the owner of a Negro man named Jim whom he considered of much value on account of his fidelity and usefulness and the general cor-

rectness of his deportment. That on the 19th of August last, the said Negro man was arrested under a warrant from the magistrate of the Parish in which your Petitioner resides on a charge of murder said to have been committed on the body of another negro of your Petitioner, who was in the act of committing depredations on the property of your Petitioner, which had been placed under the charge of the said negro man Jim.[120]

Nothing was probably more influential in preventing South Carolinian slaves from revolutionary activity than the fear of betrayals. The arms advantage of whites might be matched in the Low Country by the numerical superiority of blacks, but nothing could overcome the danger of loose tongues. One insurgent questioned during investigation of the 1816 plot admitted that he had told those who attempted to recruit him, "I thought it would be a good scheme if they could get through with it but that Negroes were so deceitful that it would not do. [Others] said the same."[121] Colonel Thomas Higginson, who risked his life with former slaves throughout the Civil War and was taken into their confidence, wrote later:

> I often asked myself why it was that with this capacity of daring and endurance, they had not kept the land in a perpetual flame of insurrection; why, especially since the opening of the war, they had kept so still. The answer was to be found in the peculiar temperament of the races, in their religious faith, and in the habit of patience that centuries had fortified. The shrewder men all said substantially the same thing. What was the use of insurrection, where everything was against them? They had no knowledge, no money, no arms, no drill, no organization, —above all, no mutual confidence. It was a tradition among them that all insurrections were always betrayed by somebody.[122]

Robert Smalls, the Civil War hero who eventually pursued an illustrious political career,[123] told Northern allies in answers to their questioning:

> Q. Do you think the colored people are anxious for their liberty, and if opportunity offered would help themselves to it? A. I do, sir; the people in Charleston—the house servants— would steal arms for themselves now if they could. They are all ready if they could trust each other. In Charleston I belonged to seven societies although the laws of South Carolina say that no more than four colored men shall meet together unless a white man is with them. These societies are for charitable purposes— to help one another in sickness and distress. Q. Were there any societies among the colored people for discussing the questions of freedom? A. No, sir; they used to talk about these things at the meetings of the charitable societies to some extent;

but they were afraid to trust each other fully. On the plantations I do not think there are any secret societies except the Church societies and they do not introduce that subject there. They pray constantly for the "day of their deliverance." Q. Did they allow their masters to hear them pray in that way? A. Oh! yes sir; the masters did not think anything would come of it.[124]

Broken links in the chain of black unity made the battle odds overwhelming. Nor did the masters or their church leaders allow the slaves to forget it. In his *Exposition of the Views of the Baptists, Relative to the Coloured Population,* the influential Reverend Dr. Richard Furman offered the governor of South Carolina some comforting thoughts and advice on Christmas Eve of 1822 about what blacks should know:

It is proper, the Convention conceives, that the Negroes should know, that however numerous they are in some parts of these Southern States, they, yet, are not even including all descriptions, bond and free, in the United States, but little more than one sixth part of the whole number of inhabitants . . . : That their destitution in respect to arms, and the knowledge of using them, with other disabilities, would render their physical force, were they all united in a common effort, less than a tenth part of that, with which they would have to contend. That there are multitudes of the best informed and truly religious among them, who, from principle, as well as from prudence, would not unite with them, nor fail to disclose their machinations, when it should be in their power to do it: That, however in some parts of our Union there are Citizens, who favour the idea of general emancipation; yet were they to see slaves in our Country, in arms, wading through blood and carnage to effect their purpose, they would do what both their duty and interest would require; unite under the government with their fellow-citizens at large to suppress the rebellion, and bring the authors of it to condign punishment.[125]

It is significant that authorities who recounted the Vesey plot said of Gullah Jack, a major figure in that conspiracy, "Such was their belief in his invulnerability, that his charms and amulets were in request, and he was regarded as a man, who could *only* be harmed but by the *treachery* of his fellows."[126] (Emphasis in the original.)

Despite such internal and external hindrances to the fruition of revolutionary quests, the slavocracy never felt comfortable with the slaves in their midst. Consequently, those who were "so turbulent and unruly as to become difficult of government"[127] were sold. What role they might have played in an armed struggle for freedom can never be known. But it is clear that masters believed the rebellious were a danger to the institution of slavery both in their disruption of labor and in the radical example they set, for, at least in the quarters, the "troublesome" were the most esteemed.[128]

It is, of course, not possible either to know the exact combination of ingredients that make a revolutionary, but if two requirements are an insatiable desire to be free and a willingness to die for it, then many runaways would have been prime candidates. Their attacks on random planters through arson, crop destructions, and even murder made clear that they were not on the defensive alone.[129] With the most fractious and courageous bondsmen removed from the quarters by sales and voluntary departures,[130] the human resources for antebellum rebellions were depleted. To the dismay of planters, however, nothing they did seemed able to control completely either the most radical or the most conservative of slaves. It was this realization that kept the masters in such constant fear and inspired the constant devising of new modes of control.

CHAPTER SEVEN

Born a Child of Freedom, Yet a Slave

Dependence is the lot of a great portion of the human race—Providence seems to have established it to preserve the order of the system of things. The wants of the poor create the duties of the rich. The inequality of conditions generates the sympathy which while it relieves the indigent, rewards the benefactor. Thus also, the relation of master and slave generates the kindly affections by which it was intended to be maintained. . . . We often relieve the beggar merely to relieve ourselves from an uneasy sensation, and dismiss him forever from our thoughts. . . . But the slave with whom we have been bred from our childhood, who is under our care or our roof; who contributes by his daily labor to our comfort and our wealth; whose sickness we relieve; who grows old as we grow old; who appeals to us when oppressed; who implores our pity when in fault; keeps up towards himself, on the part of his master, a constant interest and a lively sympathy.

The Pendleton *Messenger*, 1831[1]

Few historians have examined in any systematic or thorough way the necessity for slaveholders to create multiple mechanisms of control. A major cause for this neglect is the remarkably persistent image of slavery as a patriarchal institution. Such a picture misinterprets or ignores the force and coercion in the relationship between masters and slaves because the enslaved purportedly were content in their bondage and attached to masters only by a fidelity born within them to serve surrogate fathers. The recent emphasis on the autonomous and rich culture of slaves inadvertently has deflected attention further from the ruthlessly manipulative and repressive system in which it flourished. But no matter how dynamic that culture was, nor how convincing the ideology of masters, neither captures sufficiently the essence of slavery—a state of war.

Only by surveying the mechanisms of control bombarding slaves as a totality of physical and psychological control and the resilient and self-generative ways in which slaves combated or failed to combat them, can one see the reality. The danger of concentrating either on the culture of slaves, or on the ideology of masters, or on any aspect of slave existence, including mechanisms of control, without considering also the effect each had on the other is illustrated in the gross misconceptions of otherwise perceptive observers. Jean-Jacques Rousseau, for example, grasped firmly why the ultimate end of all control mechanisms was doomed to failure when he wrote in 1762:

> However strong a man, he is never strong enough to remain master always, unless he transform his Might into Right, and Obedience into Duty. Hence we have come to speak of the Right of the Strongest, a right which, seemingly assumed in irony, has, in fact, become established in principle. But the meaning of the phrase has never been adequately explained. Strength is a physical attribute, and I fail to see how any moral sanction can attach to its effects. To yield to the strong is an act of necessity, not of will. At most it is the result of a dictate of prudence. How, then, can it become a duty?
>
> It follows, therefore that the word Right adds nothing to the idea of Might . . . the convention, in short, which sets up on one side an absolute authority, and on the other an obligation to obey without question, is vain and meaningless. Is it not obvious that where we can demand everything, we owe nothing?[2]

Rousseau never studied or explored adequately the culture of New World slaves or the irrepressible spirit which gave them endurance and hope. As a result, he failed to see the absurdity of this further assertion:

> Nothing is more certain than that a man born into a condition of slavery is a slave by nature. A slave in fetters loses everything—even the desire to be freed from them. He grows to love his slavery, as the companions of Ulysses grew to love their state of brutish transformation.
>
> If some men are by nature slaves, the reason is that they have been made slaves *against* nature. Force made the first slaves: cowardice has perpetuated the species.[3] (Emphasis in the original.)

Richard Hildreth, the abolitionist and scholar who knew well how the master retained "his authority . . . by the constant exercise of violent means," nevertheless concluded that slaves were "cowards," for "were it not so, slavery" would have been "very short lived." Thus, he could with apparent consistency proclaim, "passion often supplies the place of courage; and we frequently hear of terrible acts of vengeance committed upon the person or family of the master, by outraged and infuriated servants."[4] The error of Rousseau in the eighteenth century and Hildreth in the nineteenth has not precluded individuals from following their lead even today. Eugene Genovese resurrected the bones of paternalism in a book subtitled *The World the Slaves Made*. Although he portrayed brilliantly the ideological tenets of patriarchal planters, he failed to capture the worldview of slaves and the control mechanisms that helped to shape it. There is a long trail of white scholars who have ensnarled slaves in a paternalistic garble that continues effectively to blur the harsh day-to-day realities of slavery. A return to the source of this imaginary servitude may help to explain the ongoing debate about masters and slaves.

Simultaneous with the growth and entrenchment of the Southern plantocracy, another body of men and women became increasingly vocal in its criticism of the institution upon which slaveholders depended. These abolitionists were in part responsible for the war of words that slaveowners mounted to rationalize and defend their enslavement of blacks. In order "to counteract the existing prejudice against slavery," no doubt referring to antislavery Northerners, Zaphaniah Kingsley, a Southern patriot, wrote a treatise in 1829 on the "patriarchal, or co-operative system of society." Under this mode of government, slaves were "discretely restrained" by, among other things, "kind treatment when sick, and fair words when well." He elaborates further on this paternalistic ideal:

> A patriarchal feeling of affection is due to every slave from his owner, who should consider the slave as a member of his family, whose happiness and protection is identified with that of his own family, of which his slave constitutes a part, according to his scale of condition. This affection creates confidence which becomes reciprocal, and is attended with the most beneficial consequence to both.[5]

A similar theme was sounded two years later in the Pendleton (South Carolina) *Messenger*. An article in its pages, quoted at the beginning of this chapter, proclaimed the relation between master and slave to be "paternal, and its duties . . . seriously weighed by the more enlightened class of Southern planters." A "sense of common interest" between the two parties mitigated authority and invigorated labor. Slavery was, in effect, a blessing: "The toil of the slave is often no more involuntary than that of the peasant; and whether forced or gratuitous, if it supplies the wants of nature and promotes health of body and content, it is a blessing."[6]

One notes the conditional and suggestive quality of these instructions: all would be happy and good if slaveholders felt what
they "should" and "if" black labor provided certain goods. Nowhere was this theoretical construct illustrated as well as in a
ruling by Judge John Belton O'Neall of Newberry, South Carolina.
Speaking for the Court of Appeals in the 1837 case of Tennent v.
Dendy, he wrote:

> The slave *ought* to be fully aware that his master is to him what the best
> administered government is to the good citizen, a perfect security from
> injury. *When* this is the case the relation of master and servant becomes
> little short of that of parent and child—it commences in the weakness of
> the one and the strength of the other. Its benefits produce the corresponding
> consequences of deep and abiding grateful attachments from the slave to the
> master, and hence result (many) instances of devotion.[7] (Emphases added.)

Paternalism was unilateral to the core: the planter made the
rules, demanded slave compliance with them, and meted out punishment for any transgressions.[8] Harriet Martineau, the percipient
English traveler, observed this quality of paternalism while touring
the South.

> I was frequently told of the "endearing relation" subsisting between mas-
> ter and slaves; but, at the best, it appeared to me the same "endearing
> relation" which subsists between a man and his horse, between a lady and
> her dog. As long as the slave remains ignorant, docile, and contented, he is
> taken good care of, humoured, and spoken of with a contemptuous, com-
> passionate kindness. But, from the moment he exhibits the attributes of a
> rational being—from the moment his intellect seems likely to come into the
> most distant competition with that of whites, the most deadly hatred springs
> up in his oppressors.[9]

In essence, slaveholders behaved paternally only if blacks were
perfect slaves. A perfect slave ceased to be a slave and became, in
effect, a "servant" who was part of the family.[10]

It appears that most African-Americans felt no obligation to
honor such a purportedly bilateral contract between master and
slave. Charles Ball, who had been a chattel on a large South Carolina plantation early in the nineteenth century, declared:

> There can never be any affinity of feeling between master and slave, except
> in some few isolated cases, where the master has treated his slave in such a
> manner, as to have excited in him strong feelings of gratitude; or where the
> slave entertains apprehensions, that by the death of his master, or by being
> separated from him in any other way, he may fall under the power of a more

tyrannical ruler, or may in some shape be worsted by the change. I was never acquainted with a slave who believed, that he violated any rule of morality by appropriating to himself any thing that belonged to his master. . . . The master might call it theft, and brand it with the name of crime; but the slave reasoned differently. . . . The slave sees his master residing in a spacious mansion, riding in a fine carriage, and dressed in costly clothes, and attributes the possession of all these enjoyments to his own labor; whilst he who is the cause of so much gratification and pleasure to another, is himself deprived of even the necessary accommodations of human life.[11]

Slaveowners' constant resort to punitive actions is further evidence of their failure to elicit patriarchal conformity. When the slaves at Clergy Hall, a plantation rented by John C. Calhoun,[12] became "disorderly," Calhoun wrote to his brother-in-law: "I hope that they have been brought into entire subjection; but I must ask it as a favour for you to see that all is right, and if not the most decided measures be adopted to bring them to *a sense of duty*."[13] (Emphasis in the original.) "Decided measures" were all too common.

Obviously, there were many beneficial and psychologically satisfying features of paternalism for planters. In addition to their belief that it harmonized potentially dangerous and divisive relations among whites, they were comforted by the protection paternalism gave them against a hostile black majority. As Robert Olsberg explained in his excellent dissertation on the South Carolina chivalry:

To make "domestic servitude" work, the white family was turned into the godhead of social peace. The relationship between the slaves and their masters then became, in [William Henry] Trescot's phrase, "a moral one," in which obedience and labor were inspired not by contract, arms, or law but by a sense of duty. This theory placed the slave's need to obey on the reassuring level of the senses. For as soon as Trescot . . . stressed the "moral" qualities of the black laborer's obligation to his master, they made his subordination a matter of feeling, but kept the African's consciousness of subordination within the limits of his supposed irrationalism. The moment the barbarous slave became a member of the white family his masculine potential—from murdering the master to seducing the mistress—descended to the unthinkable level of patricide and incest.[14]

The perspective of the ruling class was that it had upheld its part of the "agreement" and that any punishment inflicted upon slaves stemmed from their failure to do the same. It removed in some measure any guilt certain slaveholders may have felt occasionally for their cruel and inhuman treatment of blacks. Such an outlook on the responsibilities and obligations of masters enabled James Henry Hammond to withhold Christmas celebrations from blacks and write nonchalantly: "No festivities, crops being lost— negroes not having done their duty."[15]

Even the most paternalistic planters, who felt genuine remorse at being separated from their "people," experienced no chagrin when dissolving the families of disobedient slaves. Thomas Green Clemson, for example, while U.S. chargé d'affaires in Belgium, wrote his father-in-law that he hoped his "Negroes" would not have to be sold. "If the Negroes can be retained," he asked, "I do not wish them to leave the State, or to be hired where they would be badly treated or their lives jeopardised in an unhealthy position." But, as to two slaves who had given "trouble," Clemson had "less objection to parting with them." He concluded his letter: "On reflection I should prefer if the place is sold that Charles & Spencer be sold also. They have both given some difficulty which will be a reason to the rest if they are sold."[16]

Loving patriarchs thought nothing of destroying kinship ties when "forced" to sell those who had breached the "contract." Dr. John Irving declared in his plantation journal that "Bert turned out so profitless a servant" that he "was *compelled to sell him*."[17] (Emphasis added.) Samuel Gaillard recorded that he "*had to sell* Judy," because "she would not work & was constantly going off."[18] (Emphasis added.) Nevertheless, the argument persisted that if masters took their duties seriously and if bondsmen responded correctly, a paternalistic slave society was the best of all possible societies.

The Southern plantocracy never tired of comparing the condition of slaves with that of peasants and workers throughout the world—an approach interestingly adopted by two twentieth-century scholars.[19] Much earlier than historians Robert Fogel and Stanley Engerman, South Carolina's Reverend Richard Fuller, in his *Domestic Slavery Considered As A Scriptural Institution*, proudly announced that

as a class, I believe our slaves to be now better compensated, and, in moral, intellectual, and religious condition, superior to most operatives in Europe. From parliamentary reports, it appears that in Ireland three millions and half of people live in mud hovels, having one room, and without chimney or window. In England and Wales there are three millions of people without any pastoral provision.[20]

Defenders of the Peculiar Institution argued further that bondsmen, unlike these free laborers, were well taken care of and provided for when ill. Whether these services were provided for paternal reasons is debatable. There is an abundance of evidence to corroborate the extensive medical treatment of slaves, but the day-to-day records kept by masters indicate that despite some exceptions, more planters were moved by economic interests than by patriarchal instincts when they attended sick slaves.[21] When Charles Ball, for instance, spoke highly of his owner's kindness to him when disabled, he noted its contradiction to his behavior toward healthy workers outside of the "sick room."

> The contrast between the cotton and rice fields, and this little hospital, was very great; and it appeared to me at the time, that if a part of the tenderness and benevolence, displayed here, had been bestowed upon the people whilst in good health, very many of the inmates of this infirmary, would never have been here.[22]

Ball may have been correct, but he was also lucky. One freedman recounted to Charlotte Forten, a Northern black teaching at Port Royal in 1862, "When we sick and c'ldn't work dey tuk away all our food from us; gib us nutten to eat. Dey's orful hard Missis."[23] Another ex-slave recalled that while her sister was sick, the master and a relative forced her under water "to the very point of strangulation" in an effort to "cool her fever." They broke two of her bones in the process and left the helpless woman at the scene. She was found there that evening dead.[24]

Not a few slaveholders chose simply to discard laborers whose prospects for recovery appeared slight. One planter sold a bondsman because he was "worthless and diseased."[25] Another master advertised the sale of two slaves in the following manner: "A Wench named Sylvia, with or without her Child named Sukey, which is diseased."[26] Even planters like R. F. W. Allston, who "liked to be kind to his people," dropped the stance when their pockets were affected. Allston wrote a friend that "Sary goes down for my sister to decide about, she is worse than useless on the plantation and if her mistress determines not to sell her, I think she had best leave her in the hospital of some Physician in town till she gets well."[27]

The fate of blacks who were sold to hospitals and medical schools rather than sent there for care is self-evident. Note Dr. Stillman's 1838 request to "Planters and others":

> Wanted fifty negroes. Any person having sick negroes, considered incurable by their respective physicians, and wishing to dispose them, Dr. S will pay cash for negroes affected with scrofula or King's evil, confirmed hypocondriasm, apoplexy, diseases of the liver, kidneys, spleen, stomach and intestines, bladder and its appendages, diarrhea, dysentery, &c. The highest cash price will be paid on application as above.[28]

These blacks were to be sold, "disposed of," like guinea pigs. Masters also cashed in on contributing black corpses to "science," thereby incidentally disregarding the tremendous importance African-Americans placed on the funerals of family members, relatives, and friends.

The South Carolina Medical College and the numerous anatomical schools in the state were never without an adequate supply of bodies from the slave community.[29] The college prospectus advertised this asset in recruiting new pupils.

> Some advantages of a peculiar character are connected with this Institution, which it may be proper to point out. No place in the United States offers as great opportunities for the acquisition of anatomical knowledge, Subjects being obtained from among the colored population in sufficient number for every purpose, and proper dissections carried on without offending any individuals in the community.[30]

Dr. Robert Wilson, a student at the Medical College in 1856, recalled that blacks knew well their role in that school. He said "individuals of that 'persuasion' were wont to avoid religiously the particular environment after nightfall." One can understand, therefore, why an old woman passing nearby exclaimed, "Please Gawd, when I dead, I hope I wi' dead in de summah time!"[31] The Southern sun deprived students of wholesome bodies during the summer.

Such treatment of ill, dying, and dead slaves casts grave doubts on how many planters "seriously weighed their paternal duties." The plethora of articles urging masters to develop such attitudes would not have been necessary or of much interest if they had been as widespread as contended. Nevertheless, the blatantly propagandist pronouncements by slaveholders and their descendants of romantic master/slave relationships have passed through time as reality.[32] Slaveholders like Edward Heriot of Georgetown left the proof. In a letter defending the Peculiar Institution, he declared:

> I have nearly four hundred—they cost me many anxious moments, I manage them as my children, I am safe in saying that a large majority of them love me & would defend me & my family . . . I have more than once shed a tear over the body of some one of my faithful servants after death, & I am sure many will do so over me.[33]

The last remark is of particular interest because the "deathbed-mourning" theme was a favorite among the plantocracy.

No one can deny the instances of sincere grief planters recorded in diaries, plantation books, and letters. Low Country slaveholder Thomas Chaplin, who felt a strong paternalistic responsibility for his slaves, wrote on May 3, 1850:

> Anthony very ill—Sent for Dr. Jenkins gave him caloumel—no better at night. Up with him nearly all night. I like the old fellow but he never thought so because I cursed him some times I will greatly regret his death which I hope . . . to God will not now take place. His mind is greatly worried on account of his Son.

When he died two days later, Chaplin said sadly, "I will miss him more than I would any other negro that I own—Peace be to his soul."[34] Langdon Cheves, who held 187 slaves in 1840,[35] said at the death of a bondsman, "The loss of Robin is indeed distressing, not so much for the loss of his value, however great . . . but also for the loss of so worthy & amiable a human being. I do not know how you will repair his loss as the Engineer of the threshing mill which is a matter of peculiar difficulty."[36]

While planters' expressions of sorrow at the deaths of slaves can occasionally be found, they are far outnumbered by callous and indifferent utterances. Indeed, the contrast between planters' statements in pro-slavery materials and those in daily plantation records, written without an eye toward the North, is chilling.

James Henry Hammond, perhaps the most famous defender of the South and a proponent of paternalism, was described by his son as "scarcely less" devoted to his bondsmen than to his family. Slaves owned by Hammond were, it was said, "lightly tasked, well fed, protected" and, most important, "their sufferings [were] alleviated by the kindest care."[37] Master Hammond recorded his devotion to two blacks in this manner: "We went to the plantation. Prince died on the 16 inst. & old Bella on the 27th neither a serious loss. One valuable mule has also died in my absence."[38] When "old Anthony," a slave who was more than a hundred years old and a former driver, died, Hammond's only remark was: "This is a bad beginning of the New Year—a death the first day."[39] One of the most affectionate statements Hammond ever made about a lost laborer, other than adding an infrequent "poor" before the name of the deceased,[40] was written in 1841: "A valuable woman was taken in labour yesterday. . . . In spite of every stimulant she died—She was a good creature as ever lived."[41]

Mr. Hammond was not unique in insensitivity toward those who were the source of his wealth. The testimony of planters suggests that they were more concerned with the loss of valuable laborers than with the dissolution of any paternal bonds when a chattel died.[42] Langdon Cheves, who in a rare instance could speak of a slave as a "human being," had no more than this to say at the deaths of a mother and some children: "I am afflicted by the loss of Sarah and the children, not so much for the value as the unconquerable difficulty which, as one fact, it presents in preserving the life and health and securing the increase of the people."[43] Economics was the basis also for Thomas Porcher's interest in a dead slave: "My old man Sempey died this morning. . . . He is a loss to me. As he took great care of every thing at the farm."[44]

Those planters who did not make specific remarks about deceased blacks were often illustrating their cold indifference toward them. Slaveholder Keating S. Ball mourned extensively about the death of a Mr. Gaillard, but when his "servant" died, he said practically nothing. His only entry that day was: "Breaking the mules Josey my Body servant received a kick from one, which though slight in itself was followed by a violent bilious attack, of which he died on Sunday night."[45] One would expect more than this simple acknowledgment of death about a "body servant." Large planters had infrequent contact with the majority of their slaves. It is not surprising, therefore, that most journal citations on dead bondpeople refer to elite slaves. There may be some astonishment, however, for those who believe in paternalism to discover the repeated absence of any sentiment toward servants who would have been in the best position to develop paternalistic relationships with their owners.[46]

In the July 2, 1814, travel log of a South Carolina planter en route to the North are these words:

> We left Salem dined at Mr. Waggoners, and just before sun sett arrived at the Bank of the Dan river where we were directed to ford across and assured that it was very safe, but being a little intimidated by the rapid current and the muddy appearance of the river, we thought it most prudent to send our servant across first to try the depth of the ford—after he had proceeded about 10 feet his horse plunged with him half way up the saddle, and 10 feet farther began to swim, and it was with great difficulty that he reached the opposite side of the river—after the current had carried him 100 yards at least from the usual place of landing—Had we have attempted to cross, the Carriage and horses must have been lost, and ourselves probably with them.[47]

Nowhere does the writer express any concern for the servant's life that might also have been lost in testing the "safety" of the water. The only other comment about the servant, whom he undoubtedly knew well since he trusted him enough to set foot on free soil, followed immediately. It read: "Our boy then went to the house of Major Hairston who lived on the opposite side of the river, who very politely had us taken across in a small boat."[48]

Eugene Genovese does not alter drastically the contemporary Southern theory of paternalism but qualifies it. Nineteenth-century slaveholders' racist conceptions of blacks precluded them from even considering the possibility that bondsmen might have their own ideas about paternalism. Genovese, on the other hand, writes of slaves as having demands of their own. The end result of the different outlooks, however, is the same. Whether slaves acquiesced because they were mentally incapable of anything other than blind obedience to loving patriarchs, or because they were without any alternatives or capabilities to resist the overwhelming hegemony of planters, they nevertheless accepted the paternalist ethos.[49] According to Genovese masters imposed a "hegemonic system" over slaves by developing "an elaborate web of paternalistic relationships" that encompassed "mutual obligations" such as "protection and direction" in return for "involuntary labor."[50] Slaves' internalization of this system legitimized class rule and, thereby, provided slaves "their most powerful defense against the dehumanization implicit in slavery."[51]

Unlike earlier theorists on paternalism who assumed that blacks accepted the patriarchal contract, Genovese makes no such assumption. He seeks to prove slave concurrence, but has little proof.[52] I believe the testimony of slaves is most decisive in determining the type of relationship that existed between the majority of masters and slaves and whether their behavior stemmed more from a sense of loyalty to captors than from a fear of those oppressors' wrath. In South Carolina, at least, the exceedingly rich accounts and narratives of slaves indicate that only a minuscule number of captive workers felt that they owed their masters anything. If there was any real sense of "mutual obligations" between more than a minority of slaves and their enslavers, the records I examined failed to expose it. Throughout the lore, recollections, and contemporary expressions of slaves were repeated assertions that coercion and force were the principal factors that shaped their feelings for and relations with their owners. And most slaves concurred that these sentiments and connections were those of combatants at war against an implacable foe. Indeed, only an endemic vacuousness within the slave community would have permitted its members to accept any patriarchal pronouncements or gestures as anything other than clever ploys in an endless war. Furthermore, it does not appear that planters generally felt obligated to do any more for their laborers than fulfill, as cheaply as possible, the basic physical needs necessary for them to labor. As some slaveholders understood, or, perhaps more accurately, admitted, the principle that not only regulated their relation with the enslaved but vice versa was, as Reverend Jones said, "on the part of the master, *get all, and give back as little as you can,*' and on the part of the servant, *'give as little, and get back all you can.'*"[53] (Emphases in the original.)

Slaves were constantly aware that a key component to their survival was the ability to gratify, or at least appear to gratify, the innermost wishes of masters. This undoubtedly explains, to a degree, the pronouncement by some bondsmen of love for their owners: an avowal at once meant and at the same time reversed. Adeptness at exploiting the misconceptions and desires of their oppressors was crucial in slave existence and resistance. That North American slaves fought for, acquired, and maintained certain customary rights within the system like well-defined work loads and after-hour privileges in no way proves that they accepted the paternalism ethos. From the slaves' perspective, if declarations of alleged bilateral agreements about mutual obligations helped to preserve these gains, so be it. Evidence from other slave societies indicates that comparable developments could occur without the presence of planters whose proximity obviously was key. Because of the pervasive absenteeism among Jamaican slaveowners, most slaves lived on plantations under the directorship and control of attorneys and overseers. Nevertheless, slaves in Jamaica had extremely entrenched and respected customary rights. Bondage on that island was not known to be paternalistic.[54] The legendary brutality of slavery in Jamaica and the high slave mortality there justified Southern slaves' special terror at the prospect of being shipped to that or any West Indian setting.

Just as slaves sometimes felt compelled to express kind words about their owners, they knew that it was in their best interests to wear masks of loyalty and docility.[55] Deaths of slaveholders were the occasion for the grandest slave performances. Jacob Stroyer said that when his owner died

all the slaves were allowed to stop at home that day to see the last of him, and to lament with mistress. After all the slaves who cared to do so had seen his face, they gathered in groups around mistress to comfort her, they shed false tears, saying, "never mind, misses, massa gone home to heaven," while some were saying this, others said, "Thank God, massa gone home to hell." Of course the most of them were glad that he was dead; but they were gathered there for the express purpose of comforting mistress.[56]

In the endless struggle between master and slave, each opponent used whatever was at his or her disposal: both used falsehoods, but planters sometimes believed their own deceptions and, very frequently, those of others.

How persuasive slaves could be, as well as their customary cautiousness, was demonstrated brilliantly during the tense years before and throughout the Civil War when freedom seemed so near. Uncertain of the war's outcome and skeptical about Northern intentions, blacks increased their vigilance of Confederate and Union movements, listening closely for any news that would be of help in deciding the best course of action. Because the blacks were so careful in concealing their designs, whites were either satisfied with surface appearances or helplessly perplexed in trying to discern the feelings of blacks. Mary Boykin Chesnut wrote on July 27, 1861:

> Now if slavery is as disagreeable to negroes as we think it, why don't they all march over the border where they would be received with open arms? It all amazes me. I am always studying these creatures. They are to me inscrutable in their way and past finding out.[57]

Former slaves in Beaufort, South Carolina, spoke to Elizabeth Botume, a teacher with the New England Freedmen's Aid Society, of their strategy during the war. She recorded this conversation among some black women:

> "My father and the other boys used to crawl under the house an' lie on the ground to hear massa read the newspaper to missis when they first began to talk about the war."
> "See that big oak-tree there?" said another. "Our boys used to climb into that tree an' hide under the long moss while massa was at supper, so as to hear him an' his company talk about the war when they come out on the piazza to smoke."
> "I couldn't read, but my uncle could," said a third. "I was waiting-maid, an' used to help missis to dress in the morning. If massa wanted to tell her something he didn't want me to know, he used to spell it out. I could remember the letters, an' as soon as I got away I ran an' spelled them over to him, an' he told me what they meant."[58]

In this manner, slaves were kept well posted on military developments and, most important, on the location of troops. All the while, however, they masked feelings of dissatisfaction.

According to Henry Ravenel, black Carolinians "kept to themselves" any information pertaining to "their future freedom." Indeed, he added, "they never alluded to it, or acted in any manner so as to exhibit exultation or elation at the prospect."[59] Other eyewitnesses spoke also of the stolid and "sphinx-like" posture slaves maintained during the war.[60] It is for this reason that many planters were caught off guard and shocked when slaves' moment of action came. Mrs. O. T. Porcher, a South Carolinian stranded in Pineville, S.C., wrote to her children that "the plantations are filled with rebellion, we do not know who to rely upon, those who are for you today are against you tomorrow."[61] H. H. Manigault described his own experience:

The Raid occurred here on Friday last whereby I lost every Negro on my place and have now only my House Servants. . . . The Negroes as soon as they heard the guns rushed to my house and pillaged it of many things. . . . Though my injuries are bad enough those of the Col's are complete, his Negroes robbed him of everything, and ripped up the feather beds for sacks to carry off the things. . . . The Col's Jimmy left his wife, and Dianna with many others were ready waiting for the boats to come for them, *everything tends to show the whole affair was prearranged.*[62] (Emphasis added.)

The newly free exhibited caution with their purported friends from the North also. When Prince Rivers, a former slave who became a sergeant in the First Regiment of South Carolina Volunteers, was asked whether blacks would rebel against their masters if they had military equipment and knowledge to give such an attack at least a "chance" of success, he replied, "*Yes, sah . . . only let 'em know for sure—for sure,* mine you—dat de white people means right; let 'em know for sure dat dey's fightin' for themselves, and I *know* dey will fight."[63] (Emphases in the original.) Years of struggle had taught slaves to be suspect of all whites and they were not going to support Yankees without scrutinizing them carefully and prudently weighing their options and alternatives.[64] Such shrewdness proved fruitful because, in not a few instances, the behavior of Union soldiers and conditions elsewhere indicated to blacks that it was in their best interests to remain on the plantation.[65]

For generations, the enslaved had learned painfully the making and nature of Southern planters. Conforming to their demands could buy protection, but still there were sales. A former Blackstock, South Carolina, slave remembered "Marse Ed didn't 'low patarollers on de June place. He tell them to stay off and they knowed to stay off." The same master had "slave drovers often come on de June place, just lak mule drovers and hog drovers. They buy, sell, and swap niggers, just lak they buy, sell, and swap hosses, mules, and hogs."[66] These sales and swaps did more than anything else to preclude slave internalization of the paternalist ethos.

It bears repeating that even if one had the superhuman selflessness to abide by the contractual fantasies of one's master, there remained a long list of reasons for heart-rending separations besides noncompliance. There is no evidence that Ball, his wife, or their children had done anything wrong when, without warning, his Maryland master destroyed his family forever. Ball would be sold again, but that earlier sale was perhaps the most haunting:

> This man came up to me, and, seizing me by the collar, shook me violently, saying I was his property, and must go with him to Georgia. At the sound of these words, the thoughts of my wife and children rushed across my mind, and my heart died away within me. I saw and knew that my case was hopeless, and that resistance was vain, as there were near twenty persons present, all of whom were ready to assist the man by whom I was kidnapped. I . . . [then was] ordered . . . to cross my hands behind, which were quickly bound with a strong cord; and . . . told . . . that we must set out that very day for the south. I asked if I could not be allowed to go to see my wife and children, or if this could not be permitted, if they might not have leave to come to see me; but was told that I would be able to get another wife in Georgia.[67]

The economic welfare and happiness of slaveholding families was more important than protecting slave kinship ties. Daniel C. Webb was genuinely saddened by having to part with his laborers of thirty-five years, but he felt comforted by noting that it was "a duty to myself and family to render their labor more contributive to my Comfort than heretofore."[68] Whether financial distress stemmed from illness, death, or extravagance, the remedy usually entailed the dissolution of family relationships into cash.[69] When E. Montague Grimke tired of complying with his father's will, which forbade the sale of three sons he had sired through a slave, Montague disregarded his dead father's stipulation and sold one of his half-brothers.[70] George De Busse, an ex-slave from Charleston District, recalled the common practice of masters using "servants" as stakes in horse races. De Busse said of his owner: "He put up Pappy on one race 'gainst a nigger f 'um 'nother plantation. Massa loss—an' Pappy didn't get back till freedom!"[71]

Because African-Americans tended to be perceived as mindless automatons, many planters felt no guilt in deciding it was "best" for certain slaves to be separated from their mates. John Bratton, for one, told his wife not to be concerned about a servant whose husband was being sent away. He declared, "As to Sallie's distress about Isaacs trip to the west, you need not worry yourself. She will be a better and happier negro without him."[72] Some masters did not even wait for children to be conceived or born before giving them away. John Row left his daughter Nancey a slave named Rachel, whose first child was to be given to Sarah, another daughter, and any others to her sister Frances—at least the three children of Row were to be provided for.[73]

During the first half of the nineteenth century, the period when Genovese believes the enslaved and the enslaver were weaving themselves into an intricate web of paternalistic relationships, American cotton was in high demand and the interregional slave trade was increasing.[74] Thus, there were the dual pressures on masters to work their slaves harder and to capitalize on their marketability. The sale of their children would not demonstrate that slaveowners meant to "protect." Nevertheless, the myth of paternalism has persisted. In a 1976 essay entitled "Slavery—The White Man's Burden," historian William Scarborough praised Genovese for his "remarkable perception" in elucidating "the paternalistic relationship which bound together masters and slaves." But Scarborough was critical of what he perceived as Genovese's "distressing propensity to assign to [planters] only base and ignoble motives for acts of genuine benevolence." "Just as the slaves exhibited certain common traits," he wrote, "so too did those who governed them. It is my contention that the class as a whole, especially at the highest level, was permeated by a sense of honor, noblesse oblige, chivalry, justice, Christian compassion; in a word, the typical planter was a gentleman, a term which is ubiquitous in the correspondence of the period."[75]

Slaves thought somewhat differently, but they did not leave much written evidence. Planters left volumes. Their propaganda, then as today, reached far and wide. It influenced even abolitionists. Thomas Higginson, for example, "expected to find" paternalistic relationships between masters and slaves when he arrived in South Carolina to lead a black regiment against the Confederates. He discovered otherwise:

> I never heard one speak of the masters except as natural enemies. Yet they were perfectly discriminating as to individuals; many of them claimed to have had kind owners, and some expressed great gratitude to them for particular favors received. It was not the individuals, but the ownership, of which they complained. That they saw to be wrong which no special kindnesses could right. On this, as on all points connected with slavery, they understood the matter as clearly as Garrison or Phillips; the wisest philosophy could teach them nothing as to that, nor could any false philosophy befog them. After all, personal experience is the best logician.[76]

There is no evidence that most slaves ever accepted, internalized, or legitimized the paternalist ideology.

On the contrary, an 1852 document held by a South Carolinian planter portrays more accurately the threatening world shaped by, but also shaping, the slaves whom antebellum Southerners sought physically and spiritually to control. It was an insurance policy to himself and stipulated that

the said Company do hereby promise to pay the said Thomas C. Gower within sixty days after due proof of the death of the above named Slaves. . . . [If, however,] the application signed by the said Thomas C. Gower . . . shall be in any respect fraudulent or untrue; or if the said slave or slaves, or any of them shall die by his, her or their own hands, or by intemperance, or by the hands of justice, or in the violation of law, or by or in consequence of a mob, a riot, a foreign invasion, a civil war, or an insurrection, or any military or usurped power, or by the mal-treatment or neglect of the owner, or of any person to whom he, she or they may be entrusted; or if the said slave or slaves, or any of them, are now, or shall be hereafter insured in any other Company, without the written consent of this Company, or shall abscond or be kidnapped, or shall, without the written consent of the said Company, either be sold or given to a new owner, or be removed one hundred miles from their present residence, or be employed in a more hazardous occupation than their present one; or if, in case of the sickness of the said slave or slaves, or any of them, he, she or they shall fail to receive all due and proper care, promptly and without delay . . . then, and in all such cases, *the said Company shall not be liable* to pay the sum insured and set opposite the name or names of the said slave or slaves.[77] (Emphasis added.)

Certainly, the potential terrors always lingering over the heads of slaves, as well as the horrors they did experience through family separations, brutal punishments, and the stratagems to divide and rule them, were not made any more bearable by the paternalism of masters. What shielded them significantly from the psychic and physical assaults so much a part of their daily reality was the culture they forged and imparted. William J. Faulkner poignantly observed in *The Days When the Animals Talked*:

Hundreds of thousands of Africans died in the squalid holds of slave ships crossing the Atlantic, or committed suicide by jumping overboard, or were killed by the breaking-in whippings of their overlords. Those who survived met the powerful armed force of the American slave system with a matching degree of soul force, which enabled them not only to live but to grow strong and multiply. This soul force found voice in many of the slaves' religious songs and folktales. .... While the slave system tried to destroy him, the Afro-American kept his spirit alive and hopeful through his faith in a God of love and justice and through his imagination, which allowed him to escape his destitute reality. Whether working or resting, whether in joy or in suffering, he managed to pray and sing and tell folktales.[78]

Perhaps the most moving and telling support of these views of Faulkner is found in this eulogy for a South Carolinian ex-slave:

> She's at rest, asleep and free;
> Her soul from sorrow is lifted
> Far above the trials
> Of this world
> With its joys and its tears.
> Born a child of freedom,
> Yet a slave;
> Full of pride and grief,
> Yet a slave
> In a land of freedom—
> Freedom to the slave that was;
> Free when freedom was not.
>
> A slave to love and friendship
> Guided by her conscience,
> Loved by those she loved.
> True to every trust, she's dead.
> She sleeps as she lived—
> Above the lowly things of earth.
> She's at rest where the angels
> Sweetly sing, and Christ
> Has kissed the clouds away,
> And her spirit rests
> Far above the mists.[79]

Until the culture of slaves and all other crucial influences on their lives are studied in a holistic and thorough way, no accurate picture of slavery will be drawn. But unless it is drawn, yet another generation will suffer the fate predicted by an anonymous nineteenth-century pamphleteer, who commented on an insurgent convicted and hanged with Denmark Vesey:

I sympathize most sincerely with the very respectable and pious clergyman whose heart must still bleed at the recollection that his confidential classleader, but a week or two before his just conviction, had received the communion of the Lord's Supper from his hand. This wretch had been brought up in his pastor's family! and was treated with the same Christian attention as was shown to their own children. To us who are accustomed to the base and proverbial ingratitude of these people, this ill return of kindness and confidence is not surprising; but they who are ignorant of their real character will read and wonder.[80]

Sadly, many since and even today still apparently can only "read and wonder." That tragedy is inextricably linked to why, more than a century after our anonymous writer's insight, the reality dictating the black American struggle for freedom remains blurred, confused, and frequently denied by countless numbers of men and women throughout the United States.

When the Confederate Army surrendered in 1865, two former enemies had much to resolve, but, in one crucial sense, they never were opponents; although Northern and Southern whites differed on the specific place blacks should occupy in the social, political, and economic hierarchy of America, they always had been united in keeping that "place" somewhere beneath their own privileged rung. Hence, as the Confederates capitulated, blacks—North and South—held their own pact: the war would not end until *full* freedom and dignity were won.

Notes

Abbreviations

Manuscript Collections

APL   Anderson Public Library, Anderson, South Carolina
CCL   College of Charleston Library, Charleston, South Carolina
CLS   Charleston Library Society, Charleston, South Carolina
LC   Library of Congress, Washington, D.C.
MU   Medical University of South Carolina Library, Charleston, South Carolina
NA   National Archives, Washington, D.C.
PL   William R. Perkins Library, Duke University, Durham, North Carolina
SC   South Caroliniana Library, University of South Carolina, Columbia, South Carolina
SCA   South Carolina Department of Archives and History, Columbia, South Carolina
SCHS   South Carolina Historical Society, Charleston, South Carolina
SHC   Southern Historical Collection, University of North Carolina, Chapel Hill, North Carolina
WHL   Waring Historical Library, Charleston, South Carolina

Periodicals

AHR   *The American Historical Review*
AJ   *The American Journal of Religious Psychology and Education*
AM   *The Atlantic Monthly*
AQ   *American Quarterly*
BEM   *Blackwood's Edinburgh Magazine*
BHR   *Business History Review*
CH   *Church History*
CJM   *The Carolina Journal of Medicine, Science and Agriculture*
CP   *Carolina Planter*
CWH   *Civil War History*
DR   *DeBow's Review*
FP   *Farmer and Planter*
FW   *First World*
HNM   *Harper's New Monthly Magazine*
HTR   *Harvard Theological Review*
JAF   *Journal of American Folk-Lore*
JAH   *Journal of American History*
JAS   *Journal of American Studies*
JCR   *The Journal of Conflict Resolution: A Quarterly for Research Related to War and Peace*
JNH   *Journal of Negro History*
JOSH   *Journal of Social History*
JSH   *Journal of Southern History*
JWH   *Journal of World History*

NCA   *The Nashville Christian Advocate*
NCHR   *North Carolina Historical Review*
RHR   *Radical History Review*
SA   *Southern Agriculturist*
SAUS   *South Atlantic Urban Studies*
SC   *Southern Cultivator*
SCHM   *The South Carolina Historical and Genealogical Magazine*
SFQ   *Southern Folklore Quarterly*
SL   *Studies on the Left*
SQR   *Southern Quarterly Review*
SSH   *Social Science History*
SW   *Southern Workman*
TH   *The Historian*
TSC   *The Southern Cabinet*
TYR   *The Yale Review*
WMQ   *The William and Mary Quarterly*

Introduction

1. For three excellent chapter-length treatments, see Herbert Aptheker, *American Negro Slave Revolts* (New York: International Publishers, 1969), chapter 3 (originally published in 1943); Kenneth M. Stampp, *The Peculiar Institution: Slavery in the Ante-Bellum South* (New York: Vintage Books, 1956), chapter 4; Peter Wood, *Black Majority: Negroes in Colonial South Carolina From 1670 Through the Stono Rebellion* (New York: Alfred A. Knopf, 1974), chapter 10.

2. Two notable exceptions are George M. Fredrickson and Herbert G. Gutman, who not only suggest the influence of such threats, but make clear the wide-ranging ramifications of any particular sale. George M. Fredrickson, "Masters and Mudsills: The Role of Race in the Planter Ideology of South Carolina," *SAUS*, 2 (1978), 40; Herbert G. Gutman, *Slavery and the Numbers Game: A Critique of Time on the Cross* (Urbana: University of Illinois Press, 1975), pp. 124–40.

3. H. M. Henry, *The Police Control of the Slave in South Carolina* (New York: Negro Universities Press, 1968), p. 5 (originally published in 1914).

4. 2 Strobhart Law, 43: Ex parte Boylston, quoted in Henry, *Police Control*, p. 11.

5. Ulrich B. Phillips, *American Negro Slavery: A Survey of the Supply, Employment and Control of Negro Labor As Determined by the Plantation Regime*, with a foreword by Eugene Genovese (Baton Rouge: Louisiana State University Press, 1966), preface, pp. 291–330, 416 (originally published in 1918); Henry, *Police Control*, pp. 5–6, 79–83.

6. Walter L. Fleming, *Civil War and Reconstruction in Alabama* (New York, 1905), p. 210, quoted in William L. Van Deburg, *The Slave Drivers: Black Agricultural Labor Supervisors in the Antebellum South* (Westport, Conn.: Greenwood Press, 1979), p. 30.

7. Stampp, *Peculiar Institution*, p. 343.

8. Eugene D. Genovese, *Roll, Jordan, Roll: The World the Slaves Made* (New York: Pantheon Books, 1974), pp. 4–7 and passim; Eugene D. Genovese, "A Reply to Criticism," *RHR*, 4 (Winter 1977), 102–3.

9. Peter Kolchin, *Unfree Labor: American Slavery and Russian Serfdom* (Cambridge, Mass.: The Belknap Press of Harvard University Press, 1987), pp. 119–40.

10. South Carolina was also where some of the South's most influential and artic- ulate defenders of slavery made their home. Consequently, a study of South Carolina allows one to explore the far too infrequently considered intellectual impact of slaves on the mind of their masters. For a discussion of the white intellectual community and its more prominent members, see Michael O'Brien and David Moltke-Hansen, eds., *Intellectual Life in Antebellum Charleston* (Knoxville: The University of Tennessee Press, 1986); Drew Gilpin Faust, *James Henry Hammond and the Old South: A Design for Mastery* (Baton Rouge: Louisiana State University Press, 1982); William H. Pease and Jane H. Pease, *The Web of Progress: Private Values and Public Styles in Boston and Charles- ton, 1828–1843* (New York: Oxford University Press, 1985).

11. James Stirling, *Letters From the Slave States* (London: John W. Parker and Son, 1857), p. 344; Fredrika Bremer, *The Homes of the New World: Impressions of America*, Trans. Mary Howitt (New York: Harper & Brothers, 1868), I, p. 382; Rosser T. Taylor, *Antebellum South Carolina: A Social and Cultural History* (The James Sprunt Studies in History and Political Science, Chapel Hill: The University of North Carolina Press, 1942), pp. 41–42; Clement Eaton, *The Growth of Southern Civilization* (New York: Harper & Brothers, 1961), p. 10, cited in Charles M. Clark, "Plantation Overseers in South Carolina, 1820– 1860" (M.A. thesis, University of South Carolina, 1966), p. 80.

12. Guion Griffis Johnson, *A Social History of the Sea Islands: With Special Ref- erence to St. Helena Island, South Carolina* (Chapel Hill: The University of North Carolina Press, 1930), p. 38; Clark, "Plantation Overseers," p. 2; Stir- ling, *Letters*, p. 247.

13. Wood, *Black Majority*, p. 36; Taylor, *Ante-Bellum South Carolina*, p. 178; Charles W. Joyner, "Slave Folklife of the Waccamaw Neck: Antebellum Black Culture in the South Carolina Lowcountry" (Ph.D. dissertation, University of Pennsylvania, 1977), pp. 1, 326; George Rogers, Jr., *The History of George- town County, South Carolina* (Columbia: University of South Carolina Press, 1970), p. 343; Darold D. Wax, "'The Great Risque We Run': The Aftermath of Slave Rebellion at Stono, South Carolina, 1739–1745," *JNH*, LXVII (Sum- mer 1982), 136–37; Richard C. Wade, "The Vesey Plot: A Reconsideration," in John H. Bracey, Jr., et al., *American Slavery: The Question of Resistance* (Belmont, Cal.: Wadsworth Publishing Company, 1971), p. 136.

14. George P. Rawick, ed., *The American Slave: A Composite Autobiography* (Westport, Conn.: Greenwood Publishing Company, 1972), II, ii, p. 130, III, iv, p. 45; Charles Ball, *Fifty Years in Chains*, with an introduction by Philip S. Foner (New York: Dover Publications, 1970), pp. 298–300 (originally pub- lished in 1837); Thomas Wentworth Higginson, *Army Life in a Black Regiment* (Boston: Beacon Press, 1962), p. 249 (originally published in 1869). Some idea of this sentiment appears in the statement of an elite slave, the coachman of a prominent Sea Island planter, who noted that "his master was kind" but that masters collectively were "unjust." He explained, "They take all our labor for their use and get rich on it and then say we are lazy and can't take care of ourselves. That's not just, and they were not just." See Rupert Sargent Holland, ed., *Letters and Diary of Laura M. Towne: Written From the Sea Islands of South Carolina, 1862–1884* (Cambridge, Mass.: Riverside Press, 1912), p. 31.

15. Thomas D. Condy, *A Digest of the Laws of the United States and the State of South Carolina . . .* (Charleston: A. E. Miller, 1830), p. 173; "The Petition of Sundry Citizens of Orangeburg Praying That Tickets to Slaves May Be Made More Specific," October 15, 1854, (Folder 135), Slavery Files, SCA; John C.

Calhoun, Washington, to John Ewing Colhoun, January 15, 1827, John C. Calhoun Family Correspondence Typescripts (The author is indebted to Dr. Clide Wilson for generously sharing these documents when editing them at the University of South Carolina. They will hereinafter be cited as the Calhoun Family Typescripts); Holland, *Letters*, pp. 57–58.

16. Rawick, *The American Slave*, II, ii, pp. 138–40, 143–45, 150; E. C. L. Adams, *Nigger to Nigger* (New York: Charles Scribner's Sons, 1928), pp. 234–36; Elsie Clews Parsons, "Folk-Lore From Aiken, S.C.," *JAF*, 34 (January–March 1921), 22; Moses Roper, *A Narrative of the Adventures and Escape of Moses Roper From American Slavery* (New York: Negro Universities Press, 1970), pp. 8–13 (originally published in 1838).

17. Roper, *A Narrative*, pp. 1–2; Rawick, *The American Slave*, II, i, pp. 149–50, II, ii, pp. 36, 168, 304–6, III, iii, pp. 194–95; George W. Knepper, ed., *Travels in the Southland, 1822–1823: The Journal of Lucius Versus Bierce* (Columbus: Ohio State University Press, 1966), p. 78.

18. George Rawick has done a superb job of editing these narratives. See Rawick, *The American Slave*, II, III, and George P. Rawick, ed., *The American Slave: A Composite Autobiography*, Supplement, Series 1 (Westport, Conn.: Greenwood Press, 1977), 11.

19. Eric Perkins, "Roll, Jordan, Roll: A 'Marx' for the Master Class," *RHR*, 3 (Fall 1976), 48.

20. Mary Boykin Chesnut, *A Diary From Dixie*, eds. Isabella D. Martin and Myrta Locket Avery (Gloucester, Mass.: Peter Smith, 1961), p. 390.

21. William L. Van Deburg, "Slave Drivers and Slave Narratives: A New Look at the Dehumanized Elite," *TH*, 39 (1979), 729; C. Vann Woodward, "History From Slave Sources," *AHR*, 79 (April 1974), 473; John Blassingame, "Using the Testimony of Ex-Slaves: Approaches and Problems," *JSH*, XLI (November 1975), 481–82, 486–89; Rawick, *The American Slave*, sup., 11, pp. xxx–xxxiv; Norman R. Yetman, ed., *Life Under the "Peculiar Institution": Selections From the Slave Narrative Collection* (New York: Holt, Rinehart, and Winston, Inc., 1970), p. 222; Rawick, *The American Slave*, III, iv, p. 199, II, ii, p. 30.

22. Blassingame, *JSH*, 482; Rawick, *The American Slave*, II, ii, p. 228, III, iv, pp. 154, 157, II, i, p. 36.

23. See, for example, William J. Faulkner, *The Days When the Animals Talked: Black American Folktales and How They Came to Be* (Chicago: Follet Publishing, 1977), pp. x–xv, 3–5; Sterling A. Brown et al., *The Negro Caravan* (New York: Arno Press and The New York Times, 1969), pp. 413–14, 416–18, 420, 422, 434–36, 440–41 (originally published in 1941); Henry Edward Krehbiel, *Afro-American Folksongs: A Study in Racial and National Music* (New York: G. Schirmer, 1914), pp. 2–4, 29; Howard Odum, "Religious Folk-Songs of the Southern Negroes," *AJ*, 3 (July 1909), 265–69; Richard M. Dorson, *American Folklore and the Historian* (Chicago: The University of Chicago Press, 1971), pp. 18, 57, 61, 71, 141, 143–44; Daryl Dance, "In the Beginning: A New View of Black American Etiological Tales," *SFQ*, 40 (1977), 60–61; Joyner, "Slave Folklife of the Waccamaw Neck," pp. 158–59, 171–72, 175; Sterling Stuckey and Joshua Leslie, "Reflections on Reflections About the Black Intellectual, 1930–1945," *FW*, 2 (1979), 26.

24. Sterling Stuckey, "Through the Prism of Folklore: The Black Ethos in Slavery," in Anne J. Lane, ed., *The Debate Over Slavery: Stanley Elkins and His Critics* (Urbana: University of Illinois Press, 1971), pp. 246–47.

25. Frederick Douglass, *My Bondage and My Freedom,* with a new introduction by Philip S. Foner (New York: Dover Publications, 1969), p. 253 (originally published in 1855).
26. Rawick, *The American Slave,* III, iv, p. 173.
27. Edward Adams, *Congaree Sketches: Scenes From Negro Life in the Swamps of Congaree and Tales by Tad and Scip of Heaven and Hell With Other Miscellany* (Chapel Hill: The University of North Carolina Press, 1927), pp. 50–51.
28. Martha M. Pingel, *An American Utilitarian: Richard Hildreth as a Philosopher* (New York: Columbia University Press, 1948), pp. ix, 4, 6; Richard Hildreth, *Despotism in America; or An Inquiry Into the Nature and Results of the Slave-Holding System in the United States* (Boston: Whipple and Damrell, 1840), pp. 37–38.
29. Hildreth, *Despotism,* pp. 44, 50–56, 86, 160.
30. Ibid., pp. 54–55.
31. Ibid., p. 82.

Chapter 1. The Challenge of Control

1. Ernest Barker, ed., *Social Contract: Essays by Locke, Hume and Rousseau* (London: Oxford University Press, 1979), pp. 15–16.
2. Earl E. Thorpe, *The Old South: A Psychohistory* (Durham, N.C.: Seeman Printery, 1972), p. 30; Vincent Harding, *There Is a River: The Black Struggle for Freedom in America* (New York: Harcourt Brace Jovanovich, 1981), pp. xix–xx, 3–23, 60, 333; Angela Davis, *Lectures on Liberation* (New York: New York Committee to Free Angela Davis, n.d.), pp. 5–6, 9–14, 17–18; William L. McCaa, "Observations on the Manner of Living and Diseases on the Wateree River, S.C." (Sr. thesis, University of Pennsylvania, 1823), pp. 4–5, WHL; Edward Pettingill, Master of Brig, New York, off Charleston, to Langdon Cheves, by Pilot Boat, Georgia, June 22, 1837, Cheves Family Papers, SCHS; J. S. Buckingham, *The Slave States of America* (London: Fisher, Son, & Co., 1842), II, pp. 168–69; E. C. L. Adams, *Nigger to Nigger* (New York: Charles Scribner's Sons, 1928), pp. 16–17; George P. Rawick, ed., *The American Slave: A Composite Autobiography,* Supplement, Series 1 (Westport, Conn.: Greenwood Press, 1977), 11, pp. 98–100, 261–63; Frances Ann Kemble, *Journal of a Residence on a Georgian Plantation in 1838–1839,* ed. John A. Scott (New York: Alfred A. Knopf, 1961), pp. 118–19.
3. F. N. Boney, "The Ante-bellum Elite," in Charles M. Hudson, ed., *Red, White, and Black: Symposium on Indians in the Old South* (Athens, Ga.: Southern Anthropological Society, 1971), pp. 77–82; Harding, *There Is a River,* pp. 7, 76, 108–9, 143.
4. Robert F. W. Allston, Chicora Wood, to Sarah Carr, January 14, 1859, in J. H. Easterby, ed., *The South Carolina Rice Plantation as Revealed in the Papers of Robert F. W. Allston* (Chicago: University of Chicago Press, 1945), p. 152.
5. Edward Thomas Heriot, George Town, South Carolina, to [unknown], [Great Britain?], April 20, 1853, Edward Thomas Heriot Papers, PL; Jacob Stroyer, *My Life in the South* (Salem, Mass.: Salem Observer and Job Print, 1885), p. 31; A. M. French, *Slavery in South Carolina and the Ex-Slaves: Or, The Port Royal Mission* (New York: Negro Universities Press, 1969), p. 143 (originally published in 1862); "The Petition of Elly Godbold, A. Q. McDuffie and Other Citizens of Marion District," n.d., (Folder 123), Slavery Files, SCA; William Elliot, Adam's Run, to William Elliot, Jr., August 25, 1862, Elliot-

Gonzales Papers, SHC; Jane Pringle, White House, to Adele Petigru Allston, April 1 [1865], in Easterby, *South Carolina Rice Plantation,* pp. 210–11.

6. Herbert C. Kelman, "Compliance, Identification, and Internalization: Three Processes of Attitude Change," *JCR,* II (1958), 51–54. See also John W. Thibaut and Harold H. Kelley, *The Social Psychology of Groups* (New York: John Wiley & Sons, 1959), pp. 126, 128–29, 135, 147, 239, 242–45, 254; John W. McDavid and Herbert Harari, *Social Psychology: Individuals, Groups, Societies* (New York: Harper & Row, 1968), pp. 305, 326, 330. The author is indebted to Professor Victoria Swigert for bringing these sources to his attention.

7. As Thibaut and Kelley have noted: "Norms provide a means of controlling behavior without entailing the costs, uncertainties, resistances, conflicts, and power losses involved in the unrestrained, *ad hoc* use of interpersonal power." Thibaut and Kelley, *Social Psychology of Groups,* pp. 135–47.

8. According to Peter Wood, between 1730 and 1740 alone, more than "20,000 slaves had been imported from Africa." Peter Wood, *Black Majority: Negroes in Colonial South Carolina From 1670 Through the Stono Rebellion* (New York: Alfred A. Knopf, 1974), p. 302.

9. Ibid., pp. 298–303, 308–10, 322; Michael P. Johnson, "Runaway Slaves and the Slave Communities in South Carolina, 1799 to 1830," *WMQ,* 38 (July 1981), 419, 436, 441; Darold D. Wax, " 'The Great Risque We Run': The Aftermath of Slave Rebellion at Stono, South Carolina, 1739–1745," *JNH,* LXVII (Summer 1982), 137, 142, 145.

10. Wood, *Black Majority,* pp. 274–75, 280–81, 286–97, 304–7.

11. South Carolina Commons House Journals, 1736–1739, pp. 628, 631–32, 680, 681; cf. p. 707, cited in Wood, *Black Majority,* p. 310.

12. Wax, *JNH,* 136; Wood, *Black Majority,* p. 314.

13. Wood, *Black Majority,* pp. 308, 315.

14. Wax, *JNH,* 138–39; "A Ranger's Report of Travels with General Oglethorpe, 1739–1742," quoted in Wood, *Black Majority,* p. 317.

15. Michael S. Hindus, "Black Justice Under White Law: Criminal Prosecutions of Blacks in Antebellum South Carolina," *JAH,* LXIII (December 1976), 576; H. M. Henry, *The Police Control of the Slave in South Carolina* (New York: Negro Universities Press, 1968), p. 6 (originally published in 1914); Wood, *Black Majority,* p. 324.

16. Wood, *Black Majority,* pp. 290, 324–25; Wax, *JNH,* 138–39, 141–42.

17. Wood, *Black Majority,* p. 323; John Belton O'Neall, *The Negro Law of South Carolina* (Columbia: John G. Bowman, 1848), p. 20.

18. Thomas D. Condy, *A Digest of the Laws of the United States and the State of South Carolina . . .* (Charleston: A. E. Miller, 1830), p. 163.

19. Anonymous, "Itinerant Observations in America," *London Magazine* (1745–46), quoted in Wood, *Black Majority,* p. 287.

20. Charles Ball, *Fifty Years in Chains,* with an introduction by Philip S. Foner (New York: Dover Publications, 1970), p. 256 (originally published in 1837); Stroyer, *My Life,* pp. 71–72; George P. Rawick, ed., *The American Slave: A Composite Autobiography* (Westport, Conn.: Greenwood Publishing Company, 1972), II, ii, pp. 24, 110–11, III, iii, p. 227, III, iv, p. 171; Thomas Wentworth Higginson, *Army Life in a Black Regiment* (Boston: Beacon Press, 1962), pp. 158, 230–31 (originally published in 1869); Robert F. W. Allston, Columbia, to Adele Petigru Allston, November 27, 1853, in Easterby, *South Carolina Rice Plantation,* p. 117; "Petition of J. Malachi Ford, Colleton Dis-

trict," November 24, 1854, (Folder 88), Slavery Files, SCA; N. Goethe, Poctotaligo, S.C., to Captn. Ed. Barnwell, January 14, 1863, Francis W. Pickens and Milledge L. Bonham Papers, pp. 392–93, LC; George W. Onil [?], Jasper County, to I. L. Brooks [sic], November 17, 1846, Iveson Lewis Brookes Papers, SHC.

21. Hindus, *JAH*, 584; Plantation Book of William Lowndes, from 1802 to 1822, October [?], 1820, William Lowndes Papers, LC; Thomas D. Turpin, *Christian Advocate and Journal*, VIII (January 31, 1834), cited in Mason Crum, *Gullah: Negro Life in the Carolina Sea Islands* (Durham, N.C.: Duke University Press, 1940), p. 220; Rawick, *The American Slave*, III, iv, p. 2.

22. Ball, *Fifty Years in Chains*, pp. 195, 205, 305–6; Henry William Ravenel, "Recollections of Southern Plantation Life," *TYR*, XXV (June 1936), 764.

23. Charles Cotesworth Pinckney, *An Address Delivered in Charleston Before the Agricultural Society of South Carolina . . . The 18th August, 1829* (Charleston: A. E. Miller, 1829), p. 11.

24. Hortense Powdermaker, "The Channeling of Negro Aggression by the Cultural Process," in August Meier and Elliott Rudwick, eds., *The Making of Black America: Essays in Negro Life and History* (New York: Atheneum, 1973), II, pp. 95–96; Charles W. Joyner, "Slave Folklife of the Waccamaw Neck: Antebellum Black Culture in the South Carolina Lowcountry" (Ph.D. dissertation, University of Pennsylvania, 1977), pp. 163–64, 204–5; Drew G. Faust, "Culture, Conflict and Community: The Meaning of Power on an Antebellum Plantation," *JOSH*, 14 (Fall 1980), 88; Journal of Thomas B. Chaplin, 1845–1886, January 17, 1851, p. 330, SCHS; "Crime Among Slaves," *The Southern Enterprise*, October 19, 1855.

25. "A Series of True Incidents Connected With Sherman's March to the Sea . . . ," n.d. (typescript), p. 3, Grace Pierson (James) Beard Reminiscences, SHC.

26. Adam Hodgson, *Remarks During a Journey Through North America in the Years 1819, 1820, and 1821 . . .* (New York: Samuel Whiting, 1823), pp. 134–35; Winyaw *Intelligencer*, February 12, 1825; Dr. John Peyre Thomas Diary of Weather and Occurences [sic], St. Johns Parish (Berkeley), May 22, 1829, II, p. 95, Thomas Family Papers, SC; David Gavin Diary, 1855–1871, January 24, 1856, February 6, 1857, I (typescript), pp. 65–66, 121, SHC; Mary Boykin Chesnut, *A Diary From Dixie*, eds. Isabella D. Martin and Myrta Locket Avery (Gloucester, Mass.: Peter Smith, 1961), p. 145; Mary W. Milling, Bairds Hill, to Dr. J. S. Milling, Collingsburg, La., August 8, 1865, James S. Milling Papers, SHC.

27. Plantation Journal, 1856–1858, May 9, 1856, Samuel Porcher Gaillard Plantation Journals, 1835–1868, SC.

28. Ibid., November 24, 1856.

29. Floride Calhoun, Fort Hill, to John C. Calhoun, February 15, 1842, John C. Calhoun Family Correspondence Typescripts.

30. "Petition of John Jones, Edgefield District," July 17, 1838, (Folder 105), Slavery Files, SCA; "Petition of Stephen G. Deveaux for Compensation for a Slave Executed, (Charleston District)," 1840, (Folder 78), Slavery Files, SCA; William Cinque Henderson, "Spartan Slaves: A Documentary Account of Blacks on Trial in Spartanburg, South Carolina, 1830–1865" (Ph.D. dissertation, Northwestern University, 1978), pp. 128, 130–36; Harding, *There Is a River*, pp. 49, 229.

31. Henry L. Hall, "The Charleston Fire Scare of 1826," in Charles Joyner, ed.,

"Black Carolinians: Studies in the History of South Carolina Negroes in the Nineteenth Century" (typescript), pp. 1–6, SC.

32. Rawick, *The American Slave,* II, ii, p. 81.

33. Sidney W. Mintz, "Toward an Afro-American History," *JWH,* XIII (1971), 320–22.

34. Stroyer, *My Life,* pp. 22–23.

35. Joel Williamson, *After Slavery: The Negro in South Carolina During Reconstruction, 1861–1877* (Chapel Hill: The University of North Carolina Press, 1965), p. 39.

36. For a discussion of the autonomy slaves derived from their labor, extra toils, trading, and culture, see Norrece T. Jones, Jr., "Control Mechanisms in South Carolina Slave Society, 1800–1865" (Ph.D. dissertation, Northwestern University, 1981), pp. 71–77, 91–93, 111; and Philip D. Morgan, "Work and Culture: The Task System and the World of Lowcountry Blacks, 1700 to 1880," *WMQ* XXXIX (October 1982), 578–79, 591–92.

37. Lorenzo Turner, *Africanisms in the Gullah Dialect* (Chicago: University of Chicago Press, 1949), pp. 4–5, 9, 11–12; David Dalby, *Black Through White: Patterns of Communication* (Bloomington: African Studies Program, Indiana University, 1970), pp. 2–3, 14, 16, 20–21; Mintz, *JWH,* 323–26.

38. Crum, *Gullah,* p. 27.

39. Laura M. Towne, "Pioneer Work on the Sea Islands," *SW,* XXX (July 1901), 400.

40. Turner, *Africanisms,* pp. 11–12.

41. Charles C. Jones, *The Religious Instruction of the Negroes* (New York: Negro Universities Press, 1969), p. 110 (originally published in 1842).

42. Rawick, *The American Slave,* III, iv, p. 192; Thomas L. Webber, *Deep Like the Rivers: Education in the Slave Quarter Community, 1831–1865* (New York: W. W. Norton and Company, 1978), pp. 31, 49–50; Rev. Dr. Richard Furman, *Exposition of the Views of the Baptists, Relative to the Coloured Population . . . ,* 3d ed. (Charleston: A. E. Miller, 1835), pp. 4–5; Richard Hildreth, *Despotism in America; or An Inquiry Into the Nature and Results of the Slave-Holding System in the United States* (Boston: Whipple and Damrell, 1840), p. 63.

43. E. A. Ayandele, *African Historical Studies* (London: Frank Cass and Company, 1979), pp. 79–80.

44. Pinckney, *An Address,* pp. 10–11; *Proceedings of the Meeting in Charleston, S.C., May 13–15, 1845, on the Religious Instruction of the Negroes . . .* (Charleston: Published by Order of the Meeting, 1845), pp. 27, 54, 61; "Report on Management of Slaves, Duty of Overseers, and Employers to Darlington County Agricultural Society," August 1852, p. 3, Thomas Cassels Law Papers, SC.

45. Webber, *Deep Like the Rivers,* pp. 14, 19–21.

46. Ibid., pp. 9, 14, 19, 24, 152–53, 156–57, 189, 262; Sterling Stuckey, "Through the Prism of Folklore: The Black Ethos in Slavery," in Ann J. Lane, ed., *The Debate Over Slavery: Stanley Elkins and His Critics* (Urbana: University of Illinois Press, 1971), pp. 262–63, 268; Daryl Dance, "In the Beginning: A New View of Black American Etiological Tales," *SFQ,* 40 (1977), 60–62; Herbert Aptheker, "Afro-American Superiority: A Neglected Theme in Literature," *Phylon,* XXVI (Winter 1970), 336–37; Stroyer, *My Life,* pp. 22–23; Rawick, *The American Slave,* XIX, pp. 147, 161–62.

47. U.S.W.P.A., Federal Writers' Project, S.C.: Folklore MSS (typescript), SC.

48. John R. Miller, Columbia, S.C., to Mr. Joshua Miller, Lexington, S.C., August 10, 1838, John Fox Papers, PL.

49. John Durant Ashmore Plantation Journal, 1853–1859, February 5, 1856 (typescript), p. 123, SHC.

50. For a small but representative sampling of such attempts, see the following: "Letter to Peter Frigg," December 4, 1803, General Assemby/Accounts—Constables, SCA; (Case 237), July 30, 1851, Pendleton/Anderson District Court of Magistrates and Freeholders Records (microfilm), SCA; Dr. Thomas Diary, April 7, 1829, II, pp. 69–70, Thomas Family Papers, SC; Baptist Church: Church of Christ Records, 1794–1937, Poplar Springs, Laurens County, August 19, September 9, 1837 (typescript), p. 29, SC; "The Petition of William Boyd Praying Compensation for Injuries Received in the Arrest of Certain Runaway Slaves, Laurens District," November 29, 1858, (Folder 54), Slavery Files, SCA; Rawick, *The American Slave*, II, ii, pp. 234–35; Anderson *Gazette*, April 2, 1847, p. 3.

51. "Domestic," The Pendleton *Messenger*, October 5, 1831, n.pag.; "Petition of Edward L. Roche," 1831, (Folder 147), Slavery Files, SCA.

52. Hindus, *JAH*, 595–96; Jane W. Gwinn, "The Georgetown Slave Insurrection of 1829," in Joyner, "Black Carolinians," pp. 1–2, SC; "Report of Committee of Ways and Means . . . ," n.d., (Folder 230), Slavery Files, SCA; "The Petition of William Cregsmily of the parish of St. Andrews, Planter," December 6, 1800, General Assembly Petitions, SCA (The official response was attached to the petition). The last source not only reveals the type of individual who generally sought compensation, but hints at the difficulty in getting some slaveholders to report dangerous slaves. Authorities urged the legislature to grant Cregsmily, "a poor man," his "valuation without abatement" of two slaves executed for "Robbery & Murder." Their generosity was spurred by "the determined manner" in which Cregsmily brought "the Said Negroes to condign punishment" and "*as an example and encouragement to others to do so.*" (Emphasis added.)

53. Anderson *Gazette*, April 2, 1847, p. 3; William Thomson, *A Tradesman's Travels in the United States and Canada . . .* (Edinburgh: Oliver & Boyd, 1842), pp. 173–81, in Willie Lee Rose, ed., *A Documentary History of Slavery in North America* (New York: Oxford University Press, 1976), pp. 365–66; "Memoirs," n.d. (typescript), pp. 86–90, John O'Neale Papers, PL.

54. "The Petition of Alexander Colhoun, Abbeville District," 1825, General Assembly Petitions, SCA; Dr. Thomas Diary, March 25, April 7, 1829, II, pp. 62, 65, 69–70, Thomas Family Papers, SC; "Petition of G. S. McLane, Charleston," November 21, 1831, (Folder 121), Slavery Files, SCA; "Petition of Jacques Bishop Praying Compensation for a Negro Executed," November 1833, (Folder 51), Slavery Files, SCA; Rawick, *The American Slave*, III, iii, p. 158.

55. "Memoirs," pp. 88–90, John O'Neale Papers, PL.

56. "The Petition of Robert A. Cuningham Praying Payment for a Negro Executed," (1831), (Folder 74), Slavery Files, SCA.

57. "State vs. Eddy (a Negro Slave)," August 8, 1849, (Case 97), Spartanburg Court of Magistrates and Freeholders Records (microfilm), SCA.

58. "Petition of Martha Hancock, Edgefield District," November 24, 1820, General Assembly Petitions, SCA; "Petition of Wm. Speer, Administrator of Estate of Daniel Anderson for Compensation for Execution of 3 Negroes: Certificate of Appraisement of Negroes," July 28, 1834, (Folder 40), Slavery Files, SCA; Mary E. Bothwell, Louisville, to Uncle Willie, January 12, 1842, William W. Renwick

Papers, PL; "Petition of James Wideman, Abbeville District," 1847, (Folder 183), Slavery Files, SCA.

59. "Memoirs," p. 87, John O'Neale Papers, PL.

60. Rawick, *The American Slave*, II, ii, p. 234.

61. Hildreth, *Despotism*, pp. 47–49, 89–90, 92; Diary of Edward Hooker, 1805–1808, December 19–21, 1805, cited in American Historical Association, *Report of Historical Manuscripts Commission of the AHA for 1896* (Washington: Government Printing Office, 1897), pp. 881–82; Rachel Blanding, Camden, S.C., to Hannah Lewis [Philadelphia], July 4, 1816, William Blanding Papers, SC; Anna Hayes Johnson, Charleston, S.C., to Eliza Eagles Haywood, Raleigh, N.C., July 24, 1822, Ernest Haywood Collection, SHC; "Petition of Sundry Citizens of Marlboro Against Impressment for the Defence of Pee Dee Region," (1864), Milledge Luke Bonham Papers, PL; Hindus, *JAH*, 593, 596.

62. Howard A. Ohline, "Georgetown, South Carolina: Racial Anxieties and Militant Behavior, 1802," *SCHM*, 73 (July 1972), 130–32, 134–36; "Melancholy Effect of Popular Excitement," The Charleston *Courier*, July 21, 1822; William Johnson, *To the Public of Charleston* (C. C. Sebring, 1822), pp. 4–6; Rosannah P. Rogers, Union District, to David L. Rogers, Tallahassee, Fla., October 29, 1831, William W. Renwick Papers, PL; Adele Petigru Allston, Chicora Wood, to Benjamin Allston, January 1, 1857, in Easterby, *South Carolina Rice Plantation*, p. 136; Roi Ottley and William J. Weatherby, eds., *The Negro in New York: An Informal Social History* (New York: The New York Public Library and Oceana Publications, 1967), pp. 111–12.

63. Gwinn, "The Georgetown Insurrection," in Joyner, "Black Carolinians," pp. 1–3, SC; Marina Wikramanayake, *A World in Shadow: The Free Black in Antebellum South Carolina* (Columbia: University of South Carolina Press, 1973), p. 158; L. Glen Inabinet, "'The July Fourth Incident' of 1816: An Insurrection Plotted by Slaves in Camden, South Carolina," pp. 13–14, paper presented at the Reynolds Conference on South Carolina Legal History, University of South Carolina, December 1977.

64. Anna Hayes Johnson, Charleston, S.C., to Eliza Eagles Haywood, Raleigh, N.C., July 24, 1822, Ernest Haywood Collection, SHC.

65. Hodgson, *Remarks*, pp. 134–35.

66. S.A., "Management of Negroes," *SC*, XVIII (July 1860), 214; Stroyer, *My Life*, p. 77.

67. Herbert Aptheker, *American Negro Slave Revolts* (New York: International Publishers, 1969), pp. 53, 78.

68. Richard Waterhouse, "Merchants, Planters and Lawyers: Political Leadership in South Carolina, 1721–1775," in Bruce C. Daniels, ed., *Power and Status: Officeholding in Colonial America* (Middletown, Conn.: Wesleyan University Press, 1986), pp. 149, 152, 155–56, 171–72; Ira Berlin, *Slaves Without Masters: The Free Negro in the Antebellum South* (New York: Vintage Books, 1974), pp. 86–87, 364; An Inhabitant of Florida, Zaphaniah Kingsley, *A Treatise of the Patriarchal, or Co-Operative System of Society as It Exists in Some Governments . . . Under the Name of Slavery With Its Necessity and Advantages*, 2d ed. (Freeport, N.Y.: Books for Libraries Press, 1970), pp. 3–4, 11 (originally published in 1829).

69. "Southern Slavery," The Pendleton *Messenger*, August 31, 1831; Edward Thomas Heriot, Dirleton, on the Great Pee Dee near Georgetown, S.C., to [unknown], [Great Britain?], April 1854, Edward Heriot Papers, PL; James L. Huston, "The Panic of 1857, Southern Economic Thought, and the Patriarchal

Defense of Slavery," *TH*, XLVI (February 1981), 164, 167–68, 181–83; "Religious Instruction of Slaves: Twelfth Annual Report of the Liberty County Association for the Instruction of Slaves, 1847," *SQR*, XIV (July 1848), 176. For an engaging discussion of the functions and roles ideologies can play, see David Joravsky, *The Lysenko Affair* (Cambridge, Mass.: Harvard University Press, 1970), pp. 1–17.

70. Gillam v. Caldwell, 11 Rich. Eq. 73, May 1859, in Helen T. Catterall, ed., *Judicial Cases Concerning American Slavery and the Negro* (Washington, D.C.: Carnegie Institute of Washington, 1929), II, p. 464; Bell Irvin Wiley, *Southern Negroes, 1861–1865* (Baton Rouge: Louisiana State University Press, 1965), pp. 4, 7; "Governor Hammond's Letters on Slavery, no. 3 . . ." *DR*, o.s., VIII (February 1850), 122; Leslie Howard Owens, *This Species of Property: Slave Life and Culture in the Old South* (New York: Oxford University Press, 1976), p. 184; "Memoirs," p. 83, John O'Neale Papers, PL.

71. Rawick, *The American Slave*, sup., 11, pp. 129, 132.

72. "Report on Management of Slaves," p. 5, Thomas Cassels Law Papers, SC.

73. R. King, Jr., "On the Management of the Butler Estate, and the Cultivation of the Sugar Cane," *SA*, I (December 1828), 523–25; A Planter, "Rules Adopted On A Plantation, To Be Observed by the Overseer," *CP*, I (July 8, 1840), 203; W. W. Gilmer, "Management of Servants," *FP*, III (July 1852), 110. It is important to note that according to Southern patriarchs slaves themselves were frequently to blame for their plight: no whippings or sales would have been necessary if slaves had lived up to the obligations in the mythical contract enslavers and slaves supposedly sealed.

74. James D. Anderson, "Aunt Jemima in Dialectics: Genovese on Slave Culture," *JNH*, LXI (January 1976), 111–13.

75. A careful perusal of *Roll, Jordan, Roll* reveals that the control of slaves was founded more on the reciprocal feelings of obligations and responsibility between master and slave than on the coercive and manipulative tactics practiced by planters. See Eugene D. Genovese, *Roll, Jordan, Roll: The World the Slaves Made* (New York: Pantheon Books, 1974), pp. 3–7, 658–60, and passim.

76. W[illia]m Jones, Goshen, Ga., to Langdon Cheves, Charleston, S.C., June 18, 1830, Cheves Family Papers, SCHS; Journal of Thomas B. Chaplin, 1845–1886, May 3–5, 1845, pp. 28–29, SCHS; A. M. Lawrence, Marietta, Ga., to Gen. J. H. Howard, Grahamville, S.C., January 30, 1851, John H. Howard Papers, PL.

77. Arney Robinson Childs, ed., *The Private Journal of Henry William Ravenel, 1859–1887* (Columbia: University of South Carolina Press, 1947), p. 240.

78. Elizabeth W. Allston Pringle, *Chronicles of Chicora Wood* (New York: Charles Scribner's Sons, 1922), p. 67; Lawrence F. Brewster, "Planters From the Low-Country and Their Summer Travels," in *The Proceedings of the South Carolina Historical Association* (Columbia: South Carolina Historical Association, 1943), p. 35; Higginson, *Army Life*, p. 244.

79. Genovese, *Roll, Jordan, Roll*, p. 5.

80. *American Slavery As It Is: Testimony of a Thousand Witnesses* (New York: American Anti-Slavery Society, 1839), pp. 52–53; Ball, *Fifty Years in Chains*, pp. 136, 280; I. Jenkins Mikell, *Rumbling of the Chariot Wheels* (Columbia, S.C.: The State Company, 1923), pp. 129–37; John S. A. A. Legare Memoirs, n.d. (typescript), pp. 4–5, SHC; "My Reminiscences," n.d. (typescript), pp. 3–4, Charles W. Hutson Papers, SHC.

81. Edward Spann Hammond Diary, 1857–1858, January 7, 20, 1857, pp. 6, 11,

Edward Spann Hammond Papers, SC; Diary of Natalie de Delage Sumter, 1840–1841, September 7, 1840, SC; Pringle, *Chronicles*, pp. 77, 79, 82.

82. Pringle, *Chronicles*, pp. 77, 79, 82.

83. Amelia M. Murray, *Letters from the United States, Cuba and Canada* (New York: G. P. Putnam & Company, 1856), pp. 195–96.

84. Elizabeth H. Botume, *First Days Amongst the Contrabands* (New York: Arno Press and The New York Times, 1968), pp. 128–29, 132–33; Rosser T. Taylor, *Antebellum South Carolina: A Social and Cultural History* (The James Sprunt Studies in History and Political Science, Chapel Hill: The University of North Carolina Press, 1942), pp. 19–20; Wiley, *Southern Negroes*, pp. 134–35, 141–44; Jessie W. Parkhurst, "The Role of the Mammy in the Plantation Household," *JNH*, XXIII (July 1938), 351, 356–57, 367.

85. Genovese, *Roll, Jordan, Roll*, pp. 351–61.

86. Journal of Meta Morris Grimball: South Carolina, December 1860–February 1866, February 20, 1866 (typescript), pp. 112–13, CLS.

87. French, *Slavery*, p. 143.

88. George M. Fredrickson, "Masters and Mudsills: The Role of Race in the Planter Ideology of South Carolina," *SAUS*, 2 (1978), 41–42, 44; William J. Harris, *Plain Folk and Gentry in a Slave Society: White Liberty and Black Slavery in Augusta's Hinterlands* (Middletown, Conn.: Wesleyan University Press, 1985), pp. 6, 66–67, 72–76; Berlin, *Slaves Without Masters*, pp. 88, 193, 369. At no time was the race and class consciousness of ruling-class whites in sharper focus than during the decade before and throughout the Civil War. Nervousness about increasing desertions among lower-class soldiers and about the antielite sentiments expressed by the poor no doubt prompted some of the vehemence in a newspaper editor's protest against the arming of slaves. He warned, "The poor man" will be "reduced to the level of a nigger" and "his wife and daughter" will be "hustled on the street by black wenches, their equals. . . . Swaggering buck niggers are to ogle them and elbow them. . . . Gracious God, is this what our brave soldiery are fighting for?" Editor, "Men Run Mad," Charleston *Mercury*, January 26, 1865, quoted in Wiley, *Southern Negroes*, pp. 153, 155–57.

89. Michael S. Hindus, *Prison and Plantation: Crime, Justice, and Authority in Massachusetts and South Carolina, 1767–1878* (Chapel Hill: University of North Carolina Press, 1980), pp. 242, 244–45; Daniel J. Flanigan, "Criminal Procedure in Slave Trials in the Antebellum South," *JSH*, XL (November 1974), 551; William O. Prentiss, *A Sermon Preached at St. Peter's Church, . . . 2* (Charleston 1860, pp. 12–13, quoted in Michael P. Johnson and James L. Roark, eds., *No Chariot Let Down: Charleston's Free People of Color on the Eve of the Civil War* (Chapel Hill: The University of North Carolina Press, 1984), pp. 140–41.

90. Rachel N. Klein, "Ordering the Backcountry: The South Carolina Regulation," *WMQ*, 38 (October 1981), 677–78; Ball, *Fifty Years in Chains*, pp. 308, 313; "Report to the Darlington County Agricultural Society," n.d., Thomas Cassels Law Papers, SC; Herbert Aptheker, *"We Will Be Free": Advertisements for Runaways and the Reality of American Slavery* (Santa Clara, Cal.: Ethnic Studies Program, University of Santa Clara, 1984), pp. 8, 10; Elizabeth Ware Pearson, ed., *Letters from Port Royal, 1862–1868* (New York: Arno Press and The New York Times, 1969), p. 207; (Case 231), December 11, 1860, Spartanburg Court Records, SCA.

91. Petition to Governor & Council from Marion District, South Carolina, May 12, 1862, Chesnut-Miller-Manning Papers, SCHS.
92. Sister, Cokesbury, to [Joe?], December 30, [between 1852 and 1863], Lalla Pelot Papers, PL.
93. Ohline, *SCHM*, 134; Lionel H. Kennedy and Thomas Parker, *An Official Report of the Trials of Sundry Negroes, Charged with An Attempt to Raise An Insurrection . . . And in An Appendix, A Report of the Trials of Four White Persons on Indictments for Attempting to Excite the Slaves to Insurrection* (Charleston: James R. Schenck, 1822), pp. i–vii; Wikramanayake, *World In Shadow,* pp. 147–48; Aptheker, *American Negro Slave Revolts,* pp. 363–64.
94. James Oakes, *The Ruling Race: A History of American Slaveholders* (New York: Alfred A. Knopf, 1982), pp. 37–41.
95. Hildreth, *Despotism,* p. 167; Ball, *Fifty Years in Chains,* pp. 190–91; Stroyer, *My Life,* p. 28; Rawick, *The American Slave,* III, iv, p. 166.
96. "Petition of Sundry Citizens of Barnwell District to Increase the Punishment for Illicit Traffic With Slaves," December 14, 1850, (Folder 43), Slavery Files, SCA.
97. Charleston South-Carolina *Gazette and County Journal,* June 17, 1766, in Lathan A. Windley, *Runaway Slave Advertisements: A Documentary History from the 1730s to 1790* (Westport, Conn.: Greenwood Press, 1983), III, pp. 604–5; Williams S. Harvey, "100 Dollars Reward," The Georgetown *Gazette,* February 14, 1826; T. W. Kinman, "Ranaway," Greenville *Mountaineer,* August 20, 1847; Daniel C. Littlefield, *Rice and Slaves: Ethnicity and the Slave Trade in Colonial South Carolina* (Baton Rouge: Louisiana State University Press, 1981), pp. 165–67; Aptheker, *"We Will Be Free,"* pp. 8, 10.
98. Eugene D. Genovese, *From Rebellion to Revolution: Afro-American Slave Revolts in the Making of the Modern World* (Baton Rouge: Louisiana State University Press, 1979), pp. 26–27; Harris, *Plain Folk,* pp. 5–7, 71–72, 90–93. Some indication of the discomfort and fear caused by nonelite whites—particularly those without slaves—is reflected in the extraordinary suggestions on how the latter could join the ranks of enslavers. A writer calling himself simply "A Minuteman," for example, urged every large slaveholder to "sell one in ten slaves, on credit," to a nonslaveholder and hence "make *interest* supply the deficiency of patriotism." Edgefield *Advertiser,* November 28, 1860, quoted in Harris, *Plain Folk,* p. 91. See also Berlin, *Slaves Without Masters,* p. 371.
99. Memorial of the Citizens of Charleston to the Senate and House of Representatives of the State of South Carolina (Charleston, 1822), in Ulrich B. Phillips, ed., *Plantation and Frontier Documents, 1649–1863: Illustrative of Industrial History in the Colonial and Ante-Bellum South* (Cleveland: The Arthur H. Clark Company, 1909), II, pp. 109–13; Harris, *Plain Folk,* pp. 5–7, 67; Randall M. Miller, "The Fabric of Control: Slavery in Antebellum Southern Textile Mills," *BHR,* LV (Winter 1981), 479–80; "An Ordinance for the Government of Negroes and Other Persons of Color, Within the City of Charleston, . . ." Ratified October 28, 1806, in George B. Eckhard, *A Digest of the Ordinances of the City Council of Charleston, From the Year 1783 to Oct. 1844* (Charleston: Walker & Burke, 1844), pp. 169–72; Berlin, *Slaves Without Masters,* pp. 269–318.
100. William Kauffman Scarborough, *The Overseer: Plantation Management in the Old South* (Baton Rouge: Louisiana State University Press, 1966), p. 94.
101. Rochester *Union and Advertiser,* August 9, 1893, in John W. Blassingame, ed., *Slave Testimony: Two Centuries of Letters, Speeches, Interviews and Autobio-*

graphies (Baton Rouge: Louisiana State University Press, 1977), p. 512; Rawick, *The American Slave*, II, i, pp. 338–39, 344, II, ii, pp. 57, 65–66.

102. B. T. Sellers to (Williams) Middleton, June 16, 1860, Williams Middleton Papers, SC.

103. Langdon Cheves, Delta, to Huger, Hamilton, and Habersham, April 6, 1834, Cheves Family Papers, SCHS; Rawick, *The American Slave*, II, ii, p. 36; "Petition of Richard Singleton," [1848], (Folder 159), Slavery Files, SCA.

104. "Memoirs," p. 90, John O'Neale Papers, PL.

105. Rawick, *The American Slave*, II, i.

106. Both John Hope Franklin and, most recently, Orville Vernon Burton have established the explosive pugnaciousness of Southern whites. See John Hope Franklin, *The Militant South, 1800–1861* (Cambridge: Harvard University Press, 1956), and Orville Vernon Burton, *In My Father's House Are Many Mansions: Family and Community in Edgefield, South Carolina* (Chapel Hill: The University of North Carolina Press, 1985).

107. Louis Manigault, Gowrie (Savannah River) to Mr. C. W. Jones, Ricedale, December 17, 1855, Louis Manigault Papers, PL.

108. Kingsley, *A Treatise*, pp. 12–13; Bell ads. Graham, 1 N. and McC. 278, November 1818, Smith v. McCall, 1 McCord 220, May 1821, State v. Mazyk, 2 McCord 473, May 1823, in Catterall, *Judicial Cases*, II, pp. 310–11, 318, 322; Editor, Charleston *Mercury*, December 1, 1841, cited in Henry, *Police Control*, p. 60; "Petition of Citizens of Marion District," November 1, 1858, (Folder 123), Slavery Files, SCA; "L. Witsell v. J. Earnest and J. Parker. Tried before Mr. Justice Johnson, at Colleton" (1818), in Henry J. Nott and David J. McCord, *Reports of Cases Determined in the Constitutional Court of South Carolina* (Charleston: W. Riley, 1842), I, pp. 182–84.

109. Condy, *Digest of the Laws*, p. 163; Hindus, *JAH*, 578–89; Henry, *Police Control*, pp. 73–74, 78; O'Neall, *Negro Law*, p. 20.

110. John Evans, Pinckney Island, to General Charles Cotesworthy Pinckney, November 25, 1824; (C. C. Pinckney), Charleston, to (Mr. T. Dawsey), December 6, 1824; Mr. T. Dawsey, Pinckney Island,to Charles Cotesworth Pinckney, November 25, 1824; (C. C. Pinckney) to Cotesworth, December 17, 1824, The Pinckney Family Papers, LC; Henderson, "Spartan Slaves," pp. 111–14.

111. J. M. Johnson, Charleston, to Henry Ellison, August 20, 1860, Ellison Family Papers, South Caroliniana Library, quoted in Johnson, *No Chariot Let Down*, pp. 86, 98.

Chapter 2. The Threat of Sale: The Black Family as a Mechanism of Control

1. Foby, "Management of Servants," *SC*, XI (August 1853), 226.

2. George P. Rawick, ed., *The American Slave: A Composite Autobiography*, Supplement, Series 1 (Westport, Conn.: Greenwood Press, 1977), 11, p. 283.

3. Bobby Frank Jones, "A Cultural Middle Passage: Slave Marriage and Family in the Ante-Bellum South" (Ph.D. dissertation, University of North Carolina, 1965), pp. 6–7; J. G. Clinkscales, *On the Old Plantation: Reminiscences of His Childhood* (New York: Negro Universities Press, 1969), pp. 37–38 (originally published in 1916); George P. Rawick, ed., *The American Slave: A Composite Autobiography* (Westport, Conn.: Greenwood Publishing Company, 1972), III, iii, pp. 218–20, II, ii p. 77; Jacob Stroyer, *My Life in the South*

(Salem, Mass.: Observer and Job Print, 1885), pp. 42–43; A. M. French, *Slavery in South Carolina and the Ex-Slaves; Or, the Port Royal Mission* (New York: Negro Universities Press, 1969), p. 94 (originally published in 1862).

4. Charles Ball, *Fifty Years in Chains*, with an introduction by Philip S. Foner (New York: Dover Publications, 1970), p. 68 (originally published in 1837).

5. Nowel v. O'Hara, 1 Hill 150, April 1833. (151), in Helen T. Catterall, ed., *Judicial Cases Concerning American Slavery and the Negro* (Washington, D.C.: Carnegie Institute of Washington, 1929), II, p. 352.

6. Hinton v. Kennedy, 3 S.C. 459, November 1871. Will, 1855: (480), in Ibid., p. 477.

7. Robert Pringle, Charles Town, to Edward & John Mayne & Co., Lisbon, September 19, 1740, in Walter B. Edgar, ed., *The Letterbook of Robert Pringle* (Columbia: The University of South Carolina Press, 1972), I, p. 247.

8. Plantation Book of Charles Cotesworth Pinckney and Successors, 1812–1861, "Slave List," pp. 1–11, The Pinckney Family Papers, LC; John Chesnut, Camden, to Charles Chesnut, Philadelphia, September 25, 1835, Williams-Chesnut-Manning Papers, SC; James R. Sparkman Plantation Book, 1845, II, Sparkman Family Papers, SHC; Douglass v. Price, 4 Rich. Eq. 322, May 1852. (326), in Catterall, *Judicial Cases*, II, p. 433; David Golightly Harris Farm Journals, June 9, 11, 1860 (microfilm), SHC; Elizabeth Collins, *Memories of the Southern States* (Taunton: Barnicott, 1865), p. 71; William Elliot, Adam's Run, to William Elliot, Jr., August 25, 1862, Elliot-Gonzales Papers, SHC; "State vs. Frank, Hannah, and Matilda, slaves of Charles J. Colcock, Beaufort District, S.C.," June 16, 1862, Francis W. Pickens and Milledge L. Bonham Papers, LC; William Capers, Gowrie Plantation, to Charles Manigault, Charleston, S.C., September 15, 28, 1863, in Ulrich B. Phillips, ed., *Plantation and Frontier Documents, 1649–1863: Illustrative of Industrial History in the Colonial & Ante-Bellum South* (Cleveland: The Arthur H. Clark Company, 1909), II, pp. 32–33.

9. Charles C. Jones, *The Religious Instruction of the Negroes* (New York: Negro Universities Press, 1969), p. 133 (originally published in 1842); "Religious Instruction of Slaves," DR, o.s., XXVI (January 1859), 108; Rev. Andrew Flinn Dickson, *Plantation Sermons, or Plain and Familiar Discourses for Instruction of the Unlearned* (Philadelphia: Presbyterian Board of Publication, 1856), pp. 13–14.

10. H. Shelton Smith, *In His Image, But . . . Racism in Southern Religion, 1780–1910* (Durham, N.C.: Duke University Press, 1972), pp. 43–47, 53–55, 59–60, 69, 138.

11. John B. Adger, *The Christian Doctrine of Human Rights and Slavery* (Columbia, S.C., 1849), p. 15, quoted in Ibid., p. 138.

12. Rawick, *The American Slave*, II, ii, pp. 234–35.

13. Una Pope-Hennessy, *The Aristocratic Journey: Being the Outspoken Letters of Mrs. Basil Hall Written During a Fourteen Months' Sojourn in America, 1827–1828* (New York: G. P. Putnam's Sons, 1931), p. 210; John C. Calhoun, Cane Brake (Edgefield County, S.C.), to Thomas Green Clemson, Brussels, December 13, 1845, Calhoun Family Typescripts; Frederick Douglass, *Life and Times of Frederick Douglass* (1962), p. 97, cited in Herbert G. Gutman, *The Black Family in Slavery & Freedom, 1750–1925* (New York: Pantheon Books, 1976), pp. 357–58; *Preliminary Report Touching the Condition and Management of Emancipated Refugees; Made to the Secretary of War, by the American Freedmen's Inquiry Commission, June 30, 1863* (New York: John F. Trow, 1863),

p. 13; Elizabeth Hyde Botume, *First Days Amongst the Contrabands* (New York: Arno Press and The New York Times, 1968), pp. 84, 209–10 (originally published in 1892); Elizabeth Ware Pearson, ed., *Letters From Port Royal, 1862–1868* (New York: Arno Press and The New York Times, 1969), p. 97 (originally published in 1906); Ray Allen Billington, ed., *The Journal of Charlotte L. Forten: A Free Negro in the Slave Era* (New York: Collier Books, 1961), p. 211.

14. Charles Nordhoff, "The Freedmen of South-Carolina," in Frank Moore, ed., *Papers of the Day* (New York: Charles T. Evans, 1863), p. 11.

15. Rupert Sargent Holland, ed., *Letters and Diary of Laura M. Towne: Written From the Sea Islands of South Carolina, 1862–1884* (Cambridge: Riverside Press, 1912), pp. 74–75.

16. Joel Williamson, *After Slavery: The Negro in South Carolina During Reconstruction, 1861–1877* (Chapel Hill: The University of North Carolina Press, 1965), pp. 39–44; Guion Griffis Johnson, *A Social History of the Sea Islands: With Special Reference to St. Helena Island, South Carolina* (Chapel Hill: The University of North Carolina Press, 1930), p. 190; Julia Peterkin, *Roll, Jordan, Roll. Photographic Studies by Doris Ulmann* (New York: Robert O. Ballou, 1933), p. 28.

17. Elsie Clews Parsons, *Folk-Lore of the Sea Islands, South Carolina* (Cambridge, Mass.: The American Folk-Lore Society, 1923), pp. 213–16; "Memoirs of S. W. Ferguson: Family History and Boyhood," April 26, 1900 (typescript), pp. 15, 20, Heyward and Ferguson Family Papers (typescript and microfilm), SHC; Anne Sinkler Fishburne, *Belvidere: A Plantation Memory* (Columbia: University of South Carolina Press, 1949), pp. 106–7; Leon Stone Bryan, Jr., "Slavery On a Peedee River Rice Plantation, 1825–1865" (M.A. thesis, Johns Hopkins University, 1963), p. 186.

18. Patience Pennington (E. W. A. Pringle), *A Woman Rice Planter* (Cambridge: The Belknap Press of Harvard University Press, 1961), p. 59, quoted in Bryan, "Slavery On a Peedee River Rice Plantation," pp. 183–84, 186.

19. George Rogers, Jr., *The History of Georgetown County, South Carolina* (Columbia: University of South Carolina Press, 1970), p. 328; Gutman, *The Black Family*, pp. 357–58; Austin Bearse, *Reminiscences of Fugitive-Slave Law Days* (Boston: Warren Richardson, 1880), pp. 8–10; Abream Scriven to Dinah Jones, Savannah (Ga.), September 19, 1858, Charles Colcock Jones Papers, Special Collections Division, Tulane University Library, New Orleans, in Robert S. Starobin, ed., *Letters of American Slaves* (New York: New Viewpoints, 1974), p. 58; French, *Slavery in South Carolina*, p. 125; Rawick, *The American Slave*, II, i, pp. 180, 188; E. C. L. Adams, *Nigger to Nigger* (New York: Charles Scribner's Sons, 1928), pp. 235–36.

20. Thomas Wentworth Higginson, *Army Life in a Black Regiment* (Boston: Beacon Press, 1962), pp. 52–53 (originally published in 1869).

21. "Petition of Certain Citizens of Charleston Praying to Prohibit the Introduction of Slaves Merely for Sale and for Certain Other Amendments of the Law in Relation to Slaves," 1847, (Folder 64), Slavery Files, SCA.

22. "Memoirs of S. W. Ferguson," p. 3, Heyward and Ferguson Family Papers, SHC; Harriet Martineau, *Society in America* (London: Saunders and Otley, 1837), II, pp. 333–34; William P. Harrison, ed., *The Gospel Among the Slaves* (Nashville: Publishing House of the M. E. Church, South, 1893), p. 359.

23. Robert F. W. Allston, Plantersville, to Adele Petigru Allston, April 10, 1863, in J. H. Easterby, ed., *The South Carolina Rice Plantation as Revealed in the*

Papers of Robert F. W. Allston (Chicago: University of Chicago Press, 1945), p. 184.

24. Thomas Cooper and David J. McCord, eds., *The Statutes at Large of South Carolina* (Columbia, 1836–41), VII, p. 370, quoted in Peter Wood, *Black Majority: Negroes in Colonial South Carolina From 1670 Through the Stono Rebellion* (New York: Alfred A. Knopf, 1974), p. 280.

25. Wood, *Black Majority*, pp. 25–26, 140, 159–60.

26. Rawick, *The American Slave*, sup., 11, pp. 132–33; Gutman, *The Black Family*, pp. 145–46, 148–49, 153, 357–58; Leslie Howard Owens, *This Species of Property: Slave Life and Culture in the Old South* (New York: Oxford University Press, 1976), pp. 184–85; "Memoirs," n.d. (typescript), pp. 66–67, 77, John O'Neale Papers, PL.

27. Manigault Letter Book, 1846–1848 (typescript), Charles Izard Manigault, Paris, to Mr. Haynes, (Savannah River), March 1, 1847, pp. 26–27, Charles Manigault Papers, SC.

28. Rawick, *The American Slave*, II, i, p. 159.

29. Collins, *Memories of the Southern States*, p. 71.

30. Ray Allen Billington, ed., *The Journal of Charlotte L. Forten: A Free Negro in the Slave Era* (New York: Collier Books, 1961), pp. 151–52, 160; Holland, *Letters and Diary of Laura M. Towne*, p. 28; Stroyer, *My Life in the South*, pp. 43–44; Thomas H. Jones, *The Experience and Personal Narrative of Uncle Tom Jones: Who Was for Forty Years a Slave; also, the Surprising Adventures of Wild Tom, a Fugitive Negro from South Carolina* (New York: G. C. Holbrook, 1854), pp. 7–8, cited in Stanley Feldstein, "The Slave's View of Slavery" (Ph.D. dissertation, New York University, 1969), p. 35.

31. Ball, *Fifty Years in Chains*, pp. 17–18.

32. Rawick, *The American Slave*, II, i, pp. 229–30.

33. Stroyer, *My Life in the South*, pp. 42–44; Rawick, *The American Slave*, II, i, pp. 65–67, II, ii, pp. 144–45; Orland Kay Armstrong, *Old Massa's People: The Old Slaves Tell Their Story* (Indianapolis: Bobbs-Merrill Company, 1931), pp. 258–59.

34. Rawick, *The American Slave*, II, i, pp. 180, 188.

35. Sidney Mintz and Richard Price, *An Anthropological Approach to the Afro-American Past: A Caribbean Perspective* (Philadelphia: Institute for the Study of Human Issues, 1976), p. 34.

36. Arney Robinson Childs, ed., *The Private Journal of Henry William Ravenel, 1859–1887* (Columbia: University of South Carolina Press, 1947), p. 240; George W. Williams, ed., *Incidents In My Life: The Autobiography of the Rev. Paul Trapier, S.T.D. With Some of His Letters* (Charleston: Dalcho Historical Society, 1954), p. 32; Charles I. Manigault Book Containing Loose Papers, 1776–1872 (typescript) p. 17, Charles Manigault Papers, SC.

37. Rogers, *History of Georgetown County*, pp. 328, 343; Charles W. Joyner, "Slave Folklife of the Waccamaw Neck: Antebellum Black Culture in the South Carolina Lowcountry" (Ph.D. dissertation, University of Pennsylvania, 1977), p. 30.

38. Armstrong, *Old Massa's People*, pp. 44–45; Rawick, *The American Slave*, III, iii, p. 14; Billington, *Journal of Charlotte Forten*, pp. 160, 178; Fredrika Bremer, *The Homes of the New World: Impressions of America*, trans. Mary Howitt (New York: Harper & Brothers, 1868), I, p. 394; Holland, *Letters and Diary of Laura M. Towne*, p. 177.

39. Fishburne, *Belvidere*, p. 25.

40. Herbert G. Gutman, *The Black Family in Slavery & Freedom, 1750–1925* (New York: Pantheon Books, 1976), pp. 36, 45–46, 52, 88, 93, 101–2, 154, 196–97, 199, 217–18, 220.

41. Sidney Mintz, *Caribbean Transformations* (Chicago: Aldine Publishing Company, 1974), p. 77.

42. Pearson, *Letters From Port Royal,* pp. 44, 97, 133–35; Holland, *Letters and Diary of Laura M. Towne,* pp. 45–54.

43. "150 Reward," The Charleston *Mercury,* January 6, 1829; Thomas L. Shaw, "Ten Dollars Reward," Georgetown *Gazette,* December 16, 1825; "Forty Dollars Reward," The Charleston *Mercury,* January 6, 1829; "Absconded," The Charleston *Courier,* July 27, 1829; *American Slavery As It Is: Testimony of A Thousand Witnesses* (New York: American Anti-Slavery Society, 1839), p. 23; J. S. Buckingham, *The Slave States of America* (London: Fisher, Son, & Co., 1842), I, p. 571; Langdon Cheves, Pendleton, to Langdon Cheves, Jr., Savannah, May 2, 1844, Cheves Family Papers, SCHS; Anderson *Gazette,* June 5, 1846, III, p. 3.

44. The Charleston *Courier,* February 17, 1849.

45. John Davis, *Travels of Four Years and a Half in the United States of America: During 1798, 1799, 1800, 1801, and 1802* (London: 1803), pp. 92–93.

46. "John's Island," The Charleston *Mercury,* July 1, 1829.

47. Frances Lance, "Ranaway on the 29th," *The Southern Patriot,* April 18, 1829; *American Slavery As It Is,* p. 63; Jno. Cothran, "$20 Reward!" Greenville *Mountaineer,* September 21, 1838; Anne King Gregorie, *History of Sumter County, South Carolina* (Sumter: Library Board of Sumter County, 1954), p. 144; Henry Sills, "$30.00 Reward," Cheraw *Intelligencer and Southern Register,* March 5, 1824.

48. Samuel Tayler, Mobile, Ala., to Mrs. Elizabeth Blythe, [Georgetown], September 2, 1838, R. F. W. Allston Papers, SCHS.

49. "Information Wanted," *South Carolina Leader,* May 12, 1866, I, n.pag.; Leon F. Litwack, *Been in the Storm So Long: The Aftermath of Slavery* (New York: Vintage Books, 1979), pp. 230–32.

50. "Information Wanted," *New Era,* July 28, 1870, I, n.pag.

51. Cuba, like other sugar-producing societies, was feared by North American slaves as a destination little worse than hell. Not only did rumors abound of unrelenting labor, but of masters whose brutality made American slaveholders seem benign. See Holland, *Letters and Diary of Laura M. Towne,* pp. 53–54.

52. Nordhoff, "Freedmen of South-Carolina," p. 20.

53. "Testimony of Col. Higginson," American Freedmen's Inquiry Commission (microfilm), Reel 200, File III, p. 192, NA; Holland, *Letters and Diary of Laura M. Towne,* pp. 45–46, 49, 53–54, 107; Billington, *Journal of Charlotte L. Forten,* pp. 165–66, 178, 182; Botume, *First Days Amongst the Contrabands,* pp. 54–57, 68, 154, 163. While ministering among the contrabands, the Reverend Mansfield French declared that blacks' herculean search for relatives was a "sacred work" that deserved every possible assistance. Unfortunately, as Leon Litwack discovered, neither the extraordinary skill of blacks in tracking down each clue and rumor, nor their steadfast determination to remain on trails that "suddenly appeared to vanish," led many to find their families. See French, *Slavery in South Carolina,* p. 27, and Litwack, *Been in the Storm So Long,* pp. 230–31.

54. Edward L. Pierce, "Freedmen at Port Royal," *AM,* XII (September 1863), 311.

55. Stephen Moore, Camp on James Island, to Rachel, July 8, 1862, Thomas John Moore Papers, SC.

56. Ulrich B. Phillips, *American Negro Slavery: A Survey of the Supply, Employment and Control of Negro Labor As Determined by the Plantation Regime*, with a foreword by Eugene Genovese (Baton Rouge: Louisiana State University Press, 1966), pp. 264–68, 279, 286; Kenneth M. Stampp, *The Peculiar Institution: Slavery in the Ante-Bellum South* (New York: Vintage Books, 1956), pp. 282–89; Eugene D. Genovese, "Rejoinder," *SL*, 6 (November–December 1966), 58, 61; Robert W. Fogel and Stanley L. Engerman, *Time On the Cross: The Economics of American Negro Slavery* (Boston: Little, Brown and Company, 1974), I, pp. 109–17. In challenging the Fogel and Engerman thesis that "slavery provided a better diet for blacks than did freedom for most whites," Richard Sutch argues: "The slave *diet* may have generally been nutritionally balanced even when the *ration* provided by the master was not," for slaves, despite their masters, made it so. See Richard Sutch, "The Care and Feeding of Slaves," in Paul A. David et al., *Reckoning With Slavery: A Critical Study in the Quantitative History*, with an introduction by Kenneth M. Stampp (New York: Oxford University Press, 1976), pp. 268, 281–82.

57. Ball, *Fifty Years in Chains*, p. 194; George W. Knepper, ed., *Travels in The Southland, 1822–1823: The Journal of Lucius Versus Bierce* (Columbus: Ohio State University Press, 1966), p. 81; William L. McCaa, "Observations on the Manner of Living and Diseases of the Slaves on the Wateree River, S.C." (Sr. thesis, University of Pennsylvania, 1823), p. 1, WHL; Moses Roper, *A Narrative of the Adventures and Escape of Moses Roper From American Slavery* (New York: Negro Universities Press, 1970), p. 60 (originally published in 1838); H. Perry Pope, "A Dissertation on the Professional Management of Negro Slaves" (Sr. thesis, Medical College of the State of South Carolina, 1837), pp. 3–4, MU; *American Slavery As It Is*, p. 28; Henry William Ravenel, "Recollections of Southern Plantation Life," *TYR*, XXV (June 1936), 753; Nordhoff, "Freedmen of South Carolina," p. 5; French, *Slavery in South Carolina*, pp. 67, 118–20.

58. Charles M. Clark, "Plantation Overseers in South Carolina, 1820–1860" (M.A. thesis, University of South Carolina, 1966), p. 30; Ball, *Fifty Years in Chains*, pp. 205–7, 262–63; William E. Sparkman Plantation Record, 1844–1866, March 31, 1844, to December 29, 1844, SHC; Dr. J. Rhett Motte's Exeter Plantation Work Book, St. Johns, Berkeley, January 1, 1850, to July 7, 1850, I, Motte Family Papers, SC; Mulberry Journal for 1853–1857, December 3, 1853, to April 25, 1857, Mulberry Plantation Journals, 1853–1889, SCHS; Knepper, *Travels in the Southland*, p. 81; Ravenel, *TYR*, 751; Roper, *A Narrative*, p. 60; Manigault Letter Book, Charles Izard Manigault, Naples, to Mr. J. F. Cooper, Gowrie, January 10, 1848, pp. 59–60, Charles Manigault Papers, SC.

59. Duncan Clinch Heyward, *Seed From Madagascar* (Chapel Hill: The University of North Carolina Press, 1937), pp. ix, 182; Gutman, *The Black Family*, p. 237.

60. Phillips, *American Negro Slavery*, p. 265.

61. Chalmers Gaston Davidson, *The Last Foray: The South Carolina Planters of 1860, A Sociological Study* (Columbia: University of South Carolina Press, 1971), p. 252; Sparkman Plantation Record, January 1, 1845, SHC.

62. Sparkman Plantation Record, March 31, 1844, to December 26, 1844, SHC.

63. Dr. Motte's Work Book, January 1, 1850, to June 30, 1850, I, Motte Family Papers, SC.

64. Helen G. McCormack, "A Provisional Guide to Manuscripts in the South Carolina Historical Society," SCHM, 47 (July 1946), 173.

65. Mulberry Journal, December 3, 1853, to April 25, 1857, Mulberry Plantation Journals, SCHS.

66. "Report of the Committee on Colored Population," December 4, 1856 (Folder 217), Slavery Files, SCA.

67. Clark, "Plantation Overseers," p. 30; Stampp, The Peculiar Institution, pp. 283–84; Robert [Cox?], Head Quarters, [Sullivan's Island], 20th Regt. S.C.V., to Brother, September 29, 1862, I, Cox Papers (typescript), p. 167, SC; H. D. McCloud, "Hints on the Medical Treatment of Negroes" (Sr. thesis, Medical College of South Carolina, 1850), pp. 15–16, MU.

68. Farmer's Club (ABC Farmer's Club) Records, 1846–1893, Beech Island, Aiken County, November 6, 1847 (typescript), p. 45, SC.

69. A Planter, "Notions on the Management of Negroes, &c.," SA, IX (November 1836), 582; Dr. Roderick Murchison, New York, to Elizabeth Murchison, Orangeburg, S.C., February 1, 1817, Bruce, Jones, and Murchison Papers, SC.

70. H. Perry Pope, "A Dissertation on the Professional Management of Negro Slaves," pp. 3–4, MU.

71. Stroyer, My Life in the South, p. 11.

72. Ball, Fifty Years in Chains, pp. 54, 207, 262–63, 323; Roper, A Narrative, p. 60; Anti-Slavery Advocate, II (February 1, 1862), 498–99, in John W. Blassingame, ed., Slave Testimony: Two Centuries of Letters, Speeches, Interviews and Autobiographies (Baton Rouge: Louisiana State University Press, 1977), p. 359; "Rosa Barnwell to the Editor," Liberator, November 7, 1862, in Blassingame, Slave Testimony, p. 698; Billington, Journal of Charlotte Forten, p. 149; Nordhoff, "Freedmen of South Carolina," p. 5; French, Slavery in South Carolina, pp. 118–19; Rawick, The American Slave, III, iii, pp. 8–10, 272; Dorothy Sterling, Captain of the Planter, The Story of Robert Smalls (New York, 1958), pp. 16, 24, 29–31, cited in Willie Lee Rose, Rehearsal for Reconstruction: The Port Royal Experiment (New York: Vintage Books, 1964), p. 131.

73. Rochester Union and Advertiser, August 9, 1893, in Blassingame, Slave Testimony, pp. 511–12.

74. Rawick, The American Slave, II, i, p. 125.

75. Joyner, "Slave Folklife," pp. 158–59, 162–64, 321.

76. John Drayton, A View of South Carolina, As Respects Her Natural and Civil Concerns (Charleston: W. P. Young, 1802), p. 145; Ball, Fifty Years in Chains, p. 194; Bremer, Homes of the New World, I, p. 297; Ravenel, TYR, 762; D. E. Smith, A Charlestonian's Recollections, 1846–1913 (Charleston: Carolina Art Association, 1950), pp. 27, 29; Rawick, The American Slave, III, iii, pp. 8–10, 272; Joyner, "Slave Folklife," pp. 194, 321; Lawton v. Hunt, 4 Rich. Eq. 233, January, 1852. (234), in Catterall, Judicial Cases, II, pp. 431–32.

77. Sutch, "Care and Feeding of Slaves," p. 282; Charles Joyner, Down by the Riverside: A South Carolina Slave Community (Urbana: University of Illinois Press, 1984), p. 99; Adam Hodgson, Remarks During a Journey Through North America in the Years 1819, 1820, and 1821 . . . (New York: Samuel Whiting, 1823), p. 117; Bremer, Homes of the New World, I, pp. 297, 305; Charles A. Raymond, "The Religious Life of the Negro Slave," HNM, XXVII (September 1863), 676; Alice R. Huger Smith, A Carolina Rice Plantation of

the Fifties ... With Chapters From the Unpublished Memoirs of D. E. Huger Smith (New York: William Morrow and Company, 1936), pp. 71–72; Holland, Letters and Diary of Laura M. Towne, pp. 27–28; Rawick, The American Slave, III, iii, pp. 200–1, II, i, p. 244, II, ii, p. 76; Jones, "A Cultural Middle Passage," pp. 126, 131; Ball, Fifty Years in Chains, pp. 194–95, 205, 257, 274–75; Kneppler, Travels in the Southland, p. 81; Nordhoff, "Freedmen of South Carolina," pp. 5–16, 18; Heyward, Seed From Madagascar, p. 182.

78. Charles Cotesworth Pinckney, An Address Delivered in Charleston Before the Agricultural Society of South-Carolina ... The 18th August, 1829 (Charleston: A. E. Miller, 1829), p. 4.

79. Holland, Letters and Diary of Laura M. Towne, p. 25.

80. Stroyer, My Life in the South, pp. 23–24; "Have Manners: Grandma Kit and Aunt Maria Heywood," (D-4-33a), Federal Writers' Project, S.C.: Folklore MSS (typescript), SC; Jones, "A Cultural Middle Passage," p. 107.

81. Rawick, The American Slave, II, i, pp. 224–25.

82. William Howard Russell, My Diary North and South (New York: Harper & Brothers, 1863), p. 55; Collins, Memories of the Southern States, p. 31; Rawick, The American Slave, III, iii, pp. 261–62.

83. W. W. Gilmer, "Management of Servants," FP, III (July 1852), 110.

84. "Report on Management of Slaves, Duty of Overseers, and Employers to Darlington County Agricultural Society," August 1852, pp. 1–2, Thomas Cassels Law Papers, SC; Bremer, Homes of the New World, I, pp. 291–92; Charles I. Manigault Book Containing Loose Papers, p. 16, Charles Manigault Papers, SC; Armstrong, Old Massa's People, p. 200; Pinckney, An Address, pp. 10–12; Charles Cotesworth Pinckney, El Dorado, to William Capers, January 23, 1835, Conference Papers, Methodist Collection, Wofford College, quoted in Rogers, History of Georgetown County, pp. 352–53; Joyner, "Slave Folklife," pp. 159–75; E. C. L. Adams, Nigger to Nigger (New York: Charles Scribner's Sons, 1928), pp. 175–76; Parsons, Folk-Lore of the Sea Islands, pp. xvii, 22–23, 97, 102; Charles C. Jones, Negro Myths From the Georgia Coast (Columbia: The State Company, 1925), pp. 53–54.

85. Julia Peterkin, Roll, Jordan, Roll. Photographic Studies by Doris Ulmann (New York: Robert O. Ballou, 1933), p. 231; Archie Vernon Huff, Langdon Cheves of South Carolina (Columbia: University of South Carolina Press, 1977), pp. 192, 194–96.

86. Rawick, The American Slave, II, i, p. 220, III, iii, pp. 77–99, 145, 153; Ravenel, TYR, 757, 761, 764; Pearson, Letters From Port Royal, p. 215; Joyner, "Slave Folklife," pp. 167, 169; Jones, Negro Myths, pp. 53–54; Holland, Letters and Diary of Laura M. Towne, pp. 107, 148, 150; Botume, First Days Amongst the Contrabands, pp. 48–49, 68–69, 139, 190, 237–43; "Manners Will Carry You," (D-4-331), Federal Writers' Project, S.C., SC; William Francis Allen and others, Slave Songs of the United States (New York: A. Simpson & Co., 1867), pp. xxix–xxx, 39; Mintz, An Anthropological Approach, pp. 35, 37; Gutman, The Black Family, pp. 154, 216–18, 226–28.

87. Gutman, The Black Family, p. 220.

88. Joyner, "Slave Folklife," p. 169; Hodgson, Remarks, p. 130; Botume, First Days Amongst the Contrabands, p. 36; Thomas L. Webber, Deep Like the Rivers: Education in the Slave Quarter Community, 1831–1865 (New York: W. W. Norton and Company, 1978), pp. 19, 221, 225, 318; John W. Blassingame, "Status and Social Structure in the Slave Community: Evidence From

New Sources," in Harry P. Owens, ed., *Perspectives and Irony in American Slavery* (Jackson: University Press of Mississippi, 1976), p. 147.

89. Thomas Webber argues, for instance, that by the time slaveholders began any serious efforts to shape the worldview of slave youths, the latter already had learned how "to adopt the roles required by plantation etiquette *without an identification with* the reality suggested by the role." (Emphasis added.) See Webber, *Deep Like the Rivers*, p. 261.

90. Hodgson, *Remarks*, p. 130; Smith, *Carolina Rice Plantation*, p. 71.

91. Stephen Gudeman, "Herbert Gutman's The Black Family in Slavery and Freedom, 1750–1925: An Anthropologist's View," *SSH*, 3 (October 1979), 60–61; Cheryll Ann Cody, "Naming, Kinship, and Estate Dispersal: Notes on Slave Family Life on a South Carolina Plantation, 1786 to 1833," *WMQ*, XXXIX (January 1982), 202–3; John C. Inscoe, "Carolina Slave Names: An Index to Acculturation," *JSH*, XLIX (November 1983), 553–54.

92. Autobiography of Gabriel Manigault, 1836–1899 (typescript), pp. 44–45, SC.

93. Inscoe, *JSH*, 533; South-Carolina *Gazette*, September 27, 1773, in Lathan A. Windley, *Runaway Slave Advertisements: A Documentary History from the 1730s to 1790* (Westport, Conn.: Greenwood Press, 1983), III, pp. 329–30.

94. Stroyer, *My Life in the South*, p. 16.

95. Ibid., pp. 33–34; James Henry Hammond to John C. Calhoun, May 10, 1844, John C. Calhoun Papers, Clemson University, quoted in Drew G. Faust, "Culture, Conflict and Community: The Meaning of Power on an Antebellum Plantation," *JOSH*, 14 (Fall 1980), 92, 96; Pope-Hennessy, *The Aristocratic Journey*, p. 221; "Remonstrance," Greenville *Mountaineer*, November 2, 1838.

96. "Remonstrance," Greenville *Mountaineer*, November 2, 1838. The concerns expressed by those citizens probably explain the great exertions taken to assure that slaves received no information on military formations and organization. See "An Ordinance to Amend an Ordinance Passed to Prevent Slaves or Free Persons of Color from Assembling at Military Parades," in George B. Eckhard, *A Digest of the Ordinances of the City Council of Charleston, From the Year 1783 to Oct. 1844* (Charleston: Walker & Burke, 1844), p. 175.

97. Condy, *Digest of the Laws*, pp. 170, 180; *The Suppressed Book About Slavery!* (New York: Carleton, 1864), p. 245; James Lardner, "Liberating Lessons of War," Washington *Post*, January 12, 1982, B 1, 11; Rawick, *The American Slave*, III, iii, p. 14, III, iv, pp. 5, 165.

98. Rawick, *The American Slave*, sup., 11, pp. 98, 100.

99. Ibid., pp. 261–62.

100. Rawick, *The American Slave*, III, iv, p. 45.

101. Ibid., p. 9.

102. Ibid., II, i, p. 235.

103. Adele Petigru Allston to Colonel Francis Heriot, July 1864, in Easterby, *South Carolina Rice Plantation*, pp. 199–200.

104. Adele Petigru Allston to Jesse Belflowers, July 16, 1864, in Easterby, *South Carolina Rice Plantation*, p. 292.

105. An Inhabitant of Florida, Zaphaniah Kingsley, *A Treatise on the Patriarchal, or Co-operative System of Society as it Exists in Some Governments . . . Under the Name of Slavery, With Its Necessity and Advantages,* 2d ed. (Freeport, N.Y.: Books for Libraries Press, 1970), p. 9 (originally published in 1829); Jones, "A Cultural Middle Passage," pp. 76–78; Plantation Manual of James H. Hammond of Beech Island, South Carolina, circa 1834 (typescript), p. 4, WHL.

106. Quoted in Gutman, *The Black Family*, pp. 79–80.
107. Basil Hall, *Travels in North America, in the Years 1827 and 1828* (Edinburgh: Cadell and Co., 1829), III, pp. 128–29.
108. Richard Konetzke, ed., *Colección de Documentos para la historia de la formación social de Hispanoamerica, 1493–1810* (Madrid, 1962), Real Cedula, February 1, 1570, vol. 1, p. 451, quoted in Gwendolyn Midlo Hall, *Social Control in Slave Plantation Societies: A Comparison of St. Domingue and Cuba* (Baltimore: The Johns Hopkins Press, 1971), p. 94.
109. Bryan Edwards, *The History, Civil and Commercial of the British Colonies in the West Indies* (London: John Stockdale, 1801), 2, pp. 155–56; John Stewart, *A View of the Past and Present State of the Island of Jamaica* . . . (New York: Negro Universities Press, 1969), p. 281 (originally published in 1823); A Gentleman, *An Account of Jamaica, and Its Inhabitants* (London: Longman, Hurst, Rees, and Orme, 1808), p. 250.
110. Gutman, *The Black Family*, p. 154.
111. Ball, *Fifty Years in Chains*, pp. 142, 192, 195.
112. Rochester *Union and Advertiser*, August 9, 1893, in Blassingame, *Slave Testimony*, p. 512.
113. Botume, *First Days Amongst the Contrabands*, pp. 55–57, 179–80; Lloyd v. Monpoey, 2N. and McC. 446, May 1820, in Catterall, *Judicial Cases*, II, p. 315; Watson v. Hamilton, 6 Richardson 75, November 1852, in Catterall, *Judicial Cases*, II, pp. 434–35; "State vs Eddy (a Negro Slave)," August 8, 1849, (Case 97), Spartanburg Court of Magistrates and Freeholders Records (microfilm), SCA; William Wyndham Malet, *An Errand to the South in the Summer of 1862* (London: Richard Bentley, 1863), pp. 203–5; "Testimony of Harry McMillan," American Freedmen's Inquiry Commission, pp. 128–29, NA; Pierce, *AM*, 302–3; Jolliffe v. Fanning, 10 Richardson 428, May 1856, in Catterall, *Judicial Cases*, II, p. 451; E. Perry, Greenville, to B. F. Perry, November 29, 1843, Benjamin F. Perry Papers (typescript), p. 2, SC; George I. Crafts, Thebes, to Miss Maria [R. Campbell?], January 1, 1847, George I. Crafts Correspondence, 1846–1847 (typescript), CLS; Holland, *Letters and Diary of Laura M. Towne*, pp. 224–25; Rawick, *The American Slave*, II, i, p. 110; Pearson, *Letters From Port Royal*, pp. 55–56; Eric Perkins, *Roll, Jordan, Roll: A 'Marx' for the Master Class*," *RHR*, 3 (Fall 1976), 48–49.
114. Gutman, *The Black Family*, pp. 75–76.
115. John Gabriel Guignard, II, Evergreen, to James Sanders Guignard, I, November 24, 1829, Guignard Family Papers, SC; Caldwell v. Wilson, 2 Speers 75, December 1843. (77), in Catterall, *Judicial Cases*, II, p. 387; Bryan v. Robert, 1 Strob. Eq. 334, May 1847, in Catterall, *Judicial Cases*, II, p. 403; Owens v. Simpson, 5 Rich. Eq. 405, May 1853, in Catterall, *Judicial Cases*, II, p. 438; Young ads. Plumeau, Harper (second edition), 543, March 1827, in Catterall, *Judicial Cases*, II, p. 336.
116. Jones, "A Cultural Middle Passage," pp. 211–18; Stroyer, *My Life in the South*, pp. 19–23.
117. Rawick, *The American Slave*, II, ii, pp. 75–76.
118. Harris Farm Journals, January 6, 1858, SHC.
119. Ibid., March 6, 1858.
120. Holland, *Letters and Diary of Laura M. Towne*, pp. 109–10.
121. Eugene D. Genovese, *Roll, Jordan, Roll: The World The Slaves Made* (New York: Pantheon Books, 1974), pp. 648–49.
122. Peter Lewis, "50 Dollars Reward," The Georgetown *Gazette*, November 19,

1800; "Petition of Edward Brailsford," November 26, 1816, General Assembly Petitions, SCA; James Sanders Guignard, I, Columbia, to John Gabriel Guignard, II, December 9, 1833, Guignard Family Papers, SC; "The State vs. Negro Jim," October 10, 1849, (Case 109), Spartanburg Court Records, SCA; (Case 252), May 19, 1852, Pendleton/Anderson District Court of Magistrates and Freeholders Records (microfilm), SCA; Deloach v. Turner, 6 Richardson 117, January 1853. (119), in Catterall, *Judicial Cases,* II, p. 435; Stroyer, *My Life in the South,* pp. 64–68; Philo Tower, *Slavery Unmasked: Being a Truthful Narrative of a Three Years' Residence and Journeying in Eleven Southern States* (Rochester: Darrow & Brothers, 1856), pp. 119–21; (Case 231), October 11, 1860, Spartanburg Court Records, SCA; Rawick, *The American Slave,* II, ii, p. 36.

123. Jones, "A Cultural Middle Passage," p. 52; Cloud v. Calhoun, 10 Rich. Eq. 358, November 1858. (363), in Catterall, *Judicial Cases,* II, p. 461; Plowden C. J. Weston, "Rules and Management for the Plantation, 1859," cited in Collins, *Memories of the Southern States,* pp. 104–5.

124. E. Perry, Greenville, to B. F. Perry, November 29, 1843, Benjamin Perry Papers, p. 2, SC.

125. William Jones, Goshen, Ga., to Langdon Cheves, Charleston, S.C., June 18, 1830, Cheves Family Papers, SCHS; Caldwell v. Wilson, 2 Speers 75, December 1843. (77), in Catterall, *Judicial Cases,* II, p. 387; Bryan v. Robert, 1 Strob. Eq. 334, May 1847, in Catterall, *Judicial Cases,* II, p. 403; John Bratton, Camp near Richmond, to Bette Bratton, January 27, 1865, John Bratton Correspondence, 1861–1865 (typescript), p. 200, SHC.

126. *Proceedings of the Meeting in Charleston, S.C., May 13–15, 1845, on the Religious Instruction of the Negroes Together With the Report of the Committee, and the Address to the Public* (Charleston: Published by Order of the Meeting, 1845), pp. 53–55; Manigault Letter Book, Charles Izard Manigault, Paris, to Anthony Barclay Esqr, British Consul, New York, April 15, 1847, p. 36, Charles Manigault Papers, SC.

Chapter 3. A System of Rewards and Punishments

1. The Editor (at parting), "Our Slaves," *SA,* II (December 1829), 575.

2. Snee v. Trice, 2 Bay 345, November 1802 (1 Brevard 178), in Helen T. Catterall, ed., *Judicial Cases Concerning American Slavery and the Negro* (Washington, D.C.: Carnegie Institute of Washington, 1929), II, p. 282; George W. Knepper, ed., *Travels in the Southland 1822–1823: The Journal of Lucius Versus Bierce* (Columbus: Ohio State University Press, 1966), p. 80; Charles Cotesworth Pinckney, *An Address Delivered in Charleston Before the Agricultural Society of South-Carolina . . . The 18th August, 1829* (Charleston: A. E. Miller, 1829), p. 12; Langdon Cheves, Delta, to Huger, Hamilton, and Habersham, April 6, 1834, Cheves Family papers, SCHS; Moses Roper, *A Narrative of the Adventures and Escape of Moses Roper, From American Slavery* (New York: Negro Universities Press, 1970), pp. 8–9 (originally published in 1838); Charles Lyell, *Travels in North America, In the Years 1841–2; With Geological Observations on the United States, Canada, and Nova Scotia* (New York: Wiley and Putnam, 1845), I, p. 144; E. Perry, Greenville, to B. F. Perry, November 29, 1843, Benjamin F. Perry Papers (typescript), pp. 1–2, SC; Cornhill Plantation Book, 1827–1873, p. 104, McDonald Furman Papers, PL; E. Perry, Greenville, to B. F. Perry, Charleston, January 24, 1845, Benjamin Perry Papers, pp. 3–4, SC;

Francis W. Pickens, Edgewood, S.C., to John C. Calhoun, May 4, 1845, Calhoun Family Typescripts; Plantation Records, Silver Bluff, S.C., December 8, 1831–December 31, 1855, December 31, 1845, p. 343, James H. Hammond Papers, SC; Mrs. Lettice Jenkins, Edisto Island, to her sister, July 21, 1835, MS, cited in Rosser T. Taylor, *Ante-Bellum South Carolina: A Social and Cultural History* (The James Sprunt Studies in History and Political Science, Chapel Hill: The University of North Carolina Press, 1942), p. 68; H. D. McCloud, "Hints on the Medical Treatment of Negroes" (Sr. thesis, Medical College of South Carolina, 1850), pp. 2–3, MU; "The Duties of An Overseer," in Thomas Affleck, *The Cotton Plantation: Record and Account Book, No. 2*, 3rd edition (New Orleans: Weld & Co., 1851), unpaged.

3. Charles Ball, *Fifty Years in Chains*, with an introduction by Philip S. Foner (New York: Dover Publications, 1970), pp. 157, 212 (originally published in 1837); A. M. French, *Slavery in South Carolina and the Ex-Slaves; Or, the Port Royal Mission* (New York: Negro Universities Press, 1969), pp. 68, 176–77 (originally published in 1862); George P. Rawick, ed., *The American Slave: A Composite Autobiography* (Westport, Conn.: Greenwood Publishing Company, 1972), II, i, pp. 110, 148, II, ii, p. 173, III, iii, p. 92, III, iv, p. 158; Elizabeth Ware Pearson, ed., *Letters From Port Royal, 1862–1868* (New York: Arno Press and The New York Times, 1969), p. 32 (originally published in 1906); Agricola, "Management of Negroes," *DR*, XIX (September 1855), 361.

4. Amelia M. Murray, *Letters From the United States, Cuba, and Canada* (New York: G. P. Putnam & Company, 1856), pp. 195–96, 209–10.

5. Frederick Law Olmsted, *A Journey in the Seaboard Slave States, With Remarks On Their Economy* (New York: Dix & Edwards, 1856), p. 388.

6. Lyell, *Travels in North America*, I, pp. 143–44; Charles C. Jones, *The Religious Instruction of the Negroes* (New York: Negro Universities Press, 1969), p. 136 (originally published in 1842).

7. McCloud, "Medical Treatment of Negroes," passim, MU.

8. Ibid., pp. 2–3, 5, 9–10. The frequency of such ploys may have been what prompted Samuel Gaillard to express such bewilderment and joy when he recorded: "May 29, 1856: *Not a Negroe* in the house to day except Eve, who was confined yesterday—a *remarkable circumstance*. . . . May 31, 1856: (Saturday) Not a negro Sick today!!!!!!!!!!!!!! . . . June 2, 1856: (Monday) Not a negro lying up to day!!!!!!" Samuel Porcher Gaillard Plantation Journals, 1835–1868, SC. (Emphases in the original.)

9. A Planter, "Notions on the Management of Negroes, &c," *SA*, IX (November 1836), 626; "Report on Management of Slaves, Duty of Overseers, and Employers to Darlington County Agricultural Society," August 1852, pp. 3–5, Thomas Cassels Law Papers, SC; Jones, *Religious Instruction of the Negroes*, p. 241; Whitemarsh B. Seabrook, "On the Causes of the General Unsuccessfulness of the Sea-Island Planters," *SA*, VII (April 1834), 180–81; Practical Planter, "Observations on the Management of Negroes," *SA*, V (April 1832), 181–82; R, "On the Management of Negroes," *TSC*, I (May 1840), 279–80; Plantation Book of Charles Pinckney and Successors, 1812–1861, November 24, 1817, p. 17, The Pinckney Family Papers, LC; An Inhabitant of Florida, Zaphaniah Kingsley, *A Treatise on the Patriarchal, or Co-operative System of Society As It Exists in Some Governments . . . Under the Name of Slavery, With Its Necessity and Advantages*, 2d ed. (Freeport, N.Y.: Books for Libraries Press, 1970), p. 15 (originally published in 1829); Alexander James Lawton Diary and Book, 1810–1840, November 25, 1833 (typescript), p. 79, Alexander

Robert Lawton Papers, SHC; Davis v. Dr. Whitridge, 2 Strobhart 232, January 1848, in Catterall, *Judicial Cases*, II, p. 405; Journal of Thomas B. Chaplin, 1845–1886, January 21, 1846, October 25, 1849, pp. 99, 252, SCHS; Robert Nicholas Olsberg, "A Government of Class and the South Carolina Chivalry, 1860–1865" (Ph.D. dissertation, University of South Carolina, 1972), p. 135; Mr. Robertson, Fording Island, to [Charles Cotesworth Pinckney], November 24, 1824, Pinckney Family Papers, LC; Herbert Gutman, *The Black Family in Slavery & Freedom, 1750–1925* (New York: Pantheon Books, 1976), p. 79; R. King, Jr., "On the Management of the Butler Estate, and the Cultivation of the Sugar Cane," *SA*, I (December 1828), 525; Plantation Journal, 1856–1858, July 24, 1856, Samuel Porcher Gaillard Plantation Journals, SC.

10. Journal of Thomas Chaplin, April 25, 1849, p. 231, SCHS.

11. King, *SA*, 524–25.

12. Philip D. Morgan, "Work and Culture: The Task System and the World of Lowcountry Blacks, 1700 to 1880," *WMQ*, XXXIX (October 1982), 569, 572–75, 579–81; "An Ordinance for the Government of Negroes and Other Persons of Color, Within the City of Charleston, and for Other Purposes Therein Mentioned; Ratified October 28, 1806," in George B. Eckhard, *A Digest of the Ordinances of the City Council of Charleston, From the Year 1783 to Oct. 1844* (Charleston: Walker & Burke, 1844), pp. 169–72. The ordinance stated in part that without the consent of the slave's owner and the Commissioners of the Markets "no negro or other slave shall be permitted to own any boat or vessel whatever, . . . [sell] fish and other acquatic [sic] animals, . . . [or] on his or her own account, buy, sell, barter, trade, traffic or deal in any goods, wares, provisions, grain, or commodities, of any kind whatsoever, upon pain of forfeiting the same."

13. Plantation Records, September 13, 1833, p. 59, James H. Hammond Papers, SC; J. H. Easterby, ed., *The South Carolina Rice Plantation as Revealed in the Papers of Robert F. W. Allston* (Chicago: University of Chicago Press, 1945), p. 34; Olmsted, *Journey in the Seaboard Slave States*, pp. 426–29; Mary B. Elliot Account Book, MS, cited in Guion Griffis Johnson, *A Social History of the Sea Islands: With Special Reference to St. Helena Island, South Carolina* (Chapel Hill: The University of North Carolina Press, 1930), p. 141; Plowden C. J. Weston, "Rules and Management for the Plantation, 1859," cited in Elizabeth Collins, *Memories of the Southern States* (Taunton: Barnicott, 1865), p. 107; Minutes of the Winyah and All Saints Agricultural Society, 1842–1861, January 25, 1855, SCHS; Rawick, *The American Slave*, III, iii, pp. 114–15; "Report," August 1852, pp. 4–5, Thomas Cassels Law Papers, SC.

14. Rawick, *The American Slave*, III, iv, p. 202.

15. Ball, *Fifty Years in Chains*, pp. 212, 217.

16. Snee v. Trice, 2 Bay 345, November 1802 (1 Brevard 178), in Catterall, *Judicial Cases*, II, p. 282; Ball, *Fifty Years in Chains*, p. 191; Foby, "Management of Servants," *SC*, XI (August 1853), 227; Charles A. Raymond, "The Religious Life of the Negro Slave," *HNM*, XXVII (September 1863), 821; Henry William Ravenel, "Recollections of Southern Plantation Life," *TYR*, XXV (June 1936), 757; Thomas Wentworth Higginson, *Army Life in a Black Regiment* (Boston: Beacon Press, 1962), p. 31 (originally published in 1869); South Carolina Agricultural Society Records, 1825–[1860], June 16, 1829, pp. 104–5, SCHS; J. E. Bonneau, Charleston, to [John Ewing Colhoun], February 17, 1829, John Ewing Colhoun Papers, SCA; "Petition of Thomas Bennett to Governor Seabrook Praying Pardon for His Slave, Peter Blackstock," December 5, 1850,

(Folder 50), Slavery Files, SCA; Harriott Pinckney, Charleston, to Mr. Winningham, February 8, 1855, Harriott Pinckney Papers, SC; "Petition of Ladies of the Eastern Portion of York District," June 28, 1853, Bratton Family Papers, SC; State v. Elrod, 12 Richardson 662, May 1860, in Catterall, *Judicial Cases,* II, p. 469.

17. [Edward] Pierce, "Report," *Rebellion Record,* sup., I. p. 310, cited in Johnson, *Social History of the Sea Islands,* pp. 86–87.

18. A Planter, "Notions on the Management of Negroes, &c." *SA,* IX (November 1836), 582. According to McCloud, some slaves went to extremes for a drink: "Negroes frequently complain of Colic and other symptoms of indigestion when there is nothing at all the matter; and this too when they have no disposition to stop work. They do this only on those plantations where the usual domestic remedy for Colic is a glass of whiskey. Their fondness for Spirits is proverbial and when given to them without hesitation for their complaints, they are very apt to take advantage of their masters." See McCloud, "Hints on the Medical Treatment of Negroes," pp. 6–8, MU.

19. D. E. Smith, *A Charlestonian's Recollections, 1846–1913* (Charleston: Carolina Art Association, 1950), p. 20; Langdon Cheves, Log Hall, to Langdon Cheves, Jr., Delta, March 11, 1847, Cheves Family Papers, SCHS; Elizabeth W. Allston Pringle, *Chronicles of Chicora Wood* (New York: Charles Scribner's Sons, 1922), pp. 15–16, 30, 80; John Taylor, "Caution," The Georgetown *Gazette,* January 15, 1800; Journal of Thomas B. Chaplin, November 7, 1845, p. 77, SCHS; Easterby, *South Carolina Rice Plantation,* p. 34.

20. Plantation Manual of James Henry Hammond of Beech Island, South Carolina, circa 1834 (typescript), p. 1, WHL.

21. John Gabriel Guignard, II, Hopewell, to James Sanders Guignard, I, April 3, 1829, Guignard Family Papers, SC.

22. Rawick, *The American Slave,* II, i, p. 222, III, iii, pp. 283–84; R. H. Marshall, Laurens, S.C., to John and Charles Marshall, April 19, 1852, Marshall Family Papers, PL; Rev. I. E. Lowery, *Life on the Old Plantation or a Story Based on Facts* (Columbia: The State Company, 1911), pp. 95–98.

23. Plantation Records, March 21, 1846, July 4, August 29, 1848, pp. 356, 398, 400, James H. Hammond Papers, SC; Editor, "Plantation Life: Duties and Responsibilities," *DR,* XXIX (September 1860), 360; Weston, "Rules and Management for the Plantation," cited in Collins, *Memories of the Southern States,* p. 107; Lowery, *Life on the Old Plantation,* p. 69; Rawick, *The American Slave,* II, ii, pp. 58–59.

24. A Planter, *SA,* 626; Rawick, *The American Slave,* III, iii, p. 273; Peggy Lamson, *The Glorious Failure: Black Congressman Robert Brown Elliott and the Reconstruction in South Carolina* (New York: W. W. Norton & Company, 1973), pp. 50–51, 68; "Testimony of Robert Smalls," American Freedmen's Inquiry Commission (microfilm), Reel 200, File III, p. 106, NA.

25. N. Herbemont, "On the Moral Discipline and Treatment of Slaves, Read Before the Society for the Advancement of Education, at Columbia," *SA,* IX (February 1836), 71–73.

26. Ball, *Fifty Years in Chains,* pp. 200, 203.

27. Weston, "Rules and Management for the Plantation," cited in Collins, *Memories of the Southern States,* pp. 8, 107; Plantation Manual of James H. Hammond, WHL, p. 4; Adele Petigru Allston, Chicora Wood, to Benjamin Allston, January 1, 1857, in Easterby, *South Carolina Rice Plantation,* p. 136; Plantation Journal, Redcliffe, 1861–1864, 1880, December 25, 1861, James Henry

Hammond Papers, SC; Frogmore Plantation Journal, 1813–1816, December 10, 1813, John Stapleton Papers, SC; Ball, *Fifty Years in Chains,* pp. 268–69; Thomas Green Clemson, Fort Hill, to John C. Calhoun, December 30, 1842, Calhoun Family Typescripts; Jacob Stroyer, *My Life in the South* (Salem, Mass.: Salem Observer and Job Print, 1885), pp. 46–47; Lowery, *Life On the Old Plantation,* pp. 64–67.

28. Rawick, *The American Slave,* II, i, p. 207.

29. Ibid., III, iii, p. 66.

30. Plantation Records, December 25, 1831, December 25, 1840, pp. 7, 228, James H. Hammond Papers, SC; Ball, *Fifty Years in Chains,* p. 26; Lowery, *Life On the Old Plantation,* pp. 66–67; Pringle, *Chronicles of Chicora Wood,* p. 133.

31. Lowery, *Life On the Old Plantation,* pp. 13, 37, 67.

32. James R. Stuart Recollections, n.d. (typescript), pp. 1–5, SHC; Pringle, *Chronicles of Chicora Wood,* p. 152; E. Perry, Greenville, to B. F. Perry, November 29, 1843, Benjamin Perry Papers, p. 2, SC.

33. David Golightly Harris Farm Journals, December 22, 28, 1858 (microfilm), SHC.

34. Plantation Records, December 25, 1831, p. 7, James H. Hammond Papers, SC.

35. "John Hamilton Cornish, 1815–1878," Survey Book #38, SHC; Diary of John Hamilton Cornish, December 26, 1839, V (typescript), p. 57, John Hamilton Cornish Papers, SHC.

36. John Belton O'Neall, *The Negro Law of South Carolina* (Columbia: John G. Bowman, 1848), p. 12.

37. Charles Fraser Commonplace Book, 1800–1819, p. 131, CCL; Will Book "C" and "A," 1791–1834, I, p. 158, Wills: Records of Old Pendleton District, Anderson County, APL; J. S. Buckingham, *The Slave States of America* (London: Fisher, Son, & Co., 1842), II, pp. 31–32; H. M. Henry, *The Police Control of the Slave in South Carolina* (New York: Negro Universities Press, 1968), p. 170 (originally published in 1914); "An Act to Restrain the Emancipation of Slaves, and to Prevent Free Persons of Color from Entering Into This State; And for Other Purposes, 1820," in David J. McCord, ed., *The Statutes at Large of South Carolina* (Columbia: A. S. Johnston, 1840), VII, p. 459.

38. "Act to Restrain the Emancipation of Slaves," in McCord, *Statutes at Large,* VII, p. 459.

39. Peter H. Wood, *Black Majority: Negroes in Colonial South Carolina From 1670 Through the Stono Rebellion* (New York: Alfred A. Knopf, 1974), pp. 101–2, 240–41.

40. John Livingston Bradley, "Slave Manumission in South Carolina, 1820–1860" (M.A. thesis, University of South Carolina, 1964), pp. 38–40, 50, 58, 59, 65, 67, 70, 73; The Heirs of David Morton vs. Thompson and Another, Executors, in J. S. G. Richardson, *Reports of Cases in Equity, Argued and Determined in the Court of Appeals and Court of Errors, of South Carolina* (Charleston: Walker, Evans, 1855), VI, p. 370; "Petition of the Delegation from Prince George, Winyah & All Saints," n.d., (Folder 139), Slavery Files, SCA.

41. Bradley, "Slave Manumission," pp. 58–59.

42. The Editor, "Our Slaves," *SA,* II (December 1829), 575.

43. An Overseer, "On the Conduct and Management of Overseers, Drivers, and Slaves," *SA,* IX (May 1836), 228; John Ewing Colhoun, Pendleton, to Mr. William Clark, Abbeville, January 27, 1825, John Ewing Colhoun Papers, SC; *Farmer & Planter,* VI (January 1855), 10–11, cited in Charles M. Clark, "Plan-

tation Overseers in South Carolina, 1820–1860" (M.A. thesis, University of South Carolina, 1966), p. 42; Herbert Aptheker, *American Negro Slave Revolts* (New York: International Publishers, 1943), pp. 53, 78; Bobby Frank Jones, "A Cultural Middle Passage: Slave Marriage and Family in the Ante-Bellum South" (Ph.D. dissertation, University of North Carolina, 1965), pp. 10, 46, 55–60.

44. Eliza C. Ervin and Horace F. Rudisill, *Darlingtoniana: A History of People, Places and Events in Darlington County, South Carolina* (Columbia: The R. L. Bryan Company, 1964), p. 177; "Report to the Darlington County Agricultural Society," n.d., Thomas Cassels Law Papers, SC.

45. Robert Mason Myers, ed., *The Children of Pride: A True Story of Georgia and the Civil War* (New Haven: Yale University Press, 1972), p. 1567; Jones, *Religious Instruction of Negroes*, p. 119.

46. Henry, *Police Control*, p. 52.

47. Ball, *Fifty Years in Chains*, p. 161.

48. McCloud, "Hints on the Medical Treatment of Negroes," pp. 9–12, MU; "The State vs Negro Jim, Charged with Stabbing and Grievously Wounding Robert F. Miles," October 23, 1849, (Case 109), Spartanburg Court of Magistrates and Freeholders Records (microfilm), SCA; Charles Lyell, *A Second Visit to the United States* (New York: Harper & Brothers, 1849), I, p. 266; Plantation Book, 1857–1858, "Punishment," James Henry Hammond Papers, LC; *The Suppressed Book About Slavery!* (New York: Carleton, 1864), p. 191; Rawick, *The American Slave*, II, ii, p. 14; Andrew Flinn Plantation Book, 1840, "Plantation Rules," SC; A Planter, "Rules Adopted On a Plantation, To Be Observed by the Overseer," *CP*, I (July 8, 1840), 203; "Articles of Agreement Between J. F. Hollingsworth & M. T. Palmer," January 13, 1857, John Hollingsworth Papers, 1807–1880, Edgefield District, S.C., PL.

49. Rawick, *The American Slave*, II, ii, p. 173.

50. Charles Nordhoff, "The Freedmen of South-Carolina," in Frank Moore, ed., *Papers of the Day* (New York: Charles T. Evans, 1863), p. 16; Pearson, *Letters From Port Royal*, p. 31; Rupert Sargent Holland, ed., *Letters and Diary of Laura M. Towne: Written From the Sea Islands of South Carolina, 1862–1884* (Cambridge: Riverside Press, 1912), p. 132; Rawick, *The American Slave*, II, ii, pp. 173, 209; Ball, *Fifty Years in Chains*, pp. 159–60; "Testimony of Robert Smalls," American Freedmen's Inquiry Commission, p. 40, NA; State v. Harlan, 5 Richardson 470, May 1852. Report of Judge O'Neall, in Catterall, *Judicial Cases*, II, pp. 432–33.

51. State v. Harlan, 5 Richardson 470, in Catterall, *Judicial Cases*, II, pp. 432–33.

52. (Case 97), November 10, 1838, Pendleton/Anderson District Court of Magistrates and Freeholders Records (microfilm), SCA; Edward Spann Hammond Diary, 1857–1858, p. 73, Edward Spann Hammond Papers, SC; (Case 53), July 20, 1830, Pendleton/Anderson Court Records, SCA; Charles Graves Diary, 1846–1855, April 17, 1854, SCHS; (Case 75), January 26, 1835, Pendleton/Anderson Court Records, SCA.

53. Andrew Flinn Plantation Book, "Plantation Rules," SC.

54. Silver Bluff Plantation: Stock and Crop Book, Values 1832–[1841], "Rules at Silver Bluff," James Henry Hammond Papers, LC; Plantation Book, "Punishment," James Henry Hammond Papers, LC.

55. Farmer's Club (ABC Farmer's Club) Records, 1846–1893, Beech Island, Aiken County, September 4, 1849 (typescript), p. 37, SC.

56. Pearson, *Letters From Port Royal*, p. 31; Stroyer, *My Life in the South*, p. 30; Rawick, *The American Slave*, II, ii, p. 209.

57. Rawick, *The American Slave*, III, iii, p. 262.

58. George P. Rawick, ed., The American Slave: A Composite Autobiography, Supplement, Series 1 (Westport, Conn.: Greenwood Press, 1977, 11, pp. xxxii–xxxiii.

59. "Rosa Barnwell to the Editor," *Liberator*, November 7, 1862, in John W. Blassingame, ed., *Slave Testimony: Two Centuries of Letters, Speeches, Interviews, and Autobiographies* (Baton Rouge: Louisiana State University Press, 1977), p. 698; Rawick, *The American Slave*, I, i, p. 344, II, ii, pp. 14–15, 24–25, 81, III, iv, pp. 110, 206; Diary of John Hamilton Cornish, December 26, 1839, V, pp. 58–59, John Hamilton Cornish Papers, SHC; Elsie Clews Parsons, "Folk-Lore From Aiken, S.C.," *JAF*, 34 (January–March 1921), 22; E. C. L. Adams, *Nigger to Nigger* (New York: Charles Scribner's Sons, 1929), pp. 232–33; Elsie Clews Parsons, *Folk-Lore of the Sea Islands, South Carolina* (Cambridge: The American Folk-Lore Society, 1923), pp. xx–xxii.

60. John Bennett, *The Doctor to the Dead: Grotesque Legends & Folk Tales of Old Charleston* (New York: Rinehart & Company, 1943), pp. vii, ix–x, xiii, 139–42.

61. Rawick, *The American Slave*, II, ii, pp. 163–64.

62. (Case 26), June 8, 1826, Pendleton/Anderson Court Records, SCA; Roper, *A Narrative*, p. 13; "Rosa Barnwell to the Editor," *Liberator*, November 7, 1862, in Blassingame, *Slave Testimony*, pp. 697–98; Rawick, *The American Slave*, II, ii, pp. 15, 77.

63. "Henry, slave of Marcus Kirby, Burglary," March 29, 1865, Spartanburg District Court of Magistrates and Freeholders Trial Papers, SCA, quoted in William Cinque Henderson, "Spartan Slaves: A Documentary Account of Blacks on Trial in Spartanburg, South Carolina 1830–1865" (Ph.D. dissertation, Northwestern University, 1978), pp. 165–66.

64. Holland, *Letters and Diary of Laura M. Towne*, pp. 57–58.

65. Rawick, *The American Slave*, II, ii, pp. 14, 25.

66. Ball, *Fifty Years in Chains*, p. 324.

67. Holland, *Letters and Diary of Laura M. Towne*, pp. 28–29.

68. Langdon Cheves, Abbeville, to Langdon Cheves, Jr., Savannah, May 4, 1844, Cheves Family Papers. SCHS; Richmond Plantation Overseer's Book, 1859–1860, May 18, June 4, 1860, SCHS; S. H. Boineau, Combahee, to (Charles) Heyward, November 26, 1863, Heyward Family Papers, SC; Rawick, *The American Slave*, II, ii, p. 240; Dr. John Peyre Thomas Diary of Weather & Occurences, St. Johns Parish (Berkeley), October 1828–August 1829, June 25, 1829, II, p. 110, Thomas Family Papers, SC; Roper, *A Narrative*, p. 13; Farm Journal, Anderson District, 1855–1857, February 5, 6, 12, 18, 19, 1856, pp. 123–24, 135, John Durant Ashmore Plantation Journal, 1853–1859 (typescript), SHC; Manigault Letter Book, 1846–1848 (typescript), Charles Izard Manigault, Paris, to Mr. Haynes, (Savannah River), March 1, 1847, p. 26, Charles Manigault Papers, SC.

69. Captain Basil Hall, *Travels in North America, in the Years 1827 and 1828* (Edinburgh: Cadell and Co., 1829), III, p. 167; Henry L. Pinckney, mayor, *Report; Containing a Review of the Proceedings of the City Authorities From the 4th September, 1837 to the 1st August, 1838. With Suggestions for the Improvement of the Various Departments of the Public Service* (Charleston: Thomas J. Eccles, 1838), p. 36; James Stirling, *Letters From the Slave States*

(London: John W. Parker and Son, 1857), p. 285; Richard C. Wade, *Slavery in the Cities: The South, 1820–1860* (London: Oxford University Press, 1964), pp. 95–96; Holland, *Letters and Diary of Laura M. Towne*, pp. 160–61.

70. William W. Freehling, *Prelude to Civil War: The Nullification Controversy in South Carolina, 1816–1836* (New York: Harper Torchbooks, 1965), p. 67.

71. Karl Bernhard, Duke of Sax-Weimar Eisenach, *Travels Through North America, During the Years 1825 and 1826* (Philadelphia: Carey, Lea & Carey, 1828), II, pp. 9–10.

72. Higginson, *Army Life*, p. 87; Dr. Thomas Diary, August 8, 1829, II, p. 133, Thomas Family Papers, SC; Rawick, *The American Slave*, III, ii, p. 274; Diary of John Berkley Grimball, Charleston, S.C., No. 6-1837-1838-1840, May 5, 1840, I (typescript), p. 26, CLS; Gabriel L. Ellis, Matanza, to Robert F. W. Allston, September 16, 1838, in Easterby, *South Carolina Rice Plantation*, p. 255; Stroyer, *My Life in the South*, p. 69.

73. *American Slavery As It Is: Testimony of a Thousand Witnesses* (New York: American Anti-Slavery Society, 1839), p. 23.

74. Rawick, *The American Slave*, II, i, p. 207.

75. "Testimony of Robert Smalls," p. 110, NA.

76. Rawick, *The American Slave*, II, i, p. 148, III, ii, p. 115.

77. Ibid., III, iv, pp. 116–17.

78. Higginson, *Army Life*, p. 87.

79. Rawick, *The American Slave*, II, ii, p. 139.

80. Herbemont, *SA*, 73.

81. *American Slavery As It Is*, p. 175; "The Duties of An Overseer," in Affleck, *The Cotton Plantation*, unpaged; A Small Farmer, "Management of Negroes," *DR*, XI (October 1851), 371.

82. H. Perry Pope, "A Dissertation on the Professional Management of Negro Slaves" (Sr. thesis, Medical College of the State of South Carolina, 1837), pp. 7–9, MU; "Testimony of Robert Smalls," p. 101, NA; W. W. Gilmer, "Management of Servants," *FP*, III (July 1852), 110; Langdon Cheves, Portman Shoals, to Langdon Cheves, Jr., Savannah, March 19, 1843, Cheves Family Papers, SCHS; Michael S. Hindus, "Black Justice Under White Law: Criminal Prosecutions of Blacks in Antebellum South Carolina," *JAH*, LXIII (December 1976), 587; George P. Rawick, "West African Culture and North American Slavery: A Study of Culture Change Among American Slaves in the Ante-Bellum South With Focus Upon Slave Religion," in *Migration and Anthropology: Proceedings of the 1970 Annual Spring Meeting of the American Ethnological Society* (Seattle: University of Washington Press, 1970), p. 150; John W. Blassingame, *The Slave Community: Plantation Life in the Antebellum South* (New York: Oxford University Press, 1972), p. 207.

83. Rev. John G. Williams, *"De Ole Plantation"* (Charleston: Walker, Evans & Cogswell, 1895), p. 61.

84. Nordhoff, "Freedmen of South-Carolina," p. 21.

85. Herbemont, *SA*, 71–74; An Edistonian, "The Successful Planter, or Memories of My Uncle Ben," *SA*, IV (November 1831), 303–4; Jones, "A Cultural Middle Passage," pp. 41–42; Smith, *A Charlestonian's Recollections*, p. 35; Hall, *Travels in North America*, III, pp. 179–80, 191; Farmer's Club Records, November 6, 1847, p. 43, SC; Hindus, *JAH*, 587; "Record of the Proceedings of the Beech Island Agricultural Club, 1856–1862 and Journal of the Proceedings of the Beech Island Agricultural and Police Society; Organized June 28, 1851," March 7, 1857, December 3, 1859, Farmer's Club Records, pp. 79, 130, SC.

86. Charleston Scrapbook: Clippings Chiefly From Charleston Newspapers, 1800–1810, August 14, 1804, SC.
87. Lyell, *Travels in North America*, I, p. 144; Ball, *Fifty Years in Chains*, pp. 18–19; Higginson, *Army Life*, p. 21.
88. Quoted in Lawrence W. Levine, *Black Culture and Black Consciousness: Afro-American Folk Thought From Slavery to Freedom* (Oxford: Oxford University Press, 1977), p. 81.
89. Parsons, *Folk-Lore of the Sea Islands*, p. 62.
90. Levine, *Black Culture*, p. 129.
91. Ball, *Fifty Years in Chains*, p. 319.
92. William Howard Russell, *My Diary North and South* (New York: Harper & Brothers, 1863), p. 60.
93. French, *Slavery in South Carolina*, pp. 62–63.
94. Jones, "A Cultural Middle Passage," p. 45.
95. Orland Kay Armstrong, *Old Massa's People: The Old Slaves Tell Their Story* (Indianapolis: The Bobbs-Merrill Company, 1931), p. 30; Henry C. Davis, "Negro Folk-Lore in South Carolina," *JAF*, XXVII (July–September 1914), 252, 254; Rawick, *The American Slave*, II, i, pp. 152, 242, 304, II, ii, p. 240, II, iii, p. 25; Stroyer, *My Life in the South*, pp. 46–48; Ravenel, *TYR*, 767; J. G. Clinkscales, *On the Old Plantation: Reminiscences of His Childhood* (New York: Negro Universities Press, 1969), pp. 10–12 (originally published in 1916).
96. A. M. H. Christensen, *Afro-American Folklore: Told Round Cabin Fires on the Sea Islands of South Carolina* (New York: Negro Universities Press, 1969), pp. 2–4 (originally published in 1892). Sterling Stuckey has recently offered more profound reasons for the importance of slave fiddlers. He argues that their mastery continued a tradition going back to the players of a one-string violin in Africa. The use of the New World violin in important black religious ceremonies not only helped to unite various African ethnic groups, but to interweave and preserve the common threads of their collective cultures. See Sterling Stuckey, *Slave Culture: Nationalist Theory and the Foundations of Black America* (New York: Oxford University Press, 1987), pp. 18–22.
97. Jones, *Religious Instruction of Negroes*, pp. 137–38; A Planter, *SA*, 582; "The Memorial of Sundry Citizens of St. Bartholomew," 1852, (Folder 153), Slavery Files, SCA; State v. Rollins, 12 Richardson, November 1859, in Catterall, *Judicial Cases*, II, p. 464; David Gavin Diary, 1855–1871, October 29, 1860, I (typescript), p. 217, SHC; Baptist Church: Church of Christ Records, 1794–1937, Poplar Springs, Laurens County, February 19, 1842 (typescript), p. 39, SC.
98. "Petition of Society of Vigilance, Edgefield District," 1831, (Folder 160), Slavery Files, SCA.
99. Edward C. L. Adams, *Tales of the Congaree*, ed. with an Introduction by Robert G. O'Mealy (Chapel Hill: The University of North Carolina Press, 1987), pp. 277–78.
100. Hennig Cohen, "A Negro 'Folk Game' in Colonial South Carolina," *Southern Folklore Quarterly*, 16 (1952), 183–84, quoted in Levine, *Black Culture*, p. 17.
101. (Case 237), July 30, 1851, Pendleton/Anderson Court Records, SCA.
102. Some masters went to extraordinary lengths to keep slaves at home. The folklorist and historian Marie-Gladys Fry found evidence in South Carolina and elsewhere that slaveholders used supernatural tales, puddles of blood, and eerie disguises to stop slaves' nocturnal travels. She argues that historians' neglect of

these ploys and what drove whites to them have caused "a blind spot in most published scholarly works on slavery." One of her informants, Mary Elizabeth Jones, who was raised by ex-slave grandparents in Clinton, S.C., reported what they told her: "Well, they said that they [masters and overseers] used to put sheets [on] and try to frighten them . . . and make them stay home. . . . When they'd pass by, they'd jump up . . . Make you think that there was something after you. I heard Grandpa say that. He said he run a many a night. Say he almost run himself to death one night, running from something he thought he saw. But it could have been someone trying to scare him, you know." See Marie-Gladys Fry, *Night Riders in Black Folk History* (Knoxville: University of Tennessee Press, 1975), pp. 59, 61, 64–65, 67–68, 72, 74, 220.

103. Weston, "Rules and Management for the Plantation," quoted in Collins, *Memories of the Southern States,* p. 108.

104. Plantation Journal, 1856–1858, July 24, 1856, Samuel Porcher Gaillard Plantation Journals, SC.

105. Mulberry Journal for 1853–1857, December 26, 27, 1853, Mulberry Plantation Journals, 1853–1889, SCHS.

106. Fairchild v. Bell, 2 Brevard 129, April 1807, in Catterall, *Judicial Cases,* II, p. 288; "Testimony of Robert Smalls," pp. 109–110, NA; Elizabeth Hyde Botume, *First Days Amongst the Contrabands* (New York: Arno Press and The New York Times, 1968), p. 243 (originally published in 1892); Rawick, *The American Slave,* III, iii, p. 228; Plantation Records, March 24, 1845, p. 320, James H. Hammond Papers, SC; Dr. Thomas Diary, August 1, 1829, II, p. 128, Thomas Family Papers, SC; Roper, *A Narrative,* pp. 11, 15, 46–47; *Anti-Slavery Reporter,* ser. 3, XII (September 1, 1864), 202–3, in Blassingame, *Slave Testimony,* pp. 450–52.

107. Langdon Cheves, Pendleton, to Langdon Cheves, Jr., May 10, 1844, Cheves Family Papers, SCHS.

108. Rawick, *The American Slave,* II, ii, p. 81; Roper, *A Narrative,* p. 18; Philo Tower, *Slavery Unmasked: Being a Truthful Narrative of a Three Years' Residence and Journey in Eleven Southern States* (Rochester: Darrow & Brother, 1856), pp. 116–17; *American Slavery As It Is,* p. 22; "Testimony of Robert Smalls," p. 110, NA; "Testimony of Harry McMillan," pp. 120–23, NA.

109. Ball, *Fifty Years in Chains,* p. 326.

110. Charleston *City Gazette and Daily Advertiser,* January 6, 1808, quoted in Michael P. Johnson, "Runaway Slaves and the Slave Communities in South Carolina, 1799 to 1830," *WMQ,* 38 (July 1981), 428.

111. "An Ordinance to Amend 'An Ordinance for the Government of Negroes and Other Persons of Color, . . .' and Also, 'An Ordinance to Prevent Dogs going at Large, . . .' Ratified July 5, 1814," in Eckhard, *A Digest of the Ordinances,* p. 174.

112. Rawick, *The American Slave,* III, iv, p. 271. A much crueler variation of this punishment was recorded by a Quaker living in the Newberry District of South Carolina during the first quarter of the nineteenth century: "The poor slave is tied across a fence just high enough to admit of the head being fastened down on one side and the feet on the other. [*sic*] with the seat that is to be the recipient of the strokes, naked, the executioner then with a heavy paddle, five or six inches in width and six or eight in length fill'd with holes. dip it into a tub of water just in reach. and applies it with all his strength to the exposed skin, which operation raises a blister for ever [*sic*] hole leaving them ready for the next stroke to break them so that by the time the poor sufferer has received

twenty or thirty strokes, the skin and flesh is so lacerated and bruised that he can not sit down until it has time to heal." "Memoirs," n.d. (typescript). pp. 1, 52–53, 72, 76, John O'Neale Papers, PL.

113. Lucy Ruggles Diary, 1845–1848, August 26, 1845, II pp. 128–29, Daniel Ruggles Papers, PL.

114. Ball, *Fifty Years in Chains*, p. 110; James Redpath, *The Roving Editor: Or, Talks With Slaves in the Southern States* (New York: Negro Universities Press, 1969), pp. 59–62 (originally published in 1859).

115. Rawick, *The American Slave*, II, i, pp. 155, 161–62.

116. Thomas Pinckney, Altamont, to Mrs. Harriott Horry, Charleston, September 2, 1822, Thomas Pinckney Papers, SC; John Gabriel Guignard, II, Evergreen, to James Sanders Guignard, I, June 2, 1829, Guignard Family Papers, SC; *American Slavery As It Is*, p. 23; Lucy Ruggles Diary, March 5, 7, 8, 1846, I, pp. 241–45, Daniel Ruggles Papers, PL; William Wyndham Malet, *An Errand to the South in the Summer of 1862* (London: Richard Bentley, 1863), p. 204; Ray Allen Billington, ed., *The Journal of Charlotte L. Forten: A Free Negro in the Slave Era* (New York: Collier Books, 1961), p. 151; French, *Slavery in South Carolina*, pp. 120–21; Rawick, *The American Slave*, III, iii, p. 92.

117. Lucy Ruggles Diary, March 5, 1846, I, pp. 240–41, Daniel Ruggles Papers, PL.

118. Nannie M. Tilley and Noma Lee Goodwin, *Guide to the Manuscript Collections in the Duke University Library* (Durham: Duke University Press, 1947), p. 9; Cornhill Plantation Book, p. 107, McDonald Furman Papers, PL.

119. Stirling, *Letters From the Slave States*, p. 289.

120. Hall, *Travels in North America*, III, p. 181; *American Slavery As It Is*, p. 117; Rev. James Jenkins, *Experience, Labours, and Sufferings of Rev. James Jenkins, of the South Carolina Conference* (By the Author, 1842), p. 32; Jones, "A Cultural Middle Passage," p. 46.

121. Olmsted, *Journey in the Seaboard Slave States*, p. 487; Henry, *Police Control*, pp. 73–74, 78; Thomas D. Condy, *A Digest of the Laws of the United States & the State of South Carolina* . . . (Charleston: A. E. Miller, 1830), p. 163.

122. O'Neall, *The Negro Law of South Carolina*, pp. 19–20.

123. Henry, *Police Control*, pp. 67–68, 70, 72–75, 78; Fredrika Bremer, *The Homes of the New World: Impressions of America*, trans. Mary Howitt (New York: Harper & Brothers, 1862), I, p. 278; Roper, *A Narrative*, pp. 22–23; E. Perry, Rosemonte, to B. F. Perry, March 8, 1847, pp. 3–6, SC; Hindus, *JAH*, 578–79, 581–82; Fairchild v. Bell, 2 Brevard 129, April 1807, in Catterall, *Judicial Cases*, II, pp. 288–89; State v. E. and R. Smith, 1 N. and McC. 13, November 1817, in Catterall, *Judicial Cases*, II, p. 306; The State vs. Guy Raines, 1826, Fairfield District, in David J. McCord, *Report of Cases Argued and Determined in the Court of Appeals of South Carolina* (Columbia: Doyle E. Sweeny, 1826), III, pp. 534–36; State v. Rhines, 3 McCord 533, May 1826, in Catterall, *Judicial Cases*, II, pp. 332–34; State v. Montgomery, Cheves 120, February 1840, in Catterall, *Judicial Cases*, II, p. 377; State v. Fleming, 2 Strobhart 464, May 1848, in Catterall, *Judicial Cases*, II, p. 408; David Gavin Diary, November 14, 20, 1856, November 4, 16, 1857, I, pp. 60, 110, 112, SHC.

124. Hindus, *JAH*, 579.

125. State v. M'Kee, 1 Bailey 651, June 1830, in Catterall, *Judicial Cases*, II, p. 343.

126. Fairchild v. Bell, 2 Brevard 129, April 1807, in Catterall, *Judicial Cases*, II, pp. 288–89.

127. James H. Hammond Plantation Manual, n.d., II (typescript), p. 5, Edward

Spann Hammond Papers, SC; Andrew Flinn Plantation Book, "Plantation Rules," SC.

128. Florence Johnson Scott, "Letters and Papers of Governor David Johnson and Family, 1810–1855," in *The Proceedings of the South Carolina Historical Association* (Columbia: The South Carolina Historical Association, 1939), p. 24.

129. Silver Bluff Plantation: Stock and Crop Book, Values 1832, James Henry Hammond Papers, LC.

130. "Rosa Barnwell to the Editor," *Liberator*, November 7, 1862, in Blassingame, *Slave Testimony*, p. 698.

131. Rawick, *The American Slave*, II, i, pp. 338–39, 344, III, iv, p. 192; Holland, *Letters and Diary of Laura M. Towne*, p. 289; Pearson, *Letters From Port Royal*, p. 192; Rev. Andrew Cornish, Abbeville, to Rev. John H. Cornish, Charleston, September 15, 1846, John Hamilton Cornish Papers, SHC; "Petition of Dr. John S. Reid, Abbeville District," November 23, 1831, (Folder 145), Slavery Files, SCA; Botume, *First Days Amongst the Contrabands* pp. 11, 138–39; *Anti-Slavery Advocate*, II (February 1, 1862), 498–99, in Blassingame, *Slave Testimony*, p. 359; Ball, *Fifty Years in Chains*, pp. 224–26, 256–57.

132. Ball, *Fifty Years in Chains*, pp. 223–26, 240, 255, 257.

133. *American Slavery As It Is*, p. 23.

134. "Moses Roper, London, to Thomas Price, June 27, 1836," *Slavery in America*, no. 2 (August 1836), 45–46, in Blassingame, *Slave Testimony*, p. 25.

135. Journal of Thomas B. Chaplin, February 19, 1849, pp. 209–11, SCHS.

136. Orlando Patterson, *Slavery and Social Death: A Comparative Study* (Cambridge: Harvard University Press, 1982), p. 5.

137. *American Slavery As It Is*, p. 54; "Memorial of the Citizens of Charleston to the Senate and House of Representatives of the State of South Carolina" (Charleston, 1822), in Ulrich B. Phillips, ed., *Plantation and Frontier Documents, 1649–1863: Illustrative of Industrial History in the Colonial & Ante-Bellum South* (Cleveland: The Arthur H. Clark Company, 1909), II, pp. 110–13; Thomas J. Kirkland and Robert M. Kennedy, *Historic Camden* (Columbia: The State Company, 1926), II, p. 191; Pee Dee, "The Management of Negroes," *SA*, XI (October 1838), 512–13; James H. Hammond Plantation Manual, II, pp. 21–22, Edward Spann Hammond Papers, SC; Farmer's Club Records, August 7, 1847, p. 34, SC; "The Duties of An Overseer," in Affleck, *The Cotton Plantation*, unpaged; Dr. Thomas Diary, May 1, 1829, II, p. 82, Thomas Family Papers, SC.

138. Weston, "Rules for the Plantation," quoted in Collins, *Memories of the Southern States*, pp. 115–16.

139. Plantation Book of Charles Pinckney, "Account of Aukland: Hogs," pp. 24–25, Pinckney Family Papers, LC; Agreement by Robert F. W. Allston to Purchase Hogs From the Slaves, 1859, in Easterby, *South Carolina Rice Plantation*, p. 350.

140. Wm. Capers, Savannah River, Chatham County, Ga., to Charles Manigault, November 14, 1861, in Phillips, *Plantation and Frontier Documents*, I, pp. 320–21; Ball, *Fifty Years in Chains*, pp. 110–19; "State vs. Eddy (a Negro Slave)," August 8, 1849, (Case 97), Spartanburg Court Records, SCA; "Alexander, slave of Owen White, Assault and battery with intent to kill, July 9, 1856, Spartanburg Trial Papers, [SCA], quoted in Henderson, "Spartan Slaves," pp. 110–11; Malet, *An Errand to the South*, pp. 204–5; B. T. Sellers, [Newport] to [Williams] Middleton, June 16, 1860, Williams Middleton Papers, SC;

Rawick, *The American Slave*, II, i, pp. 39, 344, II, ii, pp. 235, 310–11, III, iv, pp. 170–71; Rochester *Union and Advertiser*, August 9, 1893, in Blassingame, *Slave Testimony*, p. 512; "Testimony of Harry McMillan," p. 129, NA; French, *Slavery in South Carolina*, pp. 182–83; Stroyer, *My Life in the South*, pp. 19–20.

141. Rawick, *The American Slave*, III, iii, p. 261.

142. "Simmon, Levi, Sally, slaves of John C. Zimmerman, Assault and battery with intent to kill and insurrecting rebellious conduct," May 3, 1864, Spartanburg Trial Papers, [SCA], quoted in Henderson, "Spartan Slaves," pp. 112–14.

143. Ibid.

144. Ibid., pp. 112–14, 299.

145. Roper, *A Narrative*, pp. 47, 58; *American Slavery As It Is*, pp. 53–54, 98.

146. Rawick, *The American Slave*, II, i, p. 207, II, ii, pp. 36, 173, III, iv, pp. 171, 271; *American Slavery As It Is*, p. 99.

147. "Petition of Thomas Bennett to Governor Seabrook," Slavery Files, SCA; "The Petition of William Cregsmily of the Parish of St. Andrews, Planter," December 6, 1800/"State of So Carolina, Charleston District," December 6, 1800, General Assembly Petitions, SCA; William Thomson, *A Tradesman's Travels in the United States and Canada* . . . (Edinburgh: Oliver & Boyd, 1842), pp. 173–81, in Willie Lee Rose, ed., *A Documentary History of Slavery in North America* (New York: Oxford University Press, 1976), pp. 365–66; The Newberry *Rising Sun*, July 20, 1859, cited in Taylor, *Ante-Bellum South Carolina*, p. 79; *American Slavery As It Is*, p. 158; Mary E. Bothwell, Louisville, to Uncle Willie, January 12, 1842, William W. Renwick Papers, PL; Dr. Thomas Diary, April 1, 1829, II, p. 65, Thomas Family Papers, SC; "Letter to Peter Frigg," December 4, 1803, General Assembly/Accounts—Constables, SCA; "Petition of James Wideman, Abbeville District," 1847, (Folder 183), Slavery Files, SCA; Rawick, *The American Slave*, II, ii, pp. 216, 218, III, iii, p. 158; Buckingham, *The Slave States*, I, pp. 570–71.

148. Rawick, *The American Slave*, II, ii, pp. 216, 218.

149. Buckingham, *The Slave States*, I, pp. 570–71; Kirkland, *Historic Camden*, II, p. 190; Anne King Gregorie, *History of Sumter County, South Carolina* (Sumter: Library Board of Sumter County, 1954), p. 144; *American Slavery As It Is*, p. 23; William Capers, Gowrie, Chatham County, Ga., to Charles Manigault, Charleston, June 13, 1860, in Phillips, *Plantation and Frontier Documents*, II, p. 94; Ball, *Fifty Years in Chains*, p. 337.

150. William P. Hill Diary, 1846–1849, April 9, 1847, SHC.

151. Rawick, *The American Slave*, III, ii, pp. 274–75.

152. Olmsted, *Journey in the Seaboard Slave States*, pp. 435–36; Rawick, *The American Slave*, II, ii, p. 145, III, iii, p. 114; Robert William Mackay, Walnut Hill, [McPhersonville], to George Chisolm Mackay, April 27, 1828, Mackay Family Papers, SC.

153. Rawick, *The American Slave*, II, i, pp. 11, 129–30, 184; Holland, *Letters and Diary of Laura M. Towne*, pp. 224–25; John C. Calhoun, Fort Hill, to Lt. James Edward Colhoun, U.S.N., Midway, Abbeville (District, S.C.), August 27, 1831, Calhoun Family Typescripts; Lucy Ruggles Diary, March 5, 1846, I, pp. 240–42, Daniel Ruggles Papers, PL; Diary of W. Thacher, March 16, 1817, MS, cited in Taylor, *Ante-Bellum South Carolina*, p. 180; Diary of J. B. Grimball, Charleston, S.C., No. 3-1834-1835-1836, January 7, 1835, I, p. 32, CLS.

154. Manigault Letter Book, 1846–1848 (typescript), Charles Izard Manigault, Paris to Mr. Haynes, (Savannah River), March 1, 1847, p. 26, Charles Mani-

gault Papers, SC; Jones, "A Cultural Middle Passage," p. 235; "The Duties of An Overseer," in Affleck, *The Cotton Plantation,* unpaged.

155. Stroyer, *My Life in the South,* p. 69.

156. Plantation Records, October 17, 1839, p. 187, James H. Hammond Papers, SC.

157. David Gavin Diary, January 4, 1856, March 22, 1861, I, pp. 18, 231, SHC; Malet, *An Errand to the South,* p. 204; Mr. Robertson, Fording Island, to [Charles Cotesworth Pinckney], November 25, 1824, Pinckney Family Papers, LC; Lucy Ruggles Diary, March 1, 1845, I, p. 13, Daniel Ruggles Papers, PL.

158. Arney Robinson Childs, ed., *The Private Journal of Henry William Ravenel, 1859–1887* (Columbia: University of South Carolina Press, 1947), p. 169.

159. Journal of Thomas B. Chaplin, October 2, 1852, p. 456, SCHS; James Sanders Guignard, I, Columbia, to John Gabriel Guignard, II, December 9, 1833, Guignard Family Papers, SC; William R. Davie to Capt. John Singleton, April 16, 1819, William R. Davie Papers, Southern Historical Collection, cited in Eugene D. Genovese, *Roll, Jordan, Roll: The World the Slaves Made* (New York: Pantheon Books, 1974), pp. 655–56.

160. Genovese, *Roll, Jordan, Roll,* p. 656.

161. Matthew G. Lewis, *Journal of a West India Proprietor, Kept During a Residence in the Island of Jamaica* (New York: Negro Universities Press, 1969), passim (originally published in 1834); "Evidence of Reverend Peter Duncan," Report From the Select Committee on the Extinction of Slavery Throughout the British Dominions . . . 1831–1832, in *British Parliamentary Papers* (Shannon, Ireland: Irish University Press, 1968), 2, p. 125; Henry Sterne, *A Statement of Facts . . . With An Exposure of the Present System of Jamaica Apprenticeship* (New York: Negro Universities Press, 1969), p. 262 (originally published in 1837); James M. Phillippo, *Jamaica: Its Past and Present State* (Philadelphia: James M. Campbell, 1843), p. 156; Joseph Sturge and Thomas Harvey, *The West Indies in 1837 . . .* (London: Frank Cass & Company, 1968), p. 273 (originally published in 1838).

162. Mr. T. Dawsey, Pinckney Island, to Charles Cotesworth Pinckney, November 25, 1824, Pinckney Family Papers, LC; Rawick, *The American Slave,* II, ii, p. 234; John Durant Ashmore Plantation Journal, 1853–1859, February 5, 1856 (typescript), p. 123, SHC; Church of Christ Records, August 19, 1837, p. 29, SC; An Overseer, "Overseers," *SC,* VII (September 1849), 140; Adam Hodgson, *Remarks During a Journey Through North America in the Years 1819, 1820, and 1821 . . .* (New York: Samuel Whiting, 1823), p. 131; "Domestic," The Pendleton *Messenger,* October 5, 1831; "Petition of Gideon Hutto, Orangeburgh District," November 26, 1838, (Folder 101), Slavery Files, SCA; "Petition of Frederick Mole, Beaufort District," 1840, (Folder 127), Slavery Files, SCA; "Petition of Anthony and Edmond Jones, Greenville District," November 12, 1844, (Folder 106), Slavery Files, SCA; "Petition of William M. Burt, Administrator of A. W. Burt, for Compensation for a Slave Executed, Edgefield District," November 18, 1847, (Folder 58), Slavery Files, SCA; "State vs. Eddy (a Negro Slave)," August 8, 1849, (Case 97), Spartanburg Court Records, SCA; "Petition of Charles R. Caroll for Compensation for a Slave Executed, Barnwell District," 1851, (Folder 62), SCA.

163. Anderson *Gazette,* April 2, 1847, p. 3.

164. "The Petition of William Cregsmily," General Assembly Petitions, SCA; "Petition of Martha Hancock, Edgefield District," November 24, 1820, General Assembly Petitions, SCA; "Petition of Wm. Speer, Administrator of Estate of

Daniel Anderson for Compensation for Execution of 3 Negroes: Certificate of Appraisment of Negroes," July 28, 1834, (Folder 40), Slavery Files, SCA; Joseph R. Miller, Columbia, S.C., to Mr. Joshua Miller, Lexington, S.C., August 10, 1838, John Fox Papers, PL; "Petition of Richard Singleton," 1848/ "Affidavit of James D. Tradewell, Richland District," December 7, 1838, (Folder 159), Slavery Files, SCA; *American Slavery As It Is,* p. 158; Mary E. Bothwell, Louisville, to Uncle Willie, January 12, 1842, William W. Renwick Papers, PL; "Petition of James Wideman," Slavery Files, SCA.

165. Ball, *Fifty Years in Chains,* pp. 219–22; Pearson, *Letters From Port Royal,* p. 236; Joel Williamson, *After Slavery: The Negro in South Carolina During Reconstruction, 1861–1877* (Chapel Hill: The University of North Carolina Press, 1965), p. 51; Herbert Aptheker, "Afro-American Superiority: A Neglected Theme in Literature," *Phylon,* XXXI (Winter 1970), 336–37.

166. Holland, *Letters and Diary of Laura M. Towne,* p. 31.

167. Rawick, *The American Slave,* III, iii, p. 195; Julia Peterkin, *Roll, Jordan, Roll. Photographic Studies by Doris Ulmann* (New York: Robert O. Ballow, 1933), pp. 165–66; Higginson, *Army Life,* p. 216; Ball, *Fifty Years in Chains,* pp. 220–22; Williams, *"De Ole Plantation,"* pp. 27–29; Parsons, *Folk-Lore of the Sea Islands,* p. 117.

168. Harriet Martineau, *Society in America* (London: Saunders and Otley, 1837), II, pp. 158–59.

169. Pope, "A Dissertation on the Professional Management of Negro Slaves," pp. 8–9, MU; Lowery, *Life On the Old Plantation,* p. 91; Rawick, *The American Slave,* II, i, pp. 31–32, III, iv, pp. 157–58; Jones, "A Cultural Middle Passage," pp. 170–71.

170. Lowery, *Life On the Old Plantation,* pp. 89–91.

171. Ball, *Fifty Years in Chains,* pp. 215–16.

172. Eric Perkins, "Roll, Jordan, Roll: A 'Marx' for the Master Class," *RHR,* 3 (Fall 1976), 45.

173. Alexandre Kojeve, *An Introduction to the Reading of Hegel* (New York, 1969), p. 49, quoted in Perkins, *RHR,* 45.

Chapter 4. Tactics of Divide and Rule

1. An Overseer, "On the Conduct and Management of Overseers, Drivers, and Slaves," *SA,* IX (May 1836), 227–28.

2. "Testimony of Harry McMillan," American Freedmen's Inquiry Commission (microfilm), Reel 200, File III, pp. 128–29, NA.

3. Charles C. Jones, *The Religious Instruction of the Negroes* (New York: Negro Universities Press, 1969), p. 136 (originally published in 1842); Jacob Stroyer, *My Life in the South* (Salem, Mass.: Observer and Job Print, 1885), pp. 44–45; Elizabeth Hyde Botume, *First Days Amongst the Contrabands* (New York: Arno Press and The New York Times, 1968), p. 121 (originally published in 1892); J. G. Clinkscales, *On the Old Plantation: Reminiscences of His Childhood* (New York: Negro Universities Press, 1969), p. 22 (originally published in 1916).

4. Charles Ball, *Fifty Years in Chains,* with an introduction by Philip S. Foner (New York: Dover Publications, 1970), p. 275 (originally published in 1837).

5. Jones, *Religious Instruction of Negroes,* p. 136.

6. Clinkscales, *On the Old Plantation,* pp. 8–9, 22.

7. Robert W. Mackay, W[alnu]t Hill, to George C. Mackay, Charleston, March

10, 1825, Mackay Family Papers, SC; Edgefield [S.C.] Military Record, January 7, 1837, p. 2, SHC; Diary of Natalie de Delage Sumter, 1840–1841, July 12, September 7, 1840, SC; Diary of John Hamilton Cornish, June 19, 1847, V (typescript), p. 255, John Hamilton Cornish Papers, SHC; (Case 195), September 23, 1847, Pendleton/Anderson District Court of Magistrates and Freeholders (microfilm), SCA; Columbia, South Carolina; Richmond Plantation Overseer's Book, 1859–1860, September 12, 1859, SCHS; Journal/Diary of Rev. Clark B. Stewart, September 8, 1860 (typescript), p. 13, SC; Elizabeth Ware Pearson, ed., *Letters From Port Royal, 1862–1868* (New York: Arno Press and The New York Times, 1969), pp. 214–15, 241 (originally published in 1906); Anne King Gregorie, *History of Sumter County, South Carolina* (Sumter: Library Board of Sumter County, 1954), pp. 144, 200; Baptist Church: Welsh Neck Baptist Church Minutes, 1737–1935, Society Hill, Darlington County, May 21, 1826 (typescript), pp. 110–12, SC; Diary of John Berkley Grimball, Charleston, S.C., No. 6-1837-1838-1840, May 5, 1840, I (typescript), p. 26, CLS; (Case 117), March 11, 1850, Spartanburg Court of Magistrates and Freeholders Records (microfilm), SCA.

8. Mary White, ed., *Fifteen Letters of Nathalie Sumter* (Columbia, S.C.: R. L. Bryan Company, 1942), pp. 7, 15–17; Diary of Natalie de Delage Sumter, 1840–1841, July 12, 1840, SC.

9. David Gavin Diary, 1855–1871, February 28, 1860, I (typescript), p. 187, SHC.

10. "George, slave of John B. Cleveland, Murder," March 1, 1865, Spartanburg District Court of Magistrates and Freeholders Trial Papers, [SCA], quoted in William Cinque Henderson, "Spartan Slaves: A Documentary Account of Blacks on Trial in Spartanburg, South Carolina 1830–1865" (Ph.D. dissertation, Northwestern University, 1978), p. 87.

11. "The State vs. Bassett, a negro slave the property of Marriah Wofford," February 14, 1851, (Case 128), Spartanburg Court Records, SCA.

12. H. Perry Pope, "A Dissertation on the Professional Management of Negro Slaves" (Sr. thesis, Medical College of the State of South Carolina, 1837), pp. 8–9, MU.

13. "The Petition of Samuel Fairchild, Physician of the said State," November 28, 1800, General Assembly Petitions, SCA; Ball, *Fifty Years in Chains*, p. 264; John Gabriel Guignard, II, Hopewell, to James Sanders Guignard, I, October 7, 8, 1828, Guignard Family Papers, SC; "The State v Isaac, the Slave of Edward Carew—Petition, Charleston," July 3, 1834, (Folder 247), Slavery Files, SCA; Journal of Thomas B. Chaplin, 1845–1886, March 1, 1845, p. 13, SCHS; C. T. Haskell, Abbeville, to Langdon Cheves, March 30, 1862, Cheves Family Papers, SCHS; Pearson, *Letters From Port Royal*, p. 211; George P. Rawick, ed., *The American Slave: A Composite Autobiography* (Westport, Conn.: Greenwood Publishing Company, 1972), II, ii, pp. 129–30; Bobby Frank Jones, "A Cultural Middle Passage: Slave Marriage and Family in the Ante-Bellum South" (Ph.D. dissertation, University of North Carolina, 1965), pp. 170–71.

14. Rawick, *The American Slave*, II, i, pp. 42–44.

15. Baptist Church: Welsh Neck Minutes, February 5, 1815, p. 61, SC.

16. Diary of J. B. Grimball, No. 12-1858-1859, 1861-1862, November 28, [29], 1858, II, p. 10, CLS.

17. Ibid., January 12, 1859, p. 11.

18. Jones, "A Cultural Middle Passage," pp. 165–67; Thomas D. Condy, *A Digest of the Laws of the United States & the State of South Carolina . . .* (Charleston:

A. E. Miller, 1830), p. 173; John Belton O'Neall, *The Negro Law of South Carolina* (Columbia: John G. Bowman, 1848), p. 29; "Petition of Edward L. Roche," 1831, (Folder 147), Slavery Files, SCA; "Petition of Jaques Bishop Praying Compensation for a Negro Executed, Sumter" November 1833, (Folder 51), Slavery Files, SCA; "Petition of Mary Douglas Praying Compensation for Slave Executed," 1837, (Folder 80), Slavery Files, SCA; "Petition of Anthony and Edmond Jones, Greenville District," November 12, 1844, (Folder 106), Slavery Files, SCA; (Case 97), August 8, 1849, Spartanburg Court Records, SCA; Robert S. Starobin, ed., *Denmark Vesey: The Slave Conspiracy of 1822* (Englewood Cliffs, N.J.: Prentice-Hall, 1970), p. 4.

19. "Petition of Richard Singleton," [1848], (Folder 159), Slavery Files, SCA.

20. "George, Murder," Spartanburg Trial Papers, [SCA], quoted in Henderson, "Spartan Slaves," pp. 87–88.

21. Robert W. Mackay, W[alnu]t Hill, to George C. Mackay, Charleston, March 10, 1825, Mackay Family Papers, SC; Baptist Church: Welsh Neck Minutes, May 21, June 4, 1826, January 3, 1830, pp. 110–13, 124, 142, SC; "The State v Isaac, the Slave of Edward Carew—Petition, Charleston," July 3, 1834, (Folder 247), Slavery Files, SCA; State v. Toomer, Cheves 106, February 1840, in Helen T. Catterall, ed., *Judicial Cases Concerning American Slavery and the Negro* (Washington, D.C.: Carnegie Institute of Washington, 1929), II, p. 377; Diary of J. B. Grimball, No. 6, May 5–9, 1840, I, pp. 26–27, CLS; (Case 117), March 11, 1850, Spartanburg Court Records, SCA; "Petition of Thomas Bennett to Governor Seabrook Praying Pardon for His Slave, Peter Blackstock," December 5, 1850, (Folder 50), Slavery Files, SCA; Diary of J. B. Grimball, No. 11-1852-1857, October 21, 22, 1856, February 20, 23, 1857, II, pp. 31–33, No. 12, November 28, 1858, January 12, 1859, January 11, 1860, II, pp. 10–11, 18, CLS; "The State vs. George, A Slave Murder, Charleston District," July 22, 1850, (Folder 246), Slavery Files, SCA.

22. "The State v Isaac, the Slave of Edward Carew," Slavery Files, SCA.

23. Ibid.

24. Stroyer, *My Life in the South*, pp. 59–61; A. M. H. Christensen, *Afro-American Folk Lore: Told Round Cabin Fires on the Sea Islands of South Carolina* (New York: Negro Universities Press, 1969), pp. 23–25 (originally published in 1892); Charles W. Joyner, "Slave Folklife of the Waccamaw Neck: Antebellum Black Culture in the South Carolina Low-country" (Ph.D. dissertation, University of Pennsylvania, 1977), pp. 164–68, 179–80; Elsie Clews Parsons, *Folk-Lore of the Sea Islands, South Carolina* (Cambridge, Mass.: The American Folk-Lore Society, 1923), pp. 30–31; Charles C. Jones, *Negro Myths From the Georgia Coast* (Columbia: The State Company, 1925), pp. 111, 124–26, 145–46.

25. Jones, *Negro Myths*, pp. 55–58.

26. Rawick, *The American Slave*, III, iii, pp. 97–99; John/"Come With Me," (D-4-33 #15), Federal Writers' Project, S.C.: Folklore MSS (typescript), SC; Joyner, "Slave Folklife," pp. 172–75.

27. Christensen, *Afro-American Folk Lore*, pp. 23–25; Joyner, "Slave Folklife," pp. 167–69; Jones, *Negro Myths*, pp. 54, 124–26; Parsons, *Folk-Lore of the Sea Islands*, pp. 30–31.

28. William L. McCaa, "Observations on the Manner of Living and Diseases of Slaves on the Wateree River, S.C." (Sr. thesis, University of Pennsylvania, 1823), p. 5, WHL; Rev. I. E. Lowery, *Life On the Old Plantation or a Story Based on Facts* (Columbia: The State Company, 1911), pp. 81–85; Albert J. Rabo-

teau, *Slave Religion: The "Invisible Institution" in the Antebellum South* (New York: Oxford University Press, 1978), pp. 80, 82, 237–38, 275–78; Rawick, *The American Slave,* III, iii, p. 158, III, iv, pp. 247, 252.

29. McCaa, "Observations on the Slaves," p. 5, WHL.
30. Baptist Church: Welsh Neck Minutes, May 21, 1826, pp. 110–11, SC.
31. Raboteau, *Slave Religion,* p. 276.
32. Rupert Sargent Holland, ed., *Letters and Diary of Laura M. Towne: Written From the Sea Islands of South Carolina, 1862–1884* (Cambridge: Riverside Press, 1912), p. 186; Work Projects Administration, "South Carolina Folk Tales: Stories of Animals and Supernatural Beings," *University of South Carolina Bulletin* (October 1941), 46–47.
33. (Case 231), September 11, 1860, Spartanburg Court Records, SCA; Rawick, *The American Slave,* III, iv, p. 113; Joel W. Ashford, Winnsboro, S.C., to Dr. James Milling, Rocky Mount, La., December 25, 1859, James S. Milling Papers, SHC; "MS. Records of Union County," quoted in H. M. Henry, *The Police Control of the Slave in South Carolina* (New York: Negro Universities Press, 1968), pp. 97–98 (originally published in 1914); Jones, *Religious Instruction of Negroes,* p. 130. As one would expect, this devout protectiveness and code of silence found its way into the folklore of African-Americans. In the 1930s Ephriam Lawrence, a former slave from Edisto Island, told an interviewer what obviously was a John tale. He recalled how slaves on one plantation had lied to their owner about the whereabouts of Old John Drayton. John, a superior fiddler, had gone to play for the slaves on another plantation instead of mending a fence as his master instructed. When he reappeared several days later, John, "de smaa'test of all de niggers," was able—as usual—to talk his way out of the difficult situation. See Rawick, *The American Slave,* III, iii, pp. 97–98.
34. "State vs Negro Moses (property of Mr. Hays) for Harbouring T. G. Grahams Negro Woman, Barnwell District," July 29, 1840, (Folder 249), Slavery Files, SCA; "State vs. Tom, Negro (the) property of Wm. Rice, for harbouring T. G. Grahams Negro woman, Barnwell District," July 29, 1840, (Folder 251), Slavery Files, SCA; "State vs Negro Man Will, Property of Mr. Guess, for harbouring T. G. Graham's Negro woman, Barnwell District," July 29, 1840, (Folder 252), Slavery Files, SCA; (Case 128), March 1, 1842, Pendleton/Anderson Court Records, SCA; (Case 373), June 25, 1862, Pendleton/Anderson Court Records, SCA; Kenneth M. Stampp, *The Peculiar Institution: Slavery in the Ante-Bellum South* (New York: Vintage Books, 1956), p. 116.
35. Plantation Records, Silver Bluff, S.C. December 8, 1831–December 31, 1855, July 18, 1832, p. 28, James Henry Hammond Papers, SC.
36. Ball, *Fifty Years in Chains,* pp. 115–19, 252.
37. Cornhill Plantation Book, 1827–1873, p. 107, McDonald Furman Papers, PL; *American Slavery As It Is: Testimony of A Thousand Witnesses* (New York: American Anti-Slavery Society, 1839), p. 174; Ball, *Fifty Years in Chains,* p. 323; Robert F. W. Allston Diary, 1859–1860, January 14th, in J. H. Easterby, ed., *The South Carolina Rice Plantation As Revealed in the Papers of Robert F. W. Allston* (Chicago: University of Chicago Press, 1945), p. 464.
38. Thomas Pinckney, Altamont, to Mrs. Harriott Horry, Charleston, September 2, 1822, Thomas Pinckney Papers, SC.
39. Lucy Ruggles Diary, 1845–1848, May 17, 1845, March 5, 7, 8, 1846, I, pp. 64, 240–43, Daniel Ruggles Papers, PL.
40. Edward A. Pollard, *Black Diamonds: Gathered in the Darkey Homes of the South* (New York: Pudney & Russell, 1859), pp. 60–61; Moses Roper, *A Nar-*

rative of the Adventures and Escape of Moses Roper, From Slavery (New York: Negro Universities Press, 1970), pp. 46–47, 58 (originally published in 1838); *American Slavery As It Is*, pp. 54, 98; Rawick, *The American Slave*, II, ii, p. 139; Henry, *Police Control*, p. 66.

41. *American Slavery As It Is*, p. 98.

42. Edward Spann Hammond Diary, 1857–1858, June 7, 1857, Edward Spann Hammond Papers, SC.

43. Peter H. Wood, *Black Majority: Negroes in Colonial South Carolina From 1670 Through the Stono Rebellion* (New York: Alfred A. Knopf, 1974), p. 282.

44. Plantation Manual of James H. Hammond of Beech Island, South Carolina, circa 1834 (typescript), p. 3, WHL; William Thomson, *A Tradesman's Travels in the United States and Canada . . .* (Edinburgh: Oliver & Boyd, 1842), pp. 173–81, in Willie Lee Rose, ed., *A Documentary History of Slavery in North America* (New York: Oxford University Press, 1976), pp. 366–67; Lucy Ruggles Diary, January 11, 1846, I, pp. 213–14, Daniel Ruggles Papers, PL; Journal of Thomas B. Chaplin, June 18, 20, 1853, pp. 498–99, SCHS; Alice R. Huger Smith, *A Carolina Rice Plantation of the Fifties . . . With Chapters From the Unpublished Memoirs of D. E. Huger Smith* (New York: William Morrow and Company, 1936), pp. 64–65; A. M. French, *Slavery in South Carolina and the Ex-Slaves; Or, the Port Royal Mission* (New York: Negro Universities Press, 1969), pp. 57, 95–96 (originally published in 1862); Rawick, *The American Slave*, III, iii, pp. 14–15, 273, III, iv, p. 117; Jones, *Negro Myths*, pp. 124–26; Guion Griffis Johnson, *A Social History of the Sea Islands: With Special Reference to St. Helena Island, South Carolina* (Chapel Hill: The University of North Carolina Press, 1930), pp. 78–79.

45. Frederick Law Olmsted, *A Journey in the Seaboard Slave States, With Remarks on their Economy* (New York: Dix & Edwards, 1856), pp. 433, 435–36; William Van Deburg, *The Slave Drivers: Black Agricultural Labor Supervisors in the Antebellum South* (Westport, Conn.: Greenwood Press, 1979), p. 14; Johnson, *Social History*, pp. 77–79.

46. Smith, *Carolina Rice Plantation*, pp. 64–65; King, *SA*, 524; Rawick, *The American Slave*, II, i, p. 158, III, iii, pp. 15, 273; Charles Lyell, *A Second Visit to the United States* (New York: Harper & Brothers, 1849), I, pp. 265–66.

47. Clinkscales, *On the Old Plantation*, pp. 7–10, 22, 29–30, 35–36; J. H. Easterby, ed., "Charles Cotesworth Pinckney's Plantation Diary, April 6–December 15, 1818," *SCHM*, XLI (October 1940), 139–40; Louis M. DeSaussure Plantation Record, 1835–1865, November 17, 1835 (typescript), p. 3, SHC; G. Buist/Ordinary, Inventories, Appraisements and Sales—D., 1854–1857, pp. 180, 282, SCA; Rawick, *The American Slave*, II, ii, p. 166; Smith, *Carolina Rice Plantation*, p. 65.

48. Rawick, *The American Slave*, III, iii, p. 65.

49. French, *Slavery*, pp. 68–69, 109–10; Rawick, *The American Slave*, II, i, pp. 123, 125–26, II, ii, p. 166; Raboteau, *Slave Religion*, pp. 221–22.

50. French, *Slavery*, pp. 68–69, 109–10.

51. Journal of Thomas B. Chaplin, October 16, 1850, p. 306, SCHS.

52. Ira Berlin, "Time, Space, and the Evolution of Afro-American Society in British Mainland North America," *AHR*, 85 (February 1980), pp. 65–66; James C. Darby, "On Planting and Managing a Rice Crop," *SA*, II (June 1829), 248–49; Zelotus L. Holmes, Laurens, S.C., to [Mrs. Ruth Marshall], Buffalo, N.Y., January 24, 1855, Zelotus Lee Holmes Papers, SC; Olmsted, *A Journey*, p. 438; Wm. Hopkins, Richlands District, S.C., to James Gregorie, Pocotaligo, S.C.,

October 11, 1863, Gregorie-Elliot Papers, SHC; James H. Stone, "Black Leadership in the Old South: The Slave Drivers of the Rice Kingdom," (Ph.D. dissertation, Florida State University, 1976), pp. 9–11, 25, 43–44.

53. Rawick, *The American Slave*, III, iii, pp. 48–49.

54. Walter Schatz, ed., *Directory of Afro-American Resources* (New York: R. R. Bowker Company, 1970), p. 66.

55. J. M. Hawks, North Edisto Island, S.C., to Ester Hawks, May 17, 1862, Ester H. Hawks Papers, LC.

56. Rawick, *The American Slave*, II, ii, p. 338, III, iv, p. 148; Smith, *Carolina Rice Plantation*, pp. 65–67; Joyner, "Slave Folklife," pp. 50, 55; Plantation Manual of James H. Hammond, pp. 1, 3, WHL; R. King, Jr., "On the Management of the Butler Estate, and the Cultivation of the Sugar Cane," *SA*, I (December 1828), 527; Stampp, *The Peculiar Institution*, pp. 151, 330; *The Carolina Planter*, July 8, 1840, p. 203, cited in Charles M. Clark, "Plantation Overseers in South Carolina, 1820–1860" (M.A. thesis, University of South Carolina, 1966), p. 105.

57. Robert F. W. Allston, Columbia, to Adele Petigru Allston, December 1, 1844, in Easterby, *South Carolina Rice Plantation*, p. 92; Manigault Letter Book, 1846–1848 (typescript), Charles Izard Manigault, Paris, to Mr. Caward, (Silk Hope), September 1, 1847, p. 51, Charles Manigault Papers, SC; Dr. Jacob Rhett Motte Plantation Book, 1846–1871, "Negro Clothes Sent for in November, 1859," Jacob Rhett Motte Letters and Papers, PL; William Howard Russell, *My Diary North and South* (New York: Harper & Brothers, 1863), pp. 54–55; Christensen, *Afro-American Folk Lore*, pp. 2–3; Rawick, *The American Slave*, II, i, pp. 10–11, II, ii, p. 62; Lowery, *Life On the Old Plantation*, pp. 111–12; Smith, *Carolina Rice Plantation*, p. 73; Johnson, *Social History of the Sea Islands*, pp. 87–88; Arney R. Childs, ed., *Rice Planter and Sportsman: The Recollections of J. Motte Allston, 1821–1909* (Columbia: University of South Carolina Press, 1953), p. 12; John W. Blassingame, *The Slave Community: Plantation Life in the Antebellum South* (New York: Oxford University Press, 1972), pp. 192, 207.

58. Plantation Record Book, October, 1809, I, John Ball and Keating S. Ball Books, 1779–1884, SHC.

59. Francis S. Parker Plantation Record, Hayes, St. James, Goose Creek, 1850, November 10, 1850, 1851, November 8, 1856, October 29, 1859, Francis S. Parker Plantation Records, 1849–1865, SC.

60. Duncan Clinch Heyward, *Seed From Madagascar* (Chapel Hill: The University of North Carolina Press, 1937), p. 181.

61. Rawick, *The American Slave*, II, ii, pp. 54, 56, 62, 64–65.

62. Ibid., p. 36.

63. Ball, *Fifty Years in Chains*, p. 146.

64. Childs, *Rice Planter and Sportsman*, p. 12.

65. Ball, *Fifty Years in Chains*, pp. 146, 267, 269–71; Manigault Letter Book, Charles Izard Manigault, Paris, to Messrs Mathiessen & Co, (Charleston), September 1, 1847, Charles Izard Manigault, Naples, to Mr J. F. Cooper, Gowrie, January 10, 1848, pp. 52, 60, Charles Manigault Papers, SC; Lowery, *Life On the Old Plantation*, pp. 66–67; Blassingame, *The Slave Community*, p. 207.

66. Thomas J. Kirkland and Robert M. Kennedy, *Historic Camden* (Columbia: The State Company, 1926), II, p. 191.

67. "An Ordinance For the Government of Slaves and Free Persons of Color in the Town of Greenville," *The Southern Enterprise*, March 6, 1856.

68. Christensen, *Afro-American Folk Lore*, p. 3; Plantation Manual of James H. Hammond, p. 1, WHL; Ball, *Fifty Years in Chains*, p. 279; Richmond Plantation Overseer's Book, February 13, 20, June 5, 23, September 17, October 23, 1859, SCHS; Plowden, C. J. Weston, "Rules and Management For the Plantation," 1859, cited in Elizabeth Collins, *Memories of the Southern States* (Taunton: Barnicott, 1865), pp. 105–7; Rawick, *The American Slave*, II, i, pp. 245–47; Harriott Pinckney, Charleston, to Mr. Winningham, February 8, 1855, Harriott Pinckney Papers, SC; Kirkpatrick, Douglass, and Hall, Charleston, to Langdon Cheves, Philadelphia, August 9, 1820, Cheves Family Papers, SCHS; George I. Crafts, Thebes, to Miss Maria [R. Campbell?], January 1, 1847, George I. Crafts Correspondence, 1846–1847 (typescript), CLS; Rosser T. Taylor, *Ante-Bellum South Carolina: A Social and Cultural History* (The James Sprunt Studies in History and Political Science, Chapel Hill: The University of North Carolina Press, 1942), p. 20.

69. Jessie W. Parkhurst, "The Role of the Black Mammy in the Plantation Household," *JNH*, XXIII (July 1938), 356, 359; Botume, *First Days Amongst the Contrabands*, pp. 58–59; Elizabeth W. Pringle, *Chronicles of Chicora Wood* (New York: Charles Scribner's Sons, 1922), pp. 158–59; James L. Petigru, Charleston, to Robert F. W. Allston, April 3, 1855, in Easterby, *South Carolina Rice Plantation*, p. 122; Pringle v. M'Pherson, 2 Desaussure 524, November 1807. Will of General John M'Pherson, dated 1803. (528), in Catterall, *Judicial Cases*, II, p. 291; John Gabriel Guignard, II, Hopewell, to James Sanders Guignard, I, October 20, 26, November 1, 7, 1828, Guignard Family Papers, SC; Richardson v. Richardson, Dudl. Eq. 184, February 1838. James Burchell Richardson's will dated 1826 . . . (197), in Catterall, *Judicial Cases*, II, pp. 368–69; Snowden v. Logan, Rice Eq. 174, February 1839. (181), in Catterall, *Judicial Cases*, II, p. 372; Noble v. Burnett, 10 Richardson 505, January 1857, in Catterall, *Judicial Cases*, II, pp. 453–54; American Bible Society v. Noble, 11 Rich. Eq. 156, November 1859. Autograph will of John B. Bull, dated April 1843. (162), in Catterall, *Judicial Cases*, II, p. 465; Rawick, *The American Slave*, II, ii, pp. 291–93.

70. John Ewing Bonneau to John C. Calhoun, Charleston, March 13, 1828, Calhoun Family Typescripts.

71. Journal of Thomas B. Chaplin, December 26, 1849, pp. 259–60, SCHS; Fredrika Bremer, *The Homes of the New World: Impressions of America*, trans. Mary Howitt (New York: Harper & Brothers, 1868), I, p. 376; Lowery, *Life on the Old Plantation*, pp. 59–62; Taylor, *Ante-Bellum South Carolina*, p. 20; Blassingame, *The Slave Community*, p. 87.

72. Diary of J. B. Grimball, No. 1-1832-1833, August 14, 1833, I, p. 45, CLS; Olmsted, *Journey in the Seaboard Slave States*, p. 427; Botume, *First Days Amongst the Contrabands*, pp. 58–59; D. E. Smith, *A Charlestonian's Recollections, 1846–1913* (Charleston: Carolina Art Association, 1950), pp. 20–21, 25; Pringle, *Chronicles of Chicora Wood*, p. 115; James R. Stuart Recollections, n.d. (typescript), p. 6, SHC; Orland Kay Armstrong, *Old Massa's People: The Old Slaves Tell Their Story* (Indianapolis: The Bobbs-Merrill Company, 1931), p. 200; Parkhurst, *JNH*, 356; Rawick, *The American Slave*, II, i, pp. 299–301.

73. Armstrong, *Old Massa's People*, p. 180.

74. Rawick, *The American Slave*, II, i, pp. 210–12.

75. S. H. Boineau, Combahee, to (Charles) Heyward, November 24, 1864, Heyward Family Papers, SC.

76. Rawick, *The American Slave*, III, iv, pp. 121–22, 125–26, 148; E. Ophelia

Settle, "Social Attitudes During the Slave Regime: House Servants Versus Field Hands," in August Meier and Elliot Rudwick, eds., *The Making of Black America: Essays in Negro Life and History* (New York: Atheneum, 1969), I, pp. 149–52.

77. *An Account of the Late Intended Insurrection Among a Portion of the Blacks of This City, Charleston, S.C.* (Charleston: Corporation of Charleston, 1822), in *Slave Insurrections: Selected Documents* (Westport, Conn.: Negro University Press, 1970), p. 33; James Stirling, *Letters From the Slave States* (London: John W. Parker and Sons, 1857), pp. 287–88; Clinkscales, *On the Old Plantation*, pp. 37–41; Settle, "Social Attitudes During the Slave Regime," pp. 148–52; E. Franklin Frazier, *The Negro in the United States*, rev. ed. (New York: The Macmillan Company, 1957), pp. 91, 273; Taylor, *Ante-Bellum South Carolina*, pp. 17–20; Heyward, *Seed From Madagascar*, pp. 187–90; Stampp, *The Peculiar Institution*, pp. 322, 326, 333, 338; Blassingame, *The Slave Community*, pp. 155, 161, 192, 200, 210; Joyner, "Slave Folklife," pp. 79–82; Jones, "A Cultural Middle Passage," pp. 234–37; Starobin, *Denmark Vesey*, p. 5; Eugene D. Genovese, *Roll, Jordan, Roll: The World the Slaves Made* (New York: Pantheon Books, 1974), pp. 328–30; C. W. Harper, "Black Aristocrats: Domestic Servants on the Antebellum Plantation," *Phylon*, 56 (June 1985), 123–26, 130–31, 135.

78. Joseph H. Ingraham, *The Sunny South; or, The Southerner at Home, Embracing Five Years' Experience . . . in the Land of the Sugar, and the Cotton*, p. 35, quoted in C. W. Harper, "House Servants and Field Hands: Fragmentation in the Antebellum Slave Community," *NCHR*, 55 (June 1978), 43.

79. Harper, *NCHR*, 49.

80. Jones, "A Cultural Middle Passage," p. 237.

81. Blassingame, *The Slave Community*, p. 200; Jones, "A Cultural Middle Passage," pp. 236–37; Harper, *NCHR*, 43–47, 51–53; Heyward, *Seed From Madagascar*, pp. 187–89.

82. Lucy Ruggles Diary, August 8, 1845, I, p. 112; Daniel Ruggles Papers, PL; Journal of Thomas B. Chaplin, May 15, 1851, p. 353, SCHS; John S. A. Legare Memoirs, n.d. (typescript), p. 4, SHC; Pringle, *Chronicles of Chicora Wood*, pp. 115, 121–22; "My Reminiscences," n.d. (typescript), pp. 3–4, Charles W. Hutson Papers, SHC; I. Mikell Jenkins, *Rumbling of the Chariot Wheels* (Columbia: The State Company, 1923), pp. 129–32, 204–5; Rawick, *The American Slave*, II, ii, pp. 327–28, III, iii, p. 8; Parkhurst, *JNH*, 356.

83. Holland, *Letters and Diary of Laura M. Towne*, pp. 109–10; James Stuart Recollections, p. 6, SHC; Robert L. Milligan, Brooklyn, to Miss Mary Guignard, August 3, 1926, Guignard Family Papers, SC.

84. Clinkscales, *On the Old Plantation*, p. 56.

85. Rawick, *The American Slave*, II, ii, pp. 177–78.

86. John Hope Franklin, *The Militant South, 1800–1861* (Cambridge: Harvard University Press, 1956), pp. 12, 25, 33–35, 45–46, 67–71, 202–3; Jenkins, *Rumbling of the Chariot Wheels*, pp. 204–5.

87. Rawick, *The American Slave*, II, ii, p. 130.

88. Jenkins, *Rumbling of the Chariot Wheels*, pp. 130–32.

89. Ibid.

90. Lucy Ruggles Diary, August 6, December 2, 1845, I, pp. 112, 184, Daniel Ruggles Papers, PL; Rawick, *The American Slave*, II, ii, pp. 177–78; Michael S. Hindus, "Black Justice Under White Law: Criminal Prosecutions of Blacks in Antebellum South Carolina," *JAH*, LXIII (December 1976), 589.

91. Holland, *Letters and Diary of Laura M. Towne*, pp. 27–28; Russell, *My Diary North and South*, p. 55; Rawick, *The American Slave*, II, i, pp. 10–11, II, ii, p. 62; Blassingame, *The Slave Community*, p. 155.

92. Ball, *Fifty Years in Chains*, p. 281; Mary Petigru, Badwell, to Adele Petigru Allston, December 27, 1860, in Easterby, *South Carolina Rice Plantation*, p. 172; Mrs. N. B. DeSaussure, *Old Plantation Days: Being Recollections of Southern Life Before the Civil War* (New York: Duffield & Company, 1909), pp. 52–53; Pringle, *Chronicles of Chicora Wood*, p. 156; Johnson, *Social History of the Sea Islands*, p. 106; Collins, *Memories of the Southern States*, pp. 7–8; Parkhurst, *JNH*, 354; Genovese, *Roll, Jordan, Roll*, p. 337; *American Missionary*, ser. 2, 6 (June 1862), 138, cited in Raboteau, *Slave Religion*, p. 310; "Report of the Missionaries: The Missionary (Rev. Paul Trapier) at Calvary Church, Charleston," quoted in *The Forty-Fourth Annual Report of the Trustees of the Protestant Episcopal Society for the Advancement of Christianity in South-Carolina* (Charleston: A. E. Miller, 1854), p. 10.

93. State v. Harlan, 5 Richardson 470, May 1852. Report of Judge O'Neall. (471), in Catterall, *Judicial Cases*, II, pp. 432–33; E. Perry, Greenville, to B. F. Perry, Columbia, n.d, Benjamin F. Perry Papers (typescript), pp. 2–3, SC; *American Slavery As It Is*, pp. 25–26, 54; Rawick, *The American Slave*, III, iv, pp. 121–22, 125–26.

94. Rawick, *The American Slave*, II, i, p. 300.

95. Reid v. Delorme, 2 Brevard 76, May 1806. (77), in Catterall, *Judicial Cases*, II, p. 287.

96. Roper, *A Narrative*, pp. 1, 9; Stroyer, *My Life in the South*, p. 30; Jones, "A Cultural Middle Passage," p. 179; Genovese, *Roll, Jordan, Roll*, p. 333; *American Slavery As It Is*, pp. 22–24, 44; State v. Montgomery, Cheves 120, February 1840, in Catterall, *Judicial Cases*, II, p. 377; E. Perry, Greenville, to B. F. Perry, November 29, 1843, Benjamin Perry Papers, p. 2, SC; Bremer, *Homes of the New World*, I, pp. 278, 292; David Gavin Diary, November 19, 1855, I, p. 6, SHC; Arney Robinson Childs, ed., *The Private Journal of Henry William Ravenel, 1859–1887* (Columbia: University of South Carolina Press, 1947), p. 169; Rawick, *The American Slave*, II, ii, pp. 289–90, III, iii, p. 277.

97. Rawick, *The American Slave*, II, ii, p. 209.

98. Basil Hall, *Travels in North America, in the Years 1827 and 1828* (Edinburgh: Cadell and Co., 1829), III, p. 192.

99. Olmsted, *Journey in the Seaboard Slave States*, p. 421; Smith, *Carolina Rice Plantation*, pp. 70–71; Stampp, *The Peculiar Institution*, p. 336; Blassingame, *The Slave Community*, pp. 201, 203; Genovese, *Roll, Jordan, Roll*, p. 331; Pollard, *Black Diamonds*, pp. 61–62.

100. Plantation Book of William Lowndes, From 1802 to 1822, "List of House Negroes," August 1803, William Lowndes Papers, LC; Manigault Letter Book, Charles Izard Manigault, Paris, to Mr. James Caward, [Silk Hope], March 1, 1847, p. 25, Charles Manigault Papers, SC; Olmsted, *A Journey in the Seaboard Slave States*, p. 421.

101. Robert William Mackay, Walnut Hill, [McPhersonville], to George Chisolm Mackay, April 27, 1828, Mackay Family Papers, SC.

102. Mary Boykin Chesnut, *A Diary From Dixie*, eds. Isabella D. Martin and Myrta Locket Avery (Gloucester, Mass.: Peter Smith, 1961), p. 224; Ball, *Fifty Years in Chains*, p.223; Lowery, *Life On the Old Plantation*, pp. 15–16, 100, 103; Stirling, *Letters From the Slave States*, pp. 295–96; Life and Recollections of Joseph W. Barnwell, 1929, I (typescript), p. 13, CLS; Charles A. Raymond,

"The Religious Life of the Negro Slave," *HNM*, XXVII (September 1863), 682; William Wyndham Malet, *An Errand to the South in the Summer of 1862* (London: Richard Bentley, 1863), p. 50; Gregorie, *History of Sumter County*, pp. 136–37; Rawick, *The American Slave*, II, i, p. 223, III, iii, p. 168; Alfred W. Nicholson, *Brief Sketch of the Life and Labors of Rev. Alexander Bettis* (By the Author, Trenton, S.C., 1913), pp. 9–10; Pearson, *Letters From Port Royal*, p. 166; Botume, *First Days Amongst the Contrabands*, pp. 62, 221.

103. Ball, *Fifty Years in Chains*, pp. 231, 281; Joshua B. Whitridge, Charleston, S.C., to William Whitridge, Rhode Island, June 14, 1826, Dr. Joshua Barker Whitridge Letters, 1806–1864, SCHS; Roper, *A Narrative*, pp. 64–65; Journal of Thomas B. Chaplin, May 3, 1852, p. 428, SCHS; Charles Graves Diary, 1846–1855, December 1, 2, 1854, SCHS; Olmsted, *Journey in the Seaboard Slave States*, pp. 402–3; Life of Joseph W. Barnwell, I, pp. 5, 10–11, CLS; Pringle, *Chronicles of Chicora Wood*, pp. 158–59; Smith, *Carolina Rice Plantation*, p. 34; DeSaussure, *Old Plantation Days*, pp. 52–53; Lowery, *Life On the Old Plantation*, pp. 15–16, 100, 103; Johnson, *A Social History of the Sea Islands*, pp. 81, 108; Rawick, *The American Slave*, II, ii, pp. 91, 94.

104. Hall, *Travels in North America*, p. 192; Olmsted, *Journey in the Seaboard Slave States*, p. 421; Thomas John Moore, Kinston, N.C., to Mrs. Ann Means, November 19, 1862, Thomas J. Moore, Camp near Kinston, to Mr. Hill, January 30, 1863, Elihu Moore, Camp near Wilmington, N.C., to Lou, April 9, 1863, Thomas John Moore Papers, SC; Roper, *A Narrative*, pp. 8–9; Ball, *Fifty Years in Chains*, pp. 151–52, 157, 159, 265–66.

105. Botume, *First Days Amongst the Contrabands*, pp. 59, 132–33; Rev. John G. Williams, *"De Ole Plantation"* (Charleston: Walker, Evans, & Cogswell Co., 1895), p. 12; Rawick, *The American Slave*, II, i, p. 225, III, iv, pp. 147–48, 160–62.

106. Joyner, "Slave Folklife," pp. 81–82; Robert Nicholas Olsberg, "A Government of Class and the South Carolina Chivalry, 1860–1865" (Ph.D. dissertation, University of South Carolina, 1972), pp. 135–36; Life of Joseph W. Barnwell, I, pp. 10–12, CLS; Holland, *Letters and Diary of Laura M. Towne*, pp. 84–85; Elizabeth to Adele Petigru Allston, March 17, 1865, in Easterby, *South Carolina Rice Plantation*, pp. 207–8; Blassingame, *The Slave Community*, p. 210; Joel W. Ashford, Winnsboro, S.C., to Dr. James Milling, Rocky Mount, La., December 25, 1859, James S. Milling Papers, SHC; Jones, *Religious Instruction of Negroes*, pp. 130–31; Stroyer, *My Life in the South*, p. 66; *An Account of the Late Insurrection*, in *Slave Insurrections*, pp. 33–34; Letter of the late W. Hasell Wilson of Philadelphia to Rev. Dr. Robert Wilson of Charleston, n.d, Robert Wilson Correspondence, CLS; Starobin, *Denmark Vesey*, pp. 7–9; R. Blanding, Camden, S.C., to Hannah Lewis, July 25, 1816, William Blanding Papers, SC; L. Glen Inabinet, "'The July Fourth Incident' of 1816: An Insurrection Plotted by Slaves in Camden, South Carolina," pp. 10, 15–16, paper presented at the Reynolds Conference on South Carolina Legal History, University of South Carolina, December 1977.

107. "Petition of the Delegation from Prince George Winyah & All Saints," n.d, (Folder 139), Slavery Files, SCA.

108. Plantation Book of Charles Cotesworth Pinckney and Successors, 1812–1861, "Slave List," pp. 1–2, 11, The Pinckney Family Papers, LC; Alexander James Lawton Diary and Book, 1810–1840, March 8, 1816 (typescript), pp. 11–12, SHC; Reid v. Colcock, 1 N. and McC. 592. April 1819. (593), in Catterall, *Judicial Cases*, II, pp. 311–12; John Gabriel Guignard, II, Evergreen, to James

Sanders Guignard, March 1, 1830, Guignard Family Papers, SC; E. Perry, Greenville, to B. F. Perry, November 29, 1843, Benjamin Perry Papers, p. 2, SC; Keating S. Ball Plantation Daybook, Comingtree, Cooper River, St. John's Berkeley, March 9, 1850, V, p. 48, John and Keating Ball Books, SHC; Farm Journal, Sumter District, 1853–1854, April 6–8, June 10, 14, July 1, August 20, 1853, pp. 19–20, 30–31, 34, 40, John Durant Ashmore Plantation Journal, 1853–1859 (typescript), SHC; Lowery, *Life on the Old Plantation,* pp. 100, 103; Pringle, *Chronicles of Chicora Wood,* p. 354; Rawick, *The American Slave,* III, iii, pp. 201–2, III, iv, p. 18; Dorothy Sterling, *Captain of the Planter, The Story of Robert Smalls* (New York, 1958), pp. 16, 24, 29–31, cited in Willie Lee Rose, *Rehearsal for Reconstruction: The Port Royal Experiment* (New York: Vintage Books, 1964), p. 131.

109. Ball, *Fifty Years in Chains,* p. 88.
110. Rawick, *The American Slave,* III, iii, p. 201.
111. James Hopkinson's Edisto Island Account Book, 1853–1863, Hopkinson Family Papers, MSS, [SC], quoted in Clark, "Plantation Overseers," p. 56.
112. Ball, *Fifty Years in Chains,* p. 279; Lowery, *Life On the Old Plantation,* pp. 100, 103; Armstrong, *Old Massa's People,* pp. 29–30; Diary of J. B. Grimball, No. 14-1863 to 1865, March 18, 1863, II, p. 10, CLS; Rawick, *The American Slave,* II, i, pp. 240–41, 299–301, III, iii, p. 130, III, iv, pp. 202–4.
113. Rawick, *The American Slave,* II, ii, pp. 129–30.
114. Stroyer, *My Life in the South,* p. 17.
115. Lowery, *Life On the Old Plantation,* pp. 100, 103; Rawick, *The American Slave,* II, ii, pp. 12, 327–28, III, iii, pp. 1–2, 126, III, iv, pp. 25, 156; Genovese, *Roll, Jordan, Roll,* p. 340.
116. Holland, *Letters and Diary of Laura M. Towne,* p. 5.
117. Armstrong, *Old Massa's People,* pp. 29–30; Henry C. Davis, "Negro Folk-Lore in South Carolina," *JAF,* XXVII (July–September 1914), 252, 254; James Stuart Recollections, pp. 2–3, SHC; Smith, *A Charlestonian's Recollections,* pp. 30–31; Ball, *Fifty Years in Chains,* pp. 167, 194; "Agricultural Survey of the Parish of St. Mathews, (So. Car.)," *CP,* I (May 20, 1840), 149; David Golightly Harris Farm Journals, January 12, February 25, 1861 (microfilm), SHC.
118. Diary of J. B. Grimball, No. 3-1834-1835-1836, August 16, 1834, I, p. 22, CLS.
119. A. M'Kab, "Caution," Georgetown *Gazette,* February 24, 1826.
120. Ball, *Fifty Years in Chains,* pp. 115, 119–20; Langdon Cheves, Delta, to Huger, Hamilton, and Habersham, April 6, 1834, Cheves Family Papers, SCHS; Plantation Records, February 19, 1844, April 7, 1854, pp. 286, 493, James H. Hammond Papers, SC; French, *Slavery in South Carolina,* p. 68; Lucy Ruggles Diary, March 5, 1846, I, pp. 240–41, Daniel Ruggles Papers, PL; Pearson, *Letters From Port Royal,* pp. 31–32; "Rosa Barnwell to the Editor," *Liberator,* November 7, 1862, in John W. Blassingame, ed., *Slave Testimony: Two Centuries of Letters, Speeches, Interviews, and Autobiographies* (Baton Rouge: Louisiana State University Press, 1977), p. 698; Stroyer, *My Life in the South,* pp. 17–18.
121. Stroyer, *My Life in the South,* pp. 17–18.
122. Weston, "Rules for the Plantation," cited in Collins, *Memories of the Southern States,* p. 108.
123. Dr. John Peyre Thomas Diary of Weather & Occurences, St. Johns Parish

(Berkeley), October 1828–August 1829, May 1, 1829, II, p. 82, Thomas Family Papers, SC.

124. Sam A. Townes to Rachel Townes, March 9, 1829, MS, cited in Taylor, *Ante-Bellum South Carolina*, p. 67; John C. Calhoun, Fort Hill, to Lt. James Edward Colhoun, U.S.N., Midway, Abbeville (District, S.C.), August 27, 1831, Calhoun Family Typescripts; Harriet Martineau, *Society in America* (London: Saunders and Otley, 1837), II, p. 321; *American Slavery As It Is*, pp. 22–23, 25–26, 53–55; Lucy Ruggles Diary, May 19, June 24, August 8, 9, December 2, 11, 1845, January 11, February 21, May 31, 1846, I, pp. 66, 85–86, 112–13, 184, 188, 213–14, 236, 282, Daniel Ruggles Papers, PL; H. D. McCloud, "Hints on the Medical Treatment of Negroes" (Sr. thesis, Medical College of South Carolina, 1850), pp. 9–10, MU; Rawick, *The American Slave*, II, ii, pp. 209–10, 234–35, III, iii, p. 277.

125. Blassingame, *Slave Testimony*, pp. 371–72; "Testimony of Solomon Bradley," pp. 95–96, NA.

126. Rawick, *The American Slave*, II, i, pp. 39–40; *American Slavery As It Is*, p. 26; Lucy Ruggles Diary, August 21, 26, 1845, I, pp. 125, 128–29, Daniel Ruggles Papers, PL.

127. Lucy Ruggles Diary, August 21, 1845, I, p. 125, Daniel Ruggles Papers, PL.

128. Ball, *Fifty Years in Chains*, pp. 110, 115, 119–20; Plantation Records, February 19, 1844, April 7, 1854, pp. 286, 493, James H. Hammond Papers, SC; French, *Slavery in South Carolina*, pp. 68–69; Plantation Manual of James H. Hammond, p. 3, WHL; An Overseer, *SA*, 227–28.

129. Langdon Cheves, Delta, to Huger, Hamilton, and Habersham, April 6, 1834, Cheves Family Papers, SCHS.

130. Sterling, *Captain of the Planter*, pp. 16, 24, 29–31, cited in Rose, *Rehearsal for Reconstruction*, p. 131.

131. James Redpath, *The Roving Editor: Or, Talks With Slaves in the Southern States* (New York: Negro Universities Press, 1968), pp. 285–86 (originally published in 1859); W. W. Gilmer, "Management of Servants," *FP*, III (July 1852), 110; Lowery, *Life On the Old Plantation*, pp. 100, 103; Rawick, *The American Slave*, III, iv, p. 158; Armstrong, *Old Massa's People*, p. 258; Henry William Ravenel, "Recollections of Southern Plantation Life," *TYR*, XXV (June 1936), 769–70; *Anti-Slavery Reporter*, ser. 3, XII (September 1, 1864), 202–3, in Blassingame, *Slave Testimony*, pp. 451–52; Eric Perkins, "Roll, Jordan, Roll: A 'Marx' for the Master Class," *RHR*, 3 (Fall 1976), 51.

132. Rawick, *The American Slave*, III, iv, pp. 52–53.

133. Armstrong, *Old Massa's People*, pp. 258–59; Ravenel, *TYR*, 758, 769–70; John Ewing Colhoun, Millwood, Terrysville, to James Edward Calhoun, Pendleton, February 18, 1846, John Ewing Colhoun Papers, SC; *Anti-Slavery Reporter*, 202–3, in Blassingame, *Slave Testimony*, pp. 451–52; Botume, *First Days Amongst the Contrabands*, pp. 6–7; Chesnut, *Diary From Dixie*, pp. 24–25; Olmsted, *Journey in the Seaboard Slave States*, pp. 409–10; Genovese, *Roll, Jordan, Roll*, p. 342.

134. Lowery, *Life On the Old Plantation*, p. 103.

135. Holland, *Letters and Diary of Laura M. Towne*, p. 27.

136. Ball, *Fifty Years in Chains*, pp. 110, 188–89, 192–94, 305–6; Holland, *Letters and Diary of Laura M. Towne*, p. 148; Ravenel, *TYR*, 757.

137. James R. Sparkman to Benjamin Allston, March 10, 1858, in Easterby, *South Carolina Rice Plantation*, p. 346; Ravenel, *TYR*, 761; Rawick, *The American Slave*, II, i, p. 110; Joyner, "Slave Folklife," pp. 44–45.

138. Rawick, *The American Slave,* III, iii, p. 153.

139. Ravenel, *TYR,* 761.

140. Ball, *Fifty Years in Chains,* pp. 325–28, 335–37; Roper, *A Narrative,* pp. 49–51; Stroyer, *My Life in the South,* pp. 64–68, 72; (Case 231), October 11, 1860, Spartanburg Court Records, SCA; *Anti-Slavery Reporter,* 202–3, in Blassingame, *Slave Testimony,* pp. 451–52; Smith, *A Charlestonian's Recollections,* p. 35; Rawick, *The American Slave,* III, iv, pp. 112–13.

141. James H. Hammond Diary and Account Books, July 1, 18, 19, 1832, South Caroliniana, cited in Stampp, *The Peculiar Institution,* p. 116.

142. Thomas Turpin, *Christian Advocate and Journal,* 8 (January 31, 1834), cited in Raboteau, *Slave Religion,* pp. 298–99; Jones, *Religious Instruction of Negroes,* pp. 130–31; MS records of Union County, 1857, cited in Henry, *Police Control,* p. 98.

143. Thomas Parker, Rocky Grove, to Edward Frost, Charleston, May 16, 1825, Edward Frost Papers, LC; Hall, *Travels in North America,* III, p. 177; Diary of Natalie de Delage Sumter, 1840–1841, September 7, 1840, SC; E. Perry, Greenville, to B. F. Perry, November 14, [1841?], E. Perry, Greenville, to B. F. Perry, Charleston, January 24, 1845, Benjamin Perry Papers, pp. 1–4, SC; Francis W. Pickens, Edgewood, S.C., to John C. Calhoun, May 4, 1845, Calhoun Family Typescripts; Lucy Ruggles Diary, May 29, 1846, I, p. 282, Daniel Ruggles Papers, PL; Lyell, *Second Visit,* I, p. 224; William Elliot to Mrs. Wm. Elliot, Oak Lawn, November 15, 1851, Elliot-Gonzales Papers, SHC; Bremer, *Homes of the New World,* I, pp. 391–92; Amelia M. Murray, *Letters From the United States, Cuba, and Canada* (New York: G. P. Putnam & Company, 1856), pp. 195–96, 209–10; Olmsted, *Journey in the Seaboard Slave States,* pp. 409–10; French, *Slavery in South Carolina,* pp. 80–81, 83, 85, 88; Collins, *Memories of the Southern States,* p. 5; Pringle, *Chronicles of Chicora Wood,* pp. 78–79, 82; Charles Spalding Wylly, *The Seed That Was Sown in the Colony of Georgia* (New York, 1910), pp. 24–25, cited in Johnson, *A Social History of the Sea Islands,* p. 120.

144. Stirling, *Letters From the Slave States,* pp. 295–98; The Editor, "Our Slaves," *SA,* II (December 1829), p. 575; John D. Long, *Pictures of Slavery in Church and State* (Philadelphia, 1857), pp. 20–21, cited in Raboteau, *Slave Religion,* p. 176; James C. Darby, "On Planting and Managing a Rice Crop," *SA,* II (June 1829), 248–49; Louisa S. McCord, Columbia, to Langdon Cheves, Jr., April 13, 21, December 18, 20, 1856, Cheves Family Papers, SCHS; "Correspondence of the Enterprise," *The Southern Enterprise,* July 27, 1855; "The Confession of Mr. Enslows Boy John," 1822, William and Benjamin Hammet Papers, PL; *Account of the Late Insurrection,* in *Slave Insurrections,* p. 38; Starobin, *Denmark Vesey,* pp. 3, 5; Donald Taylor, "20 Dollars Reward," The Georgetown *Gazette,* June 18, 1800; Dr. Thomas Diary, August 1827–September 1828, September 2, 6, 1827, I, pp. 12–13, Thomas Family Papers, SC; John C. Calhoun, Fort Hill, to Lt. James Edward Colhoun, U.S.N., Midway, Abbeville (District, S.C.), August 27, 1831, Calhoun Family Typescripts; Lucy Ruggles Diary, March 5, 1846, I, pp. 240–41, Daniel Ruggles Papers, PL; Rawick, *The American Slave,* II, ii, pp. 234–35, III, iv, p. 2; Plantation Records, October 16, 1835, p. 120, James H. Hammond Papers, SC; The Georgetown *Gazette,* July 25, 1826; Diary of J. B. Grimball, No. 14, August 6, 1863, II, p. 24, CLS; Thomson, *A Tradesman's Travels,* pp. 173–81, in Rose, *A Documentary History,* pp. 365–66; Dr. Thomas Diary, June 8, 1829, II, p. 103, Thomas Family Papers, SC.

145. James D. Erwin, "150 Dollars Reward," *The Southern Patriot,* January 2, 1829.
146. Thomas R. S. Elliot, Bethel, to "My Dear Mother," 1861, Elliot-Gonzales Papers, SHC; William E. Sparkman Plantation Record, 1844–1866, October 1862, SHC; Adele Petigru, Plantersville, to Benjamin Allston, October 30, 1862, in Easterby, *South Carolina Rice Plantation,* p. 190; *Anti-Slavery Advocate,* II (February 1, 1862), 498–99, in Blassingame, *Slave Testimony,* pp. 359–60; H. H. Manigault, Adams Run, to John Berkley Grimball, July 14, 1863, John Berkley Grimball Papers, PL; Adele Petigru Allston to Colonel Francis Heriot, July, 1864, in Easterby, *South Carolina Rice Plantation,* p. 200; Elizabeth to Adele Petigru Allston, March 17, 1865, in Easterby, *South Carolina Rice Plantation,* pp. 206–7; John A. Inglis, Cheraw, S.C., to Carrie, June 28, July 28, 1865, John Auchintoss Inglis Papers, LC; Collins, *Memories of the Southern States,* pp. 70–72; Charles I. Manigault Book Containing Loose Papers, 1776–1872 (typescript), pp. 16–19, 21–22, 26–27, Charles Manigault Papers, SC; Pringle, *Chronicles of Chicora Wood,* pp. 171–73, 252–53; Chesnut, *A Diary From Dixie,* pp. 82, 313, 365, 397; Smith, *A Charlestonian's Recollections,* pp. 20–21; John Legare Memoirs, pp. 4–5, SHC; George W. Williams, ed., *Incidents in My Life: The Autobiography of The Rev. Paul Trapier, S.T.D. With Some of His Letters* (Charleston: Dalcho Historical Society, 1954), pp. 31–32; Joel Williamson, *After Slavery: The Negro in South Carolina During Reconstruction, 1861–1877* (Chapel Hill: The University of North Carolina Press, 1965), pp. 8, 34–39.
147. "The State vs Charles a slave The Property of Widow Newberry For Gambling & Fighting on the 23rd of March Last." [April 1851], (Case 135), Spartanburg Court Records, SCA; Dr. John Peyre Thomas Diary, April 7, 1829, II, pp. 69–70, Thomas Family Papers, SC; "The State vs Ceasar for Receiving Stolen Goods," March 10, 1832, (Case 7), Spartanburg Court Records, SCA; Diary of J. B. Grimball, No. 12, May 2, 1859, II, p. 13, CLS; Joel W. Ashford, Winnsboro, S.C., to Dr. James Milling, Rocky Mount, La., December 25, 1859, James Milling Papers, SHC; Collins, *Memories of the Southern States,* pp. 70–71; "South Carolina/ Abbeville District/ October 11, 1860. Military Vigilance Police," Fouche Family Papers, SC; Letters of An American Traveler . . . Written During An Excursion in the Year 1810, I (typescript), p. 5, CLS; Inabinet, "'The July Fourth Incident,'" pp. 2–5; Jane W. Gwinn, "The Georgetown Slave Insurrection of 1829," in Charles Joyner, ed., "Black Carolinians: Studies in the History of South Carolina Negroes in the Nineteenth Century" (typescript), pp. 1–2, SC; "The Confession of Mr. Enslows Boy John," 1822, William and Benjamin Hammet Papers, PL; *An Account of the Late Insurrection,* in *Slave Insurrections,* pp. 3–5; Ball, *Fifty Years in Chains,* pp. 325–37; Holland, *Letters and Diary of Laura M. Towne,* pp. 84–86; Smith, *A Charlestonian's Recollections,* p. 35; Rawick, *The American Slave,* III, iv, p. 113.
148. "The State vs. Charles a slave of Widow Newberry, Spartanburg Court Records, SCA.
149. Dr. Thomas Diary, March 25, 1829, April 1, 1829, II, pp. 62, 65, Thomas Family Papers, SC.
150. Pineville Association: Treasurer's Book, 1823–1839, 1827, Pineville Association–St. John's & St. Stephens, Berkeley, 1823–1840, and Police Association, St. John's Berkeley, 1839–1852, SCHS; "Petition of the Town Council of Georgetown Praying that Negroes Jack and Tom May be Rewarded for Taking and Dispersing a Gang of Runaways Who Had Murdered Their Master," n.d., (Folder 91), Slavery Files, SCA; David Gavin Diary, November 19, 1862, II,

p. 337, SHC; Wood, *Black Majority*, pp. 324–25; John Livingston Bradley, "Slave Manumission in South Carolina, 1820–1860" (M.A. thesis, University of South Carolina, 1964), pp. 38–40, 50; Inabinet, "'The July Fourth Incident,'" pp. 13–14; Starobin, *Denmark Vesey*, p. 8.

151. Pineville Association: Secretary's Book, 1823–1829–1840, October 2, 5, 1823, Pineville Association and Police Association, SCHS.

152. (Case 231), Spartanburg Court Records, SCA; Starobin, *Denmark Vesey*, p. 7; "Melancholy Effect of Popular Excitement," The Charleston *Courier*, July 21, 1822; "The Confession of Mr. Enslows Boy John," 1822, William and Benjamin Hammet Papers, PL; "Petition of Joseph L. Enslow for Compensation for a Slave (named John) Dying in Jail," 1831, (Folder 83), Slavery Files, SCA; Inabinet, "'The July Fourth Incident,'" pp. 6, 10; Anna Hayes Johnson, Charleston, S.C., to Eliza Eagles Haywood, Raleigh, N.C., July 18, 1822, Ernest Haywood Collection, SHC; Lionel H. Kennedy and Thomas Parker, *An Official Report of the Trials of Sundry Negroes, Charged With An Attempt to Raise An Insurrection . . . And In An Appendix, A Report of the Trials of Four White Persons On Indictments for Attempting to Excite the Slaves to Insurrection* (Charleston: James R. Schenck, 1822), p. 127; Diary of Henry Ravenel of St. John's Parish, S.C., July 12, 1819, in Ulrich B. Phillips, ed., *Plantation and Frontier Documents, 1649–1863: Illustrative of Industrial History in the Colonial & Ante-Bellum South* (Cleveland: The Arthur H. Clark Company, 1909), II, p. 91; Edward Pettingill, Master of Brig, New York, off Charleston, to Langdon Cheves, by Pilot Boat, Georgia, June 22, 1837, Cheves Family Papers, SCHS; Jones, *Religious Instruction of Negroes*, pp. 136–37; (Case 252), May 19, 1852, Pendleton/Anderson Court Records, SCA; William Elliot, Adam's Run to William Elliot, Jr., August 25, 1862, Elliot-Gonzales Papers, SHC.

153. W. Hasell Wilson, Philadelphia, to Rev. Dr. Robert Wilson, Charleston, n.d., Robert Wilson Correspondence, CLS.

154. E. C. L. Adams, *Nigger to Nigger* (New York: Charles Scribner's Sons, 1928), pp. 232–33; "Memoirs of S. W. Ferguson: Family History and Boyhood," April 26, 1900 (typescript), pp. 13–14, Heyward and Ferguson Family Papers (typescript and microfilm), SHC; "Petition of the Delegation from Prince George Winyah," Slavery Files, SCA; Inabinet, "'The July Fourth Incident,'" pp. 2, 14–16.

155. Ball, *Fifty Years in Chains*, p. 334.

Chapter 5. Slave Religion: The Dialectics of Faith

1. Charles Cotesworth Pinckney, *An Address Delivered in Charleston Before the Agricultural Society of South Carolina . . . The 18th August, 1829* (Charleston: A. E. Miller, 1829), p. 8.

2. Quoted in Mary A. Livermore, *My Story of the War: A Woman's Narrative of Four Years Personal Experience* (Williamstown, Mass.: Corner House Publishers, 1978), p. 261 (originally published in 1887).

3. Captain Basil Hall, *Travels in North America, in the Years 1827 and 1828* (Edinburgh: Cadell and Co., 1829), III, p. 154; C. E. Gadsden, *An Essay on the Life of the Right Reverend Theodore Dehon, D.D.* (Charleston: A. E. Miller, 1833), p. 143; Moses Roper, *A Narrative of the Adventures and Escape of Moses Roper, From American Slavery* (New York: Negro Universities Press, 1970), pp. 59, 63–64 (originally published in 1838); E. F. Perry, Greenville, to B. F. Perry, November 14, [1841?], Benjamin F. Perry Papers (typescript),

pp. 1–2, SC; *Proceedings of the Meeting in Charleston, S.C., May 13–15, 1845, On the Religious Instruction of the Negroes* . . . (Charleston: Published by Order of the Meeting, 1845), p. 10; "Religious Instruction of Slaves: Twelfth Annual Report of the Liberty County Association for the Instruction of Slaves, 1847," *SQR*, XIV (July 1848), 176; Farmer's Club (ABC Farmer's Club) Records, 1846–1893, Beech Island, Aiken County, September 4, 1849 (typescript), pp. 36–38, SC; James Stacy, "Missions in South Carolina: How the Work Is Done," *NCA*, XX (April 24, 1856); R. F. W. Allston, *Essay On Sea Coast Crops* (Charleston, 1854), in Ulrich B. Phillips, ed., *Plantation and Frontier Documents, 1649–1863: Illustrative of Industrial History in the Colonial and Ante-Bellum South* (Cleveland: The Arthur H. Clark Co., 1909), I, p. 264; Philo Tower, *Slavery Unmasked: Being a Truthful Narrative of A Three Year's Residence and Journeying in Eleven Southern States* (Rochester: Darrow and Brother, 1856), pp. 120–21, 131; Edward Thomas Heriot, Georgetown, S.C., to [unknown], [Great Britain?], April 20, 1853, Edward Thomas Heriot Papers, PL; David Gavin Diary, 1855–1871, November 21, 1857, I (typescript), p. 115, SHC; Nathaniel Bowen, *A Pastoral Letter, On the Religious Instruction of the Slaves of Members of the Protestant Episcopal Church in the State of South Carolina* . . . (Charleston: A. E. Miller, 1835), p. 7; Rev. John B. Adger, *The Religious Instruction of the Colored Population: A Sermon* (Charleston: T. W. Haynes, 1847), p. 3; Charles C. Jones, *The Religious Instruction of the Negroes* (New York: Negro Universities Press, 1969), p. 198 (originally published in 1842); *The Suppressed Book About Slavery!* (New York: Carleton, 1864), p. 263.

4. Luther P. Jackson, "Religious Instruction of Negroes, 1830 to 1860, with Special Reference to South Carolina," *JNH*, XV (January 1930), 83.

5. Plantation Journals of Daniel Cannon Webb, 1818–1850, December 31, 1840, IV, SCHS; "Record of Windsor Plantation," October 18, 1845, John B. Irving Record of Windsor and Kensington Plantations, CLS; Plantation and Record Book, 1839–1854, February 19, 1852, Witherspoon Family Papers, SC; David Gavin Diary, November 21, 1857, I, p. 115, SHC; David Milling, Mill View, Fairfield Dist., S.C., to James Milling, February 26, 1864, James S. Milling Papers, SHC; Elizabeth Collins, *Memories of the Southern States* (Taunton: Barnicott, 1865), p. 30.

6. Rachel Blanding, Camden, S.C., to Hannah Lewis, [Philadelphia], July 4, 1816, William Blanding Papers, SC.

7. Donald G. Morgan, *William Johnson, The First Dissenter: The Career and Constitutional Philosophy of a Jeffersonian Judge* (Columbia: University of South Carolina Press, 1954), p. 25; Anna Hayes Johnson, Charleston, S.C., to Eliza Eagles Haywood, Raleigh, N.C., July 18, 1822, Ernest Haywood Collection, SHC.

8. Rev. Dr. Richard Furman, *Exposition of the Views of the Baptists, Relative to the Coloured Population* . . . *In A Communication to the Governor of South Carolina*, 3d ed. (Charleston: A. E. Miller, 1835), pp. 3–4.

9. Peter H. Wood, *Black Majority: Negroes in Colonial South Carolina From 1670 Through the Stono Rebellion* (New York: Alfred A. Knopf, 1974), pp. 134–35; Albert J. Raboteau, *Slave Religion: The "Invisible Institution" in the Antebellum South* (New York: Oxford University Press, 1978), pp. 66, 102–3, 122–23, 149; Susan Markey Fickling, "The Christianization of the Negro in South Carolina, 1830–1860" (M.A. thesis, University of South Carolina, 1923), pp. 1–4; Charles Ball, *Fifty Years in Chains*, with an introduction

by Philip S. Foner (New York: Dover Publications, 1970), pp. 162–66 (originally published in 1837); Leah Townsend, *South Carolina Baptists, 1670–1805* (Florence, S.C.: The Florence Printing Company, 1935), p. 118; Jacob Read, Charleston, S.C., to Charles Pinckney, June 18, 1807, Pinckney Letter, MS, SC; Stacy, *The Nashville Christian Advocate*; Jackson, *JNH*, pp. 84–85; Edward R. Laurens, "An Address Delivered Before the Agricultural Society of South Carolina," *SA*, V (November 1832), 565; "Remonstrance," Greenville *Mountaineer*, November 2, 1838; William Goodell, *The American Slave Code in Theory and Practice: Judiciary Decisions and Illustrative Facts* (New York, 1852), p. 329, cited in W. E. Burghardt Du Bois, *The Negro Church: Report of a Social Study Made Under the Direction of Atlanta University* (Atlanta: The Atlanta University Press, 1903), pp. 22, 25; Francis Asbury, *The Journal and Letters of Francis Asbury*, eds. Elmer T. Clark et al. (Nashville: Abingdon Press, 1958), II, p. 591, cited in Milton C. Sernett, *Black Religion and American Evangelicalism: White Protestants, Plantation Missions, and the Flowering of Negro Christianity, 1787–1865* (Metuchen, N.J.: The Scarecrow Press and The American Theological Library Association, 1975), p. 37; "Record of the Proceedings of the Beech Island Agricultural Club, 1856–1862 and Journal of the Proceedings of the Beech Island Agricultural and Police Society; Organized June 28, 1851," December 3, 1859, Farmer's Club Records, pp. 130–31, SC; Richard C. Wade, *Slavery in the Cities: The South 1820–1860* (London: Oxford University Press, 1964), p. 172; William Howard Russell, *My Diary North and South* (New York: Harper & Brothers, 1863), p. 60; Jones, *Religious Instruction of Negroes*, p. 198; Rosser T. Taylor, *Ante-Bellum South Carolina: A Social and Cultural History* (The James Sprunt Studies in History and Political Science, Chapel Hill: The University of North Carolina Press, 1942), p. 163.

10. Laurens, *SA*, 565; "Remonstrance," Greenville *Mountaineer*, November 2, 1838; Fickling, "Christianization of the Negro," pp. 7, 24–25; Taylor, *Ante-Bellum South Carolina*, pp. 159–61, 163; Haven P. Perkins, "Religion for Slaves: Difficulties and Methods," *CH*, X (1941), 229–30; Albert M. Shipp, *The History of Methodism in South Carolina* (Nashville: Southern Methodist Publishing House, 1883), pp. 449–52; A Planter, "Notions on the Management of Negroes, etc.," *SA*, IX (December 1836), 626–27; William P. Harrison, ed., *The Gospel Among the Slaves* (Nashville: Publishing House of the M. E. Church, South, 1893), pp. 297–99, 328; Jackson, *JNH*, 73–74, 84–85, 95–96.

11. Quoted in Harrison, *The Gospel Among Slaves*, pp. 172, 204–5, 210.

12. Rev. I. E. Lowery, *Life On the Old Plantation Or A Story Based on Facts* (Columbia: The State Company, 1911), p. 70.

13. Diary of Natalie de Delage Sumter, 1840–1841, July 12, August 9, 1840, SC; Vestry Journal of All Saints, Waccamaw, Georgetown, 1844–1872, April 24, 1848 (typescript), SC; Susan Lowndes Allston, "All Saints', Waccamaw," *The News and Courier*, Charleston, December 28, 1930, p. 6-A; James R. Sparkman to Benjamin Allston, March 10, 1858, in J. H. Easterby, ed., *The South Carolina Rice Plantation as Revealed in the Papers of Robert F. W. Allston* (Chicago: University of Chicago Press, 1945), p. 349; Elizabeth W. Allston Pringle, *Chronicles of Chicora Wood* (New York: Charles Scribner's Sons, 1922), pp. 34–35; Lowery, *Life On the Old Plantation*, pp. 16, 42; George P. Rawick, ed., *The American Slave: A Composite Autobiography* (Westport, Conn.: Greenwood Publishing Company, 1972), II, i, pp. 119–20, 152, 301, 311, II,

ii, pp. 18–19, 329, III, iii, pp. 19, 202, 221, III, iv, pp. 83–84, 89; George Rogers, Jr., *The History of Georgetown County, South Carolina* (Columbia: University of South Carolina Press, 1970), pp. 349–55; Shipp, *History of Methodism*, pp. 449–53; John Randolph Logan, *Sketches of the Broad River and King's Mountain Baptist Association From 1800–1882* (Shelby, N.C., 1887), p. 47, cited in Annie Hughes Mallard, "Religious Work of South Carolina Baptists Among the Slaves From 1781 to 1830" (M.A. thesis, University of South Carolina, 1946), p. 42; William M. Wightman, *Life of William Capers* (Nashville: Publishing House of the M. E. Church, South, 1902), pp. 291–93, 297; J. G. Clinkscales, *On the Old Plantation: Reminiscences of His Childhood* (New York: Negro Universities Press, 1969), pp. 27, 136–37 (originally published in 1916); Alice R. Huger Smith, *A Carolina Rice Plantation of the Fifties . . . With Chapters From the Unpublished Memoirs of D. E. Huger Smith* (New York: William Morrow and Company, 1936), p. 75; Jackson, *JNH*, 72–75, 77–83; Randall Hunt, Journal of a Traveller from Charleston, So. Ca.; to New Haven, Connecticut, 1832, pp. 63–68, SCHS; Fickling, "Christianization of the Negro," pp. 12–14; Jones, *Religious Instruction of Negroes*, pp. 93–94.

14. Presbyterian Church: Records of Salem Presbyterian Church, Black River, 1808–1860, April 10, 1825, II (typescript), p. 4, SC; Harriet Martineau, *Society in America* (London: Saunders and Otley, 1837), II, pp. 159–60; An Edistonian, "The Successful Planter or Memoirs of My Uncle Ben," *SA*, V (June 1832), 303; E. F. Perry, Greenville, to B. F. Perry, November 14, [1841?], Benjamin Perry Papers, pp. 1–2, SC; Whiteford Smith, Columbia, to Wade Hampton, II, September 6, 1842, in Charles E. Cauthen, ed., *Family Letters of the Three Wade Hamptons, 1782–1901* (South Caroliniana Series, Columbia: University of South Carolina Press, 1953), pp. 32–33; Rev. Andrew Flinn Dickson, *Plantation Sermons, or Plain and Familiar Discourses for the Instruction of the Unlearned* (Philadelphia: Presbyterian Board of Publication, 1856), pp. 13–14, 129–37; Richard Hildreth, *Despotism in America; Or An Inquiry into the Nature and Results of the Slave-Holding System in the United States* (Boston: Whipple and Damrell, 1840), p. 43; Rawick, *The American Slave*, II, i, pp. 43, 193, II, ii, pp. 77–78, 80–81, 184–85, III, iv, pp. 192, 199–201; Shipp, *History of Methodism*, pp. 461–62, 497–98; Gadsden, *Essay on Theodore Dehon*, pp. 142–43, 151–52, 168–70, 201; Adger, *Religious Instruction of the Colored*, p. 3; Rev. Alexander Glennie, *Sermons Preached On Plantations to Congregations of Negroes* (Charleston: A. E. Miller, 1844), pp. 26–27, cited in Leon Stone Bryan, Jr., "Slavery on A Peedee River Rice Plantation, 1825–1865" (M.A. thesis, Johns Hopkins University, 1963), p. 113; A. M. French, *Slavery in South Carolina and the Ex-Slaves; Or, the Port Royal Mission* (New York: Negro Universities Press, 1969), pp. 123, 127 (originally published in 1862); Jackson, *JNH*, 101, 104–5, 109, 111–12; Gwendolyn Midlo Hall, *Social Control in Slave Plantation Societies: A Comparison of St. Domingue and Cuba* (Baltimore: The Johns Hopkins Press, 1971), pp. 33–34; Vincent Harding, "Religion and Resistance Among Antebellum Negroes, 1800–1860," in August Meier and Elliot Rudwick, eds., *The Making of Black America: Essays in Negro Life and History* (New York: Atheneum, 1969), I, pp. 180–82; Rogers, *History of Georgetown*, p. 358; Raboteau, *Slave Religion*, p. 151; Bowen, *Pastoral Letter*, pp. 7, 10, appendix.

15. Jackson, *JNH*, 107.

16. Raboteau, *Slave Religion*, pp. 176, 209–10, 212, 217, 219; Mallard, "Religious

Work Among the Slaves," pp. 82–83, 85, 87; Jackson, *JNH*, p. 107; Rawick, *The American Slave*, II, i, p. 246.

17. Rawick, *The American Slave*, II, ii, pp. 184–85.

18. Ibid.

19. Pinckney, *An Address*, pp. 10–11; Allston, *Essay On Sea Coast Crops*, in Phillips, *Plantation and Frontier Documents*, I, p. 264; Rogers, *History of Georgetown*, pp. 357–58; Rawick, *The American Slave*, II, ii, p. 185; Wightman, *Life of William Capers*, p. 300; Shipp, *History of Methodism*, pp. 461–62; Jackson, *JNH*, 104, 107; *Proceedings of the Meeting in Charleston*, pp. 60–61; "Christianity Among the Slaves," *The Southern Enterprise*, January 10, 1856.

20. Minutes of the Charleston Baptist Association, November 3, 1835, Baptist Historical Collection, Furman University, cited in Taylor, *Ante-Bellum South Carolina*, p. 174; Jackson, *JNH*, pp. 78–83; Thomas J. Kirkland and Robert M. Kennedy, *Historic Camden* (Columbia: The State Company, 1926), II, p. 190; Rogers, *History of Georgetown*, pp. 353–55; Shipp, *History of Methodism*, pp. 497–98; Methodist Church: Darlington Circuit Quarterly Conference Minutes, 1841–1863, Florence County, August 10, 1844 (typescript), p. 20, SC.

21. Martineau, *Society in America*, II, pp. 158–61; Roper, *A Narrative*, pp. 58–60, 63–64; Rev. John G. Williams, *"De Ole Plantation"* (Charleston: Walker, Evans & Cogswell, 1895), pp. 2–5, 11, 46; Ball, *Fifty Years in Chains*, pp. 220–22; Henry H. Mitchell, *Black Belief: Folk Beliefs of Blacks in America and West Africa* (New York: Harper & Row, 1975), p. 11, cited in Lewis V. Baldwin, "A Home in Dat Rock: Afro-American Folklore and the Slaves' Vision of Heaven and Hell, 1750–1860" (Seminar paper, Northwestern University, 1977), p. 9; Julia Peterkin, *Roll, Jordan, Roll. Photographic Studies by Doris Ulmann* (New York: Robert O. Ballow, 1933), pp. 165–66; Gayraud S. Wilmore, *Black Religion and Black Radicalism* (Garden City, N.Y.: Anchor Press, 1973), pp. 11, 14; Raboteau, *Slave Religion*, pp. 122, 293, 295; Rawick, *The American Slave*, III, iii, pp. 194–95; E. C. L. Adams, *Nigger to Nigger* (New York: Charles Scribner's Sons, 1928), pp. 5–7, 70, 133–34.

22. Elsie Clews Parsons, *Folk-Lore of the Sea Islands, South Carolina* (Cambridge, Mass.: The American Folk-Lore Society, 1923), p. 117.

23. Adams, *Nigger to Nigger*, pp. 235–36.

24. Rachel Blanding, Camden, S.C., to Hannah Lewis [Philadelphia], July 4, 1816, William Blanding Papers, SC.

25. "Confession of Bacchus, the Slave of Mr. [Benjamin] Hammet," William and Benjamin Hammet Papers, PL. See also *Memorial of the Citizens of Charleston to the Senate and House of Representatives of the State of South Carolina* (Charleston, 1822), in Phillips, *Plantation and Frontier Documents*, II, pp. 104–5.

26. Benjamin Drew, *The Refugee: A North-Side View of Slavery* (Boston, 1856), pp. 68, 234–35, cited in Raboteau, *Slave Religion*, p. 293; Thomas R. S. Elliot, Bethel, to "My Dear Mother," 1861, Elliot-Gonzales Papers, SHC.

27. W. St. Julien Mazyck, "St. Mary's Chapel, Hagley Plantation," n.d. (typescript), p. 2, CLS.

28. Ibid., p. 1.

29. Mazyck, "St. Mary's Chapel," p. 1, CLS; Rogers, *History of Georgetown*, p. 358.

30. Chalmers G. Davidson, *The Last Foray: The South Carolina Planters of 1860: A Sociological Study* (Columbia: University of South Carolina Press, 1971),

pp. 85, 91; Smith, *Carolina Rice Plantation*, p. 75; Jones, *Religious Instruction of Negroes*, pp. 93–94; *Proceedings of the Meeting in Charleston*, p. 35; Raboteau, *Slave Religion*, p. 295; David F. Thorpe, St. Helena, to [unknown], January 25, 1863, James M. Dabbs Papers: David F. Thorpe Series, SHC; Fickling, "Christianization of the Negro," pp. 25–26; Mazyck, "St. Mary's Chapel," pp. 1–2, CLS; Bryan, "Slavery On A Peedee River," p. 114.

31. Jones, *Religious Instruction of Negroes*, pp. 126–27; Adams, *Nigger to Nigger*, pp. 216–17; Lawrence Levine, "Slave Songs and Slave Consciousness: An Exploration in Neglected Sources," in Tamara K. Hareven, ed., *Anonymous Americans: Explorations in Nineteenth-Century Social History* (Englewood Cliffs, N.J.: Prentice-Hall, 1971), pp. 111–19; James H. Cone, *The Spirituals and the Blues: An Interpretation* (New York: The Seabury Press, 1972), pp. 39, 47–48, 54–55.

32. E. F. Perry to B. F. Perry, November 14, [1841?], Benjamin Perry Papers, p. 2, SC.

33. Martineau, *Society in America*, II, pp. 159–60; Baptist Church: Welsh Neck Baptist Church Minutes, 1737–1935, Society Hill, Darlington County, February 3, 1816, January 19, 1822, June 5, 1836 (typescript), pp. 64, 87, 198, SC; Raboteau, *Slave Religion*, pp. 102–3, 122–23, 145–46, 294–95, 298–99; Townsend, *South Carolina Baptists*, p. 259; Donald Taylor, "20 Dollars Reward," The Georgetown *Gazette*, June 18, 1800; Jones, *Religious Instruction of Negroes*, pp. 126–27, 130–31, 136; Ball, *Fifty Years in Chains*, p. 205; Paul D. Escott, *Slavery Remembered: A Record of Twentieth-Century Slave Narratives* (Chapel Hill: The University of North Carolina Press, 1979), pp. 113–14.

34. "Report on Management of Slaves, Duty of Overseers, and Employers to Darlington County Agricultural Society," August, 1852, pp. 1–2, Thomas Cassels Law Papers, SC.

35. Williams, *"De Ole Plantation,"* p. 11.

36. Charles W. Joyner, "Slave Folklife of the Waccamaw Neck: Antebellum Black Culture in the South Carolina Lowcountry" (Ph.D. dissertation, University of Pennsylvania, 1977), p. 185; Charles A. Raymond, "The Religious Life of the Negro Slave," *HNM*, XXVII (September 1863), 821–23; Baptist Church: Welsh Neck Minutes, June 16, 1839, p. 220, SC; N. Herbemont, "On the Moral Discipline and Treatment of Slaves, Read Before the Society for the Advancement of Education, at Columbia," *SA*, IX (February 1836), 71.

37. Raymond, *HNM*, 680, 816–20; Jones, *Religious Instruction of Negroes*, pp. 125–26; Wightman, *Life of William Capers*, pp. 345, 363; George P. Rawick, "West African Culture and North American Slavery: A Study of Culture Change Among American Slaves in the Ante-Bellum South With Focus Upon Slave Religion," in *Migration and Anthropology: Proceedings of the 1970 Annual Spring Meeting of the American Ethnological Society* (Seattle: University of Washington Press, 1970), pp. 160–61; Parsons, *Folk-Lore of the Sea Islands*, p. 204; Joel Williamson, *After Slavery: The Negro in South Carolina During Reconstruction, 1861–1877* (Chapel Hill: The University of North Carolina Press, 1965), pp. 201–3; Dickson D. Bruce, Jr., "Religion, Society, and Culture in the Old South: A Comparative View," *AQ*, XXVI (October 1974), 399, 401–8.

38. Raymond, *HNM,* 479, 680.

39. Clifton H. Johnson, ed., *God Struck Me Dead: Religious Conversion Experi-*

ences and Autobiographies of Ex-Slaves (Nashville, 1945; paperback, Philadelphia: Pilgrim Press, 1969), p. 123, quoted in Bruce, *AQ,* 405.

40. "Testimony of Col. Higginson," American Freedmen's Inquiry Commission
(microfilm), Reel 200, File III, p. 181, NA; Lowery, *Life On the Old Plantation,*
pp. 54, 57; H. Perry Pope, "A Dissertation on the Professional Management
of Negro Slaves" (Sr. thesis, Medical College of the State of South Carolina,
1837), pp. 7–8, MU; Diary of John Hamilton Cornish, December 26, 1839,
V (typescript), pp. 57–58, John Hamilton Cornish Papers, SHC; Hunt, Journal
of a Traveller, pp. 63–65, SCHS; Fredrika Bremer, *The Homes of the New
World: Impressions of America,* trans. Mary Howitt (New York: Harper &
Brothers, 1868), I, p. 291; Martineau, *Society in America,* II, pp. 158–60;
Parsons, *Folk-Lore of the Sea Islands,* p. 206; "Rambles at Random in the
Southern States," *BEM,* LXXXVI (January 1860), 106; Peterkin, *Roll, Jordan,
Roll,* p. 101; William F. Allen et al., *Slave Songs of the United States* (New
York: A. Simpson & Co., 1867), p. x; Clinkscales, *On the Old Plantation,*
pp. 10–12.

41. "Moses Roper, London, to Thomas Price, June 27, 1836," *Slavery in America,*
no. 2 (August 1836), 45–46, in John W. Blassingame, ed., *Slave Testimony:
Two Centuries of Letters, Speeches, Interviews, and Autobiographies* (Baton
Rouge: Louisiana State University Press, 1977), pp. 23–25; Roper, *A Narrative,*
pp. 59–60; *American Slavery As It Is: Testimony of A Thousand Witnesses*
(New York: American Anti-Slavery Society, 1839), p. 24.

42. Quoted in Harrison, *The Gospel Among Slaves,* p. 359.

43. Raymond, *HNM,* 483; Wightman, *Life of William Capers,* pp. 392–93; Rev.
James Jenkins, *Experience, Labours, and Sufferings of Rev. James Jenkins, of
the South Carolina Conference* (By the Author, 1842), p. 159; Francis Asbury,
*The Journal of the Rev. Francis Asbury, Bishop of the Methodist Episcopal
Church* (New York, 1821), cited in Miles Mark Fisher, *Negro Slave Songs in
the United States* (New York: The Citadel Press, 1963), pp. 75–76 (originally
published in 1953); Langdon Cheves, Portman Shoals, to Langdon Cheves, Jr.,
Savannah, April 19, 1845, Cheves Family Papers, SCHS; James R. Stuart Rec-
ollections, n.d. (typescript), pp. 2–3, SHC; William P. Hill Diary, 1846–1849,
November 24, 1846, SHC; Raboteau, *Slave Religion,* pp. 218, 223; Eugene D.
Genovese, *Roll, Jordan, Roll: The World the Slaves Made* (New York: Pantheon
Books, 1974), p. 237.

44. Stephen Moore, Camp on James Island, to Rachel, July 8, 1862, Thomas John
Moore Papers, SC; Rawick, *The American Slave,* II, i, p. 120, II, ii, p. 63;
Williams, *"De Ole Plantation,"* p. 1; "Slave Songs of the United States," *The
Nation,* V (November 21, 1867), 411; Elizabeth Ware Pearson, ed., *Letters
From Port Royal, 1862–1868* (New York: Arno Press and The New York
Times, 1969), pp. 34, 135 (originally published in 1906); Rupert Sargent Hol-
land, ed., *Letters and Diary of Laura M. Towne: Written From the Sea Islands
of South Carolina, 1862–1884* (Cambridge: Riverside Press, 1912), pp. 36,
55; Williamson, *After Slavery,* pp. 201–2; Parsons, *Folk-Lore of the Sea Islands,* p. 205.

45. H. F. F. to *The Times* (Charleston), July 17, 1816, quoted in H. M. Henry,
The Police Control of the Slave in South Carolina (New York: Negro Universities Press, 1968), p. 141 (originally published in 1914).

46. Mary Stevenson, ed., *The Diary of Clarissa Adger Bowen, Ashtabula Plantation, 1865* (Pendleton, S.C., 1973), p. 48 (and) John B. Adger, *My Life and
Times, 1810–1899* (Richmond, 1899), pp. 346–48, quoted in William L. Van

Deburg, *The Slave Drivers: Black Agricultural Labor Supervisors in the An-tebellum South* (Westport, Conn.: Greenwood Press, 1979), pp. 20–22, 146; Jacob Stroyer, *My Life in the South* (Salem, Mass.: Salem Observer and Job Print, 1885), pp. 48, 51–52; Raboteau, *Slave Religion*, pp. 176, 314; Adams, *Nigger to Nigger*, pp. 97–101, 107–9, 133–34.

47. John D. Long, *Pictures of Slavery in Church and State* (Philadelphia, 1857), p. 127, quoted in Raboteau, *Slave Religion*, p. 314.

48. Parsons, *Folk-Lore of the Sea Islands*, pp. 68–69.

49. Rawick, *The American Slave*, II, i, pp. 1–3.

50. David Thorpe, St. Helena to William [Weld], October 31, 1862, Dabbs Papers, SHC; Jones, *Religious Instruction of Negroes*, pp. 131–32, 136–37. The Reverend C. C. Jones spoke frequently of these "falsehoods" among slaves: "Duplicity is one of the most prominent traits in the character, practiced between themselves, but more especially towards their masters and managers. . . . When criminal acts are under investigation, the sober, strenuous falsehood, *sometimes the direct and awful appeal to God, of the transgressor,* averts the suspicion, and by his own tact or collusion with others, perhaps, fixes the guilt upon some innocent person. The number, the variety and ingenuity of falsehoods that can be told by them in a few brief moments, is most astonishing." (Emphasis added.)

51. "Remonstrance," Greenville *Mountaineer*, November 2, 1838; Raboteau, *Slave Religion*, p. 223; Rawick, *The American Slave*, II, ii, pp. 328–29.

52. Guion Griffis Johnson, *A Social History of the Sea Islands: With Special Reference to St. Helena Island, South Carolina* (Chapel Hill: The University of North Carolina Press, 1930), p. 153; William W. Freehling, *Prelude to Civil War: The Nullification Controversy in South Carolina, 1816–1836* (New York: Harper Torchbooks, 1965), p. 67; *The Suppressed Book*, p. 263.

53. "Petition of the Sundry Citizens of Abbeville District," December 1838, (Folder 36), Slavery Files, SCA; "Petition of the Reverend R[ichard] Fuller Praying for the Alteration of the 1ˢ Section of the Act of 1834," December 9, 1850, (Folder 89), Slavery Files, SCA.

54. "The Petition of Sundry Citizens of Chester District Praying An Alteration of the Law in Relation to Slaves and Free Persons of Color Passed in December, 1834," 1838, (Folder 66), Slavery Files, SCA.

55. "Petition of Sundry Citizens of Abbeville," Slavery Files, SCA; "Petition of Reverend Fuller," Slavery Files, SCA.

56. Clear Spring Baptist Church Minutes, January 21, 1815, cited in Mallard, "Religious Work Among the Slaves," pp. 75, 79; Baptist Church: Barnwell Baptist Church Minutes, 1803–1912, Barnwell County, June 4, July 2, August 6, 1831 (typescript), pp. 28–29, SC.

57. Baptist Church: Big Creek Baptist Church [Records], 1801–1936, Anderson County, September 17, 1823 (typescript), pp. 24–25, SC.

58. Ibid., September 10, 1823, p. 25, SC.

59. (Case 155), June 15, 1844, Pendleton/Anderson District Court of Magistrates and Freeholders Records (microfilm), SCA; (Case 86), October 14, 1847, Spartanburg Court of Magistrates and Freeholders Records (microfilm), SCA; Rawick, *The American Slave*, III, iv, p. 165.

60. Rogers, *History of Georgetown*, pp. 356–57; *Proceedings of the Meeting in Charleston*, pp. 25–26; I. Jenkins Mikel, *Rumbling of the Chariot Wheels* (Columbia: The State Company, 1923), pp. 238–39; Rawick, *The American Slave*, II, i, p. 306, II, ii, pp. 18, 39, 78, III, iv, p. 84; David F. Thorpe, St. Helena,

to [unknown], January 25, 1863, Dabbs Papers, SHC; Gadsden, *Essay on Theodore Dehon*, p. 199.

61. Rogers, *History of Georgetown*, pp. 356–57.

62. Rawick, "West African Culture," pp. 152, 154; Rawick, *The American Slave*, III, iii, p. 19; *Proceedings of the Meeting in Charleston*, p. 54; Wilmore, *Black Religion*, p. 72; Bremer, *Homes of the New World*, I, pp. 289–90; Williams, *"De Ole Plantation,"* pp. 3, 12; G. R. Wilson, "The Religion of the American Negro Slave: His Attitude Toward Life and Death," *JNH*, VII (January 1923), 71; Genovese, *Roll, Jordan, Roll*, pp. 6, 231, 265, 283, 659–60; Gadsden, *Essay on Theodore Dehon*, p. 199; Baptist Church: Ebenezer Baptist Church Records, 1823–1860, Darlington County, March 22, July 19, 1829 (typescript), pp. 20, 24, SC.

63. Presbyterian Church: Records of Salem Presbyterian, August 28, 1831, III, p. 6, SC.

64. Baptist Church: Welsh Neck Minutes, September 3, 1825, p. 106, SC.

65. Pearson, *Letters From Port Royal*, p. 61; Minutes of the Session of Hopewell Congregation, Keowee, Pendleton Village, December 4, 1832, cited in Richard Newman Brackett, ed., *The Old Stone Church, Oconee County, South Carolina* (Pendleton, S.C.: The Old Stone Church and Cemetery Commission, 1972), pp. 45, 49–50 (originally published in 1905); Baptist Church: Barnwell Baptist Minutes, June 25, 1854, p. 98, SC; Baptist Church: Welsh Neck Minutes, September 3, 1825, February 3, 1827, January 3, 1830, pp. 106, 117, 142, SC; Baptist Church: Euhaw Baptist Church Book, 1831–1875, Euhaw, Beaufort District, February 5, 18, 1832, June 22, 1833, June 21, 1834, pp. 11–12, 33–34, 45, SC; Taylor, *Ante-Bellum South Carolina*, pp. 164–65; Henry Rowe Schoolcraft, *Plantation Life: The Narratives of Mrs. Henry Rowe Schoolcraft, 1852–1860* (New York: Negro Universities Press, 1969), pp. 84–85; Smith, *Carolina Rice Plantation*, p. 75; Lowery, *Life On the Old Plantation*, pp. 14, 16; "Records of Methodist Episcopal Church in Georgetown, S.C., 1815," Methodist Collection, Wofford College Library, Spartanburg, S.C., cited in Rogers, *History of Georgetown*, pp. 349–51; Jones, *Religious Instruction of Negroes*, pp. 93–94; Wightman, *Life of William Capers*, pp. 138–49; *Proceedings of the Meeting in Charleston*, pp. 27–29, 34, 43, 46–47, 59–60; Williams, *"De Ole Plantation,"* p. x; David F. Thorpe, St. Helena, to [unknown], January 25, 1863, Dabbs Papers, SHC; William Hill Diary, November 24, 1846, SHC; Peterkin, *Roll, Jordan, Roll*, p. 335; Perkins, *CH*, 232–35; Fickling, "Christianization of the Negro," p. 14.

66. Raymond, *HNM*, 481.

67. Perkins, *CH*, 234; Edward Lathrop to Mrs. De Saussure, July 23, 1903, cited in Mrs. N. B. De Saussure, *Old Plantation Days: Being Recollections of Southern Life Before the Civil War* (New York: Duffield & Company, 1909), p. 22; Genovese, *Roll, Jordan, Roll*, pp. 231, 283; Baptist Church: Barnwell Baptist Minutes, October 5, 1833, p. 40, SC; Baptist Church: Black Creek Church Book, 1828–1922, Beaufort County, November 10, 1855 (typescript), p. 30, SC; Baptist Church: Church of Christ Records, 1794–1937, Poplar Springs, Laurens County, June 19, July 16, 1841 (typescript), p. 37, SC; Baptist Church: Welsh Neck Minutes, February 18, 1820, March, 1831, April 6, 1839, pp. 79, 152, 220, SC; Bobby Frank Jones, "A Cultural Middle Passage: Slave Marriage and Family in the Ante-Bellum South" (Ph.D. dissertation, University of North Carolina, 1965), p. 157; Diary of John Hamilton Cornish, January 26, 1845, V, p. 8, John Hamilton Cornish Papers, SHC.

68. Plantation Records, Silver Bluff, S.C., December 8, 1831–December 31, 1855, December 26, 1840, p. 228, James H. Hammond Papers, SC.

69. One notable exception is John Blassingame, who in his revised and enlarged edition of *The Slave Community* examined church records for statistics on slave marriages, church memberships, funerals, catechumens, and confirmations. See John W. Blassingame, *The Slave Community: Plantation Life in the Antebellum South*, rev. ed. (New York: Oxford University Press, 1979), pp. 336–39, 344–60).

70. Baptist Church: Euhaw Church Book, December 9, 1838, March 26, 1848, January 28, 1849, pp. 66, 75, 78, SC; Baptist Church: New Providence Baptist Church Minutes, 1808–1922, Darlington County, November 23, 1839, April 23, 1864 (typescript), pp. 42, 87, SC; Baptist Church: Church of Christ Records, February 19, 1842, p. 39, SC; Baptist Church: Black Creek Church Book, September 8, 1861, p. 36, SC; Baptist Church: Welsh Neck Minutes, September 3, 1825, April 6, 1839, pp. 106, 221, SC; Baptist Church: Barnwell Baptist Minutes, December 31, 1814, October 4, 1828, February 1, 1834, November 5, 1836, October 6, 1838, December 1848, pp. 8, 21, 41, 51, 53, 88, SC; Cedar Spring Church Book, December 1794–December 1804, Spartanburg County, cited in Townsend, *South Carolina Baptists*, pp. 239, 241, 243; Minute Book, Siloam (Baptist) Church, Abbeville District, June 24, 1810, December, 1811, February 22, 1812, November 17, 1818, cited in Taylor, *Ante-Bellum South Carolina*, pp. 160–61.

71. Baptist Church: Barnwell Baptist Minutes, April 4, 1835, May 2, 1835, March 6, 1842, July 1, 1860, July, 1861, pp. 47, 65, 117, 120, SC; Minute Book, Siloam (Baptist) Church, November 17, 1818, cited in Taylor, *Ante-Bellum South Carolina*, p. 161; Baptist Church: Church of Christ Records, February 19, 1842, p. 39, SC; Rogers, *History of Georgetown*, p. 351; Milford Baptist Church Minutes, 1831–1868, Greenville District, August 31, 1833, p. 46, PL.

72. Baptist Church: Welsh Neck Minutes, June 5, 1836, p. 198, SC.

73. "Memorial to Military Commander of Federal Troops at Georgetown by Rev. Alex^r Glennie, Jas. R. Sparkman, Charles Alston, W. Allan Allston, Francis Weston," March 6, 1865, Sparkman Family Papers, SHC; Mallard, "Religious Work Among the Slaves," pp. 66, 75; Hildredth, *Despotism in America*, p. 43; Rogers, *History of Georgetown*, p. 358; Pinckney, *An Address*, pp. 10–11; Baptist Church: Barnwell Baptist Minutes, October 4, 1828, April 7, 1844, June 25, 1854, June 31, 1860, July, 1861, pp. 21, 72, 97–98, 117, 120, SC; Baptist Church: Big Creek [Records], September 30, 1865, p. 107, SC; Baptist Church: Welsh Neck Minutes, February 3, 1816, May 31, 1828, June 16, 1839, pp. 64, 125, 220–21, SC; Baptist Church: Ebenezer Records, July, 1824, March 22, 1829, pp. 6, 19–20, SC; Lowery, *Life On the Old Plantation*, pp. 41–42; Harrison, *The Gospel Among the Slaves*, pp. 204–5; Journal/Diary of Rev. Clark B. Steward, September 8, 1860 (typescript), p. 13, SC; Baptist Church: New Providence Minutes, November 23, 1839, p. 42, SC; Baptist Church: Euhaw Church Book, September 16, 1860, p. 126, SC.

74. Baptist Church: Church of Christ Records, August 19, 1837, September 9, 1837, p. 29, SC; Baptist Church: Welsh Neck Minutes, April 28, 1833, p. 169, SC; Baptist Church: Barnwell Baptist Minutes, October 6, 1832, October 6, 1838, pp. 36, 53, SC; Presbyterian Church: Fishing Creek Presbyterian Church [Records], 1799–1859, Chester District, August 12, 1851 (typescript), p. 46, SC.

75. Baptist Church: Barnwell Baptist Minutes, June 4, 1831, pp. 28–29, SC; Pres-

byterian Church: Records of Salem Presbyterian, May 3, 1842, III, p. 11, SC; Baptist Church: Welsh Neck Minutes, March, 1831, p. 152, SC.

76. Harding, "Religion and Resistance," pp. 180–82, 184–86, 188, 190–91, 196–97; Rawick, "West African Culture," pp. 151, 155, 163; Raboteau, *Slave Religion*, pp. 291, 293, 305; Angela Davis, *Lectures on Liberation* (New York: New York Committee to Free Angela Davis, n.d.), pp. 10–18; Wilmore, *Black Religion*, pp. xiii, 32–33, 39, 63, 69–73, 79–82, 100–2, 312; Willie Lee Rose, ed., *A Documentary History of Slavery in North America* (New York: Oxford University Press, 1976), p. 462; Genovese, *Roll, Jordan, Roll*, pp. 183, 222, 254, 259, 271–73; Joe R. Feagin, "Book Review Essay—The Black Church: Inspiration or Opiate," *JNH*, LX (October 1975), 538; Joseph R. Washington, *Black Religion: The Negro and Christianity in the United States* (Boston: Beacon Press, 1964), pp. 33–34, 202–3; Cone, *The Spirituals*, pp. 35–41; *An Account of the Late Intended Insurrection Among a Portion of the Blacks of This City, Charleston, S.C.* (Charleston: Corporation of Charleston, 1822), in *Slave Insurrections: Selected Documents* (Westport, Conn., 1970), pp. 3–5, 7–8, 15–16, 25–26, 29–30, 32–34, 36, 39, 42; "The Confession of Mr. Enslows Boy John," 1822, "Confession of Bacchus, the Slave of Mr. (Benjamin) Hammet," William and Benjamin Hammet Papers, PL; A South-Carolinian, *Practical Considerations Founded on the Scriptures, Relative to the Slave Population of South-Carolina* (Charleston: A. E. Miller, 1823), pp. 34–36; W. Hasel Wilson, Philadelphia, to Rev. Dr. Robert Wilson, Charleston, n.d., Robert Wilson Correspondence, CLS; Robert S. Starobin, ed., *Denmark Vesey: The Slave Conspiracy of 1822* (Englewood Cliffs, N.J.: Prentice-Hall, 1970), pp. 2–5; A South-Carolinian [Edwin C. Holland], *A Refutation of the Calumnies Circulated Against the Southern & Western States . . . Together With Historical Notices of All the Insurrections That Have Taken Place Since the Settlement of the Country* (Charleston: A. E. Miller, 1822), pp. 75–76; "Remonstrance," Greenville *Mountaineer*, November 2, 1838.

77. Rachel Blanding, Camden, S.C., to Hannah Lewis, [Philadelphia], July 25, 1816, William Blanding Papers, SC.

78. Dickson, *Plantation Sermons*, pp. ix, 13–14.

79. Williams, *"De Ole Plantation,"* pp. 1–5, 11; Adams, *Nigger to Nigger*, pp. 235–36; Raymond, *HNM*, 821–23; Townsend, *South Carolina Baptists*, p. 259; Donald Taylor, "20 Dollars Reward," The Georgetown *Gazette*, June 18, 1800; Elizabeth [Blyth Weston] to Adele Petigru Allston, March 17, 1865, in Easterby, *South Carolina Rice Plantation*, pp. 206–7.

80. Baptist Church: Barnwell Baptist Minutes, October 6, November 3, 1832, pp. 36–37, SC.

81. Diary of John Berkley Grimball, Charleston, S.C., No. 3-1834-1835-1836, July 11, 1834, I (typescript), p. 19, CLS.

82. Ann Sinkler Fishburne, *Belvidere: A Plantation Memory* (Columbia: University of South Carolina Press, 1949), pp. 25–26; Raymond, *HNM*, 481; Rawick, *The American Slave*, II, i, pp. 125–26; Bremer, *Homes of the New World*, I, pp. 289–90; Williams, *"De Ole Plantation,"* pp. 29, 31–32, 40, 46; Escott, *Slavery Remembered*, pp. 116–17; Alfred W. Nicholson, *Brief Sketch of the Life and Labors of Rev. Alexander Bettis* (Trenton, S.C.: By the Author, 1913), pp. 14, 45, 50; Holland, *Letters and Diary of Laura M. Towne*, p. 42; Genovese, *Roll, Jordan, Roll*, pp. 222–23, 244, 249; Lowery, *Life On the Old Plantation*, pp. 73–80.

83. Wilmore, *Black Religion*, pp. 69–73; Cone, *The Spirituals*, pp. 24–25, 147;

Genovese, *Roll, Jordan, Roll,* pp. 222–23, 254, 259, 266, 272–73, 278, 283–84; Eric Perkins, "Roll, Jordan, Roll: A 'Marx' For the Master Class," *RHR,* 3 (Fall 1976), 54–55.

84. "Record of the Beech Island Agricultural Club," December 3, 1859, Farmer's Club Records, pp. 130–31, SC; Jones, *Religious Instruction of Negroes,* p. 157; Lowery, *Life On the Old Plantation,* p. 16; Harding, "Religion and Resistance," p. 190; Perkins, *CH,* 232; Genovese, *Roll, Jordan, Roll,* p. 259.

85. John Dixon Long, *Pictures of Slavery in Church and State* (Philadelphia: By the Author, 1857), p. 233, cited in Sernett, *Black Religion,* pp. 93–94, 97–98.

86. Hall, *Travels in North America,* III, p. 191; Wightman, *Life of William Capers,* pp. 138–39; Baptist Church: New Providence Minutes, September 26, 1836, p. 35, SC; Baptist Church: Barnwell Baptist Minutes, October 6, November 3, 1832, June 25, 1854, pp. 36–37, 98, SC; James Redpath, *The Roving Editor: Or Talks With Slaves in the Southern States* (New York: Negro Universities Press, 1968), p. 260 (originally published in 1859); Cedar Spring Church Book, May, June, November, 1804 [and] Tyger River Church Book, March, May, June, 1802, October, 1804, cited in Townsend, *South Carolina Baptists,* pp. 258–59.

87. Benjamin Elijah Mays and Joseph William Nicholson, *The Negro's Church* (New York: Negro Universities Press, 1969), p. 7 (originally published in 1933).

88. Plantation Records, January 14, 1851, p. 455, James H. Hammond Papers, SC; David Thorpe Diary, 1861/1862, "Memoranda: Notes From M. Pierces Report," Dabbs Papers, SHC; H. D. Spaulding, "Under the Palmetto," *Continental Monthly,* IV (New York, 1863), 195–200, in Bruce Jackson, ed., *The Negro and His Folklore in Nineteenth-Century Periodicals* (Austin: University of Texas Press, 1967), pp. 66–67; Henry William Ravenel, "Recollections of Southern Plantation Life," *TYR,* XXV (June 1936), 765–66; Williamson, *After Slavery,* pp. 13, 194–95; Rawick, "West African Culture," pp. 155; Raboteau, *Slave Religion,* pp. 237–39; Escott, *Slavery Remembered,* p. 68.

89. Rawick, *The American Slave,* III, iv, p. 159.

90. Howard Odum, "Religious Folk-Songs of the Southern Negroes," *AJ,* 3 (July 1909), 266, 268, 270, 273–75; Henry Edward Krehbiel, *Afro-American Folksongs: A Study in Racial and National Music* (New York: G. Schirmer, 1914), pp. 2–4, 29; W. E. Burghardt DuBois, *The Souls of Black Folk: Essays and Sketches* (Chicago: A. C. McClurg & Company, 1924), pp. 250–51, 253–55; Sterling A. Brown et al., *The Negro Caravan* (New York: Arno Press and The New York Times, 1969), p. 414 (originally published in 1941); Sterling Stuckey, "Through the Prism of Folklore: The Black Ethos in Slavery," in Ann J. Lane, ed., *The Debate Over Slavery: Stanley Elkins and His Critics* (Urbana: University of Illinois Press, 1971), pp. 247–48, 268.

91. Allen, *Slave Songs,* pp. xix, 7, 46–48, 53; Thomas Wentworth Higginson, *Army Life in A Black Regiment* (Boston: Beacon Press, 1962), pp. 199, 200, 202–5, 207–11, 214–17 (originally published in 1869); James Miller McKim, "Negro Songs," *Dwight's Journal of Music,* XIX (Boston: August 9, 1862), 148–49, in Jackson, *The Negro and His Folklore,* pp. 57–58, 62; James M. McKim, *The Freed Men of South Carolina* (Philadelphia: Willis P. Hazard, 1862), pp. 11–12; Rawick, *The American Slave,* II, i, pp. 43, 180, 265–66, II, ii, pp. 51, 169–70; Holland, *Letters and Diary of Laura M. Towne,* p. 35; Wilson, *JNH,* 60–61, 64–65; Odum, *AJ,* 321–23, 334–36; DuBois, *Souls of Black Folk,* pp. 253–55, 258–63; Raboteau, *Slave Religion,* pp. 217–19, 250,

258, 260; Cone, *The Spirituals,* pp. 77, 86–87, 90–91; Stuckey, "Through the Prism of Folklore," pp. 249, 259.

92. Higginson, *Army Life,* p. 216.

93. "James M. Dabbs Papers: David F. Thorpe Series," Survey Book #41, SHC.

94. David F. Thorpe [Notebook], "Songs of Contraband," 1862, Dabbs Papers, SHC.

95. McKim, "Negro Songs," pp. 57–58, 62; Higginson, *Army Life,* pp. 217–18, 221–22; Benjamin E. Mays, *The Negro's God As Reflected in His Literature* (Boston: Chapman & Grimes, Inc., 1938), pp. 14–15, 20–25; Cone, *The Spirituals,* pp. 34–37, 77, 86–87, 90–91; Wilmore, *Black Religion,* pp. 51–52; Ball, *Fifty Years in Chains,* pp. 220–22; Raboteau, *Slave Religion,* p. 260; Genovese, *Roll, Jordan, Roll,* pp. 244, 248–49; Brown, *The Negro Caravan,* pp. 420, 440–41; Levine, "Slave Songs," pp. 115–17, 119–22.

96. Higginson, *Army Life,* p. 217.

97. Raboteau, *Slave Religion,* p. 247; Fisher, *Negro Slave Songs,* pp. viii–ix, 25, 112, 185; Harding, "Religion and Resistance," pp. 196–97; Genovese, *Roll, Jordan, Roll,* pp. 248–49; Bryan, "Slavery On A Peedee River," p. 114; E. Franklin Frazier, *The Negro Church in America* (New York: Schocken Books, 1963); Mays, *The Negro's God,* p. 2; Washington, *Black Religion,* pp. 207, 209, 217; Harold Courlander, *Negro Folk Music, U.S.A.* (New York: Columbia University Press, 1963), pp. 41–43; Cone, *The Spirituals,* pp. 39, 90–91; John Lovell, Jr., "The Social Implications of the Negro Spiritual," *Journal of Negro Education* (October 1939), 634–43, in Bernard Katz, ed., *The Social Implications of Early Negro Music in the United States* (New York: Arno Press and The New York Times, 1969), pp. 130, 134–36; Brown, *The Negro Caravan,* pp. 419–20; Levine, "Slave Songs," pp. 114–15, 121–22.

98. Raboteau, *Slave Religion,* p. 247.

99. Ibid.

100. "Testimony of Solomon Bradley," p. 97, NA.

101. "Testimony of Robert Smalls," American Freedmen's Inquiry Commission, p. 106, NA; Rawick, *The American Slave,* III, iii, p. 261; French, *Slavery in South Carolina,* pp. 133–34; Raboteau, *Slave Religion,* pp. 218–19, 250, 258, 260; Wilmore, *Black Religion,* pp. 51–52, 70–73; Escott, *Slavery Remembered,* pp. 112, 116–17; Stroyer, *My Life in the South,* pp. 22–24.

102. Stroyer, *My Life in the South,* pp. 19, 22–24.

103. Rawick, *The American Slave,* III, iv, p. 171; French, *Slavery in South Carolina,* pp. 14, 22–23, 133–34, 143, 179; Freeman Pugh, U.S.C. [G.], Picklatet, Fla., to Mrs. Ester H. Hawkes, Jacksonville, Fla., June 23, 1864, Ester H. Hawks Papers, pp. 362–63, LC; McKim, *The Freed Men,* p. 27; Higginson, *Army Life,* pp. 172–73; Cone, *The Spirituals,* p. 45; Escott, *Slavery Remembered,* pp. 112, 116–17.

104. Thomas L. Johnson, *Twenty-eight Years a Slave* (Bournemouth, England: W. Mate & Sons, 1909), pp. 29–30, quoted in Raboteau, *Slave Religion,* p. 312.

105. "Slave Songs," *The Nation,* 411; Higginson, *Army Life,* pp. 172–74, 256; French, *Slavery in South Carolina,* pp. 22–23, 133–34, 143, 179; Freeman Pugh, Picklatet, Fla., to Mrs. Ester H. Hawkes, Jacksonville, Fla., June 23, 1864, Hawks Papers, pp. 362–63, LC; Elizabeth Hyde Botume, *First Days Amongst the Contrabands* (New York: Arno Press and The New York Times, 1968), pp. 76, 204 (originally published in 1892); Holland, *Letters and Diary of Laura M. Towne,* pp. 57, 61–62, 162.

106. Holland, *Letters and Diary of Laura M. Towne,* pp. 159–60.

107. French, *Slavery in South Carolina*, pp. 22–23.
108. Harrison, *The Gospel Among Slaves*, pp. 297–99, 328.
109. Raymond, *HNM*, 481, 676; Bruce, *AQ*, 410, 412–14.
110. Rev. James Jenkins, *Experience, Labours, and Sufferings of Rev. James Jenkins, of the South Carolina Conference* (By the Author, 1842), p. 10; Diary of John Hamilton Cornish, November 20, December 1, 1857, pp. 312, 315, John Hamilton Cornish Papers, SHC; "Rambles at Random," *BEM*, 106–7; Wightman, *Life of William Capers*, pp. 299, 392–94, 396–97; E., "Correspondence of the Southern Guardian," *The Daily Southern Guardian*, April 23, 1863; Higginson, *Army Life*, pp. 53–54, 256; Botume, *First Days Amongst the Contrabands*, pp. 104–7, 121; French, *Slavery in South Carolina*, pp. 36, 46–47, 182–83; Wilson, *JNH*, 62–64, 71; Rawick, *The American Slave*, III, iv, p. 2; Pearson, *Letters From Port Royal*, p. 61; Rochester *Union and Advertiser*, August 9, 1893, in Blassingame, *Slave Testimony*, pp. 512–13; Spaulding, "Under the Palmetto," p. 72; Ball, *Fifty Years in Chains*, pp. 265–66.
111. G. G. Gibbs, "Southern Slave Life," *DR*, XXIV (January 1858), 322, quoted in Genovese, *Roll, Jordan, Roll*, p. 637.
112. "Rambles at Random," *BEM*, 106–7.
113. Botume, *First Days Amongst the Contrabands*, pp. 104–5.
114. Stroyer, *My Life in the South*, pp. 42–44; Botume, *First Days Amongst the Contrabands*, p. 155; Allen, *Slave Songs*, pp. 44, 46–47; Higginson, *Army Life*, p. 200; Pringle, *Chronicles of Chicora Wood*, p. 69; Wilson, *JNH*, 64–65; Odum, *AJ*, 336–37; Baldwin, "A Home in Dat Rock," pp. 3, 19–22, 29; Jessie McElroy to His Sister, April 22, 1868, Bonds Conway Papers, SC.
115. Allen, *Slave Songs*, p. 11.
116. Stuckey, "Prism of Folklore," pp. 263, 268; Higginson, *Army Life*, pp. 209–10; Cone, *The Spirituals*, pp. 16, 30–33; Allen, *Slave Songs*, pp. 7, 11, 13; Stroyer, *My Life in the South*, pp. 42–44; Wilson, *JNH*, pp. 59–64; Odum, *AJ*, 278–79, 298–99, 320–23.
117. Levine, "Slave Songs," pp. 115, 118; Williams, *"De Ole Plantation,"* pp. 31–32; Raymond, *HNM*, 481, 676, 680–82; Rawick, "West African Culture," p. 160; Rawick, *The American Slave*, III, iii, p. 19; Wilson, *JNH*, 53–55; Charles H. Long, "The Oppressive Elements in Religion and the Religions of the Oppressed," *HTR*, 69 (July–October 1976), 402, 405; Raboteau, *Slave Religion*, p. 318; Bruce, *AQ*, 404–8, 410, 412–15.
118. Bruce, *AQ*, 412–15; Rawick, *The American Slave*, III, iv, p. 192; Collins, *Memories of the Southern States*, p. 30; Baldwin, "A Home in Dat Rock," pp. 22, 29; French, *Slavery in South Carolina*, pp. 143, 183, 187; Mays, *The Negro's Church*, p. 2; Mays, *The Negro's God*, pp. 21–24; McKim, *The Freed Men*, pp. 14–15; Genovese, *Roll, Jordan, Roll*, pp. 7, 183, 251, 265, 283–84, 659–60; Escott, *Slavery Remembered*, pp. 110–11; Sernett, *Black Religion*, p. 108; Krebiel, *Afro-American Folksongs*, p. 29; *American Missionary* (ser. 2), 6 (June 1862), 138, cited in Raboteau, *Slave Religion*, p. 310.
119. French, *Slavery in South Carolina*, p. 183.
120. Sernett, *Black Religion*, p. 108; Wilson, *JNH*, 66; Williams, *"De Ole Plantation,"* pp. 27–29, 46; Cone, *The Spirituals*, pp. 55, 58, 62–63, 86–87; Raboteau, *Slave Religion*, p. 301.
121. Rawick, *The American Slave*, II, ii, p. 181.
122. Raboteau, *Slave Religion*, p. 301.
123. William Grimes, *Life of William Grimes* (New Haven, Conn., 1855), cited in Raboteau, *Slave Religion*, pp. 301–2.

124. Mays, *The Negro's Church*, pp. 1–2.
125. Rawick, "West African Culture," p. 151.
126. Taylor, *Ante-Bellum South Carolina*, pp. 159–61; Jones, "A Cultural Middle Passage," p. 157; Mikell, *Rumbling of the Chariot*, pp. 238–40; "Testimony of Robert Smalls," p. 106, NA; Editor, "Plantation Life: Duties and Responsibilities," *DR*, XXIX (September 1860), 367; Raymond, *HNM*, 676, 680.
127. Plantation Records, December 16, 1831, January 14, 1851, pp. 7, 455, James H. Hammond Papers, SC; Raymond, *HNM*, 680–81; Roper, *A Narrative*, p. 59; Sernett, *Black Religion*, p. 85; Rawick, *The American Slave*, III, iv, p. 192; Holland, *Letters and Diary of Laura M. Towne*, p. 81.
128. Plantation Records, December 15, 1831, p. 5, James H. Hammond Papers, SC.
129. Plantation Records, January 14, 1851, p. 455, James H. Hammond Papers, SC.
130. Nicholson, *Brief Sketch of Rev. Bettis*, pp. 12–14; Baptist Church: New Providence, September 26, 1836, p. 35, SC; Baptist Church: Black Creek Church Book, July 12, 1856, p. 31, SC; Sernett, *Black Religion*, pp. 97–98.
131. Cedar Spring Church Book, May, June, November 1804, quoted in Townsend, *South Carolina Baptists*, p. 258.
132. Baptist Church: "Letter of Dismission," May 17, 1823, SC; Presbyterian Church: Bethesda Presbyterian Church, 1806–1937, Camden, S.C., January 23, 1853 (typescript), p. 81, SC; Baptist Church: Euhaw Church Book, August 4, 1832, March 26, April 23, 1848, January 28, 1849, pp. 19, 75, 78, SC; Baptist Church: Barnwell Baptist Minutes, June 31, July 1, 1860, August 27, October 1, 1865, pp. 117, 134, SC; Baptist Church: Welsh Neck Minutes, January 3, 1830, October 5, 1839, pp. 142, 223, SC; Presbyterian Church: Records of Salem Presbyterian, May 6, 1843, III, p. 11, SC.
133. Baptist Church: Barnwell Baptist Minutes, April 7, 1844, p. 72, SC.
134. Baptist Church, Church of Christ Records, August 19, October 23, 1853, pp. 70–71, SC.
135. Mikell, *Rumbling of the Chariot*, p. 240.
136. Raboteau, *Slave Religion*, p. 302.
137. Solomon Bayley, *A Narrative of Some Remarkable Incidents in the Life of Solomon Bayley* (London, 1825), pp. 25–26, quoted in Raboteau, *Slave Religion*, p. 302.
138. Raboteau, *Slave Religion*, p. 302.

Chapter 6. Combatants Suppressed, But Not Controlled

1. George P. Rawick, ed., *The American Slave: A Composite Autobiography* (Westport, Conn.: Greenwood Publishing Company, 1972), II, ii, p. 150.
2. The Charleston (S.C.) *Religious Telegraph*, n.d., quoted in *The Suppressed Book About Slavery!* (New York: Carleton, 1864), p. 88.
3. Herbert Aptheker, *To Be Free: Studies in American Negro History* (New York: International Publishers, 1969), pp. 30–31 (originally published in 1948); William L. McCaa, "Observations on the Manner of Living and Diseases of Slaves on the Wateree River, S.C." (Sr. thesis, University of Pennsylvania, 1823), pp. 4–5, WHL; Richard Hildreth, *Despotism in America; Or an Inquiry Into the Nature and Results of the Slave-Holding System in the United States* (Boston: Whipple and Damrell, 1840), pp. 17, 81–82; Harvey Wish, "American Slave Insurrections Before 1861," in John H. Bracey, Jr., et al., eds., *American Slavery: The Question of Resistance* (Belmont, Cal.: Wadsworth Publishing Company, 1971), p. 22; Gayraud S. Wilmore, *Black Religion and Black Rad-*

icalism (Garden City, N.Y.: Anchor Press, 1973), p. 1; Angela Davis, *Lectures on Liberation* (New York: New York Committee to Free Angela Davis, n.d.), pp. 5–6, 9–10; Lionel H. Kennedy and Thomas Parker, *An Official Report of the Trials of Sundry Negroes, Charged With An Attempt to Raise An Insurrection . . . And in An Appendix, A Report of the Trials of Four White Persons On Indictments for Attempting to Excite the Slaves to Insurrection* (Charleston: James R. Schenck, 1822), pp. 30–31; "Testimony of Robert Smalls," American Freedmen's Inquiry Commission (microfilm), Reel 200, File III, pp. 105–6, NA; State v. Martin Posey, 4 Strobhart 103 and 142, November 1849, in Helen T. Catterall, ed., *Judicial Cases Concerning American Slavery and the Negro* (Washington, D.C.: Carnegie Institute of Washington, 1929), II, pp. 413–14; George Rogers, Jr., *The History of Georgetown County, South Carolina* (Columbia: University of South Carolina Press, 1970), p. 346.

4. Frances Anne Kemble, *Journal of a Residence on a Georgian Plantation in 1838–1839*, ed. John A. Scott (New York: Alfred A. Knopf, 1961), pp. xviii–xix, 118–19.

5. Act of December 20, 1800, sects. 7–9. 7 The Statutes at Large of South Carolina 442, 443, in Catterall, *Judicial Cases*, II, pp. 267–68; J. S. Buckingham, *The Slave States of America* (London: Fisher, Son, & Co., 1842), II, pp. 31–32; Hildreth, *Despotism in America*, pp. 71–72, 92; Vinyard v. Passalaigue, 2 Strobhart 536, November 1847–May 1848, in Catterall, *Judicial Cases*, II, p. 404; Dougherty v. Dougherty, 2 Strob. Eq. 63, January 1848, in Catterall, *Judicial Cases*, II, p. 407; Finley v. Hunter, 2 Strob. Eq. 208, May 1848, in Catterall, *Judicial Cases*, II, p. 409; Broughton v. Telfer, 3 Rich. Eq. 431, May 1851, in Catterall, *Judicial Cases*, II, p. 426; Peter H. Wood, *Black Majority: Negroes in Colonial South Carolina From 1670 Through the Stono Rebellion* (New York: Alfred A. Knopf, 1974), p. 324; H. M. Henry, *The Police Control of the Slave in South Carolina* (New York: Negro Universities Press, 1968), pp. 153–54, 168 (originally published in 1914).

6. The Heirs of David Morton vs. Thompson and Another, Executors, (July 1853), in J. S. G. Richardson, *Reports of Cases in Equity, Argued and Determined in the Court of Appeals and Court of Errors, of South-Carolina* (Charleston: Walker, Evans, 1855), IV, p. 370; Morton v. Thompson, 6 Rich. Eq. 370, May 1854, in Catterall, *Judicial Cases*, II, pp. 441–42; John Livingston Bradley, "Slave Manumission in South Carolina, 1820–1860" (M.A. thesis, University of South Carolina, 1964), pp. 49–50, 59, 65, 67, 70, 73.

7. Gordon v. Blackman, 1 Rich. Eq. 61, December 1844, in Catterall, *Judicial Cases*, II, p. 392.

8. "Petition of James Gill for the Freedom of a Slave Named Andy and That He Be Allowed to Remain in the State, Chester District," 1847, (Folder 93), Slavery Files, SCA.

9. Louisa S. McCord, Columbia, to Langdon Cheves, Jr., April 21, 1856, Cheves Family Papers, SCHS.

10. Ibid., April 13, 1856.

11. Ibid., December 18, 1856.

12. Ibid., December 20, 1856.

13. Gwendolyn Midlo Hall, *Social Control in Slave Plantation Societies: A Comparison of St. Domingue and Cuba* (Baltimore: The Johns Hopkins Press, 1971), p. 114; Wood, *Black Majority*, pp. 101–2, 324; John W. Blassingame, *The Slave Community: Plantation Life in the Antebellum South* (New York: Oxford University Press, 1972), pp. 192–200; Richard C. Wade, "The Vesey

Plot: A Reconsideration," in Bracey, *American Slavery,* pp. 137, 139; John Belton O'Neall, *The Negro Law of South Carolina* (Columbia: John G. Bowman, 1848), p. 12; L. Glen Inabinet, " 'The July Fourth Incident' of 1816: An Insurrection Plotted by Slaves in Camden, South Carolina," pp. 14–16, paper presented at the Reynolds Conference on South Carolina Legal History, University of South Carolina, December, 1977; Bradley, "Slave Manumission," pp. 38–40, 49–50.

14. Wood, *Black Majority,* pp. 248, 253–54, 263–64, 268, 274–75; John B. Irving, *A Day on Cooper River* (Charleston: A. E. Miller, 1842), p. 21; Eugene D. Genovese, *Roll, Jordan, Roll: The World the Slaves Made* (New York: Pantheon Books, 1974, pp. 648–52; Elizabeth Fox-Genovese, "Strategies and Forms of Resistance: Focus on Slave Women in the United States," in Gary Y. Okihiro, ed., *In Resistance: Studies in African, Caribbean, and Afro-American History* (Amherst: The University of Massachusetts Press, 1986), p. 155; "Petition of Edward Brailsford," November 1816, General Assembly Petitions, SCA; Daniel E. Meaders, "South Carolina Fugitives As Viewed Through Local Colonial Newspapers With Emphasis on Runaway Notices, 1732–1801," *JNH,* LX (April 1975), 288, 292, 298; Thomas L. Shaw, "Ten Dollars Reward," Georgetown *Gazette,* December 16, 1825.

15. Philo Tower, *Slavery Unmasked: Being a Truthful Narrative of A Three Years' Residence and Journeying in Eleven Southern States* (Rochester: Darrow and Brother, 1856), pp. 120–21; Anne Sinkler Fishburne, *Belvidere: A Plantation Memory* (Columbia: University of South Carolina Press, 1949), p. 55; "John's Island," The Charleston *Mercury,* July 1, 1829; Buckingham, *The Slave States,* I, p. 571; Anderson *Gazette,* June 5, 1846, p. 3; The Charleston *Mercury,* February 17, 1849; The Charleston *Courier,* July 27, 1829, February 17, 1849.

16. Langdon Cheves, Pendleton, to Langdon Cheves, Jr., Savannah, May 2, 1844, Cheves Family Papers, SCHS.

17. Buckingham, *The Slave States,* I, p. 572; Genovese, *Roll, Jordan, Roll,* pp. 650–52; "The Petition of James McKinney, Colleton District," November 17, 1825, General Assembly Petitions, SCA; Diary of Henry Ravenel of St. John's Parish, S.C., July 12, 1819, in Ulrich B. Phillips, ed., *Plantation and Frontier Documents, 1649–1863: Illustrative of Industrial History in the Colonial and Ante-Bellum South* (Cleveland: The Arthur H. Clark Company, 1909), II, p. 91; "Petition of David G. Rodgers, Williamsburgh District," November 21, 1820, General Assembly Petitions, SCA; David Gavin Diary, 1855–1871, February 28, May 5, 7, 1856, I (typescript), pp. 25–26, 36, SCH; Diary of W. Thacher, March 16, 1817, MS, cited in Rosser T. Taylor, *Ante-Bellum South Carolina: A Social and Cultural History* (The James Sprunt Studies in History and Political Science, Chapel Hill: The University of North Carolina Press, 1942), p. 180; Journal of Thomas B. Chaplin, 1845–1886, May 15, 1845, p. 32, SCHS; Harvey T. Cook, *Life and Legacy of David Rogerson Williams* (New York, 1916), p. 130, cited in Herbert Aptheker, *American Negro Slave Revolts* (New York: International Publishers, 1969), pp. 258–59, 277 (originally published in 1943); Rawick, *The American Slave,* II, ii, pp. 24, 110–11; Charles Ball, *Fifty Years in Chains,* with an introduction by Philip S. Foner (New York: Dover Publications, 1970), p. 256 (originally published in 1837); Robert F. .W. Allston, Columbia, to Adele Petigru Allston, November 25, 1853, in J. H. Easterby, ed., *The South Carolina Rice Plantation as Revealed in the Papers of Robert F. W. Allston* (Chicago: University of Chicago Press, 1945), p. 117.

18. *Anti-Slavery Reporter*, ser. 3, XII (September 1, 1864), 202–3, in John W. Blassingame, ed., *Slave Testimony: Two Centuries of Letters, Speeches, Interviews, and Autobiographies* (Baton Rouge: Louisiana State University Press, 1971), pp. 451, 453.

19. Genovese, *Roll, Jordan, Roll*, pp. 650–52; Plantation Journal, 1856–1858, May 5, 6, 9, 1856, Samuel Porcher Gaillard Plantation Journals, 1835–1868, SC; Diary of John Berkley Grimball, Charleston, S.C., No. 3-1834-1835-1836, January 7, 1835, I (typescript), p. 32, CLS; Plantation Records, Silver Bluff, S.C., December 8, 1831–December 31, 1855, July 5, 1835, p. 111, James Henry Hammond Papers, SC; Rawick, *The American Slave*, II, i, p. 184; Meaders, *JNH*, 309–10; *The Suppressed Book*, p. 315; Journal of Thomas B. Chaplin, May 15, June 8, 1845, pp. 32, 37, SCHS.

20. Rawick, *The American Slave*, II, i, p. 184.

21. Ibid., III, iii, p. 130.

22. James Gabriel Guignard, II, Lodimont, to James Sanders Guignard, I, July 30, 1828, Guignard Family Papers, SC.

23. The State v. Guy Raines, 1826, Fairfield District, in David J. McCord, *Report of Cases Argued and Determined in the Court of Appeals of South Carolina* (Columbia: Doyle E. Sweeney, 1826), III, pp. 534–35.

24. Ibid., pp. 534–36.

25. Ibid., p. 535.

26. Plantation Journal, 1856–1858, May 9, 1856, Samuel Porcher Gaillard Plantation Journals, SC; David Gavin Diary, July 4, 1857, I, p. 87, SHC; *American Slavery As It Is: Testimony of A Thousand Witnesses* (New York: American Anti-Slavery Society, 1839), p. 23; Alice R. Huger Smith, *A Carolina Rice Plantation of the Fifties . . . With Chapters From the Unpublished Memoirs of D. E. Huger Smith* (New York: William Morrow and Company, 1936), pp. 78–79; D. E. Smith, *A Charlestonian's Recollections, 1846–1913* (Charleston: Carolina Art Association, 1950), p. 35; Leslie Howard Owens, *This Species of Property: Slave Life and Culture in the Old South* (New York: Oxford University Press, 1976), pp. 87–88; James D. Anderson, "Aunt Jemima in Dialectics: Genovese on Slave Culture," *JNH*, LXI (January 1976), 109; [Petition of 23 Christ Church, S.C. Planters, 1829], MS, cited in Aptheker, *To Be Free*, pp. 22–24; Rawick, *The American Slave*, III, iv, pp. 112–13; Jacob Stroyer, *My Life in the South* (Salem, Mass.: Salem Observer and Job Print, 1885), pp. 64–66.

27. Stroyer, *My Life in the South*, pp. 71–72.

28. "Petition of the Town Council of Georgetown Praying that Negroes Jack and Tom May Be Rewarded for Taking and Dispersing a Gang of Runaways Who Had Murdered Their Master," n.d., (Folder 91), Slavery Files, SCA; Diary of J. B. Grimball, No. 12-1858-1859, 1861-1862, November 28, 1858, January 12, 1859, II, pp. 10–11, CLS; Pineville Association: Secretary's Book, 1823–1839-1840, October 2, 5, 1823, October, 1827, Pineville Association—St. John's and St. Stephens, Berkely, 1823–1840 and Police Association—St. John's Berkely, 1839–1852, SCHS; Pineville Association: Treasurer's Book, 1823–1839, 1827, Pineville Association and Police Association, SCHS.

29. Eugene D. Genovese, *From Rebellion to Revolution: Afro-American Slave Revolts in the Making of the Modern World* (Baton Rouge: Louisiana State University Press, 1979), pp. 77–79.

30. (Case 231), October 11, 1860, Spartanburg Court of Magistrates and Freeholders Records (microfilm), SCA.

31. Ibid.
32. Buckingham, *The Slave States,* I, pp. 86–87.
33. W. E. B. DuBois, *Black Reconstruction in America, 1800–1880* (New York: Atheneum, 1973), p. 13; Genovese, *Roll, Jordan, Roll,* p. 657; George M. Fredrickson and Christopher Lasch, "Resistance to Slavery," in Ann J. Lane, ed., *The Debate Over Slavery: Stanley Elkins and His Critics* (Urbana: University of Illinois Press, 1971), p. 228; Owens, *This Species of Property,* p. 87; Anderson, *JNH,* 109.
34. "The Petition of Major Browns Widow, St. Paul's Parish," [1800], General Assembly Petitions, SCA; "Petition of Dr. Louis Raoul, Charleston District," 1823, (Folder 142), Slavery Files, SCA; "Petition that Negroes Jack and Tom Be Rewarded for Taking and Dispersing a Gang of Runaways," Slavery Files, SCA.
35. "Petition of David G. Rodgers," General Assembly Petitions, SCA.
36. [Petition of 23 Christ Church Planters], MS, quoted in Aptheker, *To Be Free,* p. 24.
37. "The Petition of James B. Richardson of Sumter District," [1800], General Assembly Petitions, SCA; Peter Lewis, "Fifty Dollars Reward," Georgetown *Gazette,* November 19, 1800; Charleston Scrapbook: Clippings Chiefly From Charleston Newspapers, 1800–1810, Augusta, July 31, 1806, SC; Plantation Book, April 30, May 26, June 9, 1813, Coffin Point Records, 1800–1821, SCHS; William S. Harvey, "100 Dollars Reward," The Georgetown *Gazette,* February 14, 1826; "For the Mercury-Travellers Beware of Runaway Negroes and Robbers," The Charleston *Mercury,* August 4, 1829; "Committed to the Work-House, as Runaways," The Charleston *Mercury,* August 14, 1829; Rockingham Plantation Journal, 1828–1829, May 28, June 17, July 23, 1828, PL; Genovese, *From Rebellion to Revolution,* pp. 68–69; G. W. Featherstonhaugh, *Excursion Through the Slave States* (London: John Murray, 1844), II, pp. 342, 344; Rawick, *The American Slave,* III, iii, pp. 15, 130; "The Petition of William Boyd Praying Compensation for Injuries Received in the Arrest of Certain Runaway Slaves, Laurens District," November 29, 1858, (Folder 54), Slavery Files, SCA; "Petition that Negroes Jack and Tom Be Rewarded for Taking and Dispersing a Gang of Runaways," Slavery Files, SCA; W. M. Bateman, Robertson Plantation, to Mrs. S. B. Manning, October 8, 1862, Chesnut-Miller-Manning Papers, SCHS.
38. "The Petition of Major Browns Widow," General Assembly Petitions, SCA.
39. Charleston Scrapbook: Clippings Chiefly From Charleston Newspapers, 1800–1810, Augusta, July 31, 1806, SC.
40. "Petition of John Rose, Richland District," 1831, (Folder 149), Slavery Files, SCA.
41. (Case 252), May 19, 1852, Pendleton/Anderson Court of Magistrates Records (microfilm), SCA.
42. Charles T. Haskell, Abbeville, to Langdon Cheves, June 16, 1862, Cheves Family Papers, SCHS.
43. Genovese, *Roll, Jordan, Roll,* p. 650.
44. Stroyer, *My Life in the South,* p. 65; Anne King Gregorie, *History of Sumter County, South Carolina* (Sumter: Library Board of Sumter County, 1954), p. 144; Cook, *Life of David Williams,* p. 130, cited in Aptheker, *American Slave Revolts,* pp. 258–59; "Petition that Negroes Jack and Tom Be Rewarded for Taking and Dispersing a Gang of Runaways," Slavery Files, SCA; "Petition of Dr. Louis Raoul," Slavery Files, SCA; Charleston Scrapbook, Augusta, July

31, 1806, SC; "The Petition of Major Browns Widow," General Assembly Petitions, SCA; W. M. Bateman, Robertson Plantation, to Mrs. S. B. Manning, October 1862, Chesnut-Miller-Manning Papers, SCHS; Smith, *A Charlestonian's Recollections*, p. 35; Rawick, *The American Slave*, II, i, p. 184.

45. Johnson v. Wideman, Rice 325, May 1839, in Catterall, *Judicial Cases*, II, pp. 372–73.

46. David Gavin Diary, February 28, 1856, I, pp. 25–26, SHC.

47. Pineville Association: Secretary's Book, October, 1827, Pineville Association and Police Association, SCHS.

48. "Petition of William Boyd," Slavery Files, SCA.

49. Hildreth, *Despotism in America*, p. 77; Aptheker, *To Be Free*, p. 11; Ball, *Fifty Years in Chains*, pp. 325–26; Plantation Records, October 17, 1839, p. 187, James H. Hammond Papers, SC; Elizabeth Hyde Botume, *First Days Amongst the Contrabands* (New York: Arno Press and The New York Times, 1968), p. 243 (originally published in 1892); *American Slavery As It Is*, p. 153.

50. Rawick, *The American Slave*, II, i, pp. 338–39.

51. Manigault Letter Book, 1846–1848 (typescript), Charles Izard Manigault, Paris, to Anthony Barclay Esqⁱ British Consul, New York, April 15, 1847, p. 36, Charles Manigault Papers, SC.

52. David Gavin Diary, July 4, 1857, I, p. 87, SHC; Plantation Journal, 1856–1858, May 9, 1856, Samuel Porcher Gaillard Plantation Journals, SC; Manigault Letter Book, Charles Manigault to Anthony Barclay, April 15, 1847, p. 36, Charles Manigault Papers, SC.

53. John Chesnut, Camden, to Charles Chesnut, Philadelphia, September 25, 1835, Williams-Chesnut-Manning Papers, SC.

54. E. C. L. Adams, *Nigger to Nigger* (New York: Charles Scribner's Sons, 1928), pp. 16–17.

55. Rev. John G. Williams, *"De Ole Plantation"* (Charleston: Walker, Evans & Cogswell, 1895), p. 40.

56. Sterling Stuckey, *Slave Culture: Nationalist Theory and the Foundations of Black America* (New York: Oxford University Press, 1987), pp. 48–49; Robert S. Starobin, ed., *Denmark Vesey: The Slave Conspiracy of 1822* (Englewood Cliffs, N.J.: Prentice-Hall, 1970), pp. 2–3.

57. William W. Freehling, "Denmark Vesey's Peculiar Reality," in Robert H. Abzug and Stephen E. Maizlish, eds., *New Perspectives on Race and Slavery in America: Essays in Honor of Kenneth M. Stampp* (Lexington: The University Press of Kentucky, 1986), p. 29.

58. Quoted in Aptheker, *American Slave Revolts*, pp. 269–70.

59. Starobin, *Denmark Vesey*, pp. 5, 178–79; Freehling, "Denmark Vesey's Reality," p. 29; Stuckey, *Slave Culture*, p. 47.

60. Starobin, *Denmark Vesey*, pp. 5, 178–79; Aptheker, *American Slave Revolts*, p. 269; Freehling, "Denmark Vesey's Reality," pp. 38–39.

61. Martha Procter to "My Dear James," August 7, 1822, Arnold-Screven Papers, Southern Historical Collection, University of North Carolina at Chapel Hill, quoted in Freehling, "Denmark Vesey's Reality," p. 31.

62. "The State of South-Carolina vs. William Allen," quoted in Starobin, *Denmark Vesey*, pp. 4, 58–59.

63. Starobin, *Denmark Vesey*, pp. 4–5, 17; Freehling, "Denmark Vesey's Reality," p. 30.

64. Quoted in Freehling, "Denmark Vesey's Reality," pp. 29, 40.

65. Quoted in Starobin, *Denmark Vesey*, p. 7.

66. Ibid., p. 5.
67. Aptheker, *American Slave Revolts*, p. 271; Starobin, *Denmark Vesey*, pp. 5, 8, 17.
68. Sterling Stuckey, "Remembering Denmark Vesey—Agitator or Insurrectionist?" *Negro Digest*, XV (February 1966), quoted in Starobin, *Denmark Vesey*, p. iii.
69. Bruce Morgan, "In Georgia: Through the Gospel Grapevine," *Time*, 132 (September 12, 1988), 12–13.
70. Aptheker, *American Slave Revolts*, p. 3.
71. Quoted in Herbert Aptheker, *Resistance and Afro-American History: Some Notes on Contemporary Historiography and Suggestions for Further Research,"* in Okihiro, *In Resistance*, p. 11.
72. William Styron, "Overcome," *The New York Review of Books,* 1 (September 26, 1963), 18–19.
73. Philip Schwarz, "Forging the Shackles: The Development of Virginia's Criminal Code for Slaves," in David Bodenhamer and James W. Ely, Jr., eds., *Ambivalent Legacy: A Legal History of the South* (Jackson: University Press of Mississippi, 1984), p. 134.
74. Mr. J. Dawsey, Pinckney Island, to Charles Cotesworth Pinckney, November 25, 1824, Pinckney Family Papers, LC.
75. Ibid.
76. John Evans, Pinckney Island, to General Charles Cotesworth Pinckney, November 25, 1824, Pinckney Family Papers, LC.
77. Ibid.
78. Starobin, *Denmark Vesey*, p. 3; Rachel Blanding, Camden, S.C., to Hannah Lewis, [Philadelphia], July 25, 1816, William Blanding Papers, SC; Inabinet, "'The July Fourth Incident,'" pp. 2–6, 9–14; A South-Carolinian (Edwin C. Holland), *A Refutation of the Calumnies Circulated Against the Southern & Western States . . . Together With Historical Notices of All the Insurrections That Have Taken Place Since the Settlement of the Country* (Charleston: A. E. Miller, 1822), pp. 75–77.
79. *An Account of the Late Intended Insurrection Among a Portion of the Blacks of This City, Charleston, S.C.* (Charleston: Corporation of Charleston, 1822), in *Slave Insurrections: Selected Documents* (Westport, Conn.: Negro Universities Press, 1970), pp. 3–8, 15–16, 25–39; Rev. Dr. Richard Furman, *Exposition of the Views of the Baptists, Relative to the Coloured Population . . . In A Communication to the Governor of South Carolina*, 3d ed. (Charleston: A. E. Miller, 1835), pp. 3–6; "Memoirs of S. W. Ferguson: Family History and Boyhood," April 26, 1900 (typescript), p. 13, Heyward and Ferguson Family Papers (typescript and microfilm), SHC; Anna Hayes Johnson, Charleston, S.C., to Eliza Eagles Haywood, Raleigh, N.C., July 18, 1822, Ernest Haywood Collection, SHC; W. Hasell Wilson, Philadelphia, to Rev. Dr. Robert Wilson, Charleston, n.d., Robert Wilson Correspondence, CLS; William Jones, Goshen, Lincoln County, Ga., to Langdon Cheves, Philadelphia, July 28, 1822, Cheves Family Papers, SCHS; Edward L. Pierce, "The Freedmen at Port Royal," *AM*, XII (September 1863), 301; Kennedy, *Official Report*, pp. 29–31, 44–46, 127; Henry, *Police Control*, pp. 153–54; William W. Freehling, *Prelude to Civil War: The Nullification Controversy in South Carolina, 1816–1836* (New York: Harper Torchbooks, 1965), p. 56; Thomas Wentworth Higginson, *Black Rebellion* (New York: Arno Press and The New York Times, 1969), pp. 106–9,

122–23 (originally published as a series of articles in the *Atlantic Monthly* during the 1850s and 1860s); Wade, "The Vesey Plot," pp. 128–30, 132–34, 139–40.

80. Kinloch v. Harvey, 2d ed. 508, January 1830, in Catterall, *Judicial Cases*, II, pp. 340–41; James Petigru Carson, *Life, Letters and Speeches of James Louis Petigru: The Union Man of South Carolina* (Washington, D.C.: W. H. Lowdermilk & Co., 1920), p. 66; "Petition of the Delegation from Prince George Winyah & All Saints," n.d., (Folder 139), Slavery Files, SCA; Jane W. Gwinn, "The Georgetown Slave Insurrection of 1829," in Charles Joyner, ed., "Black Carolinians: Studies in the History of South Carolina Negroes in the Nineteenth Century" (typescript), pp. 1–3, SC; Bradley, "Slave Manumission," pp. 57–58; Wish, "American Slave Insurrections," p. 30; New York *Evening Post*, August 28, 1829, cited in Aptheker, *American Slave Revolts*, p. 286.

81. Diary of Edward Hooker, 1805–1808, December 19–21, 1805, cited in American Historical Association, *Report of Historical Manuscripts Commission of the AHA for 1896* (Washington: Government Printing Office, 1897), pp. 881–82; Letters of An American Traveller . . . Written During An Excursion in the Year 1810, I (typescript), pp. 5–6, CLS; Rosannah P. Rogers, Union District, to David L. Rogers, Tallahassee, Fla., October 29, 1831, William W. Renwick Papers, PL; "The Petition of Robert A. Cuningham Praying Payment for a Negro Executed," [December 1831], (Folder 74), Slavery Files, SCA.

82. Gwinn, "The Georgetown Insurrection," in Joyner, "Black Carolinians," p. 3, SC; Aptheker, *American Slave Revolts*, pp. 155–57; T. W. Higginson, "Gabriel's Defeat," *AM*, X (July 1862), 340, 343; Inabinet, "'The July Fourth Incident,'" pp. 9–10; M. Foster Farley, "The Fear of Negro Slave Revolts in South Carolina, 1690–1865," *Afro-American Studies*, III (1972), 199; Genovese, *From Rebellion to Revolution*, p. 4; Wish, "American Slave Insurrections," p. 21.

83. New York *Evening Post*, August 28, 1829, quoted in Aptheker, *American Slave Revolts*, p. 286.

84. Quoted in Carson, *Life of James Petigru*, p. 66.

85. Gwinn, "The Georgetown Insurrection," in Joyner, "Black Carolinians," p. 2, SC.

86. "Report of Comm on Claims on the Petition of Robert A. Cunningham: Senate—10 December 1831/House of Representatives, December 16, 1831," in "The Petition of Robert Cuningham," Slavery Files, SCA.

87. Rosannah P. Rogers, Union District, to David L. Rogers, Tallahassee, Fla., October 29, 1831, William W. Renwick Papers, PL.

88. Taylor, *Ante-Bellum South Carolina*, pp. 7–8; Guion Griffis Johnson, *A Social History of the Sea Islands: With Special Reference to St. Helena Island, South Carolina* (Chapel Hill: The University of North Carolina Press, 1930), p. 106; Charles W. Joyner, "Slave Folklife of the Waccamaw Neck: Antebellum Black Culture in the South Carolina Lowcountry" (Ph.D. dissertation, University of Pennsylvania, 1977), pp. 1, 326; Rogers, *History of Georgetown*, p. 343; Leon Stone Bryan, Jr., "Slavery On a Peedee River Rice Plantation, 1825–1865" (M.A. thesis, Johns Hopkins University, 1963), pp. 2, 178; Eliza Ervin Cowan and Horace Fraser Rudisill, *Darlingtoniana: A History of People, Places, and Events in Darlington County, South Carolina* (Columbia: The R. L. Bryan Company, 1964), p. 177; David Thorpe Diary, 1861/1862, "Memoranda: Notes From M. Pierces Report," Dabbs Papers, SHC; Easterby, *South Carolina Rice Plantation*, p. 8; Joel R. Williamson, "Black Self-Assertion Before and

After Emancipation," in Nathan I. Huggins et al., *Key Issues in the Afro-American Experience* (New York: Harcourt Brace Jovanovich, 1971), I, p. 218; "Petition to His Excellency F. W. Pickens of the State of South Carolina, [1861?]," Francis W. Pickens and Milledge L. Bonham Papers, pp. 341–42, LC.

89. "The Confession of Mr. Enslows Boy John—1822," William and Benjamin Hammet Papers, PL.

90. Diary of Edward Hooker, December 19, 1805, quoted in AHA, *Report*, p. 881.

91. Starobin, *Denmark Vesey*, pp. 1–3, 180; *Account of the Late Insurrection*, in *Slave Insurrections*, pp. 10, 13, 32–33, 36, 38–39; Inabinet, "'The July Fourth Incident,'" pp. 1–2; A South-Carolinian, *A Refutation*, pp. 75–76; Higginson, *Black Rebellion*, pp. 108–9, 121–23, 125; Wade, "The Vesey Plot," p. 10; Robert S. Starobin, "Denmark Vesey's Slave Conspiracy of 1822: A Study in Rebellion and Repression," in Bracey, *American Slavery*, pp. 142, 154; Freehling, *Prelude to Civil War*, p. 56; Richard C. Wade, *Slavery in the Cities: The South 1820–1860* (London: Oxford University Press, 1964), pp. 55–59; John Potter, Charleston, to Langdon Cheves, Philadelphia, July 5, 1822, Cheves Family Papers, SCHC; "The Confession of Mr. Enslows Boy John—1822," William and Benjamin Hammet Papers, PL; Lawrence F. Brewster, "Planters From the Low-Country and Their Summer Travels," in *The Proceedings of the South Carolina Historical Association* (Columbia: South Carolina Historical Association, 1943), p. 35.

92. "Document B, copy 2, accompanying Gov. Thomas Bennett's MS message no. 2 to the Senate and House of Representatives," Legislative Papers, South Carolina Archives, June-July trials, p. 21, quoted in Freehling, "Denmark Vesey's Reality," pp. 38–39.

93. Freehling, "Denmark Vesey's Reality," p. 39.

94. Higginson, *Black Rebellion*, pp. 174, 180.

95. "The Confession of Mr. Enslows Boy John—1822," William and Benjamin Hammet Papers, PL; Starobin, *Denmark Vesey*, pp. 1–2; Genovese, *From Rebellion to Revolution*, p. 48.

96. Easterby, *South Carolina Rice Plantation*, p. 7; Genovese, *From Rebellion to Revolution*, pp. 69, 76; Aptheker, *To Be Free*, pp. 11, 17; Gregorie, *History of Sumter*, p. 144.

97. Captain Thomas G. Allen, Combahee Rangers, Camp Hanckel, to General Walker, February 3, 1863, Francis W. Pickens and Milledge L. Bonhan Papers, p. 410, LC.

98. James M. McKim, *The Freed Men of South Carolina* (Philadelphia: Willis P. Hazard, 1862), p. 19; Thomas Wentworth Higginson, *Army Life in a Black Regiment* (Boston: Beacon Press, 1962), p. 248 (originally published in 1869); Wilmore, *Black Religion*, pp. 69–72; James H. Cone, *The Spirituals and the Blues: An Interpretation* (New York: The Seabury Press, 1972), pp. 25, 90–91, 147; Eric Perkins, "Roll, Jordan, Roll: A 'Marx' for the Master Class," *RHR*, 3 (Fall 1976), 55; Eugene D. Genovese, "The Legacy of Slavery and the Roots of Black Nationalism," *SL*, 6 (November–December 1966), 6, 10; Genovese, *Roll, Jordan, Roll*, pp. 259, 657; Genovese, *From Rebellion to Revolution*, pp. 7–8, 28, 49–50; Peter Kolchin, *Unfree Labor: American Slavery and Russian Serfdom* (Cambridge: The Belknap Press of Harvard University Press, 1987), pp. 252–53.

99. Genovese, *From Rebellion to Revolution*, pp. 15–17; *The Rising Sun*, November 14, 1860, cited in Henry, *Police Control*, p. 161; Stroyer, *My Life in the*

South, p. 65; Cook, *Life of David Williams*, p. 130, cited in Aptheker, *American Slave Revolts*, pp. 258–59; Rachel Blanding, Camden, to Hannah Lewis, [Philadelphia], July 4, 1816, William Blanding Papers, SC; *An Account of the Late Insurrection*, in *Slave Insurrections*, p. 25; "The Confession of Mr. Enslows Boy John—1822," William and Benjamin Hammet Papers, PL; Anna Hayes Johnson, Charleston, S.C., to Eliza Eagles Haywood, Raleigh, N.C., July 24, 1822, Ernest Haywood Collection, SHC; Inabinet, " 'The July Fourth Incident,' " p. 11.

100. Hildreth, *Despotism in America*, pp. 89–90; Kershaw County: MS, July 3–17, 1816, SC; Michael S. Hindus, "Black Justice Under White Law: Criminal Prosecutions of Blacks in Antebellum South Carolina," *JAH*, LXIII (December 1976), 594; Inabinet, " 'The July Fourth Incident,' " pp. 4–5; Rachel Blanding, Camden, to Hannah Lewis, [Philadelphia], July 4, 1816, William Blanding Papers, SC; *An Account of the Late Insurrection*, in *Slave Insurrections*, p. 28; Buckingham, *The Slave States*, I, p. 570; W. Hasell Wilson, Philadelphia, to Rev. Dr. Robert Wilson, Charleston, n.d., Robert Wilson Correspondence, CLS; Gwinn, "The Georgetown Insurrection," in Joyner, "Black Carolinians," pp. 1–2, SC.

101. L. Kennedy, Thomas Parker, William Drayton, Nathaniel Heyward, J. R. Pringle, H. Deos, and Robert J. Turnbull to Governor Thomas Bennett, July 24, 1822, South Carolina Archives Division, cited in Wade, "The Vesey Plot," p. 129; Buckingham, *The Slave States*, I, p. 570.

102. Anna Hayes Johnson, Charleston, S.C., to Eliza Eagles Haywood, Raleigh, N.C., July 27, 1822, Ernest Haywood Collection, SHC.

103. Starobin, *Denmark Vesey*, p. 8.

104. Ibid.

105. Kershaw County: MS, July 5, 1816, SC; Hindus, *JAH*, 593.

106. "Memoirs of S. W. Ferguson," pp. 13–14, Heyward and Ferguson Family Papers, SHC; Kinlock v. Harvey, Harper, 2d ed. 508, January 1830, in Catterall, *Judicial Cases*, II, pp. 340–41; *Account of the Late Insurrection*, in *Slave Insurrections*, p. 26.

107. Inabinet, " 'The July Fourth Incident,' " p. 12.

108. An Inhabitant of Florida, Zaphaniah Kingsley, *A Treatise on the Patriarchal, or Co-operative System of Society as it Exists in Some Governments . . . Under the Name of Slavery, With Its Necessity and Advantages*, 2d ed. (Freeport, N.Y.: Books for Libraries Press, 1970), pp. 8–9 (originally published in 1829); "Petition of Edward Brailsford," November 26, 1816, General Assembly Petitions, SCA; E. Franklin Frazier, "The Negro Slave Family," *JNH*, 15 (1930), 233–34, 255, cited in John White, "Review Article: Whatever Happened to the Slave Family in the Old South?" *JAS*, 8 (1974), 385–86, 388; DuBois, *Black Reconstruction*, p. 12; *Account of the Late Insurrection*, in *Slave Insurrections*, p. 26.

109. Harriott Pinckney, Charleston, to Mr. Winningham, Pinckney Island, March 25, 1855, Harriott Pinckney Papers, SC.

110. Furman, *Exposition*, p. 6.

111. Higginson, *Black Rebellion*, p. 132.

112. Wood, *Black Majority*, pp. 300–4; W. E. Burghardt DuBois, *The Suppression of the African Slave Trade to the United States of America, 1638–1870* (New York: Schocken Books, 1969), pp. 5–6, 9–11 (originally published in 1896); Wish, "American Slave Insurrections," pp. 26–27; Starobin, "Denmark Vesey's Conspiracy," p. 145; Genovese, *From Rebellion to Revolution*, pp. 42–43,

113–14; Saunders Redding, *They Came in Chains: Americans From Africa* (Philadelphia: J. B. Lippincott Company, 1950), pp. 29–31.

113. Meaders, *JNH*, 288, 292; Genovese, *Roll, Jordan, Roll,* pp. 648–49; Wood, *Black Majority,* pp. 248, 301–2; DuBois, *The Suppression,* pp. 5–6; Eugene D. Genovese, "Rebelliousness and Docility in the Negro Slave: A Critique of the Elkins Thesis," *CWH,* 13 (1967), 307; Genovese, *SL,* 5; Freehling, *Prelude to the Civil War,* p. 53; Ball, *Fifty Years in Chains,* pp. 219–21; Buckingham, *The Slave States,* II, p. 30; Pierce, *AM,* 300–1.

114. Letters of An American Traveller, I, p. 5, CLS.

115. Farley, *Afro-American Studies,* 199; Thomas J. Kirkland and Robert M. Kennedy, *Historic Camden* (Columbia: The State Company, 1926), II, pp. 188–89; Rachel Blanding, Camden, to Hannah Lewis, [Philadelphia], July 4, 1816, William Blanding Papers, SC; *Account of the Late Insurrection,* in *Slave Insurrections,* pp. 3–8; William Jones, Goshen, Lincoln County, Ga., to Langdon Cheves, Philadelphia, July 28, 1822, Cheves Family Papers, SCHS; Gwinn, "The Georgetown Insurrection," in Joyner, "Black Carolinians," pp. 1–2, SC; "Petition of the Delegation from Prince George Winyah," Slavery Files, SCA.

116. Bradley, "Slave Manumission," pp. 38–40, 58; "Petition for the Pardon of Monday Gell, Charles Drayton, and Harry Haig to the Governor of South Carolina, July 24, 1822," South Carolina Archives Division, cited in Wade, "The Vesey Plot," pp. 130, 133–34; "Melancholy Effect of Popular Excitement," The Charleston *Courier,* July 21, 1822; "Petition of Joseph L. Enslow for Compensation for a Slave Dying in Jail," 1831, (Folder 83), Slavery Files, SCA; (Case 231), October 11, 1860, Spartanburg Court Records, SCA; Rawick, *The American Slave,* III, iv, pp. 112–13; Smith, *A Charlestonian's Recollections,* p. 35; Dr. John Peyre Thomas Diary of Weather and Occurences, St. John's Parish (Berkeley), October 1828–August 1829, April 7, 1829, II, pp. 69–70, Thomas Family Papers, SC; David Gavin Diary, November 19, 1862, II, p. 337, SHC.

117. "Petition that Negroes Jack and Tom Be Rewarded for Taking and Dispersing a Gang of Runaways," Slavery Files, SCA.

118. Inabinet, "'The July Fourth Incident,'" pp. 2–3, 14–16.

119. Kenneth M. Stampp, *The Peculiar Institution: Slavery in the Ante-Bellum South* (New York: Vintage Books, 1956), p. 327.

120. "Petition of the Rev. Richard Johnson, St. Matthew's Parish," December 12, 1838, (Folder 104), Slavery Files, SCA.

121. Inabinet, "'The July Fourth Incident,'" p. 5.

122. Higginson, *Army Life,* p. 248.

123. Thomas Holt, *Black Over White: Negro Political Leadership in South Carolina During Reconstruction* (Urbana: University of Illinois Press, 1977), pp. 48, appendix A.

124. "Testimony of Robert Smalls," pp. 105–6, NA.

125. Furman, *Exposition,* p. 5.

126. *Account of the Late Insurrection,* in *Slave Insurrections,* p. 24.

127. Gillam v. Caldwell, 11 Rich. Eq. 73, May 1859, in Catterall, *Judicial Cases,* II, p. 464.

128. Hildreth, *Despotism in America,* p. 43; Nowell v. O'Hara, 1 Hill 150, April 1833, in Catterall, *Judicial Cases,* II, p. 352; D'Oyley v. Loveland, 1 Strobhart 45, November 1846, in Catterall, *Judicial Cases,* II, p. 401; Deloach v. Turner, 6 Richardson 117, January 1853, in Catterall, *Judicial Cases,* II, p. 435; Hinton

v. Kennedy, 3 S.C. 459, November 1871; Will, 1855, in Catterall, *Judicial Cases*, II, p. 477; The Editor, "Our Slaves," *SA*, 2 (December 1829), 575; Plantation Journal, May 9, November 24, December 29, 1856, Samuel Porcher Gaillard Plantation Journals, SC; Smith, *A Charlestonian's Recollections*, p. 36; James Stirling, *Letters From the Slave States* (London: John W. Parker and Son, 1857), p. 298; William Capers, Gowrie Plantation, to Charles Manigault, Charleston, S.C., September 15, 1863, in Phillips, *Plantation Documents*, II, pp. 32–33; John W. Blassingame, "Status and Social Structure in the Slave Community: Evidence From New Sources," in Harry P. Owens, ed., *Perspectives and Irony in American Slavery* (Jackson: University Press of Mississippi, 1976), pp. 149–51.

129. Plantation Journal, May 9, November 24, 1856, Samuel Porcher Gaillard Plantation Journals, SC; Owens, *This Species of Property*, p. 87; [Petition of 23 Christ Church Planters], MS, cited in Aptheker, *To Be Free*, pp. 22–24; Gregorie, *History of Sumter*, p. 144.

130. It may very well be that these were also the brightest slaves. As a Southern editor observed regarding South Carolina and Georgia captives: "It is a melancholy fact, that a large proportion of our ablest and most intelligent slaves are annually sent out of the State for misconduct, . . . and we earnestly call the attention of the legislature to this view of the subject." The Editor, *SA*, 575.

Chapter 7. Born a Child of Freedom, Yet a Slave

1. "Southern Slavery," The Pendleton *Messenger*, August 31, 1831.

2. Sir Ernest Barker, ed., *Social Contract: Essays by Locke, Hume and Rousseau* (London: Oxford University Press, 1979), pp. 172–73, 175.

3. David Brion Davis, *The Problem of Slavery in Western Culture* (Ithaca: Cornell University Press, 1966), pp. 413–14; Barker, *Social Contract*, pp. 171–72.

4. Richard Hildreth, *Despotism in America; Or An Inquiry Into the Nature and Results of the Slave-holding System in the United States* (Boston: Whipple and Damrell, 1840), pp. 89, 164.

5. An Inhabitant of Florida, Zaphaniah Kingsley, *A Treatise on the Patriarchal, or Co-operative System of Society As It Exists in Some Governments . . . Under the Name of Slavery, With Its Necessity and Advantages*, 2d ed. (Freeport, N.Y.: Books for Libraries Press, 1970), pp. 3, 6–9, 16 (originally published in 1829).

6. "Southern Slavery," Pendleton *Messenger*.

7. 1 Dudley (Law), 84, quoted in H. M. Henry, *The Police Control of the Slave in South Carolina* (New York: Negro Universities Press, 1968), p. 13 (originally published in 1914).

8. Robert F. W. Allston, Chicora Wood, to Sarah Carr, January 14, 1859, in J. H. Easterby, ed., *The South Carolina Rice Plantation as Revealed in the Papers of Robert F. W. Allston* (Chicago: University of Chicago Press, 1945), p. 152.

9. Harriet Martineau, *Society in America* (London: Saunders and Otley, 1837), II, pp. 152–53.

10. Charles Ball, *Fifty Years in Chains*, with an introduction by Philip S. Foner (New York: Dover Publications, 1970), p. 87 (originally published in 1837); Alice R. Huger Smith, *A Carolina Rice Plantation of the Fifties . . . With Chapters From the Unpublished Memoirs of D. E. Huger Smith* (New York: William Morrow and Company, 1936), p. 34.

11. Ball, *Fifty Years in Chains*, pp. 268, 298–99. ·

12. Charles M. Wiltse, *John C. Calhoun: Nationalist, 1782–1823* (New York: The Bobbs-Merrill Company, 1944), p. 342.

13. John C. Calhoun, Washington, to John Ewing Colhoun, January 15, 1827, Calhoun Family Typescripts.

14. Robert Nicholas Olsberg, "A Government of Class and the South Carolina Chivalry, 1860–1865" (Ph.D. dissertation, University of South Carolina, 1972), p. 132.

15. Plantation Records, Silver Bluff, S.C., December 8, 1831–December 31, 1855, December 25, 1854, p. 500, James Henry Hammond Papers, SC.

16. Thomas Green Clemson, Terveuren, Belgium, to John C. Calhoun, September 1845, Calhoun Family Typescripts.

17. "Record of Windsor Plantation," January 4, 1841, John B. Irving Record of Windsor and Kensington Plantations, CLS.

18. Plantation Journal, 1835–1845, "List of Slaves," January 18, 1836, Samuel Porcher Gaillard Plantation Journals, 1835–1868, SC.

19. A.S.D., "On Raising Negroes," *SA*, XI (February 1838), 77–78; An Inhabitant of Florida, *A Treatise*, p. 3; "Governor Hammond's Letters on Slavery, no. 3: Physical and Moral Condition of Southern Slaves Compared With English Laborers; Schemes of Abolition; Moral Suasion; Force; Competition of Free Labor; West India Emancipation," *DR*, o.s., VIII (February 1850), 122–25; Robert W. Fogel and Stanley L. Engerman, *Time On the Cross: The Economics of American Negro Slavery* (Boston: Little, Brown, and Company, 1974), pp. 106–26, 145–47, 244.

20. Rev. Richard Fuller and Rev. Francis Wayland, *Domestic Slavery Considered As A Scriptural Institution* (New York: Lewis Colby, 1845), p. 163.

21. Account Book Kept by Dr. W. W. Anderson, 1815–1819 [and] Slave Book & Notes on Operation by W. W. Anderson, June 14, 1830, Borough House Papers (microfilm), SHC; George P. Rawick, ed., *The American Slave: A Composite Autobiography* (Westport, Conn.: Greenwood Publishing Company, 1972), III, iii, p. 269; Henry Rowe Schoolcraft, *Plantation Life: The Narratives of Mrs. Henry Rowe Schoolcraft, 1852–1860* (New York: Negro Universities Press, 1969), p. 113; Wade Hampton, III, to Mary Fisher Hampton, Wild Woods, [Miss.], February 14, 1857, in Charles E. Cauthen, ed., *Family Letters of the Three Wade Hamptons, 1782–1901* (South Caroliniana Series, Columbia: University of South Carolina Press, 1953), p. 43; James Ladson, Charleston, to William Elliot, May 14, 1851, Elliot-Gonzales Papers, SHC.

22. Ball, *Fifty Years in Chains*, pp. 207–8, 319.

23. Ray Allen Billington, ed., *The Journal of Charlotte L. Forten: A Free Negro in the Slave Era* (New York: Collier Books, 1961), pp. 32, 151.

24. A. M. French, *Slavery in South Carolina and the Ex-Slaves: Or, The Port Royal Mission* (New York: Negro Universities Press, 1969), pp. 49–50 (originally published in 1862).

25. Smelie v. Reynolds, 2 Desaussure 66, January 1802, (70), in Helen T. Catterall, ed., *Judicial Cases Concerning American Slavery and the Negro* (Washington, D.C.: Carnegie Institute of Washington, 1929), II, p. 281.

26. "For Sale, Belonging to An Estate," The Charleston *Mercury,* September 24, 1829.

27. Robert F. W. Allston, Matanza, to Alexander W. Campbell, February 2, 1837, in Easterby, *South Carolina Rice Plantation*, pp. 152, 384.

28. "Dr. T. Stillman's Medical Infirmary for Diseases of the Skin," The Charleston *Mercury,* October 12, 1838.

29. *Annual Announcement of the Trustees and Faculty of the Medical College of*

the State of South Carolina, for the Session of 1837–38 (Charleston: James S. Burges, 1837), p. 16; Robert W. Gibbes, Jr., Charleston, to James Sanders Guignard III, December 14, 1850, Guignard Family Papers, SC; "Medical College of South Carolina," The Charleston *Mercury,* January 10, 1829; "Medical Intelligence," *CJM,* n.s., I (1826), 200.

30. Prospectus of South Carolina Medical College, quoted in *American Slavery As It Is: Testimony of a Thousand Witnesses* (New York: American Anti-Slavery Society, 1839), p. 169.

31. Rev. Robert Wilson, M.D., D.D., "Their Shadowy Influence Still Hovers About Medical College," Charleston *News & Courier,* April 13, 1913.

32. "Southern Slavery," The Pendleton *Messenger,* August 31, 1831; Bobby Frank Jones, "A Cultural Middle Passage: Slave Marriage and Family in the Ante-Bellum South" (Ph.D. dissertation, University of North Carolina, 1965), pp. 6–8.

33. Edward Thomas Heriot, George Town, South Carolina, to [unknown], [Great Britain?], April 20, 1853, Edward Thomas Heriot Papers, PL.

34. Journal of Thomas B. Chaplin, 1845–1886, May 3, 5, 1850, p. 285, SCHS.

35. Archie Vernon Huff, *Langdon Cheves of South Carolina* (Columbia: University of South Carolina Press, 1977), p. 156.

36. Langdon Cheves, Portman Shoals, to Langdon Cheves, Jr., Savannah, April 19, 1845, Cheves Family Papers, SCHS.

37. Harry Hammond, "Biography of James Henry Hammond," 1908 (transcript), p. 1, James Henry Hammond Papers, SC.

38. Plantation Records, Silver Bluff, SC., December 8, 1831–December 31, 1855, April 29, 1844, p. 291, James H. Hammond Papers, SC.

39. Plantation Records, January 2, 1843, p. 245, James H. Hammond Papers, SC.

40. Ibid., January 11, 1848, August 7, 1849, pp. 389, 423.

41. Diary: 1841–1846, September 4, 1841, James Henry Hammond Papers, LC.

42. David Gavin Diary, 1855–1871, November 25, 1855, I (typescript), p. 11, SHC; Charlotte Ann Allston, Mantanza, to Robert F. W. Allston, April 3, 1823, in Easterby, *South Carolina Rice Plantation,* p. 59; Hal Sonbeck to I. L. Broods [sic], Hamburg, S.C., April 17, 1850, Ivenson Lewis Brookes Papers, SHC; W. Sweet, N[ightin]gale Hall, to Adele Petigru Allston, November 23, 1864, in Easterby, *South Carolina Rice Plantation,* p. 316.

43. Langdon Cheves, Portman Shoals, to Langdon Cheves, Jr., Savannah, February 14, 1842, Cheves Family Papers, SCHS.

44. Thomas Porcher of Ophir: Plantation Diary, Notes, and Records, April 17, 1824, III, Stoney and Porcher Papers (microfilm), SHC.

45. Keating S. Ball Plantation Daybook, Comingtree, Cooper River, St. John's Berkeley, March 5, 1849, March 9, 1850, V, pp. 13, 48, John Ball and Keating S. Ball Books, 1779–1884, SHC.

46. Plantation Journal, 1856–1858, May 5, 1856, Samuel Porcher Gaillard Plantation Journals, SC; "Kensington," March 1, 1846, John B. Irving Record of Windsor and Kensington Plantations, CLS; Plantation Journals of Daniel Cannon Webb, 1818–1850, June 15, 1823, I, SCHS.

47. Journal of Dr. James Stuart of Beaufort, S.C., 1814, July 2, 1814 (typescript), pp. 4–5, SCHS.

48. Ibid., p. 5.

49. Eugene D. Genovese, *Roll, Jordan, Roll: The World the Slaves Made* (New York: Pantheon Books, 1974), pp. 3–7, 658–60.

50. Ibid., pp. 5, 658.

51. Ibid., p. 7.

52. Eric Perkins, "Roll, Jordan, Roll: A 'Marx' for the Master Class," *RHR*, 3 (Fall 1976), 47; Herbert G. Gutman, *The Black Family in Slavery & Freedom, 1750–1925* (New York: Pantheon Books, 1976), p. 313.

53. Charles C. Jones, *The Religious Instruction of the Negroes* (New York: Negro Universities Press, 1969), p. 207 (originally published in 1842).

54. Bryan Edwards, *The History, Civil and Commercial of the British Colonies in the West Indies* (London: John Stockdale, 1801), 2, pp. 162–63; R. R. Madden, *A Twelve-month's Residence in the West Indies, During the Transition From Slavery to Apprenticeship* . . . (Westport, Conn.: Negro Universities Press, 1970), II, pp. 181–82 (originally published in 1835); Sidney Mintz and Richard Price, *An Anthropological Approach to the Afro-American Past: A Caribbean Perspective* (Philadelphia Institute for the Study of Human Issues, 1976), p. 38; Orlando Patterson, *The Sociology of Slavery: An Analysis of the Origins, Development and Structure of Negro Slave Society, in Jamaica* (London: Macgibbon & Kee, 1967), pp. 80, 171, 216, 221; John Bigelow, *Jamaica in 1850: The Effects of Sixteen Years of Freedom on a Slave Colony* (Westport, Conn.: Negro Universities Press, 1970), p. 79 (originally published in 1851); H. P. Jacobs, *Sixty Years of Change, 1806–1866: Progress and Reaction in Kingston and the Countryside* (Jamaica: Institute of Jamaica, 1973), p. 12.

55. French, *Slavery in South Carolina*, pp. 56, 60–61; Elizabeth W. Allston Pringle, *Chronicles of Chicora Wood* (New York: Charles Scribner's Sons, 1922), pp. 252–53.

56. Jacob Stroyer, *My Life in the South* (Salem, Mass.: Observer and Job Print, 1885), p. 31.

57. Mary Boykin Chesnut, *A Diary From Dixie*, eds. Isabella D. Martin and Myrta Locket Avery (Gloucester, Mass.: Peter Smith, 1961), p. 93.

58. Elizabeth Hyde Botume, *First Days Amongst the Contrabands* (New York: Arno Press and The New York Times, 1968), pp. 6–7 (originally published in 1892).

59. Henry William Ravenel, "Recollections of Southern Plantation Life," *TYR*, XXV (June 1936), 758.

60. Chesnut, *A Diary From Dixie*, p. 225; William Watts Ball, *The State That Forgot: South Carolina's Surrender to Democracy* (Indianapolis: The Bobbs-Merrill Company, 1932), pp. 117, 127; S. H. Boineau, Combahee, to [Charles] Heyward, January 6, 1865, Heyward Family Papers, SC.

61. Mrs. O. T. Porcher, Pineville, to "My Dear Children," March 29, 1865, Octavius Thomas Porcher Papers, SC.

62. H. H. Manigault, Adams Run [St. Paul's Parish, S.C.], to John Berkley Grimball, July 14, 1863, John Berkley Grimball Papers, PL.

63. James M. McKim, *The Freed Men of South Carolina* (Philadelphia: Willis P. Hazard, 1862), p. 19.

64. Botume, *First Days Amongst the Contrabands*, p. 55.

65. Pringle, *Chronicles of Chicora Wood*, p. 233; Leon Stone Bryan, Jr., "Slavery On a Peedee River Rice Plantation, 1825–1865" (M.A. thesis, Johns Hopkins University, 1963), pp. 166–67; Patton, Frog Line, S.C., to Brother William, June 21, 1865, Young Family Papers, SCHS; Joe M. Richardson, *Christian Reconstruction: The American Missionary Association and Southern Blacks, 1861–1890* (Athens: The University of Georgia Press, 1986), pp. 6–8; Chesnut, *A Diary From Dixie*, p. 397.

66. Rawick, *The American Slave*, II, i, p. 231.

67. Ball, *Fifty Years in Chains*, p. 36.

68. Plantation Journals of Daniel Cannon Webb, 1818–1850, December 31, 1850, IV, SCHS.

69. J. A. Hemingway, Chiney Grove, to Robert F. W. Allston, May 7, 1855, in Easterby, *South Carolina Rice Plantation*, p. 260; F. W. Pickens, Edgewood, S.C., to John C. Calhoun, October 2, 1841, in Chauncey S. Boucher and Robert P. Brooks, eds., "Correspondence Addressed to John C. Calhoun, 1831–1849," in *Annual Report of the American Historical Association for the Year 1929* (Washington, D.C.: Government Printing Office, 1930), p. 161; George W. Williams, ed., *Incidents In My Life: The Autobiography of The Rev. Paul Trapier, S.T.D. With Some of His Letters* (Charleston: Dalcho Historical Society, 1954), p. 12; Journal of Thomas Chaplin, May 3, 1845, p. 28, SCHS.

70. Billington, *Journal of Charlotte L. Forten*, p. 37.

71. Orland Kay Armstrong, *Old Massa's People: The Old Slaves Tell Their Story* (Indianapolis: The Bobbs-Merrill Company, 1931), p. 207.

72. John Bratton, Camp Near Germantown, to Bettie Bratton, October 13, 1861, John Bratton Correspondence, 1861–1865 (typescript), p. 41, SHC.

73. Will Book "C" and "A," 1791–1834, I, p. 32, Wills: Records of Old Pendleton District, Anderson County, APL.

74. Fred Siegal, "Paramaters for Paternalism," *RHR*, 3 (Fall 1976), 61–64; Gutman, *The Black Family*, pp. 309–16; Perkins, *RHR*, 56–57. One should also note, as James Oakes observed in his discussion of the compulsive migrations of slaveowners, that "it was not uncommon for planters to sell all their slaves before a major move." James Oakes, *The Ruling Race: A History of American Slaveholders* (New York: Alfred A. Knopf, 1982), p. 178.

75. William K. Scarborough, "Slavery—The White Man's Burden," in Harry P. Owens, ed., *Perspectives and Irony in American Slavery* (Jackson: University Press of Mississippi, 1976), pp. 108–9.

76. Thomas Wentworth Higginson, *Army Life in A Black Regiment* (Boston: Beacon Press, 1962), p. 249.

77. "Southern Mutual Insurance Company Policy," July 7, 1852, (Folder 15), Slavery Files, SCA.

78. William J. Faulkner, *The Days When the Animals Talked: Black American Folktales and How They Came to Be* (Chicago: Follett Publishing Company, 1977), p. 4.

79. E. C. L. Adams, *Nigger to Nigger* (New York: Charles Scribner's Sons, 1929), pp. 251–52.

80. Untitled pamphlet, quoted in Thomas Wentworth Higginson, *Black Rebellion* (New York: Arno Press and The New York Times, 1969), p. 129 (originally published as a series of articles in the *Atlantic Monthly* during the 1850s and 1860s).

Bibliography

Primary Sources

Manuscripts

Anderson Public Library, Anderson, South Carolina
Wills: Records of Old Pendleton District, Anderson County/Will Book "C" and "A",
1791–1834.

Charleston Library Society, Charleston, South Carolina
Life and Recollections of Joseph Barnwell. 2 volumes (Typescripts).
George I. Crafts Correspondence, 1846–1847. (Typescript).
John Berkley Grimball Diary, 1832–1884. 2 volumes (Typescript).
Meta Morris Grimball Journal, December 1860–February 1866.
John B. Irving: Record of Windsor and Kensington Plantations.
Letters of An American Traveller, Containing a Brief Sketch of the Most Remarkable
    Places in Various Parts of the United States & the Canadas . . . Written During an
    Excursion in the Year 1810. (Typescript).
W. St. Julian Mazyck: "St. Mary's Chapel, Hagley Plantation," n.d. (Typescript).
Robert Wilson Correspondence.

College of Charleston Library, Charleston, South Carolina
Charles Fraser: Commonplace Book, 1800–1819.

Duke University, Durham, North Carolina: William R. Perkins Library
Milledge Luke Bonham Papers.
John Fox Papers.
McDonald Furman Papers.
John Berkley Grimball Papers.
William and Benjamin Hammet Papers.
Edward Thomas Heriot Papers.
John Hollingsworth Papers, 1807–1880.
John H. Howard Papers, 1848–1880.
Edward Wilkinson Kinsley Papers.
Louis Manigault Papers.
Marshall Family Papers.
Milford Baptist Church Minutes, 1831–1868.
Jacob Rhett Motte Letters and Papers.
John O'Neale Papers. (Typescript).
Lalla Pelot Papers.
William W. Renwick Papers.
Rockingham Plantation Journal, 1828–1829.
Daniel Ruggles Papers.

Library of Congress, Washington, D.C.
Edward Frost Papers.
James Henry Hammond Papers.
Ester H. Hawks Papers.
John Auchintoss Inglis Papers.
William Lowndes Papers.
Francis W. Pickens and Milledge L. Bonham Papers.
The Pinckney Family Papers.

Medical University of South Carolina Library, Charleston, South Carolina
H. D. McCloud. "Hints on the Medical Treatment of Negroes." Senior Thesis, Medical College of South Carolina, 1850.
H. Perry Pope. "A Dissertation on the Professional Management of Negro Slaves." Senior Thesis, Medical College of South Carolina, 1837.

National Archives, Washington, D.C.
American Freedmen's Inquiry Commission: Testimony. (Microfilm). Reel 200, File III.

South Carolina Department of Archives and History, Columbia, South Carolina
G. Buist/Ordinary. Inventories, Appraisements and Sales—D., 1854–1857.
Court of Magistrates and Freeholders Records. (Microfilm).
General Assembly/Accounts—Constables, 1803/5–6.
General Assembly Petitions.
Slavery Files, 1830–1859.

South Carolina Historical Society, Charleston, South Carolina
R. F. W. Allston Papers.
Journal of Thomas B. Chaplin, 1845–1886.
Chesnut-Miller-Manning Papers.
Cheves Family Papers.
Coffin Point Records, 1800–1821.
Charles Graves Diary, 1846–1855.
Randall Hunt: Journal of A Traveller From Charleston, South Carolina, to New Haven, Connecticut, 1832.
Mulberry Plantation Journals, 1853–1889. 4 volumes.
Pineville Association–St. John's & St. Stephens, Berkeley, 1823–1840 and Police Association–St. John's, Berkeley, 1839–1852.
Richmond Plantation Overseer's Book, 1859–1860.
South Carolina Agricultural Society Records, 1825–1860.
Journal of Dr. James Stuart of Beaufort, S.C., 1814. (Typescript).
Vestry Journal of All Saints, Waccamaw, Georgetown, 1844–1872. (Typescript).
Daniel Cannon Webb Plantation Journals, 1818–1850. 6 volumes.
Dr. Joshua Barker Whitridge Letters, 1806–1864.
Winyah and All Saints Agricultural Society Minutes, 1842–1861.
Young Family Papers.

University of North Carolina, Chapel Hill: Southern Historical Collection
John Durant Ashmore Plantation Journal, 1853–1859. (Typescript).
John and Keating S. Ball Books, 1779–1884.
Grace Pierson (James) Beard Reminiscences, n.d. (Typescript).
Borough House Papers.
John Bratton Correspondence, 1861–1865. (Typescript).
Iveson Lewis Brookes Papers.
John Hamilton Cornish Papers. (Typescript).
James M. Dabbs Papers: David F. Thorpe Series.
Louis M. DeSaussure Plantation Record, 1835–1865. (Typescript).
Edgefield (S.C.) Military Record.
Elliot-Gonzales Papers.
David Gavin Diary, 1855–1871.
David Golightly Harris Farm Journals. (Microfilm).
Gregorie-Elliot Papers.
Ernest Haywood Collection.
Heyward and Ferguson Family Papers. (Typescripts and Microfilm).
William P. Hill Diary, 1846–1849.
Charles Woodward Hutson Papers.
Alexander Robert Lawton Papers.
John Sidney A. S. Legaré Memoirs, n.d. (Typescript).
James S. Milling Papers.
Sparkman Family Papers.
William E. Sparkman Plantation Record, 1844–1866.
Stoney and Porcher Papers. (Microfilm).
James R. Stuart Recollections. (Typescript).

University of South Carolina, Columbia: South Caroliniana Library
Baptist Church: Anderson County—Big Creek Baptist Church, 1801–1936. (Typescript).
Baptist Church: Barnwell County—Barnwell Baptist Church Minutes, 1803–1912. (Typescript).
Baptist Church: Black Creek Church Book, 1828–1922. Beaufort County. (Typescript).
Baptist Church: Church of Christ Records, 1794–1937. Poplar Springs, Laurens County. (Typescript).
Baptist Church: Ebenezer Baptist Church Records, 1823–1860. Darlington County. (Typescript).
Baptist Church: Euhaw Baptist Church Book, 1831–1875. Euhaw, Beaufort District.
Baptist Church: MS, May 17, 1823.
Baptist Church: New Providence Baptist Church Minutes, 1808–1922. Darlington County. (Typescript).
Baptist Church: Welsh Neck Baptist Church Minutes, 1737–1935. Society Hill, Darlington County.
William Blanding Papers.
Bratton Family Papers.
Bruce, Jones, and Murchison Papers.

Charleston Scrapbook: Clippings Chiefly From Charleston Newspapers, 1800–1810.
John Ewing Colhoun Papers.
Bonds Conway Papers.
Cox Papers: Transcripts and Abstracts of Miscellaneous Papers, chiefly of The Cox Family 1791–1883. 2 volumes. (Typescripts).
Farmer's Club (ABC Farmer's Club) Records, 1846–1893. Beech Island, Aiken County. (Typescript).
Andrew Flinn Plantation Book, 1840.
Fouche Family Papers.
Samuel Porcher Gaillard Plantation Journals, 1835–1868.
Guignard Family Papers.
Edward Spann Hammond Papers.
James Henry Hammond Papers.
Zelotus Lee Holmes Papers.
Heyward Family Papers.
Charles Joyner, ed. "Black Carolinians: Studies in the History of South Carolina Negroes in the Nineteenth Century." Laurinburg, North Carolina: St. Andrews Presbyterian College, 1969. (Typescript).
Kershaw County: MS, July 3–17, 1816.
Thomas Cassels Law Papers.
Mackay Family Papers.
Charles Manigault Papers.
Autobiography of Gabriel Manigault, 1836–1899. (Typescript).
Methodist Church: Darlington Circuit Quarterly Conference Minutes, 1841–1863. Florence County. (Typescript).
Methodist Church: Minutes of the Quarterly Conference, 1818–1838. The Camden M. E. Church. (Typescript).
Williams Middleton Papers.
Thomas John Moore Papers.
Motte Family Papers.
Francis S. Parker Plantation Records, 1849–1865.
Pendleton Farmer's Society Records, 1824–1919. (Typescript).
Benjamin F. Perry Papers. (Typescript).
Pinckney Letter: MS, June 18, 1807.
Harriott Pinckney Papers.
Thomas Pinckney Papers.
Octavius Theodore Porcher Papers.
Presbyterian Church: Bethesda Presbyterian Church, 1806–1937, Camden, South Carolina. (Typescript).
Presbyterian Church: Fishing Creek Presbyterian Church, 1799–1859, Chester District. (Typescript).
Presbyterian Church: Records of Salem Presbyterian Church, 1808–1860. Black River. (Typescript).
Sams Family Papers.
John Stapleton Papers.
Rev. Clark B. Steward Journal/Diary, 1859. (Typescript).
Natalie de Delage Sumter Diary, 1840–1841.
Thomas Family Papers.
United States: W.P.A., Federal Writers' Project, S.C. Folklore MSS. (Typescript).
Williams-Chesnut-Manning Papers.
Witherspoon Family Papers.

University of South Carolina: Miscellaneous

John C. Calhoun Family Correspondence Typescripts. These documents were generously made available to me in 1977 by Dr. Clide Wilson who was then editing them at the University of South Carolina.

Waring Historical Library, Charleston,
South Carolina

William L. McCaa. "Observations on the Manner of Living and Diseases of the Slaves on the Wateree River." Thesis, University of Pennsylvania, 1823. (Typescript).

Plantation Manual of James H. Hammond of Beech Island, South Carolina, circa 1834. (Typescript).

Published Materials

Slave and Freedman Testimony: Autobiographies, Narratives,
and Recollections

Armstrong, Orland Kay. *Old Massa's People: The Old Slaves Tell Their Story.* Indianapolis: The Bobbs-Merrill Company, 1931.

Ball, Charles, *Fifty Years in Chains.* Introduction by Philip S. Foner. New York: Dover Publications, Inc., 1970. Originally published in 1837.

Blassingame, John W., ed. *Slave Testimony: Two Centuries of Letters, Speeches, Interviews, and Autobiographies.* Baton Rouge: Louisiana State University Press, 1977.

Douglass, Frederick. *My Bondage and My Freedom.* New York: Dover Publications, 1969. Originally published in 1855.

Lowery, I. E., Reverend. *Life On the Old Plantation or A Story Based on Facts.* Columbia, S.C.: The State Company, 1911.

Rawick, George P., ed. *The American Slave: A Composite Autobiography.* 19 volumes. Westport, Conn.: Greenwood Publishing Company, 1972.

————., ed. *The American Slave: A Composite Autobiography.* Supplement, series 1. 12 volumes. Westport, Conn.: Greenwood Press, 1977.

Roper, Moses. *A Narrative of the Adventures and Escape of Moses Roper, From American Slavery.* New York: Negro Universities Press, 1970. Originally published in 1838.

Stroyer, Jacob. *My Life in the South.* Salem, Mass. Salem Observer and Job Print, 1885.

Williams, John B., Reverend. *"De Ole Plantation."* Charleston, S.C.: Walker, Evans & Cogswell, 1895.

Yetman, Norman R., ed. *Life Under the "Peculiar Institution": Selections From the Slave Narrative Collection.* New York: Holt, Rinehart, and Winston, 1970.

Planter Testimony: Speeches, Papers, Memoirs, Letters and Diaries

Boucher, Chauncey S., and Robert P. Brooks, eds. "Correspondence Addressed to John C. Calhoun, 1837–1849" in *Annual Report of the American Historical Association For the Year 1929.* Washington, D.C.: Government Printing Office, 1930.

Cauthen, Charles E., ed. *Family Letters of the Three Wade Hamptons, 1782–1901.* South Caroliniana Series. Columbia: University of South Carolina Press, 1953.

Chesnut, Mary Boykin. *A Diary From Dixie,* eds. Isabella D. Martin and Myrta Locket Avery. Gloucester, Mass.: Peter Smith, 1961.

Childs, Arney Robinson, ed. *The Private Journal of Henry William Ravenel, 1859–1887*. Columbia: University of South Carolina Press, 1947.

————. *Rice Planter and Sportsman: The Recollections of J. Motte Alston, 1821–1909*. Columbia: University of South Carolina Press, 1953.

Clinkscales, J. G. *On the Old Plantation: Reminiscences of His Childhood*. New York: Negro Universities Press, 1969. Originally published in 1916.

DeSaussure, N. B. *Old Plantation Days: Being Recollections of Southern Life Before the Civil War*. New York: Duffield & Company, 1909.

Easterby, J. H., ed. "Charles Cotesworth Pinckney's Plantation Diary, April 6–December 15, 1818," *The South Carolina Historical and Genealogical Magazine*, XLI (October 1940), 135–150.

————., ed. *The South Carolina Rice Plantation As Revealed in the Papers of Robert F. W. Allston*. Chicago: University of Chicago Press, 1945.

Edgar, Walter B., ed. *The Letterbook of Robert Pringle*. 2 volumes. Columbia: The University of South Carolina Press, 1972.

Fishburne, Ann Sinkler. *Belvidere: A Plantation Memory*. Columbia: University of South Carolina Press, 1949.

Irving, John B. *A Day on Cooper River*. Charleston, S.C.: A. E. Miller, 1842.

Lewis, Matthew G. *Journal of a West India Proprietor, Kept During a Residence in the Island of Jamaica*. New York: Negro Universities Press, 1969. Originally published in 1834.

Mikell, I. Jenkins. *Rumbling of the Chariot Wheels*. Columbia, S.C.: The State Company, 1923.

Myers, Robert Manson, ed. *The Children of Pride: A True Story of Georgia and the Civil War*. New Haven: Yale University Press, 1972.

Pinckney, Charles Cotesworth. *An Address Delivered in Charleston Before the Agricultural Society of South-Carolina . . . The 18th August, 1829*. Charleston: A. E. Miller, 1829.

Pringle, Elizabeth W. Allston. *Chronicles of Chicora Wood*. New York: Charles Scribner's Sons, 1922.

Ravenel, Henry Wilbam. "Recollections of Southern Plantation Life," *The Yale Review*, XXV (June 1936), 748–777.

Scott, Florence Johnson. "Letters and Papers of Governor David Johnson and Family, 1810–1855" in *The Proceeding of the South Carolina Historical Association*. Columbia: The South Carolina Historical Association, 1939.

Smith, Alice R. Huger. *A Carolina Rice Plantation of the Fifties . . . With Chatpers From the Unpublished Memoirs of D. E. Huger Smith*. New York: William Morrow and Company, 1936.

Smith, D. E. *A Charlestonian's Recollections, 1846–1913*. Charleston, S.C.: Carolina Art Association.

White, Mary, ed., *Fifteen Letters of Nathalie Sumter*. Columbia, S.C.: R. L. Bryan Company, 1942.

Contemporary Diaries, Correspondence, Memoirs, Monographs, and Political Tracts

Allen, William, and others. *Slave Songs of the United States*. New York: A. Simpson & Company, 1867.

American Historical Association. Diary of Edward Hooker, 1805–1808 in *Report of Historical Manuscripts Commission of the AHA for 1896*. Washington: Government Printing Office, 1897.

American Slavery As It Is: Testimony of A Thousand Witnesses. New York: Anti-Slavery Society, 1839.

Bearse, Austin. *Reminiscences of Fugitive-Slave Law Days.* Boston: Warren Richardson, 1880.

Bigelow, John. *Jamaica in 1850 or, The Effects of Sixteen Years of Freedom on a Slave Colony.* Westport, Conn.: Negro Universities Press, 1970. Originally published in 1851.

Billington, Ray Allen, ed. *The Journal of Charlotte L. Forten: A Free Negro in the Slave Era.* New York: Collier Books, 1961.

Botume, Elizabeth Hyde. *First Days Amongst the Contrabands.* New York: Arno Press and The New York Times, 1968. Originally published in 1892.

Carson, James Petigru. *Life, Letters and Speeches of James Louis Petigru: The Union Man of South Carolina.* Washington, D.C.: W. H. Lowdermilk & Company, 1920.

Collins, Elizabeth. *Memories of the Southern States.* Taunton: Barnicott, 1865.

Drayton, John. *A View of South-Carolina, As Respects Her Natural and Civil Concerns.* Charleston, S.C.: W. P. Young, 1802.

Edwards, Bryan. *The History, Civil and Commercial of the British Colonies in the West Indies.* 3 volumes. London: John Stockdale, 1801.

French, A. M. *Slavery in South Carolina and the Ex-Slaves or The Port Royal Mission.* New York: Negro Universities Press, 1969. Originally published in 1862.

Higginson, Thomas Wentworth. *Army Life in a Black Regiment.* Boston: Beacon Press, 1962. Originally published in 1869.

———. *Black Rebellion.* New York: Arno Press and The New York Times, 1969. Originally published as essays in the *Atlantic Monthly* during the 1850s and 1860s.

Hildreth, Richard. *Despotism in America; or An Inquiry Into the Nature and Results of the Slave-Holding System in the United States.* Boston: Whipple and Damrell, 1840.

Holland, Rupert Sargent, ed. *Letters and Diary of Laura M. Towne: Written From the Sea Islands of South Carolina, 1862–1884.* Cambridge: Riverside Press, 1912.

An Inhabitant of Florida, Zaphaniah Kingsley. *A Treatise on The Patriarchal, or Co-operative System of Society as It Exists in Some Governments . . . Under the Name of Slavery, With Its Necessity and Advantages.* 2d ed. Freeport, N.Y.: Books For Libraries Press, 1970. Originally published in 1829.

Kemble, Francis Anne. *Journal of a Residence on a Georgian Plantation in 1838–1839,* ed. John A. Scott. New York: Alfred A. Knopf, 1961.

Livermore, Mary A. *My Story of the War: A Woman's Narrative of Four Years Personal Experience.* Williamstown, Mass.: Corner House Publishers, 1978. Originally published in 1887.

McKim, James M. *The Freed Men of South Carolina.* Philadelphia: Willis P. Hazard, 1862.

Madden, R. R. *A Twelvemonth's Residence in the West Indies, During the Transition From Slavery to Apprenticeship . . .* 2 volumes. Westport, Conn.: Negro Universities Press, 1970. Originally published in 1835.

Mallett, William Wyndham. *An Errand to the South in the Summer of 1862.* London: Richard Bentley, 1863.

Nordhoff, Charles. "The Freedmen of South-Carolina" in Frank Moore, ed. *Papers of the Day.* New York: Charles T. Evans, 1863.

Pearson, Elizabeth Ware, ed. *Letters From Port Royal, 1862–1868.* New York: Arno Press and The New York Times, 1969. Originally published in 1906.

Phillippo, James M. *Jamaica: Its Past and Present State.* Philadelphia: James M. Campbell, 1843.

Pollard, Edward A. *Black Diamonds: Gathered in Darkey Homes of the South*. New York: Pudney & Russell, 1959.

Redpath, James. *The Roving Editor: or, Talks with Slaves in the Southern States*. New York: Negro Universities Press, 1968. Originally published in 1859.

Russell, William Howard. *My Diary North and South*. New York: Harper & Brothers, 1863.

Schoolcraft, Henry Rowe. *Plantation Life: The Narratives of Mrs. Henry Rowe Schoolcraft*. New York: Negro Universities Press, 1969. Originally published between 1852 and 1860.

A South-Carolinian (Edwin C. Holland). *A Refutation of the Calumnies Circulated Against the Southern & Western States . . . Together With Historical Notices of All the Insurrections That Have Taken Place Since the Settlement of the Country*. Charleston: A. E. Miller, 1822.

Sterne, Henry. *A Statement of Facts . . . With An Exposure of the Present System of Jamaica Apprenticeship*. New York: Negro Universities Press, 1969. Originally published in 1837.

Sturge, Joseph, and Thomas Harvey. *The West Indies in 1837 . . .* London: Frank Cass & Company, 1968. Originally published in 1838.

The Suppressed Book About Slavery! New York: Carleton, 1864.

Tower, Philo, Reverend. *Slavery Unmasked: Being a Truthful Narrative of A Three Years' Residence and Journeying in Eleven Southern States*. Rochester: Darrow & Brother, 1856.

Travel Accounts

Bernhard, Karl, Duke of Saxe-Weimar Eisenach. *Travels Through North America, During the Years 1825 and 1826*. 2 volumes. Philadelphia: Carey, Lea & Carey, 1828.

Bremer, Fredrika. *The Homes of the New World: Impressions of America*. Translated by Mary Howitt. 2 volumes. New York: Harper & Brothers, 1868.

Buckingham, J. S. *The Slave States of America*. 2 volumes. London: Fisher, Son, & Company, 1842.

Davis, John. *Travels of Four Years and a Half in the United States of America; During 1798, 1799, 1800, 1801, and 1802*. London, 1803.

Featherstonhaugh, G. W. *Excursion Through the Slave States*. 2 volumes. London: John Murray, 1844.

Hall, Basil, Captain. *Travels in North America, in the Years 1827 and 1828*. 3 volumes. Edinburgh: Cadell and Company, 1829.

Hodgson, Adam. *Remarks During A Journey Through North America in the Years 1819, 1820, and 1821 . . .* New York: Samuel Whiting, 1823.

Knepper, George W., ed. *Travels in the Southland, 1822–1823: The Journal of Lucius Versus Bierce*. Columbus: Ohio State University Press, 1966.

Lyell, Charles. *A Second Visit to the United States*. 2 volumes. New York: Harper & Brothers, 1849.

———. *Travels in North America, in the Years 1841–2*. 2 volumes in one. New York: Wiley & Putnam, 1845.

Martineau, Harriet. *Society in America*. 3 volumes. London: Saunders and Otley, 1837.

Murray, Amelia M. *Letters From the United States, Cuba and Canada*. 2 volumes in one. New York: G. P. Putnam & Company, 1856.

Olmsted, Frederick Law. *A Journey in the Seaboard Slave States, With Remarks on Their Economy*. New York: Dix & Edwards, 1856.

Pope-Hennessy, Una. *The Aristocratic Journey: Being the Outspoken Letters of Mrs. Basil Hall Written During a Fourteen Month's Sojourn in America, 1827–1828.* New York: G. P. Putnam's Sons, 1931.

Stirling, James. *Letters From the Slave States.* London: John W. Parker and Son, 1857.

Church Records, Religious Studies, and Clerical Accounts

Adger, John B., Reverend. *The Religious Instruction of the Colored Population: A Sermon.* Charleston: T. W. Haynes, 1847.

Bowen, Nathaniel, Bishop. *A Pastoral Letter, on the Religious Instruction of the Slaves of Members of the Protestant Episcopal Church in the State of South-Carolina . . .* Charleston: A. E. Miller, 1835.

Dickson, Andrew Flinn, Reverend. *Plantation Sermons, or Plain and Familiar Discourses for the Instruction of the Unlearned.* Philadelphia: Presbyterian Board of Publications, 1856.

The Forty-Fourth Annual Report of the Trustees of the Protestant Episcopal Society for the Advancement of Christianity in South-Carolina. Charleston: A. E. Miller, 1854.

Fuller, Richard, Reverend, and Reverend Francis Wayland. *Domestic Slavery Considered As a Scriptural Institution.* New York: Lewis Colby, 1845.

Furman, Richard, Reverend. *Exposition of the Views of the Baptists, Relative to the Coloured Population . . . In a Communication to the Governor of South Carolina.* 3d ed. Charleston: A. E. Miller, 1835.

Gadsden, C. E. *An Essay on the Life of the Right Reverend Theodore Dehon, D. D.* Charleston: A. E. Miller, 1833.

Harrison, William P., ed. *The Gospel Among the Slaves.* Nashville: Publishing House of the M.E. Church, South, 1893.

Jenkins, James, Reverend. *Experience, Labours, and Sufferings of Rev. James Jenkins, of the South Carolina Conference.* Published by the Author, 1842.

Jones, Charles C. *The Religious Instruction of the Negroes.* New York: Negro Universities Press, 1969. Originally published in 1842.

Proceedings of the Meeting in Charleston, S.C., May 13–15, 1845, On the Religious Instruction of the Negroes Together With the Report of the Committee, and the Address to the Public. Charleston: Published by Order of the Meeting, 1845.

A South-Carolinian [Dr. Dalcho]. *Practical Considerations Founded on the Scriptures, Relative to the Slave Population of South-Carolina.* Charleston: A. E. Miller, 1823.

Williams, George W., ed. *Incidents in My Life: The Autobiography of The Rev. Paul Trapier, S.T.D. With Some of His Letters.* Charleston: Dalcho Historical Society, 1954.

Legal and Miscellaneous Documents

An Account of the Late Intended Insurrection Among a Portion of the Blacks of This City, Charleston, S.C. Charleston: Corporation of Charleston, 1822 in *Slave Insurrections: Selected Documents.* Westport, Conn.: Negro Universities Press, 1970.

Annual Announcement of the Trustees and Faculty of the Medical College of the State of South-Carolina. For the Session of 1837–38. Charleston: James S. Burges, 1837.

Catterall, Helen T., ed. *Judicial Cases Concerning American Slavery and the Negro.* 5 volumes. Washington, D.C.: Carnegie Institute of Washington, 1929.

Condy, Thomas D. *A Digest of the Laws of the United States & The State of South-*

Carolina, Now of Force, Relating to the Militia; With an Appendix, Containing the Patrol Laws; The Laws for the Government of Slaves and Free Persons of Colour . . . Charleston: A. E. Miller, 1830.

Eckhard, George B. *A Digest of the Ordinances of the City Council of Charleston, From the Year 1783 to Oct. 1844.* Charleston: Walker & Burke, 1844.

Goodell, William. *The American Slave Code in Theory and Practice: Its Distinctive Features Shown By Its Statutes, Judicial Decisions, and Illustrative Facts.* 4th ed. New York, 1853.

Johnson, William. *To The Public of Charleston.* Charleston: C. C. Sebring, 1822.

Kennedy, Lionel H., and Thomas Parker. *An Official Report of the Trials of Sundry Negroes, Charged With An Attempt to Raise An Insurrection . . . And In An Appendix, A Report of the Trials of Four White Persons on Indictments for Attempting to Excite the Slaves to Insurrection.* Charleston: James R. Schenck, 1822.

McCord, David J. *Reports of Cases Argued and Determined in the Court of Appeals of South Carolina.* Columbia: Doyle E. Sweeny, 1826.

————, ed. *The Statutes At Large of South Carolina.* 10 volumes. Columbia: A. S. Johnston, 1840.

Nott, Henry J., and David J. McCord. *Reports of Cases Determined in the Constitutional Court of South Carolina.* Charleston: W. Riley, 1842.

O'Neall, John Belton. *The Negro Law of South Carolina.* Columbia: John G. Bowman, 1848.

Phillips, Ulrich B., ed. *Plantation and Frontier Documents: 1649–1863, Illustrative of Industrial History in the Colonial & Ante-Bellum South.* 2 volumes. Cleveland: The Arthur H. Clark Company, 1909.

Pinckney, Henry. *Report; Containing A Review of the Proceedings of the City Authorities From the 4th September, 1837, to the 1st August, 1838 . . .* Charleston: Thomas J. Eccles, 1838.

Preliminary Report Touching The Condition and Management of Emancipated Refugees; Made to the Secretary of War, by the American Freedmen's Inquiry Commission, June 30, 1863. New York: John F. Trow, 1863.

"Report from the Select Committee on the Extinction of Slavery Throughout the British Dominions . . . 1831–1832" in *British Parliamentary Papers.* Shannon, Ireland: Irish University Press, 1968.

Richardson, J. S. G. *Reports of Cases in Equity, Argued and Determined in the Court of Appeals and Court of Errors, of South-Carolina.* 12 volumes. Charleston: Walker, Evans, 1855.

Rose, Willie Lee, ed. *A Documentary History of Slavery in North America.* New York: Oxford University Press, 1976.

Newspapers (South Carolina)

Anderson *Gazette.*
Charleston *Courier.*
Charleston *Mercury.*
Cheraw *Intelligencer.*
The Daily Southern Guardian.
Farmer's Gazette and Cheraw Advertiser.
The Georgetown Gazette.

Greenville *Mountaineer.*
New Era.
Pendleton *Messenger.*
South Carolina Leader.
The Southern Enterprise.
The Southern Patriot.
Winyaw *Intelligencer.*

Magazines

The Atlantic Monthly.
Blackwood's Magazine.
The Carolina Journal of Medicine,
Science and Agriculture.
Carolina Planter.
De Bow's Review.
Farmer and Planter.
Harper's New Monthly Magazine.

Living Age.
The Nashville Christian Advocate.
The Nation.
Southern Agriculturist.
The Southern Cabinet.
Southern Cultivator.
Southern Quarterly Review.

Secondary Sources

Books

Adams, Edward C. L. *Congaree Sketches: Scenes From Negro Life in the Swamps of the Congaree and Tales by Tad and Scip of Heaven and Hell With Other Miscellany.* Chapel Hill: The University of North Carolina Press, 1927.
————. *Nigger to Nigger.* New York: Charles Scribner's Sons, 1928.
————. *Tales of the Congaree.* Edited with an Introduction by Robert G. O'Meally. Chapel Hill: The University of North Carolina Press, 1987.
Aptheker, Herbert. *American Negro Slave Revolts.* New York: International Publishers, 1969. Originally published in 1943.
————. *To Be Free: Studies in American Negro History.* New York: International Publishers, 1969. Originally published in 1948.
————. *"We Will Be Free": Advertisements for Runaways and the Reality of American Slavery.* Santa Clara, Cal.: Ethnic Studies Program, University of Santa Clara, 1984.
Ayandele, E. A. *African Historical Studies.* London: Frank Cass and Company, 1979.
Ball, William Watts. *The State That Forgot: South Carolina's Surrender to Democracy.* Indianapolis: The Bobbs-Merrill Company, 1932.
Barker, Ernest, Sir, ed. *Social Contract: Essays By Locke, Hume and Rousseau.* London: Oxford University Press, 1979.
Bennett, John. *The Doctor to the Dead: Grotesque Legends & Folk Tales of Old Charleston.* New York: Rinehart & Company, 1943.
Berlin, Ira. *Slaves Without Masters: The Free Negro in the Antebellum South.* New York: Vintage Books, 1974.
Blassingame, John W. *The Slave Community: Plantation Life in the Antebellum South.* New York: Oxford University Press, 1972. Revised edition, 1979.
Brackett, Richard Newman, ed. *The Old Stone Church, Oconee County, South Carolina.* Pendleton [?]: The Old Stone Church and Cemetery Commission, 1972. Originally published in 1905.
Burton, Orville Vernon. *In My Father's House Are Many Mansions: Family and Community in Edgefield, South Carolina.* Chapel Hill: The University of North Carolina Press, 1985.
Christensen, A. M. H. *Afro-American Folk Lore: Told Round Cabin Fires on the Sea Islands of South Carolina.* New York: Negro Universities Press, 1969. Originally published in 1892.
Cone, James H. *The Spirituals and the Blues: An Interpretation.* New York: The Seabury Press, 1972.
Courlander, Harold. *Negro Folk Music, U. S. A.* New York: Columbia University Press, 1963.

Crum, Mason. *Gullah: Negro Life in the Carolina Sea Islands.* Durham, N.C.: Duke University Press, 1940.

Dalby, David. *Black Through White: Patterns of Communication.* Bloomington: African Studies Program, Indiana University, 1970.

Davidson, Chalmers Gaston. *The Last Foray: The South Carolina Planters of 1860: A Sociological Study.* Columbia: University of South Carolina Press, 1971.

Davis, Angela. *Lectures on Liberation.* New York: New York Committee to Free Angela Davis, n.d.

Davis, David Brion. *The Problem of Slavery in Western Culture.* Ithaca: Cornell University Press, 1966.

Dorson, Richard M. *American Folklore and the Historian.* Chicago: The University of Chicago Press, 1971.

Dubois, W. E. B. *Black Reconstruction in America, 1800–1880.* New York: Atheneum, 1973. Originally published in 1935.

———. *The Negro Church: Report of a Social Study Made Under the Direction of Atlanta University.* Atlanta: The Atlanta University Press, 1903.

———. *The Souls of Black Folk: Essays and Sketches.* Chicago: A. C. McClurg & Company, 1924.

———. *The Suppression of the African Slave-Trade to the United States of America, 1638–1870.* New York: Schocken Books, 1969. Originally published in 1896.

Ervin, Eliza Cowan, and Horace Fraser Rudisill. *Darlingtoniana: A History of People, Places and Events in Darlington County, South Carolina.* Columbia: The R. L. Bryan Company, 1964.

Escott, Paul D. *Slavery Remembered: A Record of Twentieth-Century Slave Narratives.* Chapel Hill: The University of North Carolina Press, 1979.

Faulkner, William J. *The Days When The Animals Talked: Black American Folktales and How They Came To Be.* Chicago: Follett Publishing Company, 1977.

Faust, Drew Gilpin. *James Henry Hammond and the Old South: A Design for Mastery.* Baton Rouge: Louisiana State University Press, 1982.

Fisher, Miles Mark. *Negro Slave Songs in the United States.* New York: The Citadel Press, 1963. Originally published in 1953.

Franklin, John Hope. *From Slavery to Freedom: A History of Negro Americans.* New York: Vintage Books, 1969.

———. *The Militant South, 1800–1861.* Cambridge: Harvard University Press, 1956.

Frazier, E. Franklin. *The Negro Church in America.* New York: Schocken Books, 1963.

Freehling, William W. *Prelude to Civil War: The Nullification Controversy in South Carolina, 1816–1836.* New York: Harper Torchbooks, 1965.

Fry, Marie-Gladys. *Night Riders in Black Folk History.* Knoxville: University of Tennessee Press, 1975.

Genovese, Eugene D. *From Rebellion to Revolution: Afro-American Slave Revolts in the Making of the Modern World.* Baton Rouge: Louisiana State University Press, 1979.

———. *Roll, Jordan, Roll: The World the Slaves Made.* New York: Pantheon Books, 1974.

Gregorie, Anne King. *History of Sumter County, South Carolina.* Sumter: Library Board of Sumter County, 1954.

Gutman, Herbert G. *The Black Family in Slavery & Freedom, 1750–1925.* New York: Pantheon Books, 1976.

Hall, Gwendolyn Midlo. *Social Control in Slave Plantation Societies: A Comparison of St. Domingue and Cuba.* Baltimore: The Johns Hopkins Press, 1971.

Harding, Vincent. *There Is A River: The Black Struggle for Freedom in America.* New York: Harcourt Brace Jovanovich, 1981.

Harris, J. William. *Plain Folk and Gentry in a Slave Society: White Liberty and Black Slavery in Augusta's Hinterlands.* Middletown, Conn.: Wesleyan University Press, 1985.

Henry, H. M. *The Police Control of the Slave in South Carolina.* New York: Negro Universities Press, 1968. Originally published in 1914.

Heyward, Duncan Clinch. *Seed From Madagascar.* Chapel Hill: The University of North Carolina Press, 1937.

Holt, Thomas S. *Black Over White: Negro Political Leadership in South Carolina During Reconstruction.* Urbana: University of Illinois Press, 1977.

Hindus, Michael S. *Prison and Plantation: Crime, Justice, and Authority in Massachusetts and South Carolina, 1767–1878.* Chapel Hill: University of North Carolina Press, 1980.

Huff, Archie Vernon. *Langdon Cheves of South Carolina.* Columbia: University of South Carolina Press, 1977.

Jackson, Bruce, ed. *The Negro and His Folklore in Nineteenth-Century Periodicals.* Austin: University of Texas Press, 1967.

Jacobs, H. P. *Sixty Years of Change, 1806–1866: Progress and Reaction in Kingston and the Countryside.* Jamaica: Institute of Jamaica, 1973.

Johnson, Guion Griffis. *A Social History of the Sea Islands: With Special Reference to St. Helena Island, South Carolina.* Chapel Hill: The University of North Carolina Press, 1930.

Johnson, Michael P., and James L. Roark, eds. *No Chariot Let Down: Charleston's Free People of Color on the Eve of the Civil War.* Chapel Hill: The University of North Carolina Press, 1984.

Jones, Charles C. *Negro Myths From the Georgia Coast.* Columbia, S.C.: The State Company, 1925.

Joravsky, David. *The Lysenko Affair.* Cambridge: Harvard University Press, 1970.

Joyner, Charles. *Down by the Riverside: A South Carolina Slave Community.* Urbana: University of Illinois Press, 1984.

Katz, Bernard, ed. *The Social Implications of Early Negro Music in the United States.* New York: Arno Press and the New York Times, 1969.

Kirkland, Thomas J., and Robert M. Kennedy. *Historic Camden.* 2 volumes. Columbia: The State Company, 1926.

Kolchin, Peter. *Unfree Labor: American Slavery and Russian Serfdom.* Cambridge, Mass.: The Belknap Press of Harvard University Press, 1987.

Krehbiel, Henry Edward. *Afro-American Folksongs: A Study in Racial and National Music.* New York: G. Schirmer, 1914.

Lamson, Peggy. *The Glorious Failure: Black Congressman Robert Brown Elliott and the Reconstruction in South Carolina.* New York: W. W. Norton & Company, 1973.

Levine, Lawrence W. *Black Culture and Black Consciousness: Afro-American Folk Thought from Slavery to Freedom.* Oxford: Oxford University Press, 1977.

Littlefield, Daniel C. *Rice and Slaves: Ethnicity and the Slave Trade in Colonial South Carolina.* Baton Rouge: Louisiana State University Press, 1981.

Litwack, Leon F. *Been in the Storm So Long: The Aftermath of Slavery.* New York: Vintage Books, 1979.

Mays, Benjamin E. *The Negro's God As Reflected in His Literature.* Boston: Chapman & Grimes, 1938.

Mays, Benjamin E., and Joseph William Nicholson. *The Negro's Church.* New York: Negro Universities Press, 1969. Originally published in 1933.

McDavid, John W., and Herbert Harari. *Social Psychology: Individuals, Groups, Societies.* New York: Harper & Row, 1968.

Mintz, Sidney. *Caribbean Transformations.* Chicago: Aldine Publishing Company, 1974.

Mintz, Sidney and Richard Price. *An Anthropological Approach to the Afro-American Past: A Caribbean Perspective.* Philadelphia: Institute for the Study of Human Issues, 1976.

Morgan, Donald G. *Justice William Johnson; The First Dissenter: The Career and Constitutional Philosophy of A Jeffersonian Judge.* Columbia: University of South Carolina Press, 1954.

Nicholson, Alfred W. *Brief Sketch of the Life and Labors of Rev. Alexander Bettis.* Trenton, S.C.: By the Author, 1913.

Oakes, James. *The Ruling Race: A History of American Slaveholders.* New York: Alfred A. Knopf, 1982.

O'Brien, Michael, and David Moltke-Hansen, eds. *Intellectual Life in Antebellum Charleston.* Knoxville: The University of Tennessee Press, 1986.

Owens, Leslie Howard. *This Species of Property: Slave Life and Culture in the Old South.* New York: Oxford University Press, 1976.

Parsons, Elsie Clews. *Folk-Lore of the Sea Islands, South Carolina.* Cambridge, Mass.: The American Folk-Lore Society, 1923.

Patterson, Orlando. *The Sociology of Slavery: An Analysis of the Origins, Development and Structure of Negro Slave Society in Jamaica.* London: Mcgibbon & Kee, 1967.

————. *Slavery and Social Death: A Comparative Study.* Cambridge, Mass.: Harvard University Press, 1982.

Pease, William H., and Jane H. Pease. *The Web of Progress: Private Values and Public Styles in Boston and Charleston, 1828–1843.* New York: Oxford University Press, 1985.

Peterkin, Julia. *Roll, Jordan, Roll. Photographic Studies by Doris Ulmann.* New York: Robert O. Ballou, 1933.

Phillips, Ulrich Bonnell. *American Negro Slavery: A Survey of the Supply, Employment and Control of Negro Labor as Determined by the Plantation Regime.* Foreword by Eugene Genovese. Baton Rouge: Louisiana State University Press, 1966. Originally published in 1918.

Pingel, Martha M. *An American Utilitarian: Richard Hildreth as a Philosopher.* New York: Columbia University Press, 1948.

Raboteau, Albert J. *Slave Religion: The "Invisible Institution" in the Antebellum South.* New York: Oxford University Press, 1978.

Redding, Saunders. *They Came In Chains: Americans from Africa.* Philadelphia: J. B. Lippincott Company, 1950.

Richardson, Joe M. *Christian Reconstruction: The American Missionary Association and Southern Blacks, 1861–1890.* Athens: The University of Georgia Press, 1986.

Rogers, George, Jr. *The History of Georgetown County, South Carolina.* Columbia: University of South Carolina Press, 1970.

Rose, Willie Lee. *Rehearsal For Reconstruction: The Port Royal Experiment.* New York: Vintage Books, 1964.

Sanchez, Sonia. *homegirls & handgrenades*. New York: Thunder's Mouth Press, 1984.

Scarborough, William Kauffman. *The Overseer: Plantation Management in the Old South*. Baton Rouge: Louisiana State University Press, 1966.

Schatz, Walter, ed. *Directory of Afro-American Resources*. New York: R. R. Bowker Company, 1970.

Sernett, Milton C. *Black Religion and American Evangelicalism: White Protestants, Plantation Missions, and the Flowering of Negro Christianity, 1787–1865*. Metuchen, N.J.: The Scarecrow Press and The American Theological Library Association, 1975.

Shipp, Albert M. *The History of Methodism in South Carolina*. Nashville: Southern Methodist Publishing House, 1883.

Smith, H. Shelton. *In His Image, But . . . Racism in Southern Religion, 1780–1910*. Durham, N.C.: Duke University Press, 1972.

Stampp, Kenneth M. *The Peculiar Institution: Slavery in the Ante-Bellum South*. New York: Vintage Books, 1956.

Starobin, Robert S., ed. *Denmark Vesey: The Slave Conspiracy of 1822*. Englewood Cliffs, N.J.: Prentice-Hall, 1970.

———, ed. *Letters of American Slaves*. New York: Viewpoints, 1974.

Stuckey, Sterling. *Slave Culture: Nationalist Theory and the Foundations of Black America*. New York: Oxford University Press, 1987.

Taylor, Rosser R. *Ante-Bellum South Carolina: A Social and Cultural History*. The James Sprunt Studies in History and Political Science. Chapel Hill: The University of North Carolina Press, 1942.

Thibaut, John W., and Harold H. Kelley. *The Social Psychology of Groups*. New York: John Wiley & Sons, Inc., 1959.

Thorpe, Earl E. *The Old South: A Psychohistory*. Durham, N.C.: Seeman Printery, 1972.

Tilley, Nannie M., and Norma Lee Goodwin. *Guide to the Manuscript Collections in the Duke University Library*. Durham: Duke University Press, 1947.

Townsend, Leah. *South Carolina Baptist, 1670–1805*. Florence, S.C.: The Florence Printing Company, 1935.

Turner, Lorenzo Dow. *Africanisms in the Gullah Dialect*. Chicago: University of Chicago Press, 1949.

Van Deburg, William L. *The Slave Drivers: Black Agricultural Labor Supervisors in the Antebellum South*. Westport, Conn.: Greenwood Press, 1979.

Wade, Richard C. *Slavery in the Cities: The South 1820–1860*. London: Oxford University Press, 1964.

Washington, Joseph R., Jr. *Black Religion: The Negro and Christianity in the United States*. Boston: Beacon Press, 1964.

Webber, Thomas L. *Deep Like the Rivers: Education in the Slave Quarter Community, 1831–1865*. New York: W. W. Norton & Company, 1978.

Wightman, William M. *Life of William Capers*. Nashville: Publishing House of the M.E. Church, South, 1902.

Wikramanayake, Marina. *A World in Shadow: The Free Black in Antebellum South Carolina*. Columbia: University of South Carolina Press, 1973.

Wiley, Bell Irvin. *Southern Negroes, 1861–1865*. Baton Rouge: Louisiana State University Press, 1965.

Williamson, Joel. *After Slavery: The Negro in South Carolina During Reconstruction, 1861–1877*. Chapel Hill: The University of North Carolina Press, 1965.

Wilmore, Gayraud S. *Black Religion and Black Radicalism.* Garden City, N.Y.: Anchor Press, 1973.

Wiltse, Charles M. *John C. Calhoun: Nationalist, 1782–1828.* New York: The Bobbs-Merrill Company, 1944.

Windley, Lathan A. *Runaway Slave Advertisements: A Documentary History from the 1730s to 1790.* 3 volumes. Westport, Conn.: Greenwood Press, 1983.

Wood, Peter H. *Black Majority: Negroes in Colonial South Carolina From 1670 Through the Stono Rebellion.* New York: Alfred A. Knopf, 1974.

Work Projects Administration. South Carolina Folk Tales: Stories of Animals and Supernatural Beings in *Bulletin of University of South Carolina.* October, 1941.

Articles

Anderson, James D. "Aunt Jemima in Dialectics: Genovese on Slave Culture," *The Journal of Negro History,* LXI (January 1976), 99–114.

Aptheker, Herbert. "Afro-American Superiority: A Neglected Theme in Literature," *Phylon,* XXXI (Winter 1970), 336–43.

Berlin, Ira. "Time, Space, and the Evolution of Afro-American Society in British Mainland North America," *The American Historical Review,* 85 (February 1980), 44–78.

Blassingame, John W. "Status and Social Structure in the Slave Community: Evidence From New Sources" in Harry P. Owens, ed. *Perspectives and Irony in American Slavery.* Jackson: University Press of Mississippi, 1976.

———. "Using the Testimony of Ex-Slaves: Approaches and Problems," *The Journal of Southern History,* XLI (November 1975), 473–92.

Boney, F. N. "The Ante-bellum Elite" in Charles M. Hudson, ed. *Red, White, and Black: Symposium on Indians in the Old South.* Athens, Ga.: Southern Anthropological Society, 1971.

Brewster, Lawrence T. "Planters From the Low-Country and Their Summer Travels" in *The Proceedings of The South Carolina Historical Association, 1943.* Columbia: South Carolina Historical Society, 1943.

Bruce, Dickson D., Jr. "Religion, Society and Culture in the Old South: A Comparative View," *American Quarterly,* XXVI (October 1974), 399–416.

Cody, Cheryll Ann. "Naming, Kinship, and Estate Dispersal: Notes on Slave Family Life on a South Carolina Plantation, 1786 to 1833," *William and Mary Quarterly,* XXXIX (January 1982), 192–211.

Dance, Daryl. "In the Beginning: A New View of Black American Etiological Tales," *Southern Folklore Quarterly,* 40 (1977), 53–64.

Davis, Henry C. "Negro Folk-Lore in South Carolina," *The Journal of American Folk-Lore,* XXVII (July–September 1914), 241–54.

Farley, M. Foster. "The Fear of Negro Slave Revolts in South Carolina, 1690–1865," *Afro-American Studies,* III (1972), 199–207.

Faust, Drew Gilpin. "Culture, Conflict and Community: The Meaning of Power on an Antebellum Plantation," *Journal of Social History,* 14 (Fall 1980), 83–97.

Feagin, Joe R. "Book Review Essay—The Black Church: Inspiration or Opiate," *Journal of Negro History,* LX (October 1975), 536–40.

Flanigan, Daniel J. "Criminal Procedure in Slave Trials in the Antebellum South," *The Journal of Southern History,* XL (November 1974), 537–64.

Fox-Genovese, Elizabeth. "Strategies and Forms of Resistance: Focus on Slave Women in the United States" in Gary Y. Okihiro, ed. *In Resistance: Studies in African, Caribbean, and Afro-American History.* Amherst: The University of Massachusetts Press, 1986.

Fredrickson, George M. "Masters and Mudsills: The Role of Race in the Planter Ideology of South Carolina" in Jack R. Censer et al., eds. *South Atlantic Urban Studies*, 2 (1978), 34–48.

Fredrickson, George M., and Christopher Lasch, "Resistance to Slavery" in Ann J. Lane, ed. *The Debate Over Slavery: Stanley Elkins and His Critics.* Urbana: University of Illinois Press, 1971.

Freehling, William W. "Denmark Vesey's Peculiar Reality" in Robert H. Abzug and Stephen E. Maizlish, eds. *New Perspectives on Race and Slavery in America: Essays in Honor of Kenneth M. Stampp.* Lexington: The University Press of Kentucky, 1986.

Genovese, Eugene D. "The Legacy of Slavery and the Roots of Black Nationalism," *Studies on the Left*, 6 (November–December 1966), 3–26.

———. "Rebelliousness and Docility in the Negro Slave: A Critique of the Elkins Thesis," *Civil War History*, 13 (1967), 293–314.

———. "Rejoiner," *Studies on the Left*, 6 (November–December 1966), 55–65.

———. "A Reply to Criticism," *Radical History Review*, 4 (Winter 1977), 94–110.

Gudeman, Stephen. "Herbert Gutman's The Black Family in Slavery and Freedom, 1750–1925: An Anthropologist's View," *Social Science History*, 3 (October 1979), 56–65.

Harding, Vincent. "Religion and Resistance Among Antebellum Negroes, 1800–1860" in August Meier and Elliott Rudwick, eds. *The Making of Black America: Essays in Negro Life & History.* 2 volumes. New York: Atheneum, 1969.

Harper, C. W. "Black Aristocrats: Domestic Servants on the Antebellum Plantation," *Phylon*, 56 (June 1985), 123–35.

———. "House Servants and Field Hands: Fragmentation in the Antebellum Slave Community," *The North Carolina Historical Review*, 55 (June 1978), 42–59.

Hindus, Michael S. "Black Justice Under White Law: Criminal Prosecutions of Blacks in Antebellum South Carolina," *The Journal of American History*, LXII (December 1976), 575–99.

Huston, James L. "The Panic of 1857, Southern Economic Thought, and the Patriarchal Defense of Slavery," *The Historian*, XLVI (February 1981), 163–86.

Inscoe, John C. "Carolina Slave Names: An Index to Acculturation," *The Journal of Southern History*, XLIX (November 1983), 527–54.

Jackson, Luther P. "Religious Instruction of Negroes, 1830 to 1860, With Special Reference to South Carolina," *Journal of Negro History*, XV (January 1930), 72–114.

Johnson, Michael P. "Runaway Slaves and the Slave Communities in South Carolina, 1799 to 1830," *William and Mary Quarterly*, 38 (July 1981), 418–41.

Kelman, Herbert C. "Compliance, Identification, and Internalization: Three Processes of Attitude Change," *The Journal of Conflict Resolution: A Quarterly for Research Related to War and Peace*, II (1958), 51–60.

Klein, Rachel N. "Ordering the Backcountry: The South Carolina Regulation," *The William and Mary Quarterly*, 38 (October 1981), 661–80.

Levine, Lawrence. "Slave Songs and Slave Consciousness: An Exploration in Neglected Sources" in Tamara K. Hareven, ed. *Anonymous Americans: Explorations in Nineteenth-Century Social History.* Englewood Cliffs, N.J.: Prentice-Hall, 1971.

Long, Charles H. "The Oppressive Elements in Religion and the Religions of the Oppressed," *Harvard Theological Review*, 69 (July–October 1976), 397–412.

Meaders, Daniel E. "South Carolina Fugitives As Viewed Through Local Colonial Newspapers with Emphasis on Runaway Notices, 1732–1801," *Journal of Negro History* LX (April 1975), 288–319.

Miller, Randall M. "The Fabric of Control: Slavery in Antebellum Southern Textile Mills," *Business History Review*, LV (Winter 1981), 471–90.

Mintz, Sidney W. "Toward An Afro-American History," *Journal of World History*, XIII (1971), 317–32.

Morgan, Philip D. "Work and Culture: The Task System and the World of Low-country Blacks, 1700 to 1880," *The William and Mary Quarterly*, XXXIX (October 1982), 563–99.

Odum, Howard. "Religious Folk-Songs of the Southern Negroes." *The American Journal of Religious Psychology and Education*, 3 (July 1909), 265–365.

Ohline, Howard A. "Georgetown, South Carolina: Racial Anxieties and Militant Behavior, 1802," *The South Carolina Historical Magazine*, 73 (July 1972), 130–40.

Parkhurst, Jessie W. "The Role of the Black Mammy in the Plantation Household," *The Journal of Negro History*, XXIII (July 1938), 349–69.

Parsons, Elsie Crews. "Folk-Lore From Aiken, S.C.," *The Journal of American Folk-Lore*, 34 (January–March 1921), 2–39.

Perkins, Eric. "Roll, Jordan Roll: A 'Marx' For the Master Class," *Radical History Review*, 3 (Fall 1976), 41–59.

Perkins, Haven P. "Religion for Slaves: Difficulties and Methods," *Church History*, X (1941), 228–45.

Powdermaker, Hortense. "The Channeling of Negro Aggression By the Cultural Process" in August Meier and Elliot Rudwick, eds. *The Making of Black America: Essays in Negro Life & History*. 2 volumes. New York: Atheneum, 1969.

Rawick, George P. "West African Culture and North American Slavery: A Study of Culture Change Among American Slaves in the Ante-Bellum South With Focus Upon Slave Religion" in *Migration and Anthropology: Proceedings of the 1970 Annual Spring Meeting of the American Ethnological Society*. Seattle: University of Washington Press, 1970.

Scarborough, William K. "Slavery—The White Man's Burden" in Harry P. Owens, ed. *Perspectives and Irony in American Slavery*. Jackson: University Press of Mississippi, 1976.

Schwarz, Philip J. "Forging the Shackles: The Developments of Virginia's Criminal Code for Slaves" in David Bodenhamer and James W. Ely, Jr., eds. *Ambivalent Legacy: A Legal History of the South*. Jackson: University Press of Mississippi, 1984.

Settle, Ophelia. "Social Attitudes During the Slave Regime: House Servants Versus Field Hands" in August Meier and Elliot Rudwick, eds. *The Making of Black America: Essays in Negro Life & History*. 2 volumes. New York: Atheneum, 1969.

Siegal, Fred. "Parameters For Paternalism," *Radical History Review*, 3 (Fall 1976), 60–65.

Starobin, Robert S. "Denmark Vesey's Slave Conspiracy of 1822: A Study in Rebellion and Repression" in John H. Bracey, Jr., et al. *American Slavery: The Question of Resistance*. Belmont, Cal.: Wadsworth Publishing Company, 1971.

Stuckey, Sterling. "Through the Prism of Folklore: The Black Ethos in Slavery" in Ann J. Lane, ed. *The Debate Over Slavery: Stanley Elkins and His Critics*. Urbana: University of Illinois Press, 1971.

Stuckey, Sterling, and Joshua Leslie. "Reflections on Reflections About the Black Intellectual, 1930–1945," *First World*, 2 (1979), 26–32.

Sutch, Richard. "The Care and Feeding of Slaves" in Paul A. David et al., *Reckoning With Slavery: A Critical Study in the Quantitative History of American Negro*

Slavery. Introduction by Kenneth M. Stampp. New York: Oxford University Press, 1976.

Towne, Laura M. "Pioneer Work on the Sea Islands," XXX (July 1901), 396–97.

Van Deburg, William L. "Slave Drivers and Slave Narratives: A New Look at the 'Dehumanized Elite,'" *Historian*, 39 (1979), 717–32.

Wade, Richard C. "The Vesey Plot: A Reconsideration" in John H. Bracey, Jr., et al. *American Slavery: The Question of Resistance*. Belmont, Cal.: Wadsworth Publishing Company, 1971.

Waterhouse, Richard. "Merchants, Planters, and Lawyers: Political Leadership in South Carolina, 1721–1775" in Bruce C. Daniels, *Power and Status: Officeholding in Colonial America*. Middletown, Conn.: Wesleyan University Press, 1986.

Wax, Darold D. "'The Great Risque We Run': The Aftermath of Slave Rebellion at Stono, South Carolina, 1739–1745," *Journal of Negro History*, LXVII (Summer 1982), 136–47.

White, John. "Review Article: Whatever Happened to the Slave Family in the Old South?" *Journal of American Studies*, 8 (1974), 383–90.

Wilson, G. R. "The Religion of the American Negro Slave: His Attitude Toward Life and Death," *Journal of Negro History*, VII (January 1923), 41–71.

Wish, Harvey. "American Slave Insurrections Before 1861" in John H. Bracey, Jr., et al. *American Slavery: The Question of Resistance*. Belmont, Cal.: Wadsworth Publishing Company, 1971.

Unpublished Papers, Theses, and Dissertations

Baldwin, Lewis V. "A Home in Dat Rock: Afro-American Folklore and the Slaves' Vision of Heaven and Hell, 1750–1860." Seminar paper, Northwestern University, 1977.

Bradley, John Livingston. "Slave Manumission in South Carolina, 1820–1860." M.A. thesis, University of South Carolina, 1964.

Bryan, Leon Stone, Jr. "Slavery On a Peedee River Rice Plantation, 1825–1865." Thesis, The Johns Hopkins University, 1963.

Clark, Charles M. "Plantation Overseers in South Carolina, 1820–1860." M.A. thesis, University of South Carolina, 1966.

Feldstein, Stanley. "The Slave's View of Slavery." Ph.D. dissertation, New York University, 1969.

Fickling, Susan Markey. "The Christianization of the Negro in South Carolina, 1830–1860." M.A. thesis, University of South Carolina, 1923.

Henderson, William Cinque. "Spartan Slaves: A Documentary Account of Blacks on Trial in Spartanburg, South Carolina, 1830 to 1865." Ph.D. dissertation, Northwestern University, 1978.

Inabinet, L. Glen. "'The July Fourth Incident' of 1816: An Insurrection Plotted by Slaves in Camden, South Carolina." Paper presented at the Reynolds Conference on South Carolina Legal History, University of South Carolina, December 1977.

Jones, Bobby Frank. "A Cultural Middle Passage: Slave Marriage and Family in the Ante-Bellum South." Ph.D. dissertation, University of North Carolina, 1965.

Jones, Norrece Thomas, Jr. "Control Mechanisms in South Carolina Slave Society, 1800–1865." Ph.D. dissertation, Northwestern University, 1981.

Joyner, Charles W. "Slave Folklife of the Waccamaw Neck: Antebellum Black Culture in the South Carolina Lowcountry." Ph.D. dissertation, University of Pennsylvania, 1977.

Mallard, Annie Hughes. "Religious Work of South Carolina Baptists Among the Slaves From 1781 to 1830." M.A. thesis, University of South Carolina, 1946.

Bibliography

Oslberg, Robert Nicholas. "A Government of Class and the South Carolina Chivalry, 1860–1865." Ph.D. dissertation, University of South Carolina, 1972.

Stone, James Herbert. "Black Leadership in the Old South: The Slave Drivers of the Rice Kingdom." Ph.D. dissertation, The Florida State University College of Arts and Sciences, 1976.

Index

About the Author

Norrece T. Jones, Jr., born in Philadelphia and raised in the urban North, spent his summers with four generations of family in the rural South, where he first saw the large plantations of antebellum South Carolina, symbols of the society of slavery. He was graduated from Hampton Institute in 1974, and received his Ph.D. from Northwestern University in 1981.

Jones taught at College of the Holy Cross in Worcester, Massachusetts, from 1979 to 1982. He is now an associate professor of history at Virginia Commonwealth University, where he has taught since 1983. His home is in Richmond, Virginia.

About the Book

Born a Child of Freedom, Yet a Slave was composed on the Mergenthaler Linotron 202 in Sabon, a typeface designed in the 1960s by the Swiss scholar and book designer Jan Tschichold and named for the sixteenth-century French typefounder Jacques Sabon. The typesetting was done by Brevis Press of Bethany, Connecticut. The design is by Kachergis Book Design of Pittsboro, North Carolina.